# The Tuzuk-i-Ja



## Or, Memoirs of Ja

## (Volume 2)

Emperor of Hindustan Jahangir

(Editor: Henry Beveridge)

(Translator: Alexander Rogers)

**Alpha Editions**

This edition published in 2024

ISBN : 9789362517692

Design and Setting By
**Alpha Editions**
www.alphaedis.com
Email - info@alphaedis.com

# VOLUME 2

## PREFACE

After an interval of about five years, the second volume of Mr. Alexander Rogers' translation of Jahāngīr's Memoirs has been published by the Royal Asiatic Society. It is a smaller work than the first volume, for it only extends over six years of the reign, as against the twelve years of its predecessor. Even then it does not include the whole of the reign, for that lasted twenty-two years. The two volumes, however, contain all that Jahāngīr wrote or supervised. It will be found, I think, that the present volume is fully as interesting as its predecessor. The accounts of the Zodiacal coinage (pp. 6 and 7), and of the comet, or new star (p. 48), the notice of the Plague in Agra (pp. 65–67), and the elaborate description of Kashmīr, under the chronicle of the 15th year, are valuable, and a word should be said for the pretty story of the King and the Gardener's daughter (p. 50), and for the allusions to painters and pictures.

If Bābur, who was the founder of the Moghul Empire in India, was the Cæsar of the East, and if the many-sided Akbar was an epitome of all the great Emperors, including Augustus, Trajan, Hadrian, Marcus Aurelius, Julian, and Justinian. Jahāngīr was certainly of the type of the Emperor Claudius, and so bore a close resemblance to our James I. All three were weak men, and under the influence of their favourites, and all three were literary, and at least two of them were fond of dabbling in theology. All three were in their wrong places as rulers. Had James I. (and VI. of Scotland) been, as he half wished, the Keeper of the Bodleian, and Jahāngīr been head of a Natural History Museum, they would have been better and happier men. Jahāngīr's best points were his love of nature and powers of observation, and his desire to do justice. Unfortunately, the last of these merits was vitiated by a propensity for excessive and recondite punishments. Like his father, grandfather, and great-grandfather, he was addicted to drugs and alcohol, and he shortened his life in this way. He made no addition to the imperial territories, but, on the contrary, diminished them by losing Qandahar to the Persians. But possibly his peaceful temper, or his laziness, was an advantage, for it saved much bloodshed. His greatest fault as a king was his subservience to his wife, Nūr-Jahān, and the consequent quarrel with his son, Shah Jahan, who was the ablest and best of his male children. The last years of his reign were especially melancholy, for he suffered from asthma and other diseases; and he had to endure the ignominy of being for a while a captive to one of his own servants—Mahābat K͟hān. He died on the borders of Kashmir, when on his way to Lahore, in October, 1627, in the fifty-ninth year of his age, and was buried at Shāhdara, near Lahore, where his widow, Nūr-Jahān, and her brother are also interred. At the time of his death his son Shah Jahan was at Junair in the Deccan, and there the news was conveyed in a wonderfully short time by a Hindu courier. Jahāngīr was succeeded by Shah Jahan, who lost no time in getting rid of his relatives, for, like the Turk, he bore no kinsman near the throne. Indeed, he is strongly suspected of having killed his elder brother, Khusrau, several years before.

I am indebted to Mr. Ellis, of the India Office, for revising the proofs.

NOTE.

In the Catalogue of Manuscripts in the Library of Trinity College, Dublin, p. 416, mention is made of a history of Hindustan during the reign of Jahāngīr, in two volumes, with paintings (Ouseley MSS.). I have recently ascertained that the MS. is only a modern copy of the Iqbāl-nāma.

H. Beveridge.

# THE THIRTEENTH NEW YEAR'S FEAST

On the eve of Wednesday, the 23rd Rabīʿu-l-awwal, 1027 (March 10, 1618), after the lapse of fourteen and a half *gharīs*, the entrance of the Sun—that is, H.M. the Great Light—the Benefactor of the Universe, into the constellation of the Ram, took place. Twelve years had now passed from the august Accession of this suppliant at the throne of God, in prosperity, and the New Year began in joy and thanksgiving. On Thursday, 2 Farwardīn, Divine month, the festival of my Lunar weighment took place, and the fifty-first1 year of the age of this suppliant at God's throne began with rejoicings. I trust that my life will be spent in the doing of God's Will, and that not a breath of it will pass without remembering Him. After the weighment had been finished, a fresh feast of joy was arranged, and my domestic servants celebrated the day with brimming cups.

On this day Āṣaf K. (Nūr-Jahān's brother), who held the rank of 5,000 with 3,000 horse, was favoured by the grant of 4,000 two-horsed and three-horsed troopers, and Ṣ̤ābit K. was raised to the office of Examiner of Petitions. I bestowed the post of the Artillery on Muʿtamid K. A Kachh (Cutch) horse had been brought as an offering by the son of Dilāwar K. No horse so good as this had come into my establishment till I encamped in Gujarat, and as M. Rustam showed a great liking for it, I presented it to him. On the Jām were conferred four rings—viz., diamond, ruby, emerald, and sapphire—and two hawks. I also gave four rings—viz., ruby, cat's-eye, emerald, and sapphire—to Raja Lachmī Narāyan (of Kūch Bihār). Muruwwat K. had sent three elephants from Bengal, and two of them were included in my private stud. On the eve of Friday I ordered lamps to be placed round the tank, and this had a very good appearance. On Sunday Ḥājī Rafīq came from ʿIrāq, and had the good fortune to kiss the threshold, and laid before me a letter which my brother S̱ẖāh ʿAbbās had sent with him. The aforesaid person is a slave of Mīr Muḥammad Amīn K., the caravan leader, and the Mīr had brought him up from his childhood. In truth, he is an excellent servant. He frequently visited ʿIrāq, and became intimate with my brother S̱ẖāh ʿAbbās. This time he had brought tipchāq2 horses and fine cloth-stuffs, such that of the horses some were put into the private stables. As he is a skilful slave, and a servant worthy of favour, I honoured him with the title of *Maliku-t-tujjār* (King of Merchants). On Monday I gave Raja Lachmī Narāyan a special sword, a jewelled rosary, and four pearls for ear-rings. On *Mubārak-s̱ẖamba* (Thursday) I increased by 500 horse the manṣab of 5,000 personal and 1,000 horse held by Mīrzā Rustam; Iʿtiqād K. was promoted to a manṣab of 4,000 and 1,000 horse; Sarfarāz K. was promoted to a manṣab of 2,500 and 1,400 horse; Muʿtamid K. to the rank of 1,000 with 350 horse. On Anīrāʾī Singh-dalan and Fidā'ī K., horses worth 100 *muhars* were conferred. As the guarding and administration of the Punjab had been entrusted to I'timādu-d-daula, I, at his request, promoted to the government (ḥukūmat) of the said Ṣubah, Mīr Qāsim, the Bakhshī of the Aḥadīs, who is related to him, and bestowed on him a manṣab of 1,000 personal with 400 horse and the title of Qāsim K. Before this I had given Raja Lachmī Narāyan an 'Irāq horse. On this day I conferred on him an elephant and a Turkī horse, and gave him leave to go to Bengal. The Jām was dismissed to his native country with a present of a jewelled waist-sword, a jewelled rosary, two horses, one from 'Irāq and the other a Turkī, and a dress of honour. Ṣāliḥ, brother's son of the deceased Āṣaf Khān,[3] was promoted to a manṣab of 1,000 with 300 horse, and allowed to go to Bengal, and a horse was conferred on him. On this date Mīr Jumla[4] came from Persia, and had the good fortune to pay his respects. The aforesaid is one of the respectable Sayyids of Isfahan and his family have always been held in honour in Persia, and now his brother's son, Mīr Riẓā, is in the service of my brother, Shāh 'Abbās, and has the rank of Ṣadr, and the Shah has married him to his own daughter. Mīr Jumla had left Persia fourteen years before this, and gone to Golconda to Muḥammad Qulī Quṭbu-l-mulk. His name is Muḥammad Amīn. Quṭbu-l-mulk gave him the title of Mīr Jumla. For ten years he had been his *Mudār 'Alaihi* (Centre of Affairs) and his *Ṣāḥib Sāmān* (factotum). After Quṭbu-l-mulk died, and the rule came to his brother's son, the latter did not treat the Mīr properly, and so he took leave and hastened to his native country. The Shah, on account of his connection with Mīr Riẓā, and the respect which he had for men[5] of merit, showed much consideration for and kindness to him. He (the Mīr) also presented fitting offerings, and passed three or four years in Persia, and amassed properties (estates?).[6] As he several times represented that he wished to enter the service of this Court, I sent a farmān and invited him. Immediately the farmān arrived he severed his connections there, and set the face of loyalty towards this Court. This day he attained the honour of kissing the carpet, and produced as offering twelve horses, nine *tuqūz*[7] of silk cloths, and two rings. As he had come with devotion and sincerity, I conferred favours and kindness on him, and presented him with 20,000 *darbs* (Rs. 10,000) for his expenses and a dress of honour. On the same day I gave the post of Bakhshī of the Aḥadīs to 'Ināyat K. in place of Qāsim K. I honoured Khwāja 'Āqil, who is one of the old servants, with the title of 'Āqil K., and presented him with a horse. On Friday, Dilāwar K., coming from the Deccan, had the good fortune to kiss the threshold, and presented an offering of 100 *muhars* and Rs. 1,000. Bāqir K., Faujdār of Multan, was promoted to a manṣab of 800 personal and 300 horse. Tijārat K. and Bāhū'ī,[8] Zamindar of Multan, were honoured with the gift of elephants. On Saturday, the 11th, marching from Doḥad with the intention of hunting elephants, I pitched at the village of

Kara Bāra (Garbara ?). On Sunday, the 12th, the village of Sajāra (Sajwara ?) became the place of alighting. It is 8 *koss* from this place to Doḥad, and 1½ *koss* to the hunting-ground. On the morning of Monday, the 13th, I went to hunt elephants with a body of my private servants. As the grazing-place of the elephants is in a hilly country, with elevations and depressions, a passage is obtained with difficulty by one on foot. Before this, a large body of horse and foot had surrounded the jungle after the manner of a *qamurgha*, and outside the jungle, on a tree, they had prepared a wooden platform for me. On all sides of this they had arranged seats on other trees for the Amirs. They had got ready 200 male elephants with strong nooses, and many female elephants. On each elephant there were seated two elephant-drivers of the tribe of *Jarga*,9 whose special employment is the hunting of elephants, and it had been arranged that they should bring the wild elephants from the jungle into my presence, that I might witness the hunt. It happened that at the time when the men from all sides entered the jungle, in consequence of the thickness of the forest and the heights and hollows, the chain was broken, and the order of the *qamurgha* did not remain perfect. The wild elephants in bewilderment turned in every direction, but twelve male and female came to this side (where J. was). As the fear was that they might escape, they drove in the tame elephants and tied them (the wild elephants) up wherever they found them. Although many elephants were not caught, at least two excellent ones were captured, very handsome in shape, of good breed, and perfect marks. As there is a hill in the jungle in which the elephants were, called Rākas (Rākshas) Pahār,10 or demon hill, I called these two elephants Rāvan Sar and Pāvan Sar, these being the names of two demons. On Tuesday, the 14th, and Kam-s͟hamba (Wednesday), the 15th, I halted.

On the eve of Thursday, the 16th, I marched, and halted at the stage of Kara Bāra. Ḥakīm Beg,11 who is one of the household of the Court, was honoured with the title of Ḥakīm K., and a sum of Rs. 3,000 was given to Sangrām, a Zamindar of the hill country of the Panjab. As the heat was very great, and marching by day was to be avoided, I marched by night. On Saturday, the 18th, a halt was made in the parganah of Doḥad. On Sunday, the 19th, the sun that bestows favour on the world attained the highest point in the constellation of Aries. On this day a great entertainment was held, and I sat on the throne. I promoted S͟hāh-nawāz K., who held a manṣab of 5,000, with the favour of 2,000 horse, of two and three horses. K͟hwāja Abū-l-Ḥasan, the Chief Bak͟hs͟hī, was given a mansab, original and increased, of 4,000 with 2,000 horse. As Ahmad Beg K., of Kabul, who had obtained the governorship of Kashmir, had promised that he would conquer in the space of two years Tibet and Kis͟htwār, and the promised time had elapsed, and he had not fulfilled this service, I removed him, and promoted Dilāwar K. Kākar to the Government of Kashmir. I gave him a dress of honour and an elephant, and sent him off. He also made a promise in writing that in the course of two years he would conquer Tibet and Kis͟htwār. Badī'u-z-Zamān, s. S͟hāhrukh͟ M. came from the jagir he held in Sulṭānpūr, and had the good fortune to kiss the threshold. Having at this time honoured Qāsim K. with a jewelled dagger and an elephant, I dismissed him to the Government of the Punjab.

On the night of Tuesday, the 21st, I marched from the stage mentioned, and turned the reins of the army of prosperity towards Aḥmadābād. As in consequence of the great heat and the corruption of the air I would have had to undergo much hardship, and would have had to traverse a long distance before reaching Agra, it occurred to me not to proceed at this hot season to the capital. As I heard much praise of the rainy season in Gujarat, and there was no report about the evil reputation of Aḥmadābād (see *infra* for account of epidemic there), I finally conceived the idea of remaining there. Inasmuch as the protection and guardianship of God (to Him be praise) was in all places and at all times extended to this suppliant, just at this crisis news arrived that signs of the plague (*wabā*) had shown themselves again at Agra, and many people were dying, my intention of not going to Agra, which had thrown its rays on my mind through Divine inspiration, was confirmed. The entertainment of Thursday, the 23rd, was held at the station of Jalod.12

Previously to this, the rule of coinage was that on one face of the metal they stamped my name, and on the reverse the name of the place, and the month and year of the reign. At this time it entered my mind that in place of the month they should substitute the figure of the constellation which belonged to that month; for instance, in the month of Farwardīn the figure of a ram, and in Urdībihis͟ht the figure of a bull. Similarly, in each month that a coin was struck, the figure of the constellation was to be on one face, as if the sun were emerging from it. This usage is my own, and has never been practised until now.13

On this day I'tiqād K. was promoted to the dignity of a standard, and a standard was also conferred on Muruwwat K., who was attached to Bengal. On the night of Monday,14 the 27th, the camp was pitched in the village of Badrwāla, in the parganah of Sahra.15 At this stage was heard the voice of the koel (*koyal*). The koel is a bird of the crow tribe, but smaller. The crow's eyes are black, and those of the koel red. The female has white spots, but the male is all black. The male has a very pleasant voice, quite unlike that of the female. It is in reality the nightingale of India. Just as the nightingale is agitated and noisy in the spring, so is the cry of the koel at the approach of the rainy season, which is the spring of Hindustan. Its cry is exceedingly pleasant and penetrating, and the bird begins its exhilaration (*masti*) when the mangoes ripen. It frequently sits on the mango-trees, and is delighted with the colour and scent of the mango. A strange thing about the koel is that it does not bring up its young from the egg, but, finding the nest of the crow unguarded at the time of laying, it breaks the crow's eggs with its beak, throws them out, and lays its own in the place of them, and flies off. The crow, thinking the eggs its own, hatches the young and brings them up. I have myself seen this strange affair at Allahabad.

On the night of *Kamshamba* (Wednesday), the 29th, the camp was on the bank of the Māhī, and the entertainment of *Mubārakshamba* was held there. Two springs appeared on the bank of the Māhī, that had very clear water, so much so that if a poppy-seed fell into them the whole of it was visible. All that day I passed with the ladies. As it was a pleasant place to walk about in, I ordered them to build a raised seat round each of the springs. On Friday I fished in the Māhī, and large fish with scales fell into the net. I first told my son, Shāh-Jahān, to try his sword on them. After this I ordered the Amīrs to strike them with the swords they had in their belts. My son's sword cut better than all of theirs. These fish were divided among the servants who were present. On the eve of Saturday, the 1st of Urdībihisht, marching from the above-mentioned stage, I ordered[16] the mace-bearers (*yasāwulān*) and *tawāchiyān* to collect the widows and poor people from the villages on the road and near it, and bring them before me, so that I might bestow charity on them with my own hand, which would be an occupation, and the helpless ones might also find grace. What better occupation could there be than this? On Monday, the 3rd, Shajā'at K. 'Arab, and Himmat K., and other servants who belonged to the Deccan and Gujarat, had the good fortune to kiss the threshold. The holy men and the possessors of blessing (faqīrs, etc.) who lived at Ahmadabad paid their respects to me. On Tuesday, the 4th, the bank of the river at Maḥmūdābād became the alighting place. Rustam K., whom my son, Shāh-Jahān, had left in the Government of Gujarat, was honoured by paying his respects. The entertainment of Thursday, the 6th, was held on the bank of the Kānkrīya tank. Nāhir K., according to order, came from the Deccan and raised the head of honour with the good fortune of prostrating himself before me.

A diamond ring was presented to my son, Shāh-Jahān, as part of the offering of Quṭbu-l-mulk. It was of the value of 1,000 muhars, and on it there appeared three letters of equal size and of good form, such that they made the word Lillahi (for God). This diamond had been sent, as it was reckoned one of the marvels of the world. In fact, veins and scratches are flaws in precious stones, but it was generally thought that the marks on this one were fabricated. Moreover, the diamond did not come from any celebrated mine. As my son, Shāh-Jahān, wished that it should be sent to my brother, Shāh 'Abbās, as a souvenir of the conquest of the Deccan it was sent to the Shah along with other gifts.[17]

On this day I presented Brikha Rāy *bād-farūsh* (panegyrist) with Rs. 1,000. He is a Gujarātī by origin, and is fully versed in the chronicles and circumstances of that country. His name was Būnṭā—that is, a sapling (*nihāl*). It seemed to me that it was anomalous to call an old man Būnṭā, especially now that he had become verdant (*sar-sabz*) and fruit-bearing through the irrigation (*saḥāb*, literally, cloud, or mirage) of our kindness. I therefore ordered that henceforth he should be called Brikha Rāy. Brikha means "tree" in Hindī. On Friday, the 7th of the aforesaid month, corresponding with the 1st Jumāda-l-awwal, at a chosen propitious hour, I entered the city of Ahmadabad with all enjoyment. At the time of mounting, my son of prosperous fortune, Shāh-Jahān, had brought 20,000 *charan*, or Rs. 5,000, for the *niṣār* (scattering), and I scattered them as I hastened to the palace. When I alighted there he laid before me by way of an offering a jewelled *ṭurra* (aigrette) of the value of Rs. 25,000, and those of his officers whom he had left in this Subah also presented offerings. They altogether amounted to nearly Rs. 40,000. As it was represented to me that Khwāja Beg Mīrzā Ṣafawī had reached the neighbourhood of the forgiveness of God—*i.e.*, had died—at Aḥmadnagar, I promoted to a mansab of 2,000 personal and horse, original and increased, Khanjar K., whom he had adopted as his son, and, indeed, held dearer than a son of his loins, and who was in truth, an intelligent, ambitious youth, and a servant worthy of patronage, and entrusted him with the charge of the fort of Ahmadnagar.

In these days, in consequence of the great heat and the corruption of the air, sickness had broken out among the people, and of those in the city and the camp there were few who for two or three days had not been ill. Inflammatory fever or pains in the limbs attacked them, and in the course of two or three days they became exceedingly ill—so much so that even after recovery they remained for a long time weak and languid. They mostly at last recovered, so that but few were in danger of their lives. I heard from old men who resided in this country that thirty years before this the same kind of fever prevailed, and passed away happily. Anyhow, there appeared some deterioration in the climate of Gujarat, and I much regretted having come here. I trust that the great and glorious God, in His mercy and grace, will lift up this burden, which is a source of uneasiness to my mind, from off the people. On *Mubārak-shamba* (Thursday), the 13th, Badīʿu-z-zamān, s. Mīrzā Shāhrukh, was promoted to the mansab of 1,500 personal and horse, and presented with a standard, and appointed faujdār of Sarkār Paṭan. Sayyid Niẓām, faujdār of Sarkār Lucknow, was raised to the manṣab of 1,000 personal and 700 horse. The manṣab of ʿAlī Qulī Darman, who was attached to the province of Qandahar, at the request of Bahādur K., the governor thereof, was ordered to be 1,000 personal and 700 horse. Sayyid Hizbar K.

Bārha was dignified with the manṣab of 1,000 personal and 400 horse. I promoted Zabardast K. to the rank of 800 personal and 350 horse. On this day Qāsim Khwāja of Dihbīd18 had sent from Mā-warā'a-n-nahr (Transoxiana) by the hand of one of his tribesmen by way of supplication five *tūyghūn* (white) falcons. One died on the road, and four arrived at Ujjain in safety. I ordered them to hand over the sum of Rs. 5,000 to someone among them, that he might purchase and take with him whatever things would be agreeable to the Khwāja, and gave a reward of Rs. 1,000 to himself. At this time Khān 'Ālam, who had been sent as ambassador to the ruler of Persia, sent an *āshyānī* falcon (bird from the nest), which in the Persian language they call *ukna.*19 Outwardly one cannot distinguish between these and *bāz dāmī*20 falcons by any particular mark, but after they have been flown the difference is clear. On Thursday, the 20th, Mīr Abū-ṣ-Ṣāliḥ, a relation (? son-in-law) of the deceased Mīrzā Yūsuf K., came from the Deccan by order, and enjoyed the good fortune of kissing the threshold. He presented as an offering 100 *muhars*21 and a jewelled plume (*kalgī*). Mīrzā Yūsuf K.22 was one of the Riẓawī Sayyids of Mashhad, and his family was always held in great honour in Khurasan, and just now my brother Shāh 'Abbās has given his daughter in marriage to the younger brother of the aforesaid Abū-ṣ-Ṣāliḥ. His father, Mīrzā Atagh,23 was the head of the attendants of the mausoleum of Riẓā, the 8th Imām. Mīrzā Yūsuf Khān, by means of the patronage of H.M. (Akbar), had risen to nobility, and attained to the manṣab of 5,000. Without doubt he was a good Mīr, and held his many servants in good order. A number of relations gathered round him. He died24 in the Deccan. Although he left many sons, who obtained favours in consideration of former services, special attention was paid to the development of his eldest son. In a short time I advanced him to the rank of nobility. Certainly there is a great difference between him and his father.

On *Mubārak-shamba* (Thursday), the 27th, I presented Ḥakīm Masīḥu-z-zamān with 20,000 *darbs* (8 anna pieces), and to Ḥakīm Rūḥu-llah 100 *muhars* and Rs. 1,000. As he had thoroughly diagnosed my constitution, he perceived that the climate of Gujarat was very inimical to it. He said: "As soon as you moderate your habit of taking wine and opium, all these troubles of yours will disappear." Indeed, when I in one day diminished (the quantity I took of) both of them, there was a great gain on that first day. On *Mubārak-shamba* (Thursday), the 3rd Khūrdād, Qizilbāsh K. was promoted to the manṣab, original and increased, of 1,500 personal and 1,200 horse. A report was received from Gajpat K., superintendent of the elephant stables, and Balūch K., chief huntsman (*Qarāwul Beg*), that up to this time sixty-nine elephants, male and female, had been caught. Whatever took place after this would be reported. I ordered them to beware not to take old or small elephants; but with this exception they should catch all they saw, male or female. On Monday, the 14th,[25] the sum of Rs. 2,000 was presented for S͟hāh ʿĀlam's anniversary, to Sayyid Muḥammad, his representative. A special Kachh horse, one of the good horses of the Jām which had been presented to me, was given to Rāja Bīr Singh Deo. I made a present of Rs. 1,000 to Balūch K., the chief huntsman, who is engaged in capturing elephants. On Tuesday, 15th, I found I had a severe headache, which at last ended in fever. At night I did not drink my usual number of cups, and after midnight crop-sickness[26] was added to my fever, and till morning I rolled about on my couch. On Wednesday, the 16th, at the end of the day, the fever diminished, and, after asking the advice of my doctors, I took my usual number of cups on the third night. Although they urged me to take some broth of pulse and rice, I could not make up my mind to do so. Since I arrived at the age of discretion, I never remember having taken *būg͟hān*[27] broth, and hope that I may not want it in future. When they brought food for me this day, I had no inclination for it. In short, for three days and two nights I remained fasting. Though I had fever for a day and a night, and my weakness was such that it appeared as if I had been confined to bed for a long time, I had no appetite left, and had no inclination towards food.

I[28] am amazed to think what pleasure or goodness the founder of this city could have seen in a spot so devoid of the favour (of God) as to build a city on it. After him, others, too, have passed their lives in precious trouble in this dustbin. Its air is poisonous, and its soil has little water, and is of sand and dust, as has already[29] been described. Its water is very bad and unpalatable, and the river, which is by the side of the city, is always dry except in the rainy season. Its wells are mostly salt and bitter, and the tanks in the neighbourhood of the city have become like buttermilk from washermen's soap. The upper classes who have some property have made reservoirs in their houses, which they fill with rainwater in the rainy season, and they drink that water until the next year. The evils of water to which the air never penetrates, and which has no way for the vapour to come out by, are evident. Outside the city, in place of green grass and flowers, all is an open plain full of thorn-brakes (*zaqqūm*), and as for the breeze that blows off the thorns, its excellence is known:

"[30]O thou, compendium of goodness, by which of thy names shall I call thee?

I had already called Aḥmadābād Gardābād (the abode of dust)."

Now, I do not know whether to call it *Samūmistān* (the place of the samūm or simoom) or Bīmāristān (abode of sickness), or Zaqqūm-zār (the thorn-bed), or Jahannamābād (the house of Hell), for it contains all these varieties. If the rainy season had not prevented me, I would not have delayed one day in this abode of trouble, but, like Solomon, would have seated myself on the throne of the wind, and hastened out, and released the people of God from this pain and trouble. As the men of this city are exceedingly weak-hearted and wretched, in order to guard against any of the men from the camp entering their houses with a view to oppress them, or interfering with the affairs of the poor and miserable: and lest the Qāẓī and Mīr ʿAdl (judge) should, from fear of the face of men (*rū-dīdagī*), temporize and not stop such oppression, I, from the date on which I entered the city, notwithstanding the heat of the air, every day, after completing the midday prayer, went and sat in the *Jharoka*. It was towards the river, and had no impediment in the shape of gate, or wall, or watch-men (*yasāwul*), or *chobdārs* (mace-bearers). For the sake of administering justice, I sat there for two or three sidereal hours and listened to the cries for redress, and ordered punishments on the oppressors according to their faults and crimes. Even in the time of weakness I have gone every day to the *jharoka*, though in great pain and sorrow, according to my fixed custom, and have looked on ease of body as something unlawful31 (*ḥarām*) for me.

"For the care of the people of God

At night I make not mine eyes acquainted with sleep;

For the ease of the bodies of all

I approve of pain for my own body."

By the grace of Allah, it has become my habit not to surrender the nychthemeron, for more than two or three sidereal hours of the coin of Time, to the plundering of sleep. In this there are two advantages—one, the knowledge of the kingdom; the other, wakefulness of heart in calling God to mind. God forbid that this life of a few days should pass in carelessness. As a heavy sleep is in front, I must reckon as a gain this time of my wakefulness, which I shall not see again in sleep, and must not be careless of recollecting God for a single wink. "Be wakeful, for a wondrous32 sleep is ahead." On the same day that I contracted fever, my son S̲h̲āh-Jahān, who is close to my heart, also contracted it. His attack lasted a long time, and for ten days he could not come to pay his respects. He came on Thursday, the 24th, and waited on me, and appeared very weak and powerless, so much so that if anyone had not explained the matter, one might have supposed he had been ill for a month or more. I am grateful that at last all ended well. On Thursday, the 31st, Mīr Jumla, who had come from Īrān—a summary of what had happened to him has been already written—was honoured with the mansab of 1,500 personal and 200 horse. On this day, in consequence of the weakness I suffered from, I bestowed as alms on deserving people an elephant, a horse, and varieties of quadrupeds, with a quantity of gold and silver and other valuable things. Most of my servants also brought alms according to their means. I told them that if their object was to parade their loyalty, their proceeding was not acceptable, and if they were acting from genuine piety there was no need for bringing their alms into the Presence; they could secretly and personally distribute them to the poor and needy. On *Mubārak-s͟hamba* (Thursday), the 7th Tīr, Divine month, Ṣādiq K. Bak͟hs͟hī was promoted to the mansab of 2,000 personal and horse, original and increased; Irādat K., the Mīr Sāmān, to that of 2,000 and 1,000 horse, Mīr Abū Ṣāliḥ Riẓawī to the mansab of 2,000 and 1,000 horse, with the title of Riẓawī K͟hān, and, being honoured with a standard and an elephant, he took leave for the Deccan.

At this time it was represented to me that the Commander-in-Chief, the Ātālīq K͟hān-k͟hānān, as a sequel to the celebrated line, "For every rose one must bear the pain of a hundred thorns," had written an ode, and that Mīrzā Rustam Ṣafawī and Mīrzā Murād, his son, had also tried their skill. An impromptu opening couplet came into my mind:

"A cup of wine should be poured33 on the cheek of the rosebud.

There are many clouds, much wine should be poured."

Of those who were present at the entertainment who had the poetic temperament each composed an ode, and presented it. It became known that the hemistich was from Maulānā ʿAbdu-r-Raḥmān Jāmī. I looked at the whole of his ode (or odes). Except this hemistich, which like a proverb has become famous over the world, he has not written anything epigrammatic. All is very simple and smooth.34 On this day arrived the news of the death of Aḥmad Beg K., governor of Kashmir. His sons, who were of the house-born ones of the Court, and on whose foreheads the signs of intelligence and zeal were manifest, obtained suitable mansabs, and were sent to do duty in the Ṣuba of Bangas͟h and Kabul. His mansab was that of 2,500; his eldest son obtained that of 3,000 (?),35 and three other sons that of 900 each. On Thursday, the 14th, K͟hwāja Bāqī K., who was adorned with the high qualities of dignity, honour, generosity, and valour, under whose rule was one of the thānas of the country of Berār, was promoted to the mansab of 1,500 and 1,000 horse, original and increased, and the title of Bāqī K. Rāy Kahnūr (Kunwar?), who was formerly Dīwān of Gujarat, was chosen for the dīwānship of Mālwa.

At this time the pairing of the *sāras*, which I had never seen before, and is reported never to have been seen by man, was witnessed by me. The *sāras* is a creature of the crane genus, but somewhat larger.36 On the top of the head it has no feathers, and the skin is drawn over the bones of the head. From the back of the eye to six finger-breadths of the neck it is red. They mostly live in pairs on the plains, but are occasionally seen in flocks. People bring a pair in from the fields, and keep them in their houses, and they become familiar with men. In fact, there was a pair of *sāras* in my establishment to which I had given the names of Lailā and Majnūn. One day a eunuch informed me that (the) two had paired in his presence. I ordered that if they showed an inclination to pair again they should inform me. At dawn he came and told me that they were about to pair again. I immediately hastened to look on. The female having straightened its legs bent down a little: the male then lifted up one of its feet from the ground and placed it on her back, and afterwards the second foot, and, immediately seating himself on her back, paired with her. He then came down, and, stretching out his neck, put his beak to the ground, and walked once round the female. It is possible they may have an egg and produce a young one. Many strange tales of the affection of the *sāras* for its mate have been heard. The following case has been recorded because it is very strange. Qiyām K., who is one of the k͟hānazāds (houseborn ones) of this Court, and is well acquainted with the arts of hunting and scouting, informed me that one day he had gone out to hunt, and found a *sāras* sitting. When he approached, it got up and went off. From its manner of walking he perceived signs of weakness and pain. He went to the place where it had been sitting, and saw some bones and a handful of feathers on which it had been sitting. He threw a net round it, and drew himself into a corner, and it tried to go and sit in the same place. Its foot was caught in the net, and he went forward and seized it. It appeared extremely light, and when he looked minutely he saw there were no feathers on its breast and belly: its flesh and skin had separated, and there were maggots. Moreover, there was no sign of flesh left on any of its members: a handful of feathers and bone came into his hand. It was clear that its mate had died, and that it had sate there from the day it lost its companion.

"My burning heart hath melted my body with separation's pang;

A soul-consuming sigh burnt me, as 'twere a lamp.

The day of my joy became black like the night of grief,

Separation from thee hath made my day like this."

Himmat K., who is one of my best servants, and whose word is worthy of reliance, told me that in the Doḥad37 pargana he had seen a pair of *sāras* on the bank of a tank. One of his gunners shot one of them, and in the same place cut off its head and stripped38 it of its feathers (?). By chance we halted two or three days at that place, and its mate continually walked round it, and uttered cries and lamentation. "My heart," he said, "ached at its distress, but there was no remedy for it save regret." By chance, twenty-five days afterwards, he passed by the same spot, and asked the inhabitants what had become of that *sāras*. They said it died on the same day, and there were still remains of feathers and bones on the spot. He went there himself, and saw it was as they said. There are many tales of this kind among the people, which it would take too long to tell.

On Saturday, the 16th, there came the news of the death of Rāwat S͟hankar, who was one of those on duty in Bihār. Mān Singh, his eldest son, was raised to the manṣab of 2,000 personal and 600 horse: his other sons and connections were also raised in manṣab, and were directed to obey him. On Thursday, the 21st, the elephant Bāvan,39 the pick of my catch, which had been left in the pargana of Doḥad to be tamed, was brought to Court. I ordered him to be kept near the jharoka on the river side, that he might be constantly under my eye. In the elephant-stables of H.M. Akbar the largest elephant I saw was Durjan Sāl. It was long the premier elephant. Its height was 4 yards (*dara*ʿ40), and 3½ quarters of the *Ilāhī gaz*, which is 8 yards and 3 fingers of the ordinary *gaz*. At present, among the elephants of my establishment, the largest athlete is ʿĀlam-Gajrāj, which H.M. Akbar himself had caught. It is the chief of my special elephants. Its height is 4⅛ yards, or 7 yards and 7 fingers41 of the ordinary yard. The ordinary *gaz* has been fixed at 24 fingers' breadth of an average-sized man, and the *Ilāhī gaz* is 40 fingers' breadth.

On this day Muẓaffar K., who had been promoted to the Subadarship of Thatta (Sind), had the good fortune to kiss the threshold. He presented 100 *muhars* and Rs. 100 as naẕr, and the equivalent of Rs. 100,000 in jewels and jewelled things. At this time news came that God Almighty had bestowed on my son Parwīz a son42 by the daughter of S͟hāh Murād, deceased. It is to be hoped that his coming will be of good omen to this State.

On Sunday, the 24th, Rāy Bihārī43 had the good fortune to kiss the threshold: there is not a greater Zamindar than this in the country of Gujarat. His country is close to the sea. Bihārī and the Jām are from one stem. They were united ten generations ago. As far as territory and forces go, the standing of Bihārī is greater than that of the Jām. They say that he never came to see any of the Sultans of Gujarat. Sulṭān Maḥmūd had sent an army against him, but in the fight the army of Maḥmūd was defeated. At the time when K͟hān Aʿẓam went to conquer the fort of Jūnāgaṛh in the country of Sūrat, Nannū, who was called Sulṭān Muẓaffar, and gave himself out as heir to the kingdom, was passing his days in a state of misery under the protection of the zamindars. After this the Jām was defeated in battle with the victorious (Royal) army, and Nannū took refuge with Rāy Bihārī. K͟hān Aʿẓam demanded Nannū from Rāy Bihārī, and as he could not oppose the Royal army, he gave him up, and by this piece of loyalty was saved from the blows of the victorious army. At the time44 when Ahmadabad was adorned by the presence of the retinue of fortune for a short time, he did not come to wait on me. His country was somewhat distant, and time did not admit of the appointing of a force (against him). When it happened that I returned there, my son S̲h̲āh-Jahān appointed Raja Bikramājīt with an army (for this purpose), and he, seeing his own safety in coming in hastened to receive the honour of kissing the threshold, giving 200 *muhars* and Rs. 2,000 as naẕr, and 100 horses. However, there was not one of his horses that I approved of. His age appeared to me to be more than eighty45 years, and he himself said he was ninety. In his senses and powers there was no appearance of decay. Among his men there was an old man with white beard, moustaches, and eyebrows. He said that Rāy Bihārī remembered him when he (the old man) was a child (infant), and that he had grown up from childhood in his service.

On this day Abū-l-Ḥasan,46 the painter, who has been honoured with the title of Nādiru-z-zamān, drew the picture of my accession as the frontispiece to the Jahāngīr-nāma, and brought it to me. As it was worthy of all praise, he received endless favours. His work was perfect, and his picture is one of the *chefs d'œuvre* of the age. At the present time he has no rival or equal. If at this day the masters ʿAbdu-l-Ḥayy and Bihzād were alive, they would have done him justice. His father, Āqā Riẓāʾī, of Herat,47 at the time when I was Prince, joined my service. He (Abū-l-Ḥasan) was a *k̲h̲ānaẓād* of my Court. There is, however, no comparison between his work and that of his father (*i.e.*, he is far better than his father). One cannot put them into the same category. My connection was based on my having reared him. From his earliest years up to the present time I have always looked after him, till his art has arrived at this rank. Truly he has become Nādira-i-zamān ("the wonder of the age"). Also, Ustād Manṣūr48 has become such a master in painting that he has the title of Nādiru-l-ʿAṣr, and in the art of drawing is unique in his generation. In the time of my father's reign and my own these two have had no third. As regards myself, my liking for painting and my practice in judging it have arrived at such a point that when any work is brought before me, either of deceased artists or of those of the present day, without the names being told me, I say on the spur of the moment that it is the work of such and such a man. And if there be a picture containing many portraits, and each face be the work of a different master, I can discover which face is the work of each of them. If any other person has put in the eye and eyebrow of a face, I can perceive whose work the original face is, and who has painted the eye and eyebrows.

On the eve of Sunday, the 31st of the month of Tīr, heavy rain fell, and it went on raining with great violence till Tuesday, the 1st of Amurdād.49 For sixteen days there were constantly clouds and (? or) rain. As this is a sandy country, and the buildings in it are weak, many houses fell, and many lives were lost. I heard from the inhabitants of the city that they remembered no rain like that of this year. Although the channel of the Sābarmatī50 appears full of water, it is in most places fordable, and elephants can always cross it. If for a day there has been no rain, horses and men can ford it. The fountain head of this river is in the hill-country of the Rānā. It comes out from the ravine of Kokra(?),51 and, having traversed 1½ *koss*, passes below Mīrpūr,52 and in this place they call it the Wākal (?). After passing 3 *koss* beyond Mīrpūr, they call it the Sābarmatī.

On Thursday, the 10th, Rāy Bihārī was exalted with the favour of a male and a female elephant, a jewelled dagger, and four rings, of red ruby and yellow ruby (topaz), sapphire, and emerald. Before this, the Ātālīq Jān-sipār (life-jeoparding), Kh̲ān-kh̲ānān (ʿAbdu-r-Raḥīm), Commander-in-Chief, by order, had sent a force under the leadership of his son Amru-llah53 towards Gondwāna, in order to seize the diamond mine of Barākar54 (?) that was in the possession of Panjū, a Zamindar of Khandesh. On this day a report came from him that the aforesaid Zamindar, knowing that opposition to the victorious army was beyond his power, had made an offering of the mine, and a royal superintendent had been appointed to manage it. The diamonds of that place are superior in kind and beauty to all other kinds of diamonds, and much esteemed by jewellers. They are of good shape, and larger, and superior. Of the second rank is the mine of Kokhra,55 which is on the borders of Bihar; but the diamonds of that place are not obtained from the mine, but from a river which in the rainy season comes down in flood from the hills. Before that they dam it up, and when the flood has passed over the dam and there is little water, a number of men who are skilled in this art go into the river bed and bring out the diamonds. It is now three years since this country came into the possession of the State. The Zamindar of the place is in confinement. The climate of that land is excessively poisonous, and strangers cannot live there. The third place is in the province of the Karnatik (Carnatic), near the frontier of Quṭbu-l-mulk. At a distance of 50 *koss*56 there are four mines. Many very fine57 diamonds are obtained there.

On Thursday, the 10th, Nāhir K. was promoted to the manṣab of 1,500 personal and 1,000 horse, and he was presented with an elephant. Maktūb K., superintendent of the *Kutub-kh̲āna* (library), was given the manṣab of 1,500 personal. As I had ordered that on the Sh̲ab-i-Barāt they should place lamps round the Kānkrīya tank, at the end of the day on Monday, the 14th Shaʿbān, I went out to look at them. The buildings all round the tank they had arranged with lanterns of different colours and all kinds of artifices that are practicable with lamps, and fireworks. Although at this season there were continually clouds and rain, by God's favour from the beginning of the night the air had become clear, and not a trace of cloud remained, and the lights shone just as one could wish. My domestic servants were regaled with the cups of joy. I ordered them to light lamps in the same manner on the eve of Friday, and a strange thing was that at the close of the day of Thursday, the

17th, it continually rained (*muttaṣil bāridagī*), but at the time of lighting the lamps the rain ceased, and the show was well seen. On this day Iʿtimādu-d-daula presented an offering of a *quṭbī* (?) sapphire exceedingly delicate, and an elephant without tusks with silver housings. As it was handsome-looking and of good shape, it was put among my private elephants. On the bank of the Kānkrīya tank a *sanyāsī*, one of the most austere sects of Hindus, had made a hut after the dervish manner, and lived as a hermit. As I was always inclined to associate with dervishes, I hastened without ceremony to interview him, and for a while enjoyed his society. He was not wanting in information and reasonableness, and was well informed according to the rules of his own faith in the doctrines of Sufism. He had conformed to the ways of people of religious poverty and mortification, and given up all desires and ambitions. One might say that a better than he of his class was never seen.

On Monday, the 21st (Amurdād), the *sāras*, the pairing of which has been related in the preceding pages, collected together some straw and rubbish in the little garden, and laid first of all one egg. On the third day (afterwards) it laid a second egg. This pair of *sāras* were caught when they were a month old,58 and had been in my establishment for five years. After five and a half years they paired, and continued doing so for a month; on the 21st of the month of Amurdād, which the Hindus call Sāwan (Srāvan) the hen laid the eggs. The female used to sit on the eggs the whole night alone, and the male stood near her on guard. It was so alert that it was impossible for any living thing to pass near her. Once a large weasel made its appearance, and he ran at it with the greatest impetuosity, and did not stop until the weasel got into a hole. When the sun illuminated the world with his rays, the male went to the female and pecked her back with his beak. The female then rose, and the male sate in her place. She returned, and in the same manner made him rise, and seated herself. In short, the female sits the whole night, and takes care of the eggs, and by day the male and female sit by turns. When they rise and sit down they take great precautions that no harm shall come to the eggs.

During this season, as there was still some of the hunting time left, Gajpat K., the darogha, and Balūch K., the head huntsman, had been left to hunt elephants, to catch as many as they possibly could. In the same manner the huntsmen of my son, S͟hāh-Jahān, had also been employed. On this day they came and waited on me. Altogether 185 elephants had been caught, male and female: of these, 73 were males and 112 females. Out of these, 47 males and 75 females, or 122, the imperial huntsmen and faujdārs had secured, while the huntsmen and elephant-drivers of my son, S͟hāh-Jahān, had taken 26 males and 37 females, or 63 altogether.

On Thursday, the 24th, I went to see the Bāgh-i-Fatḥ,[59] and spent two days there in enjoyment and pleasure. At the end of the day on Saturday I returned to the palace. As Āṣaf K. had represented that his *ḥawīlī* (house) garden was exceedingly green and pleasant, and all sorts of flowers and scented plants had bloomed there, at his request I went to it on *Mubārak-shamba* (Thursday), the 31st. In truth, it was a very nice villa, and I was much pleased. His offering of jewels and jewelled things, and cloth, of the value of Rs. 35,000, was accepted. Muẓaffar K. was favoured with a dress of honour and an elephant, and, as before, was entrusted with the charge of the government of Thatta (Sind). My brother Shāh ʿAbbās sent a letter with some trifling presents by ʿAbdu-l-Karīm of Gīlān, who had come with merchandise from Īrān. On this day I presented him with a dress of honour and an elephant, and gave him leave to return, and sent an answer to the Shah's letter with a memorandum. Khān ʿĀlam was also honoured with a gracious farman and a special dress of honour. Friday was the 1st of the month of Shahrīwar. From Sunday, the 3rd, till the eve of Thursday (the 7th) rain fell. It is strange that on other days the pair of *sāras* sate on the eggs five or six times in turn, but during this twenty-four hours, when there was constant rain and the air was somewhat cold, the male, in order to keep the eggs warm, sate from early in the morning until midday, and from that time until the next morning the female sat without an interval, for fear that in rising and sitting again the cold air should affect them, and the eggs become wet and be spoilt. Briefly, men are led by the guidance of Reason, and animals according to the Divine wisdom implanted in them by Nature. Stranger still is it that at first they keep their eggs together underneath the breast, and after fourteen or fifteen days have passed they leave a little space between them, for fear the heat should become too great from their contact with each other. Many become addled in consequence of (too great) heat.

On Thursday, the 7th, with great joy and congratulation, the advance camp was started towards Agra. The astrologers and astronomers had already fixed the auspicious hour for the march. As excessive rain fell, the main camp could not cross the river of Maḥmūdābād (the Vātrak) and the Māhī at this hour. Out of necessity, the advanced camp was started at the appointed hour, and the 21st Shahrīwar[60] was fixed for the march of the main camp.

My son Shāh-Jahān took upon himself the responsibility of the conquest of the fort of Kāngṛa, over which the noose of victory had not been thrown by any of the Sultans of lofty dignity, and an army under the leadership of Rāja Sūraj Mal, s. Rāja Bāso, and Taqī, who was one of his attached servants, had before this been sent for that purpose. It was now clear that the conquest could not be achieved by the force that had been previously appointed. Rāja Bikramājīt,[61] who was one of his principal officers, with 2,000 horse who were present of his private attendants, and a force of Jahāngīrī servants, such as Sẖāh-bāz K. Lodī, Hardī Narāyan Hāḍā, Rāy Prithī Chand, and the sons of Rām Chand, with 200 mounted musketeers and 500 foot-musketeers (*topchī*, perhaps cannoniers), in addition to the force that had previously been sent, were appointed to the duty. As the hour for departure was fixed on this day, the aforesaid (Bikramājīt) presented as an offering a rosary of emeralds of the value of Rs. 10,000. He was honoured with the gift of a dress of honour and a sword, and took his leave for this duty. As he had not a jagir in that Subah, my son Sẖāh-Jahān asked for him as a jagir the pargana of Barhāna (?),62 the revenue of which was 2,200,000 of dams, which63 he himself (? Sẖāh-Jahān) held in in'ām.64 Kẖwāja Taqī, the Dīwān-i-Buyūtāt, who had been appointed to the Dīwānī of the Deccan, was honoured with the title of Mu'taqid65 K., a dress of honour, and an elephant. I appointed Himmat K. to the faujdārship of the Sarkar of Bharūch (Broach) and that neighbourhood, with the gift of a horse and a special *parm narm* (shawl), and despatched him. The pargana of Bharūch (Broach) was also bestowed on him as jagir. Rāy Prithī Chand, who had been nominated for service at Kāngṛa, was promoted to the rank of 700 and 450 horse. As the anniversary of Sẖaikẖ Muḥammad Gẖauṣ66 had arrived, I gave his sons 1,000 *darbs* (Rs. 500) for its expense. Muẕaffar, s. Bahāduru-l-mulk, who was attached to the Deccan, was given the manṣab of 1,000 personal and 500 horse.

As the events of twelve years of *Jahāngīr-nāma* have been recorded, I ordered67 the clerks of my private library to make one volume of these twelve years, and to prepare a number of copies so that I might give them to my special servants, and that they might be sent to the various cities, so that administrators (arbāb-i-daulat) and the auspicious might adopt them as their code. On Friday, the 8th,68 one of the news-writers had written the whole and made a volume, which he produced to me. As it was the first copy that had been prepared, I gave it to my son Sẖāh-Jahān, whom I consider to be in all respects the first of my sons. On the back of it I wrote with my own hand that I had given it him on a certain day and at a certain place. I hope that the favour of the receipt of those writings which are intended for the satisfaction of the creature and for supplication to the Creator may be a cause of good fortune.

On Tuesday, the 12th, Subḥān Qulī, huntsman, was brought to punishment. The details of this are that he is the son of Ḥājī Jamāl Balūch, who was my father's best huntsman, and after his (the King's) death, he entered the service of Islām K., and went with him to Bengal. Islām Kẖān, on account of his (Subḥān Qulī's) connection with this Court, showed him proper consideration, and considering him trustworthy always kept him near him when travelling or hunting. 'Uṡmān, the Afghan, who for many years passed his days in that Subah in disobedience and stubbornness, and the end of whose affairs has been recorded in the preceding pages, being much troubled by Islām Khān, sent someone to this wretch, and made proposals for his murdering Islām. He undertook the business, and associated two or three other men with himself. By chance, before the futile idea of this ungrateful fellow was carried into execution, one of them came and informed him (Islām K.). Islām K. immediately seized and imprisoned the scoundrel. After the latter's death he came to Court. As his brothers and relatives were included among the huntsmen, he was also ordered to be enrolled among them. At this time the son (Ikrām K.) of Islām K. represented in an enigmatical way that he was unworthy of service near my person. After explanation it appeared what the charge was. Notwithstanding this, fas his brothers strenuously represented that there was only suspicion, and Balūch K., the head huntsman, became security for him, I forbore to put him to death, and ordered him to do duty with Balūch K. In spite of this grace and the gift of his life, without cause or motive he fled from the Court, and went to Agra and that neighbourhood. Balūch K., having become his security, was ordered to produce him. He sent people to inquire for him. In one of the villages of Agra, which was not wanting in sedition, and is called Jahanda,69 the brother of Balūch Khān, who had gone to make inquiries, found him, and although he endeavoured to bring him by persuasion to Court, he would in no way consent, and the people rose to assist him.

Being without remedy, he (the brother) went to Khwāja Jahān at Agra, and told him the circumstances. He sent a detachment against that village to take him by force and bring him. The people of the village, seeing their own ruin in the mirror of the case, handed him over to him. This day he came to Court in chains. I gave an order for his execution. The man of wrath (the executioner) took him to the place of punishment with all haste. After a while, through the intercession of one of the courtiers, I gave him his life, and ordered his feet to be cut off, but according to his destiny (what was written on his head) before the order arrived he had been punished. Although that doomed man was deserving of punishment, yet I regretted70 the circumstance, and directed that whenever an order was given for anyone's execution, notwithstanding that the command were imperative, they should wait till sunset before putting him to death. If up to that time no order for release arrived, he should without fail be capitally punished.

On Sunday there was a great commotion in the River Māhī, and very large waves were visible. Although there formerly had been (great) rains, yet such violence, or even the half of it, had never been known. From the beginning of the day the flood began to come, and at the end of the day began to decrease. Old inhabitants of this city represented that once, during the government of Murtaẓā K. (Farīd Bukhārī), a similar great flood had occurred. But with that exception they did not remember another such flood.

In these days mention was made of an ode by Muʿizzī,71 the panegyrist of Sulṭān Sanjar, and his Poet-laureate. It is a very smooth and equable72 composition. It begins thus:

"O thou whose commands heaven obeys

Ancient Saturn is the slave of thy young Fortune."

Saʿīdā,73 the chief goldsmith, has a poetical temperament and he imitated this ode, and presented his paraphrase to me. It was very well composed. The following are some verses from it:

"O thou, of whose threshold the nine spheres are an examplar

Aged Time hath grown young in thy reign

Thy heart is bounteous as the Sun, and like it needs no cause (for bounty).

All lives are devoted to thy gracious heart

Heaven is but a green74 orange from the garden of Power

Tossed by thy gardener into the atmosphere,

O God, Thy essence has shone from eternity

The souls of all the saints receive light from Thine,

O king, may the world ever be at thy beck,

May thy Shāh-Jahān ever rejoice in thy shade

O Shadow of God, may the world be filled with thy light

May the Light of God ever be thy canopy."

On *Mubārak-shamba*, the 14th, in reward for this ode, I ordered Saʿīdā to be weighed against money (*zar*, perhaps gold). At the end of the day I went to walk about the garden of Rustam-bārī,75 which appeared to me very green and pleasant. Sitting in a boat in the evening, I returned to the palace.

On Friday, the 15th, a Mullā of the name of Amīrī, an old man, came from Mā-warāʾa-n-nahr (Transoxiana), and had the good fortune to kiss the threshold. He represented to me that he was one of the ancient (servants) of ʿAbdu-llah Khān Uzbeg, and from the days of infancy76 and youth was brought up by the Khān until his death. He had been included among his old servants, and had been a confidential friend.77 After the death of the Khān until now he had passed his days respected in that country. He had left his native country with a view to visit the blessed house (Mecca), and had come to pay his respects to me. I made him free to remain or go. He asked to remain in attendance on me for some days. Rs. 1,000 for expenses and a dress of honour were given him. He is an old man of very pleasing face, and full of talk and anecdote. My son S_h_āh-Jahān also gave him Rs. 500 and a robe of honour.

In the middle of the garden of K_h_urram (S_h_āh-Jahān's) residence there is a bench and a reservoir. On one side78 of that bench there is a Mūlsarī-tree (*Mimusops elengi*) against which to lean the back. As in one side of its trunk there was a hollow to the extent of three-fourths of a yard, it had an ugly look. I ordered them to cut a tablet of marble and fix it firmly in that place, so that one could lean one's back on it and sit there. At this time an impromptu couplet came to my tongue, and I ordered the stone-cutters to engrave it on that stone, that it might remain as a memento on the page of time. This is the couplet:

"The seat of the S_h_āh of the seven worlds (kis_h_war),

Jahāngīr, son of Akbar S_h_āhins_h_āh.

On the eve of Tuesday,79 the 19th, a bazaar was arranged in the private palace. Up to this time the custom has been for the people of the bazaar and the artificers of the city in every place to bring their shops according to order into the courtyard of the palace (royal abode, whether in camp or elsewhere), and bring jewels and jewelled things and various kinds of cloth and other goods such as are sold in the bazaar. It occurred to me that if a bazaar were prepared in the night-time, and a number of lamps were arranged in front of the shops, it would look well. Undoubtedly it came off well and was unusual. Going round all the shops, whatever jewels and jewelled things pleased me I bought. I gave some present from each shop to Mullā Amīrī, and he received so many things that he was unable to hold them.

On *Mubārak-s_h_amba* (Thursday) the 21st of the Divine month of S_h_ahrīwar, in the thirteenth year from my accession, corresponding with the 22nd Ramaẓān (September 2, 1618), in the Hijrī year 1027, when two and a half hours of day had passed, in prosperity and happiness, the standards of purpose turned towards the capital of Agra. From the palace as far as the Kānkrīya tank, the place of alighting, I passed along in the usual manner, scattering money (*niṣār-kunān*). On the same day the feast of my solar weighment took place, and according to solar reckoning the fiftieth year of the age of his suppliant at the throne of God commenced auspiciously. According to my usual rule I weighed myself against gold and other valuables. I scattered pearls and golden roses, and looking at night at the show of lamps passed my time in the private apartments of the royal abode in enjoyment. On Friday, the 22nd, I ordered that all the S͟haik͟hs and men of piety who lived in the city should be brought in order that they might break their fast80 in attendance on me. Three nights were passed after this manner, and every night at the end of the meeting I stood up and recited with the tongue of ecstasy:

"Thou art the mighty One, O Lord,

Thou art the cherisher of rich and poor;

I'm not a world-conqueror or law-giver,

I'm one of the beggars at this gate.

Help me in what is good and right,

Else what good comes from me to any one?

I'm a master81 to my servants,

To the Lord I'm a loyal servant."

All the Faqīrs who as yet had not waited on me prayed for allowances. According to their merits I gave to each of them land or money for expenses, and gratified them.

On the eve of *Mubārak-s͟hamba* (Thursday) the 21st, the sāras hatched one young one, and on the eve of Monday, the 25th, a second: that is, one young one was hatched after thirty-four82 days, and the other after thirty-six days. One might say that they were one-tenth83 larger than the young of a goose, or equal to the young of the peafowl at the age of a month. Their skin was of a blue colour. On the first day they ate nothing, and from the second day the mother, taking small locusts (or grasshoppers) in her mouth, sometimes fed them like a pigeon, or sometimes like a fowl threw them before them for them to pick up of themselves. If the locust were small, it went off well, but if it were large, she sometimes made two or three pieces of it so that the young ones might eat it with ease. As I had a great liking for seeing them I ordered them to be brought before me with every precaution that no harm might happen to them. After I had seen them I ordered them to be taken back to the same little garden inside the royal enclosure, and to be preserved with the greatest care, and that they should be brought to me again whenever they were able to walk.

On this day Ḥakīm Rūḥu-llah was exalted with the gift of Rs. 1,000. Badī'u-z-zamān, s. M. S͟hāhruk͟h, came from his jagir and waited on me. On Tuesday, the 26th, marching from the Kānkrīya tank, I halted at the village of Kaj.84 On Wednesday, the 27th, I pitched my camp on the bank of the river at

Maḥmūdābād called the Īzak85 (now called Meshva). As the water and air of Aḥmadābād were very bad, Maḥmūd Bīgara, by the advice of his physicians, founded a city on the bank of the aforesaid river and lived there. After he conquered Chāmpāner, he made that place his capital, and until the time of Maḥmūd the martyred86 the rulers of Gujarat chiefly lived there. This Maḥmūd was the last of the Sultans of Gujarat, and he took up his residence at Maḥmūdābād. Undoubtedly the water and air of Maḥmūdābād have no resemblance to those of Aḥmadābād. By way of testing this I ordered them to hang up a sheep on the bank of the Kānkrīya tank after taking off its skin, and at the same time one at Maḥmūdābād, that the difference of the air might be ascertained. It happened that after seven *gharīs* of day had passed in that place (Aḥmadābād) they hung up the sheep. When three *gharīs* of day remained it became so changed and putrid that it was difficult to pass near it. They hung up the sheep at Maḥmūdābād in the morning, and it was altogether unchanged until the evening, and began to be putrid when one and a half watches of night had passed. Briefly, in the neighbourhood of Aḥmadābād it became putrid in eight sidereal hours, and in Maḥmūdābād in fourteen hours.

On Thursday, the 28th, Rustam K., whom my son of prosperous fortune, S̲h̲āh-Jahān, had appointed to the charge and government of Gujarat, was honoured with the gift of an elephant, a horse, and a special *parm narm* (shawl), and given leave to depart, and the Jahāngīrī officers who were attached to that Subah were presented with horses and dresses of honour according to the rank and standing of each. On Friday, 29th S̲h̲ahrīwar, corresponding with 1st Shawwāl, Rāy Bihārī was honoured with the bestowal of a dress of honour, a jewelled sword and a special horse, and took leave to go to his native place. His sons were also honoured with horses and dresses of honour. On Saturday I ordered Sayyid Muḥammad, grandson87 (?) of S̲h̲āh ʿĀlam, to ask for whatever he desired without concealment, and I took an oath on the Qoran to this effect. He said that as I had sworn on the Qoran he would ask for a Qoran that he might always have it by him, and that the merit of reading it might accrue to His Majesty. Accordingly, I gave the Mīr a Qoran in Yāqūt's88 handwriting. It was a small, elegant89 volume, and was the wonder of the age. On the back of it I wrote with my own hand that I had made this gift on a certain day and in a certain place to Sayyid Muḥammad. The real reason for this is that the Mīr is of an exceedingly good disposition, endowed with personal nobility and acquired excellencies, of good manners and approved ways, with a very pleasing face and open forehead. I have never seen a man of this country of such a pleasing disposition as the Mīr. I told him to translate this Qoran into plain language without ornament, and that without occupying himself with explanations or fine language he90 should translate the Qoran in simple language (*lughāt-i-*

*rīkhta*) word by word into Persian, and should not add one letter to its exact purport. After he had completed it he should send it by his son Jalālu-d-dīn Sayyid to the Court. The Mīr's son is also a young man of external and internal intelligence. The signs of piety and blessedness are distinct on his forehead. The Mīr is proud of his son, and in truth he is worthy, as he is an excellent youth. As I had repeatedly shown kindness to the holy men of Gujarat, according to their merits, I again bestowed on each cash and jewels, and dismissed them to their homes.

As the climate91 of this country was not suited to my temperament, the physicians thought it right that I should decrease somewhat my usual number of cups. According to their advice I began to decrease their number, and in the course of a week reduced them by the weight of one cup. At first it was six cups every evening, each cup being 7½ *tola*, or altogether 45 *tolas*. The wine was usually mixed with water. Now I drank six cups, each of which was 6 *tolas* and 3 *māshas*,92 altogether 37½ *tolas*.

Sixteen or seventeen years ago I had vowed with my God at Allahabad that when I reached fifty I would give up shooting with gun and bullet, and would injure no living thing with my own hand. Muqarrab K., who was one of my confidants, knew of my determination. At this date I have reached the commencement of my fiftieth year, and one day, in consequence of excessive fever (*dūd u bukhār*) my breath was short and I was very unwell. While in this condition the compact I had made with my God came, by Divine inspiration, into my mind, and I resolved that when my fiftieth year was completed and the period of fulfilling my vow had arrived, I would, on the day93 on which I visited my father's tomb—may the light of God be his testimony—by God's help, seek the confirmation of my resolve from my father's holy elements, and renounce the practice (of shooting). As soon as this thought occurred to me, my illness and trouble disappeared. I revived, and opened my mouth to praise God, and tasted the joy of thanksgiving for His mercies. I hope that I shall be sustained.

"How well said Firdūsī of pure nature

May mercy rest on that (his) pure tomb.

"Ah! spare yon emmet94 rich in hoarded grain,

He lives with pleasure, and he dies with pain."

On Thursday, the 4th of the Divine month, Sayyid Kabīr and Bakhtar K., the Wakils of ʿĀdil K., who had brought his offering to the exalted Court, obtained leave to return. Sayyid Kabīr was honoured with a dress of honour, a horse, and a jewelled dagger, and Bakhtar K. with a horse, a dress of honour, and a jewelled *ūrbasī*,95 which the people of that country (the Deccan?) wear round their necks, and a present of 6,000 *darbs* was given to each of them for expenses.

As 'Ādil K. was constantly asking for a likeness of myself through my prosperous son S͟hāh-Jahān, I sent him one with a ruby of great value and a special elephant. A gracious farman was issued that he should be presented with whatever territory of Niẓāmu-l-mulk or Quṭbu-l-mulk he might get into his possession, and whenever he should require any support and assistance, S͟hāh-nawāz K. should prepare an army and appoint it to assist him. In former days Niẓāmu-l-mulk was the largest of the rulers of the Deccan, a superior whom all acknowledged, and whom they considered as their eldest brother. At this period 'Ādil K. did approved service, and was honoured with the exalted title of "son." I appointed him the head and leader of the whole country of the Deccan, and wrote this quatrain on the portrait with my own hand:

"O thou towards whom is always (turned) the eye of my kindness

Repose at ease under the shadow of my fortune.

I have sent thee my own portrait,

That thou mayest see me spiritually from my picture."

My son S͟hāh-Jahān sent Ḥakīm K͟hūs͟h-ḥāl, son of Ḥakīm Humām, who was one of the excellent house-born ones of this Court, and from his early years had been in my son's service, in company with the Wakils of 'Ādil K. to convey to him the good news of the Jahāngīrī favour towards him. On the same day Mīr Jumla was honoured with the duty of *'Arẓ-mukarrir.* As Kifāyat K., the Diwan of Gujarat, at the time when he was employed in the Dīwānī of Bengal, in consequence of certain accidents, had lost property (*az sāmān uftāda*), a sum of Rs. 15,000 was presented to him.

At this time two copies of the Jahāngīr-nāma that had been prepared were laid before me. One of these I had some days previously given to the *Madāru-l-mulk* (centre of the kingdom), I'timādu-d-daula, and the other I on this day bestowed on my (adopted) son (*farzandī*), Āṣaf K. On Friday, the 5th, Bahrām, son of Jahāngīr Qulī K͟hān, came from the province of Bihar, and had the good fortune to pay his respects. He laid before me some diamonds he had obtained from the mine of Kokra. Approved service had not been performed in that province by Jahāngīr Qulī K., and it was also frequently reported that certain of his brothers and sons-in-law had stretched out the hand of tyranny in that country, and were oppressing the servants of God (the people), and that each of them, cutting out a governorship for himself, did not regard the authority of Jahāngīr Qulī. On this account a farman written with my own hand was given to Muqarrab K., one of my confidential old servants, stating that he was appointed Governor of Bihar. I ordered that immediately on receipt of the farman he should hasten to that quarter. Some of the diamonds that Ibrāhīm Fatḥ-jang had sent to Court after the taking of the mine had been given to the Government lapidaries to cut. At this time Bahrām suddenly came to Agra, and was going on to the Court (in Gujarat). K̲h̲wāja Jahān (the Governor of Agra) sent along with him some diamonds that were ready. One of them is of a violet[96] colour, and cannot be outwardly distinguished from a sapphire. Up to this time I had not seen a diamond of this colour. It weighed several *surk̲h̲*,[97] and jewellers estimated its value at Rs. 3,000, and represented that if it had been white (*safid*) and had had perfect marks, it would have been worth Rs. 20,000.

This year I had mangoes up to the 6th Mihr (middle of September). In this country there is abundance of lemons (*līmūn*), and they are large (*bālīda?*). A Hindu brought some from a garden called Kākū (or Gangū), which were very pleasant and large (*bālīda*, perhaps ripe). I ordered them to weigh the largest of them, and it came to 7 *tolas*.

On Saturday, the 6th, the Dasahrā festival took place. First, they decked out my horses, and paraded them before me. After that they produced the elephants, decorated in a similar way.

As the Māhī had not become fordable, so that the sublime camp could cross it, and the climate of Maḥmūdābād was quite different (*i.e.*, it was better) from that of other stages, I remained here for ten more days. On Monday, the 8th, I marched and encamped at Mūda.[98] I had already sent K̲h̲wāja Abū-l-Ḥasan Bak̲h̲s̲h̲ī with an active body of servants, such as boatmen, and also oars,[99] to make a bridge over the Māhī, with instructions not to wait till it was fordable, so that the victorious camp might cross at ease. On Tuesday, the 9th, there was a halt, and on *Kams̲h̲amba* (Wednesday), the 10th, the camp was at the village of Aina.[100]

At first the male *sāras* used to hold its young one by its leg upside down in his beak, and there was a fear that he might be unkind to it and it might be destroyed. I accordingly ordered them to keep the male separately, and not allow it near its young ones. I now ordered by way of experiment that it should be allowed near them, that the real degree of its unkindness and affection might be ascertained. After allowing it, he displayed much attachment and kindness, and his affection was found to be no less than that of the female; I thus knew that this performance was out of real love. On Thursday, the 11th, there was a halt, and at the end of the day I went to hunt with cheetahs, and two black buck, four does, and a *chikāra* were caught. On Sunday, the 14th, I also went to hunt with cheetahs, and caught fifteen head of male and female antelopes. I had ordered Rustam and Suhrāb[101] K̲h̲ān, his son, to go out hunting and shoot as many nilgaw as they could. The father and son together killed seven head, male and female. As it was represented to me that there was a tiger in this neighbourhood, a man-killer that had taken to eating men's flesh, and the people of God were afflicted by it, I ordered my son S͟hāh-Jahān to save them from its wickedness. He, as ordered, shot it with his gun, and brought it to me at night. I ordered them to skin it in my presence. Although large in appearance, as it was thin, it turned out less in weight than the large tigers I had myself killed. On Monday, the 15th, and Tuesday, the 16th, I went to shoot nilgaw, and on each day shot two blue bulls. On Thursday, the 18th, on the bank of a tank at which I pitched, a feast of cups was held. Rare lotus (kanwal) flowers had blossomed on the face of the water. My private servants enjoyed themselves greatly with cups of wine. Jahāngīr Qulī had sent twenty elephants from Bihar, and Muruwwat K. eight from Bengal, and these were brought before me. One of Jahāngīr Qulī's and two of Muruwwat's were placed in my private stud, and the rest were divided amongst my followers. Mīr K., s. Mīrzā Abū-l-Qāsim Namakīn, who was one of the khanazads of this Court, was promoted to the mansab, original and increased, of 800 personal and 600 horse. Qiyām K. was appointed to the duty of chief huntsman, and had given him the rank of 600 personal and 150 horse. ʿĪzzat102 K., one of the Bārha Sayyids, who was distinguished for bravery and ambition, is attached to the province of Bangash. At the request of Mahābat K., the Governor of that Subah, he was promoted to the mansab of 1,500 personal and 800 horse. Kifāyat K., Diwan of Gujarat, had an elephant given him, and was allowed to depart. I conferred a sword on Ṣafī K., Bakhshi of that Subah. On Friday, the 19th, I went to hunt, and killed a blue bull. I do not remember a bullet passing through a large male nilgaw. Many have passed through females. On this day, at a distance of forty-five paces (*qadam*), it went through both skins. In the language of hunters a *qadam* means two feet (*gām*103) placed one in front of the other. On Sunday, the 21st, I enjoyed myself with hawking, and ordered Mīrzā Rustam, Dārāb K., Mīr Mīrān, and other servants to go and shoot as many nilgaw as they could. They killed nineteen head, male and female. Ten head of antelope were also caught with cheetahs. Ibrāhīm K., Bakhshi of the Deccan, was, at the request of the Commander-in-Chief, K͟hān K͟hānān, promoted to the mansab of 1,000 personal and 200 horse. On Monday, the 22nd, a march was made, and on Tuesday, the 23rd, I again marched. The huntsmen represented that there had been seen in the neighbourhood a tigress with three cubs. As it was on the road I went myself after them and shot all four, and then went on to the next stage. I crossed the Māhī by the bridge that had been made. Though there were no boats on this river of which a bridge could be made, and the water was very deep and flowing rapidly, K͟hwāja Abū-l-Ḥasan, the chief Bakhshi, had built with great exertions a very strong bridge two or104 three days before. Its length was 140 yards and its breadth 4 yards (*dara*). By way of testing it I ordered the elephant Gun Sundar K͟hāṣṣ which is one of the large and strong elephants, with three females, to be sent across it. It was so firmly built that its supports did not shake with the weight of elephants of mountainous form.

From the most honoured lips of my father I heard as follows: "In early youth I had taken two or three cups (of wine), and had mounted a full-blooded (*mast*) elephant. Though I was in my senses, and the elephant in very good training, and was under my control, I pretended that I was out of my senses, and that the elephant was refractory and vicious, and that I was making him charge the people. After that, I sent for another elephant, and made the two fight. They fought, and in doing so went to the head of the bridge that had been made over the Jumna. It happened that the other elephant ran away, and as there was no other escape, he went towards the bridge. The elephant I was on pursued him, and although I had him under control, and he would have halted at the slightest signal, I thought that if I held him back from the bridge the people would regard those drunken ways (of mine) as a sham, and would believe that neither was I beside myself, nor was the elephant violent and headstrong. Such pretences on the part of kings are disapproved of, and so after imploring the aid of God—Glory be to Him—I did not restrain my elephant. Both of them went upon the bridge, and as it was made of boats, whenever an elephant put his forefeet on the edge of a boat, half of it sank, and the other half stood up. At each step there came the thought that the lashings might give way. People on seeing this were overwhelmed in the sea of perplexity and alarm. As the care and guardianship of the Great and Glorious God is ever and in all places the protection of this suppliant, both elephants crossed the bridge in safety."105

On Thursday, the 25th, a wine-feast was held on the banks of the Māhī, and some of my intimate servants who had admittance to such assemblies had their hearts delighted by brimming cups and ample favours. Certainly it was an entrancing halting-ground. I stayed here four days for two reasons—first, because of the beauty of the spot, and secondly in order that the people might not be confused in crossing the river.

On Sunday, the 28th, I marched from the bank of the Māhī. On Monday I marched again. On this day a strange sight was witnessed. The pair of sāras that had had young ones had been brought from Aḥmadābād on Thursday (the 25th). In the Court of the royal enclosure, which had been placed on the bank of a tank, they were walking about with their young ones. By chance both the male and female raised a cry, and a pair of wild sāras hearing it, and crying out from the other side of the tank, came flying towards them. The male with the male, and the female with the female, engaged in a fight, and although some people were standing about, the birds paid no heed to them. The eunuchs who had been told off to protect them hastened to seize them. One clung to the male and the other to the female. He who had caught the male kept hold of it after much struggling, but the one who seized the female could not hold her, and she escaped from his hand. I with my own hand put rings in his beak and on his legs, and set him free. Both went and settled in their own place.[106] Whenever the domestic sāras raised a cry they responded. I saw a sight of this kind in wild antelopes when I had gone to hunt in the pargana of Karnāl. About thirty of my huntsmen and servants were in attendance when a black buck with some does came in sight, and we let loose the decoy-antelope[107] to fight him. They butted two or three times, and then the decoy came back. A second time I wanted to put a noose on its horns and to let it go, that it might capture (the wild one). Meanwhile the wild antelope, in the excess of its rage, not looking at the crowd of men, ran without regard to anything, and butting the tame buck two or three times fought with it till it fled. The wild antelope thereupon made its escape.

On this day news came of the death of ʿInāyat K. He was one of my intimate attendants. As he was addicted to opium, and when he had the chance, to drinking as well, by degrees he became maddened with wine. As he was weakly built, he took more than he could digest, and was attacked by the disease of diarrhœa, and in this weak state he two or three times fainted. By my order Ḥakīm Ruknā applied remedies, but whatever methods were resorted to gave no profit. At the same time a strange hunger came over him, and although the doctor exerted himself in order that he should not eat more than once in twenty-four hours, he could not restrain himself. He also would throw[108] himself like a madman on water and fire until he fell into a bad[109] state of body. At last he became dropsical, and exceedingly low and weak. Some days before this he had petitioned that he might go to Agra. I ordered him to come into my presence and obtain leave. They put him into a palanquin and brought him. He appeared so low and weak that I was astonished.

"He was skin drawn over bones."

Or rather his bones, too, had dissolved. Though painters have striven much in drawing an emaciated face, yet I have never seen anything like this, nor even approaching to it. Good God, can a son of man come to such a shape and fashion? These two couplets of Ustād[110] occurred as appropriate:

"If my shadow do not hold my leg

I shall not be able to stand till the Resurrection

Nor, from weakness, does my soul see a refuge

Where it may for a while rest on my lips."

As it was a very extraordinary case I directed painters to take his portrait. In fact, I found him wonderfully changed. I said to him: "Beware; in your present state do not for a moment forget God, nor despair of His mercy! If Death grant you quarter (*amān*), regard the reprieve as a time for apologizing and for amendment. If your life has come to its close, consider every moment passed in remembrance of God as gain. Trouble not your head about those you are leaving behind. A slight claim of service is a great thing with us." As they had spoken to me about his poverty, I gave him Rs. 2,000 for road-expenses, and let him go. Next day he travelled the road of non-existence.

On Tuesday, the 30th, the bank of the River Mānab111 became the halting-place for the sublime camp. The New Year's112 feast of Thursday was prepared at this place on the 2nd of the Ilāhī month of Ābān. Amānu-llah, s. Mahābat K., at his request, was promoted to the mansab of 1,000 personal and 300113 horse, and Girdhar, s. Rāy Sāl, to that of 1,000 personal and 800 horse. ʿAbdu-llah, son of K͟hān Aʿẓạm, obtained the mansab of 1,000 personal and 300 horse. Dilīr K., who was one of the jagirdars of Gujarat, I presented with a horse and an elephant. Ran-bāz K., s. S͟hāh-bāz K. Kāmbū, came by order from the Deccan, and was promoted to the post of Bakhshi and Recorder of the army of Bangas͟h, and his mansab was fixed at 800 personal and 400 horse. I marched on Friday, the 3rd. At this stage114 Prince S͟hujāʿ, the beloved son (liver-corner) of my son S͟hāh-Jahān, who was being brought up in the chaste lap of Nūr-Jahān Begam, and towards whom I have so much affection that he is dearer to me than life, was attacked by a specially infantile disease which they call "ummu-ṣ-ṣibyān,"115 and for a long time his senses left him. Although experienced people devised many remedies, they were unprofitable, and his insensibility (*bī-hūs͟hī*) took away my senses (*hūs͟h*). As visible remedies were hopeless, by way of humility and submission I rubbed the head of supplication on the Court of the gracious Ruler who cherishes his slaves, and begged for the child's recovery. In this state it occurred to me that as I had made a vow116 to my God that after I had passed my fiftieth year, this suppliant would give up hunting with bullet and gun, and would injure no creature with his own hand, if for the sake of his safety I were to give up shooting from the present date, it were possible that his life would become the means of preserving the lives of many animals, and God Almighty might give him to me. In fine, with true purpose, and sincere belief I vowed117 to God that I would thenceforward not harm any living thing with my own hand. By the grace of Allah his illness diminished. At the time when this suppliant was in his mother's womb, one day I made no movement after the manner that other children make. The attendants were amazed, and inquiring into the cause stated the case to my father (Akbar). At that time my father was engaged in hunting with cheetahs. As that day was a Friday, for the purpose of my safety he made a vow that during his life he would not hunt with cheetahs on a Friday. Till the end of his life he remained firm in this determination, and I also in obedience to him until now have never hunted with cheetahs on a Friday. Finally, on account of the weakness of the light of my eye, S͟hāh S͟hujāʿ, for three days I halted at this stage, that God Almighty might give him his natural[118] life.

On Tuesday, the 7th, I marched. One day the son of Ḥakīm[119] ʿĀlī was praising the milk of a camel. It occurred to me that if I could continue that for some days, it was possible that it might do some good, and it might prove agreeable to me. Āṣaf K͟hān had a Persian camel in milk, and I took a little of it. Contrary to the milk of other camels, which is not devoid of saltness, it appeared to my taste sweet and delicious, and now for a month past I have been drinking every day a cup of it, equal in quantity to half a water-cup, and it is clearly advantageous, for it quenches my thirst. It is strange that two years ago Āṣaf K. bought this camel, but at that time it had not a young one, and had no sign of milk. At this time by chance milk flowed from its dugs. They gave it every day to drink four seers of cow's milk with five seers of wheat, one seer of black[120] sugar, and one seer of fennel (*bādyān*), to make its milk delicious, sweet, and profitable. Certainly it suited me admirably, and was to my taste. By way of testing it, I sent for some cow's and buffalo's milk, and tasted all three. There was no comparison in sweetness and flavour with the milk of this camel. I ordered them to give the same kind of food to some other female camels, that it might become clear whether the purity was in consequence of eating good food, or whether it was due to the natural sweetness of this (particular) camel's milk.[121]

On Wednesday, the 8th, I marched, and halted on the 9th. The royal tent was pitched near a large tank. S͟hāh-Jahān presented me with a boat made after the Kashmīr fashion, the sitting-place of which they had made of silver. At the end of that day I embarked in that boat and went round the tank. On this day ʿĀbid K., Bakhshi of Bangas͟h, who had been summoned, came and had the good fortune to kiss the threshold, and was honoured with the post of Dīwān-i-buyūtāt. Sar-farāz K͟hān, who was one of the auxiliaries of Gujarat, received a standard, a private *tipchāq* horse, and an elephant, and, overwhelmed with honour, obtained leave to go. ʿĪzzat[122] K͟hān, who was one of those attached to the army of Bangas͟h, was exalted with the gift of a standard. Marching was ordered on Friday, the 10th. Mīr Mīrān was promoted to the mansab of 2,000 personal and 600 horse. On Saturday, the 11th, the auspicious equipage alighted in the pargana of Doḥad. On the eve of Sunday, the 12th of the Ilāhī month of Ābān, in the thirteenth year from my accession, corresponding with the fifteenth Ẕī-l-Qaʿda of the Hijrī year 1027, in the nineteenth degree of Libra, the Giver of blessings gave my prosperous son S͟hāh-Jahān a precious son by the daughter of Āṣaf K. I hope that his[123] advent may be auspicious and blessed to this everlasting State. Halting for three days at this place, on Wednesday,[124] the 15th Ābān, the camp was pitched at the village of Ṣamarna.125 As it was necessary that the Mubārak-s̲h̲amba entertainment should as far as possible be arranged for on the bank of a river and a clean place, and there was in this neighbourhood no spot which met those requirements, there was no help for it but to order a start when half of the night of Thursday (*i.e.*, Wednesday), the 16th, had passed, and when the sun rose the camp was pitched on the bank of the tank of Bākhūr. At the end of the day, the feast of cups was held and I presented cups to some of my private servants. On Friday, the 17th, I ordered a march. Kes̲h̲o Dās Mārū is a jagirdar in that neighbourhood. According to orders, he came from the Deccan, and was honoured by doing homage.

On Saturday, the 18th (Ābān), the camp was at Rāmgaṛh. For some nights before this there appeared, at three *gharīs* before sunrise, in the atmosphere, a (luminous) vapour in the shape of a pillar.126 At each succeeding night it rose a *g̲h̲aṛī* earlier. When it assumed its full form, it took the shape of a spear (*ḥarba*), thin at the two ends, and thick in the middle. It was curved like a sickle, and had its back to the south, and its face to the north. It now showed itself a watch (*pahar*) before sunrise. Astronomers took its shape and size by the astrolabe, and ascertained that with differences of appearance (?) it extended over twenty-four degrees. It moved in high heaven, but it had a movement of its own, differing from that of high heaven, for it was first in Scorpio and afterwards in Libra. Its declination (*ḥarakat-i-ʿarẓ*?) was mainly southerly. Astrologers call such a phenomenon a spear (*ḥarba*) in their books, and have written that its appearance portends weakness to the kings of Arabia, and points to their enemies prevailing over them. God knows! Sixteen nights after this phenomenon, a star showed itself in the same quarter. Its head was luminous, and its tail was two or three yards long, but the tail was not luminous. It has now appeared for eight nights; when it disappears, the fact will be noticed, as well as the results of it.

I halted on Sunday, the 19th, and on Monday I alighted at the village of Sītalkhera.127 On Tuesday, the 21st, there was again a halt. I presented Ras̲h̲īd K., the Afghan, with a robe of honour and an elephant, sending them to him by Ran-bāz K. On Wednesday, the 22nd, the camp rested in pargana Madanpūr.128 On Thursday, the 23rd, I halted and had a feast of cups, and Dārāb K. had a *nādirī* dress of honour given to him. Halting on Friday, on Saturday the camp was pitched in the pargana of Nawārī.129 On Sunday, the 26th, I pitched on the bank of the River Chambal, and on Monday on the bank of the River Kahnar130 (?). On Tuesday, the 28th, the royal standards were raised in the neighbourhood of the city of Ujain. From Aḥmadābād to Ujain is a distance of ninety-eight kos. It was traversed in twenty-eight marches and forty-one halts—that is, in two months and nine days. On Wednesday, the 29th, I had an interview with Jadrūp, who is one of the austere ones of the Hindu religion, and the particulars of whose circumstances have been described in the preceding pages, and went with him to see Kāliyādaha. Certainly association with him is a great privilege.

On this day it was made known to me in the contents of a report from Bahādur K., the Governor of Qandahar, that in the Hijrī year 1026—that is, last year—the number of mice in Qandahar and the neighbourhood was so great that they destroyed all the crops and grain and cultivation and the fruits of the trees of the province, so that there had been no produce. They (the mice) cut off the ears of corn and ate them. When the cultivators gathered their crops, before they were threshed and cleaned, another131 half was destroyed, so that perhaps one-fourth of the crops only came to hand. In the same way no vestige was left of the melons (melon-beds) or garden produce. After some time the mice disappeared.

As my son S͟hāh-Jahān had not made a birthday entertainment for his son (Aurangzīb), he petitioned at Ujain, which is the place of his jagir, that the Thursday entertainment of the 30th should be held at his abode. Of necessity, having consented to the carrying out of his wish, the day was passed in enjoyment at his quarters. My private servants who have the *entrée* into this kind of parties and assemblies were delighted with brimming cups. My son S͟hāh-Jahān brought that auspicious child before me, and, presenting as offerings a tray of jewels, and jewelled ornaments, and fifty elephants, thirty male and twenty female, asked me for a name for him. Please God it will be given him in a favourable hour. Of his elephants seven were included in my private stud; the rest were distributed among the faujdārs. The value of the offerings that were accepted will be Rs. 200,000.

On this day ʿAẓudu-d-daula (Jamālu-d-dīn Ḥusain Anjū) came from his jagir, and had the good fortune to kiss the threshold. He gave eighty-one *muhars* as *naẕr*, and an elephant as an offering. Qāsim K., whom I had dismissed from the government of Bengal, had been sent for, and having had the good fortune to do homage, presented 1,000 *muhars* as *naẕr*. On Friday, the 1st of Āẕar, I amused myself with hawking. As the retinue passed along, a field of millet (*jwār*) was met with. Though generally a stem has only one head, each of them had twelve. I was astonished, and at this time the tale of "The King and the Gardener" occurred to me.

TALE OF "THE KING AND THE GARDENER."132

A King came to the gate of a garden in the heat of the day. He saw an old gardener standing at the gate, and asked him if there were any pomegranates in the garden. He said: "There are." He told him to bring a cup of pomegranate juice. The gardener had a daughter adorned with grace of person, and beauty of disposition. He made a sign to her to bring the pomegranate juice. The girl went and at once brought a cup full of pomegranate juice, and placed some leaves upon it. The King took it from her hand and drank it. Then he asked the girl what was her reason for placing leaves on the top of the juice. She, with an eloquent tongue and a sweet voice, represented that it was not wise at once to drink off a quantity of liquid when he was bathed in perspiration, and in such a hot air. On this account she had placed the leaves on the liquid by way of precaution, so that he might drink it slowly. The King was greatly pleased with her sweet ways, and it crossed his mind to admit the girl into his Palace. After this he asked the gardener: "How much profit do you derive from this garden every year?" He answered: "Three hundred *dīnārs*." The King asked: "What do you pay the Diwan (tax-collector)?" He answered: "The King takes nothing from the trees, but takes a tenth of the cultivated crops." It came into the King's mind that there were in his dominions many gardens and countless trees. If he were to get a tenth of the garden produce as well, it would amount to a large sum, and there would be no great loss to the cultivator. Hereafter he would order a tax to be levied on garden produce. He said then: "Bring me a little more pomegranate juice." The girl went, and after a long time brought a small quantity. The King said: "The first time thou camest quickly, and broughtest more. This time thou didst stay a long time, and broughtest less." The girl said: "The first time I had filled the cup with the juice of one pomegranate, and brought it; this time I pressed out five or six pomegranates and did not get as much juice." The astonishment of the King increased. The gardener represented: "The blessing of produce depends on the goodwill of the King. It occurs to me that you must be a King. At the time when you inquired of me the income from the garden, your disposition must have changed. Consequently the blessing passed away from the fruit." The Sultan was impressed, and drove that idea out of his heart. He then said: "Bring me once more a cup of pomegranate juice." The girl went again, and quickly bringing a cup full to the brim, gave it, smiling and gladly, into the Sultan's hand. He praised the intelligence of the gardener, and explained the actual state of affairs, and begged the girl of him in marriage, and married her.

This true tale of that truth-preserving King has remained as a memento on the page of time. In truth, the manifestation of such spiritual (?)133 results is the mark of good intentions, and the fruit of justice. Whenever all the energies and purposes of justice-observing Kings are devoted to the comfort of the people and the contentment of their subjects, the manifestations of well-being and the productions of fields and gardens are not far off. God be praised that in this age-enduring State no tax has ever been levied on the fruit of trees, and is not levied now. In the whole of the dominion not a *dām* nor one grain (*ḥabba*)134 on this account enters the public treasury, or is collected by the State. Moreover, there is an order that whoever makes a garden on arable land, its produce is exempted. I trust that God (to whom be glory!) will always incline this suppliant towards what is good.

"When my purpose is good, do Thou grant me good."135

On Saturday, for the second time, my desire for the company of Jadrūp increased. After performing the midday devotions, I embarked in a boat and hastened to meet him, and at the close of day I ran and enjoyed his society in the retirement of his cell. I heard many sublime words of religious duties and knowledge of divine things. Without immoderate praise, he sets forth clearly the doctrines of wholesome Sufism, and one can find delight in his society. He is sixty years old. He was twenty-two years of age, when, forsaking all external attachments, he placed the foot of determination on the highroad of asceticism, and for thirty-eight years he had lived in the garment of nakedness. When I took leave he said: "In what language can I return thanks for this gift of Allah that I am engaged in the reign of such a just King in the worship of my own Deity in ease and contentment, and that the dust of discomposure from any accident settles not on the skirt of my purpose?"

On Sunday, the 3rd, marching from Kāliyādaha, I encamped at the village of Qāsimkhera. I employed myself on the road in hawking. By chance a crane rose, and the *tūyghūn* falcon, of which I am very fond, was let fly after it. The crane sought to escape, and the falcon soared and flew so high as to disappear from sight. Although the huntsmen and the head-beaters ran after it in all directions, they found no trace of it, and it was impossible for the falcon to be caught in such a desert. Lashkar Mīr Kashmīrī, who is the head of the Kashmir huntsmen, in whose charge the falcon was, ran in a bewildered state through the desert in all directions without finding a sign or trace. Suddenly he saw a tree in the distance, and when he went up to it he found the falcon sitting on the end of a branch. Showing a domestic fowl, he called to the falcon. Three *gharīs* more had not passed when he brought it to me. This gift from the hidden world, that had entered into the thoughts of no one, increased the joy of my mind. Increasing his mansab as a reward for this service, I gave him a horse and a dress of honour.

On Monday, the 4th, Tuesday, the 5th, Wednesday, the 6th, I marched continuously, and, halting on Thursday, the 7th, I arranged a feast of pleasure on the bank of a tank. Nūr-Jahān Begam had been ill for some time, and the physicians who had the good fortune to be chosen to attend on her, Musulmans and Hindus, perceived no gain from all the medicines they gave her, and confessed their helplessness in treating her. At this time Ḥakīm Rūḥu-llah began to wait upon her, and undertook (to find) a remedy. By the aid of God (Glory be to His name!), in a short time she quite recovered. In reward for this excellent service I increased his mansab and bestowed on the Ḥakīm three villages in his native country as his private property, and an order was given that he should be weighed against silver, which should be given him as a reward. From Friday, the 8th, until Sunday,136 the 13th, I made successive marches, and every day up to the end of the stage employed myself in hunting with hawks and falcons (*bāz u jurra*). Many *durrāj* (partridges) were caught. On last Sunday, Kunwar Karan, s. Rānā Amar Singh, having enjoyed the good fortune of kissing the ground, presented his congratulations on the conquest of the Deccan, offering 100 *muhars* and Rs. 1,000 by way of *naẕr*, and the value of Rs. 21,000 in jewelled vessels, with some horses and elephants as *pīshkash*. The horses and elephants I returned to him, and the rest was accepted. The next day I presented him with a dress of honour. To Mīr Sharīf, Vakil of Quṭbu-l-mulk, and to Irādat K., the chief butler, an elephant each was given. Sayyid Hizabr K. was given the faujdāri of Mewāt, and his mansab, original and increased, was fixed at 1,000 personal and 500 horse. Having selected Sayyid Mubārak for the charge of the fort of Rohtās, I conferred on him the mansab of 500 personal and 200 horse. On Thursday, the 14th, the camp was pitched on the bank of the tank of the village of Sandhāra, and the feast of cups was held, and chosen servants were made happy with cups of pleasure. The birds of chase, "that had been shut up in Agra to moult" (*ba-kurīz basta būdand*), were this day brought to me by Khwāja 'Abdu-l-Laṭīf, the Chief Fowler. Picking out those that were fit for my own use, the rest were given to the Amīrs and other servants.

On this day the news of the revolt and ingratitude for favours of Rāja Sūraj Mal, s. Rāja Bāso, came to my ear. Bāso had several137 sons. Although the above-mentioned was the eldest, his father mostly kept him in confinement on account of his evil thoughts and mischievous tendencies, and regarded him with displeasure. After his (Bāso's) death, as this wretch was the eldest, and he had no other capable or intelligent son, I, looking to the services rendered by Rāja Bāso, for the purpose of preserving the family of a Zamindar, and the protection of his hereditary property and country, conferred on this wretch the title of Raja, with a mansab of 2,000, and gave him the position and jagir of his father, which the latter had obtained by his loyalty and good service. I also gave him the sums of money and goods that his father had collected during long years. When the deceased Murtaẓā K. was sent off on the duty of conquering Kāngṛa, as this wretch was the chief Zamindar of that hill country, he outwardly displayed zeal in the service and loyalty, and was nominated as an auxiliary. After he reached the spot, Murtaẓā K. pressed the siege tightly against the garrison. This evil-minded fellow discovered from the appearance of things that he would soon be victorious, and began to disagree and be troublesome. He took off the veil of respect from his face, and proceeded to quarrel and be hostile to Murtaẓā K.'s men. Murtaẓā K. read the writing of misery and ruin on the page of the wretch's forehead, and reported unfavourably of him to the Court, or rather wrote plainly that the signs of rebellion and want of loyalty were clear in his conduct. As there was there such an officer as Murtaẕā K. and a large army in the hill-country, the wretch did not find the time convenient for the preparation of a disturbance. He sent a report to my son S͟hāh-Jahān that Murtaẕā K., at the instigation of interested parties, had turned against him, and desired to overthrow and ruin him, and was accusing him of wrong-doing and rebellion. He hoped that he would summon him to Court, and thus provide a means for his escape and (the prolonging of) his life. Although I had every confidence in the words of Murtaẕā K., yet as he (Sūraj Mal) begged to be sent for to Court, a doubt passed into my mind that possibly Murtaẕā K., at the instigation of seditious people, might cause a confusion, and might have accused him without due reflection. Briefly, at the request of my son S͟hāh-Jahān, passing over his offence, I summoned him (Sūraj Mal) to Court. Just at this time Murtaẕā K. died, and the conquest of the fort of Kāngṛa was delayed till the dispatch of another leader. When this seditious fellow arrived at Court, I, under the pressure of affairs, rapidly encompassed him with favours and sent him off to do duty with my son S͟hāh-Jahān in the conquest of the Deccan. After this, when the Deccan had come into the possession of the servants of the enduring State, he, having acquired influence in my son's service, was appointed to superintend the taking of the fort of Kāngṛa. Although the sending back of this ungrateful and untruthful one into that hill-country showed a want of caution and care, yet as my son had taken on himself the responsibility of the undertaking, I was obliged to give in to his wish and to leave the matter to him. My fortunate son appointed him, along with one of his own servants of the name of Taqī and a suitable army of *manṣabdārs*, *aḥadīs*, and royal musketeers, as has already been related summarily in these pages. When he arrived at the place, he began to show enmity and trickery toward Taqī also, and displayed his natural disposition. He continually reported unfavourably of him (Taqī), until he wrote plainly that he could not get on with him, and that Taqī could not do the work. If another general were appointed, the fort would be quickly conquered. In fine, he (S͟hāh-Jahān) had no choice but to summon Taqī to Court, and to appoint Rāja Bikramājīt, who was one of his chief servants, with an army of fresh men on this service. When the wretch discovered that his stratagems could no longer continue, and his deceit go no farther, he, before the arrival of Bikramājīt, gave leave to a number of the servants of the Court, on the pretence that they had been on service a long time without proper arrangements (commissariat), to hasten to their jagirs and provide themselves with their equipments before the arrival of Rāja Bikramājīt. As palpably this came to a dispersion of the forces of the loyal, and most of them left for their own jagirs, only a few experienced men remained there. Seeing his opportunity, he showed the signs of revolt and sedition. Sayyid Ṣafī Bārha, who was distinguished for his bravery, with some of his brothers and relatives, advanced the feet of courage, and tasted the wholesome draught of martyrdom, and some who were wounded with severe wounds, which are the adornment of the lions of battle, that rascal took captive from the field of strife and carried off to his own house of calamity.[138] Some from love[139] of life hastily withdrew themselves to the corner of safety. That rascal stretched out the hand of oppression and possession over the parganas on the skirts of the hill-country (*daman-i-kūh*), which mostly belonged to the jagir of I'timādu-d-daula, and did not abate a hair's breadth from attacking and plundering. It is hoped that with the same swiftness, he will be caught with the reward of his deeds and the recompense of his actions, and that the spirit[140] of this State will do its work, please God!

On Sunday, the 17th, I crossed Ghāṭī Chāṇḍā. On Monday, the 18th, the Jān-sipār Ātālīq Kh̲ān-kh̲ānān, Commander-in-Chief, had the honour of kissing the threshold. As he had been absent from my presence for a long time, and the victorious retinue was passing by near the Sarkars of Khandesh and Burhānpur, he asked to wait upon me, and an order was given that if his mind were at ease in all respects, he should come unattended and return quickly. He accordingly came with all speed, and had the good fortune to pay his respects on this day, and, having been exalted by the receipt of all kinds of royal favours and kingly benefits, he presented an offering of 1,000 *muhars* and Rs. 1,000.

As the camp had undergone great hardship in crossing the Ghāṭī, I ordered a halt for the refreshment of the people on Tuesday, the 19th. I marched on Wednesday, the 20th, and on Thursday, the 21st, halted again and held a feast of cups on the bank of a river that is known as the Sind.[141] I gave a special horse, of the name of Sumer, which was one of the finest horses, to the Kh̲ān-kh̲ānān. In the Hindi language they call a hill of gold Sumer (Sumeru), and he was called by this name on account of his colour and size. On Friday, the 22nd, and Saturday, the 23rd, two successive marches were made. On this day a wonderful waterfall was seen. The water is exceedingly clear, and pours down with boiling and noise from a lofty place. On all sides of it there are halting places where one may praise God. Certainly I have not recently seen such another fine waterfall, and it is a delightful recreation-place. I was delighted with the spectacle for a while. On Sunday, the 24th, I halted, and, sitting in a boat on a tank which was in front of the royal enclosure (*daulat-kh̲āna*), were shot[142] ducks (*murgh̲ābī*). On Monday, the 25th, Tuesday, the 26th, and Wednesday, the 27th, I marched one after the other. I bestowed on the Kh̲ān-kh̲ānān the *pūstīn* (sheep-skin coat) I had on my own person, and seven horses from my stable, on which I always rode, were also given him. On Sunday, the 2nd of the Ilāhī month of Dai, the royal standards were raised at the fort of Ranthambūr. This is one of the great forts of the Indians. In the time of Sulṭān ʿAlāʾu-d-dīn Khaljī, Rāy Pitambar Deo was in possession of it. The Sultan besieged it for a long time, and conquered it with labour and great exertions, and in the beginning143 of the reign of H.M. (Akbar)—may the light of God be his witness!—Rāy Surjan Hāḍā had it in his possession. He had always 6,000 or 7,000 horse in attendance on him. That revered one, by the aid of the glorious God, conquered it in the space of one month and twelve days, and Rāy Surjan, by the guidance of fortune, having had the good fortune to kiss the threshold, was enrolled among the number of the loyal, and became one of his respectable and trusted Amīrs. After him his son Rāy Bhoj also was included among the great Amīrs. Now his grandson, Sarbuland Rāy, is among the chief officers. On Monday,144 the 3rd, I went to inspect the fort. There are two hills close to each other. They call one Ran, and the other Thanbūr. The fort is built on the top of Thanbūr, and, putting these two names together, they have called it Ranthambūr. Although the fort is exceedingly strong, and has plenty of water, the hill of Ran is a specially strong fortress (in itself), and the capture of the fortress depends upon the possession of this hill. Accordingly, my revered father ordered that they should plant cannon on the top of the hill of Ran, and aim at (*majrā gīrand*) the buildings inside the fort. The first gun they fired reached the square building (*chaukandī*)145 of the palace of Rāy Surjan. From the fall of that building, a trembling found its way into the foundations of his courage, and a great perplexity overpowered his heart, and thinking he would best consult his own safety in delivering up the fort, he rubbed the head of worship and humility on the throne of the king of kings, who forgave faults and accepted excuses.

I had intended to pass the night in the fort, and the next day to return to camp. As the buildings inside the fort had been built after the fashion of the Hindus, and the rooms were without air and with little space, they did not please me, nor was I disposed to stay there. I saw a bath house, which one of the servants of Dastam146 Khān had built near the wall of the fort. A little garden and a lodging (*nishīman*) which overlooks (*mushrif*) the open space is not wanting in space and air, and there is no better place in the whole fort.147 Dastam K. was one of the Amīrs of the late King (Akbar), and from his early years had been brought up in his service. His connection with him was confidential and intimate. H.M. had entrusted this fort to him from his exceeding confidence in him.

After completing my inspection of the fort and houses, I ordered that they should bring before me the criminals who were confined in the fort, so that I might look into the case of each of them and give an order in accordance with justice. In brief, with the exception of affairs of murder, and of any person through whose release disturbance or calamity might ensue in the country, I freed them all, and to each one in accordance with his circumstances gave his expenses and dresses148 of honour. On the eve of Tuesday, the 4th, I returned to the royal abode after a watch and three gharis had passed. On Sunday (properly Wednesday), the 5th, having marched nearly 5 koss, I halted on Thursday, the 6th. On this day the K͟hān-k͟hānān presented his offering of jewels, ornamented vessels, cloth, and an elephant. Of these I chose whatever pleased me, and returned the rest. What was accepted of his offering was of the value of Rs. 150,000. On Friday, the 7th, I marched 5 koss. I had before this captured a *sāras* with a falcon, but until now I had never seen the hunting of a *durnā*149 (crane). As my son S͟hāh-Jahān had great pleasure in *durnā* hunting with the falcon (*s͟hāhīn*), and his falcons were well grown, at his request I rode out early in the morning, and caught one *durnā* myself, whilst the falcon my son had on his wrist caught another. Certainly, of all good hunting amusements, this is the best. I was exceedingly pleased with it. Although the *sāras* is large, it is lazy and heavy on the wing. The chase of the *durnā* has no resemblance to it. I praise the heart and courage of the falcon that can seize such strong-bodied animals, and with the strength of his talons can subdue them. Ḥasan K., the chief huntsman of my son, was honoured with an elephant, a horse, and a dress of honour, as a reward for this exhibition of sport, and his son also received a horse and a dress of honour. On Saturday, the 8th, having marched 4¼ koss, I halted on Sunday, the 9th. On this day the K͟hān-k͟hānān, the Commander-in-Chief, having raised the head of dignity through the gift of a special dress of honour, a jewelled waist-sword, and a private elephant with trappings, was reappointed to Khandesh and the Deccan. The mansab of that pillar of the kingdom, original and increase, was fixed at 7,000 personal and horse. As he did not get on with Las͟hkar K., at his request I assigned to ʿĀbid K. the duty of Dīwān-i-buyūtāt,150 and having given him the mansab of 1,000 personal and 400 horse, as well as a horse, an elephant, and a dress of honour, sent him to that Subah. On the same day K͟hān Daurān arrived from Kabul, and had the good fortune to pay his respects, and presented as *naz̲r* 1,000 muhars and Rs. 1,000, as well as an offering of a pearl rosary, fifty horses, ten Persian male and female camels, and some hawks, and china,151 and porcelain (?), and other things. On Monday, the 10th, I marched 3¼ koss, and on Tuesday, the 11th, 5¾ koss. On this day the K͟hān Daurān arranged his men before me, and passed in review a thousand Mug͟hal cavalry, most of whom had Turkī horses, and some ʿIrāq and some Mujannas152 horses. Though his troopers had been mostly dispersed, some going into the service of Mahābat K. and remaining in that Subah, whilst a number left him at Lahore and went into different parts of the dominion, yet he could show this body of well-mounted men. Certainly the K͟hān Daurān for valour and generalship is one of the unique of the ages, but alas! I found he had become a decrepit old man, and his sight was very weak. He has two intelligent young sons, who are not wanting in reasonableness, but it will certainly be a great and difficult thing for them to show themselves his equals. On this day I gave him and his sons dresses of honour and swords. On Sunday, the 12th, traversing 3½ koss, I alighted on the bank of the tank of Māndū.153 In the middle of the tank there is a stone building, and on one of the pillars the quatrain of someone had been engraved. I saw it, and was amazed. In truth, it is a fine verse:

"My congenial friends have left me:

One by one they've fallen into the hands of death.

They were poor drinkers at the banquet of life.

A moment sooner than us they became drunken."154

At this time I also heard another quatrain of the same description, which I have recorded because it was very well said:

"Alas! that people of intelligence and wisdom have passed away.

They have been forgotten in the minds of their contemporaries.

Those who spoke with a hundred tongues

Ah! what heard they that they became silent."

On Thursday, the 13th, I made a halt. ʿAbdu-l-ʿAzīz K., having come from Bangash, had the good fortune to kiss the threshold. Ikrām K., who was in charge of the faujdāri of Fatḥpūr and the neighbourhood, was honoured with waiting on me. Khwāja Ibrāhīm K., Bakhshī of the Deccan, was exalted with the title of ʿAqīdat K. Mīr Ḥājj, who is one of the auxiliaries attached to that Subah, and one of the brave young officers, was promoted to the title of Sharza (tiger-whelp) K., and received a standard. On Friday, the 14th, I marched 5¼ koss. On Saturday, the 15th, having marched 3 koss, I halted in the neighbourhood of Bayānā.155 There I hastened with the ladies to see the spectacle of the top of the fort. Muḥammad, the Bakhshī of Humāyūn, who was entrusted with the charge of the fort, had built a fine house overlooking the plain, of great height and with fine air. The tomb of Shaikh Bahlūl is also in that neighbourhood, and is not wanting in excellence. The Shaikh was the elder brother of Shaikh Muḥammad Ghauṣ, and was much versed in the science of incantations by names (of God). Humāyūn had great affection for him, and the most perfect reliance on him. When he conquered the province of Bengal, he took up his abode there for some time. Mīrzā Hindāl, by his order, had remained156 at Agra. A body of avaricious servants (*qulluq-chiyān*), whose character was mischievous and seditious, taking to the way of faithlessness, came from Bengal to the Mīrzā, and, working upon his base nature (shaking the chain of his vile heart), led the Mīrzā on the road of rebellion and ingratitude for favours, and of irrecognition of duty. The thoughtless Mīrzā had the *khuṭba* recited in his own name (proclaimed himself king), and openly raised the standard of rebellion and strife. When the royal ear heard what had taken place from the reports of those who were loyal, he sent Shaikh Bahlūl to admonish the Mīrzā, and to turn him back from his vain purpose, and to establish his feet on the highroad of sincerity and concord. As these wretches had made the flavour of royalty sweet to the Mīrzā's palate, he became imbued with futile ideas, and would not be loyal. At the instigation of these seditious people he made Shaikh Bahlūl a martyr with the sword of recklessness at the Chārbāgh (garden) which H.M. Bābar had made on the bank of the Jumna. As Muḥammad Bakhshī was a disciple of the Shaikh, he carried the body into the fort of Bayānā, and buried it there.

On Sunday, the 16th, marching 4½ koss, I came to the stage of Barah.157 As the garden and well which had been built by the order of Maryam-zamānī (Jahāngīr's mother) in the pargana of Jūsat was on the road, I went to inspect them. Certainly the *bā'olī* (step-well) was a grand building, and had been built exceedingly well. I ascertained from the officials that a sum of Rs. 20,000 had been expended on this well. As there was much game in this neighbourhood, I halted on Monday, the 17th.

On Tuesday, the 18th, marching 3⅛ koss, the host of prosperity halted at the village of Dāyarm'a'ū.158 On Wednesday, the 19th, marching 2½ koss, the victorious standards were raised on the bank of the Lake of Fatḥpūr. As at the time when the conquest of the Deccan was meditated, the stages and distances from Ranthambūr to Ujain were recorded, it appears unnecessary to repeat them. From Ranthambūr159 to Fatḥpūr by the road by which I came was a distance of 234 koss, in sixty-three marches and fifty-six halts, traversed in 119 days, or, according to solar reckoning, in one day under four months, and by lunar four full months. From the date on which the army of fortune started from the capital for the conquest of the Rānā and the acquisition of the Deccan until now, when the victorious and prosperous standards have been planted again in the centre of the empire, it is five years and four months. The astrologers and astronomers chose the day of *Mubārak-shamba* (Thursday), the 28th of the Divine month of Dai, in my thirteenth year, corresponding with the last day of the Muḥarram in the Hijrī year 1028 (January 7, 1619), as the proper time at which to enter the capital of Agra.

At this time, again, it appeared from the reports of the loyal that the disease of the plague was prevalent in Agra, so that daily about 100 people, more or less, were dying of it. Under the armpits, or in the groin, or below the throat, buboes formed, and they died. This is the third year that it has raged in the cold weather, and disappeared in the commencement of the hot season. It is a strange thing that in these three years the infection has spread to all the towns and villages in the neighbourhood of Agra, while there has been no trace of it at Fatḥpūr. It has come as far as Amānābād, which is 2½ koss from Fatḥpūr, and the people of that place (Amānābād) have forsaken their homes and gone to other villages. There being no choice, and considering the observance of caution necessary, it was decided that at this propitious[160] hour the victorious army should enter the inhabited part of Fatḥpūr in all joy and auspiciousness, and after the sickness and scarcity had subsided and another auspicious hour had been chosen, I should enter the capital, please the Almighty and most holy Allah!

The Thursday entertainment took place on the bank of the Lake of Fatḥpūr. As the time for entering the town (of Fatḥpūr) was fixed for the 28th, I halted eight days in this place. I ordered them to measure the circumference of the lake,[161] and it came to 7 koss. At this stage, with the exception of the revered Maryam-zamānī, who had become very weak, all the Begams and inhabitants of the enclosure of chastity and all the palace employés came out to meet me (istiqbāl). The daughter[162] of Āṣaf K., deceased, who is in the house of ʿAbdu-llah K. (*i.e.*, is married to ʿAbdu-llah), s. K͟hān Āʿẓ̤am, told me a strange and wonderful tale, and strongly insisted upon its truth. I write it on account of its strangeness. She said: "One day in the courtyard of the house I saw a mouse rising and falling in a distracted state. It was running about in every direction after the manner of drunkards, and did not know where to go. I said to one of my girls: 'Take it by the tail and throw it to the cat!' The cat was delighted, and jumped up from its place and seized it in its mouth, but immediately dropped it and showed disgust. By degrees an expression of pain and trouble showed itself in its face. The next day it was nearly dead, when it entered into my mind to give it a little treacle[163] (*tiryāq*, opium?). When its mouth was opened, the palate and tongue appeared black. It passed three days in a state of misery, and on the fourth day came to its senses. After this the grain (*dāna*) of the plague (buboes) appeared in the girl, and from excess of temperature and increase of pain she had no rest. Her colour became changed—it was yellow inclining to black—and the fever was high (*tap muḥriq gardīd*). The next day she vomited[164] and had motions, and died. Seven or eight people in that household died in the same way, and so many were ill that I went to the garden from that lodging. Those who were ill died in the garden, but in that place there were no buboes. In brief, in the space of eight or nine days seventeen people became travellers on the road of annihilation." She also said: "Those in whom the buboes appeared, if they called another person for water to drink or wash in, the latter also caught the infection (*sirāyat*), and at last it came to such a pass that through excessive apprehension no one would come near them."

On Saturday, the 22nd, K͟hwāja Jahān, who had had the charge of Agra, having had the good fortune to kiss the threshold, presented 500 *muhars* by way of *naẕr*, and Rs. 400165 as charity. On Monday, the 24th, a special dress of honour was conferred on him. On *Mubārak-s͟hamba*166 (Thursday), the 28th (? 27th), after four *g͟haṛī*167 or nearly two sidereal hours (*sāʿat*), had passed,

"In an hour which agreed with two almanacs (?) (or which marked two events),"

the royal standards auspiciously and happily entered the inhabited part of Fatḥpūr. At the same hour the entertainment (of weighing) for my prosperous and noble son, S͟hāh-Jahān, was held. I ordered him to be weighed against gold and other things, and his twenty-eighth year according to the solar168 months began auspiciously. It is hoped that he may reach the natural169 limit of life. On the same day H.M. the revered Maryam-zamānī (his mother) came from Agra, and I acquired eternal good fortune from the blessing of waiting on her. I hope that the shadow of her bringing up and affection may be perennial on the head of this suppliant. As Ikrām K., s. Islām K., had performed the duties of faujdār of this neighbourhood in a proper manner, I bestowed on him the mansab of 1,500 personal and 1,000 horse, original and increased. Suhrāb170 K., s. Mīrzā Rustam Ṣafavī, was promoted to the mansab of 1,000 personal and 300 horse.

On this day, going over in detail the buildings of the palace of the late King (Akbar), I showed them to my son, S͟hāh-Jahān. Inside of them a large and very clear reservoir of cut stone has been constructed, and is called the *Kapūr-talāo* (camphor tank). It is a square of 36 yards by 36,171 with a depth of 4½ yards. By the order of that revered one, the officials of the public treasury had filled it with *fulūs* (copper coins) and rupees. It came to 34 krors, and 48 lakhs, and 46,000 dāms, and 1,679,400 rupees, or a total of 10,300,000 (one kror and three lakhs) according to Hindustani reckoning, and 343,000 *tūmān* according to Persian. For a long time the thirsty-lipped ones of the desert of desire were satisfied from that fountain of benignity.

On Sunday, the 1st Bahman, a reward of 1,000 *darb* (Rs. 500) was given to Ḥāfiẓ. Nād ʿAlī,172 the reciter. For a long time past Muḥibb ʿAlī, s. Budāg͟h173 K. Chikanī, and Abū-l-Qāsim Gīlānī, whom the Ruler of Īrān had blinded and driven into the desert of exile, have passed their days in ease under the refuge of this State. To each of them, according to his condition, an allowance for living had been granted. On this day they came from Agra, and had the good fortune to kiss the threshold, and each of them was presented with Rs. 1,000. The *Mubārak-s͟hamba* entertainment was held in state in the palace, and my private servants were gladdened with cups of pleasure. Naṣru-llah, whom my son, Sulṭān Parwīz, had sent to Court with the elephant Kūh-damān,174 took his leave and returned. A copy (*jild*) of the *Jahāngīr-nāma*, together with a special tipchāq horse, were given to him to take to my son. On Sunday, the 8th, Kunwar Karan, son of Rānā Amar Singh, was presented with a horse, an elephant, a dress of honour, a jewelled *khapwa*, and a *phūl-kaṭāra.* I gave him leave to go to his jagir, and sent a horse with him for the Rānā. On the same day I went out sporting to Amānābād. As there was an order that no one should kill the antelope of that region, in the course of six years many antelope had come together, and they had grown very tame. On Thursday, the 12th, I returned to the palace, and on that day, according to custom, a feast of cups was prepared.

On the eve of Friday, the 13th (Bahman), I went to the mausoleum of the refuge of pardon, Shaikh Salīm Chishtī, a little concerning whose blessed qualities has been written in the preface175 to this record of prosperity, and the *fātiḥa* was recited. Although the manifestation of miracles and wonders is not approved by the elect of the throne of God, and from humility and a feeling of their low rank (as saints) they avoid such display, yet occasionally in the excitement of ecstasy an appearance is manifested unintentionally and without control,176 or for the sake of teaching someone the exhibition is made. Among these was this, that he before my birth gave my father the good news of the advent of this suppliant and of my two brothers. Again, one day my father incidentally asked him how old he was, and when would he depart to the abiding regions. He replied: "The glorious God knows what is secret and hidden." After much urgency he indicated this suppliant (Prince Salīm), and said: "When the Prince, by the instruction of a teacher or in any other way, shall commit something to memory and shall recite it, this will be a sign of my union with God." In consequence of this, His Majesty gave strict orders to all who were in attendance on me that no one should teach me anything in prose or verse. At length when two years and seven months had passed away, it happened one day that one of the privileged177 women was in the palace. She used to burn rue constantly in order to avert the evil eye, and on this pretext had access to me. She used to partake of the alms and charities. She found me alone and regardless of (or ignorant of) what had been said (by Akbar), she taught me this couplet:

"O God, open the rosebud of hope

Display a flower from the everlasting garden."178

I went to the Shaikh and repeated this couplet. He involuntarily rose up and hastened to wait on the King, and informed him of what had occurred. In accordance with Fate, the same night the traces of fever appeared, and the next day he sent someone to the King (with the request) to call Tān Sen Kalāwant, who was unequalled as a singer. Tān Sen, having gone to wait upon him, began to sing. After this he sent some one to call the King. When H.M.

came, he said: "The promised time of union has come, and I must take leave of you." Taking his turban from his head, he placed it on mine, and said: "We have made Sulṭān Salīm our successor, and have made him over to God, the protector and preserver." Gradually his weakness increased, and the signs of passing179 away became more evident, till he attained union with the "True Beloved."

One of the greatest monuments of my father's reign is this mosque and cemetery (*rauẓa*). Certainly they are exceedingly lofty and solid buildings. There is nothing like this mosque in any other country. It is all built of beautiful stone, and five lakhs of rupees were expended from the public treasury upon it. Quṭbu-d-dīn K. Kokaltāsh made the marble railing (*maḥjar*) round180 the cemetery, the flooring (*farsh*) of the dome and portico, and these are not included in the five lakhs. The mosque has two great gateways. The one181 towards the south is extremely lofty, and is very beautiful. The archway (*pīshtāq*) is 12 yards broad, 16 long, and 52 high. One must mount thirty-two steps to get to the top of it. The other gateway is smaller, and is towards the east. The length of the mosque from east to west, including the width of the walls, is 212 yards. Out of this, the *Maqṣūra* (the chancel) is 25½ yards, the middle is 15 yards by 15, the portico (*pīshtāq*) is 7 yards broad, 14 yards long, and 25 yards high. On each side of the large dome are two smaller domes 10 yards by 10. Then there is a veranda (*aiwān*) which is pillared. The breadth of the mosque from north to south is 172 yards. Round it are ninety verandas (*aiwān*) and eighty-four cells. The breadth of each cell is 4 yards,182 and the length 5 yards. The verandas are 7½ yards broad. The courtyard (*ṣaḥn*) of the mosque, exclusive of the *maqṣūra*, and the verandas, and the gates, is 169 yards long and 143 yards broad. Above the verandas, the gates, and the mosque, small domes have been constructed, and on the eves of anniversaries and on holy days lamps are placed in these, and they are enveloped in coloured183 cloths, so that they look like lamp-shades (?). Under the courtyard they have made a well, and they fill this with rainwater. As Fatḥpūr has little water, and what there is is bad, this well184 yields a sufficient supply for the whole year for the members of the family (of Salīm Chishtī) and for the dervishes who are the *mujāwirs* (caretakers) of the mosque. Opposite the great entrance and towards the north-north-east is the tomb of the Shaikh. The middle dome is 7 yards, and round the dome is a portico of marble, and on the front side of this is a marble lattice. It is very beautiful. Opposite this tomb on the west, at a little distance, is another dome, in which are laid to rest the sons-in-law and sons of the Shaikh, such as Quṭbu-d-dīn K., Islām K., Mu'aẓẓam K.,185 and others, who were all connected with this family, and rose to the position of Amirs and to lofty rank. Accordingly, the circumstances of each have been recorded in their places. At present the son of Islām K., who is distinguished by the title of

Ikrām K., is the lord of the prayer-carpet. The signs of auspiciousness are manifest in him; I am much inclined to cherish him.

On Thursday, the 19th, I promoted ʿAbdu-l-ʿAzīz K. to the mansab of 2,000 personal and 1,000 horse, and nominated him to the duty of taking the fort of Kāngṛa, and the overthrow of the ungrateful Sūraj Mal. I bestowed on him an elephant, a horse, and a dress of honour. Tursūn Bahādur was also dispatched on this duty, and his mansab was fixed at 1,200 personal and 450 horse. He was given a horse, and took his leave. As the house of Iʿtimādu-d-daula was on the bank of a tank, and people praised it greatly as a delightful place and enchanting residence, at his request on Thursday, the 26th, an entertainment was held there. That pillar of the kingdom engaged in the dues of prostration and offerings, and prepared a grand meeting. At night, after eating food, I returned to the palace. On Thursday, the 3rd of the Divine month of Isfand-armuz, Sayyid ʿAbdu-l-Wahhāb Bārha, who had done active service in Gujarat, was promoted to the mansab of 1,000 personal and 500 horse, and was honoured with the title of Dilīr K. On Saturday, the 12th, I went out to Amānābād for sport, and until Sunday, with the ladies, employed myself in the pleasure of hunting. On the eve of Thursday, the 27th186 (17th), I returned to the palace.

By chance, on Tuesday, during the hunting, a string of pearls and rubies that Nūr-Jahān Begam had on her neck was broken, and a ruby of the value of Rs. 10,000 and a pearl worth Rs. 1,000 were lost. Although the huntsmen made every search for it on Wednesday, it did not fall into their hands. It occurred to me that as the name of the day was *Kam-s̲h̲amba*, it was impossible to find it on that day. On the contrary, as *Mubārak-s̲h̲amba* (Thursday) was always a lucky day for me, and had been blessed to me, the huntsmen on that day with but a little search found both in that track-less place (without head or foundation) and brought them to me. The best of coincidences was that on the same propitious day the entertainment for my lunar weighing and the feast of Basant-bārī (Spring festival) also took place, and the good news of the conquest of the fort of Mau and the defeat of that evil-fortuned Sūraj Mal arrived.

The particulars of this are that when Rāja Bikramājīt with the victorious army arrived in that region, the ill-fated Sūraj Mal desired to delay him for some days by trickery and babblement, but the aforesaid knew the real state of the case and did not pay attention to his words, but advanced with the foot of valour. That abandoned one, letting fall from his hand the thread of plan, neither planted the foot of intrepidity firmly for battle nor had the courage to defend the fort. After a slight struggle, and when many of his people had been slaughtered, he took to flight, and the forts of Mau187 and Mahrī (?), which were the chief reliance of that ill-fated man, were both taken without difficulty. A country which he had held by hereditary right from his fathers was trodden under foot by the victorious troops, and he became a wanderer and a vagabond. He retired to the ravines of the hills, and cast the dust of ruin and contempt on the head of his Fortune. Rāja Bikramājīt, leaving his country behind, hastened in pursuit of him with the victorious army. When the state of affairs reached the royal ears, in reward for this becoming service I ordered drums for the Raja, and a fateful farman was issued from the Sovereign of Wrath that they should overthrow from their foundation the fort and buildings that had been erected by Sūraj Mal's father and himself, and leave not a trace of them on the face of the earth. A strange thing is that the unfortunate Sūraj Mal had a brother called Jagat Singh. When I promoted Sūraj Mal to the title of Raja, and made him an Amir, and gave him dominion, etc., without a partner or sharer, I, in order to please him, gave a small mansab to Jagat Singh, who did not get on well with him, and sent him to Bengal. This wretched one was passing his days in a poor condition far from his home, in contempt, and to the delight of his enemies, and waiting for some hidden aid, until by his good fortune this affair took place, and that unblessed one struck an axe on his own foot. Summoning Jagat Singh in all haste to Court, I honoured him with the title of Raja and the mansab of 1,000 personal and 500 horse, and bestowed 20,000 *darbs*188 on him out of the public treasury for his expenses. Giving him a jewelled khapwa, a robe of honour, a horse, and an elephant, I sent him to Rāja Bikramājīt, and issued a farman that if the aforesaid, by the guidance of a good destiny, should perform laudable service, and display loyalty, that country should be given over into his hand.189

As the praise of the garden of Nūr-manzil and the buildings that had been newly-erected there continually reached me, I on Monday mounted my steed, and went to the stage of Bustān-sarāy, and passed Tuesday in pleasure and at ease in that entrancing rose-garden. On the eve of Wednesday the garden of Nūr-manzil (the abode of light) was adorned by the alighting of the hosts of prosperity. This garden contains 330 *jarībs* (*bīghās*), according to the *Ilāhī gaz*. Around it there has been built a wall, lofty and broad, of bricks and cement, exceedingly strong. In the garden there is a lofty building and a residence, highly decorated. Pleasant reservoirs have been constructed, and outside the gate a large well has been made, from which thirty-two pairs of bullocks continually draw water. The canal passes through the garden, and pours water into the reservoirs. Besides this, there are other wells, the water of which is distributed to the reservoirs and plots. The beauty is increased by all kinds of fountains and cascades and there is a tank in the exact middle of the garden which is filled by rainwater. If by chance its water should fail in the extreme heat, they supplement it by water from the wells, so that it may always be full to the brim. Nearly Rs. 150,000 have been spent up to now on this garden, and it is still unfinished, and large sums will be expended in making avenues and laying down plants. It has also been settled that the middle garden shall be newly walled190 round, and the channels for the coming and going of the water shall be made so strong that it may always remain full of water and the water shall not leak out in any way, and no damage accrue. It is possible that before it is complete nearly Rs. 200,000 will have been spent on it.

On Thursday, the 24th, Khwāja Jahān presented an offering of jewels, jewelled vessels, cloths, an elephant, and a horse, of the value of Rs. 150,000. Having made a selection from them, I gave him the remainder. Until Saturday I passed my time in that garden of delight in enjoyment. On the eve of Sunday, the 27th, I inclined the reins of returning towards Fatḥpūr, and an order was given that the great Amirs, according to annual custom, should decorate the palace. On Monday, the 28th, I found that something had gone wrong with my eye. As it arose from too much blood, I ordered ʿAlī Akbar, the surgeon, to open a vein. On the next day the benefit of this was apparent. I bestowed Rs. 1,000 on him. On Tuesday, the 29th, Muqarrab K. came from his native place, and had the good fortune to kiss the threshold, and I favoured him with many sorts of kindness.

---

1 Jahāngīr was born on Wednesday, 17 Rabīʿu-l-awwal 977 A.H., or August 31, 1569, and so on March 11, 1618, or 23 Rabīʿu-l-awwal, 1027, he was in the beginning of his fifty-first lunar year. By solar computation he was not yet fifty, that is, he was in his fiftieth year. The text wrongly has 1017 instead of 1027. ↑

2 Text wrongly has *panchāq*. In Turki dictionaries it is spelt topchāq, and means a large or long-necked horse. See P. de Courteille Dict., etc. ↑

3 Āṣaf K. III. of Blochmann; his name was Jaʿfar Beg. ↑

4 See "Iqbāl-nāma," p. 111. etc. He is not the famous Mīr Jumla, who was Aurangzeb's general, though possibly the latter was his son. According to the "Iqbāl-nāma, he was the nephew, and not the uncle, of Mīr Riẓā, but Jahāngīr's statement agrees with the ʿĀlam-ārāʾī (p. 623). Mīr Jumla's patron, Muḥammad Qulī Quṭb-Shāh, died in 1612. He himself died in 1637, while Aurangzeb's general died in 1663. ↑

5 Possibly what is meant is that Shāh ʿAbbās was greedy after Mīr Jumla's (Sāmān) wealth. Kāmgār Ḥusainī distinctly says that ʿAbbās wanted to get hold of Mīr Jumla's goods. ↑

6 The Iqbāl-nāma says that ʿAbbās only gave Mīr Jumla flattering words, and did not give him any high appointment. See also ʿĀlam-ārāʾī, 623, and Maʾāṣiru-l-umarā, III. 415. ↑

7 Tuqūz means "nine," but perhaps it is here only used to express a gift, and the pieces of cloth were perhaps only nine, and not eighty-one. See Vullers s.v., who refers to Quatremere. ↑

8 The I.O. MSS. have Māmū'ī, and the meaning may be "the maternal uncle of the Zamindar." ↑

9 Jariya in No. 181. It seems to be the Jareja tribe of Abū-l-Faẓl, Jarrett II. 250. Compare Blochmann's translation, p. 285 n., of the corresponding passage in the Iqbāl-nāma. The tribe is there called Jhariyah. ↑

10 This must be Pāvāgarh, a hill fort in the Pānch ʻMaḥāl district, which is 2,800 feet above the sea. See I.G. XX. 79, and XIX. 380. ↑

11 Son-in-law of Iʻtmādu-d-daula, being married to a sister of Nūr-Jahān. See Ma'āṣiru-l-umarā I. 573. ↑

12 Jhālod in the Doḥad ta'lūqa of the Pānch Maḥāl district, Bombay. ↑

13 The text (pp. 227, 228) has drawings of the twelve Zodiacal coins. See also Tavernier's account of their institution. ↑

14 Text wrongly has Saturday. ↑

15 Probably the Seyreh of Bayley's map, in the Lūnāvāda State, E. of Aḥmadābād. ↑

16 Quoted by Blochmann, *Calcutta Review*, 1869, p. 128. ↑

17 The text has dar *zīr-i-ān* ("under it") in mentioning the position of the letters, but the I.O. MS. No. 181, has *dar zabar* ("above" or "on it."). The words *khaṭṭ-i-muḥarraf* might mean "inverted or slanting letters," and Mr. Rogers has taken the passage to mean that two of the letters were on a line with one another, and that the third was inverted and below the other two. But *muḥrif*, as the word may also be read, has the meaning of "handsome," and I think this is the meaning here. Possibly the meaning is that there was a letter or mark *above*—viz., the *tashdīd*. Another meaning may be that all three letters were equal in size, and in a slanting position on the stone. ↑

18 Dihbīd, "the village of the willow," a well-known place in Transoxiana. It is Dihband in text. ↑

19 *Ukna*. The word appears to be Arabic, and signifies a nest. It is commonly written *wukna*. ↑

20 *Bāz dāmī* apparently means hawks reared in captivity, or it may mean hawks brought by dealers—*dāmī*. Information about hawks may be found in Blochmann, 293, etc., and in Col. Phillott's recent articles in the J.A.S.B., May, 1907, etc. ↑

21 The I.O. MS. has "rupees." ↑

22 Blochmann, 346. ↑

23 Ulugh in MSS. ↑

24 Blochmann, 346. Yūsuf died in November, 1601. His eldest son was M. Lashkarī. ↑

25 The MSS. have 24th and 25th for the following day, but 14th and 15th seem right. ↑

26 The passage is translated in Elliot, VI. 357, but the mention of Saturday and of Multan doctors there is a mistake. Text has *afzūdam*, "I increased my intoxication," but this seems wrong. The MSS. have *afzūd.* Jahāngīr means that the stoppage of his wine increased crapulousness. See Elliot, VI. 357. ↑

27 Apparently this should be *yūghān*, which is a Turki word meaning "*thick.*" ↑

28 Elliot, VI. 358. ↑

29 See Vol. I., p. 414. ↑

30 The Iqbāl-nāma, 115, has a different reading of this line. ↑

31 It should be recorded to Jahāngīr's credit that he has a reputation even at the present day for his love of justice. ↑

32 *'ajabī.* The MSS. have *'ajsī*, "lasting," which seems better. ↑

33 Compare Elliot, VI. 359. *Rukh-i-gulzār* also means the cheek of the rosebud (*i.e.*, the beloved one). Apparently the conceit is that the cheek of the fair one is clouded over, so it should be reddened by pouring wine on it. ↑

34 *hamwār.* Perhaps it means "mediocre" here, but we have the word a little lower down, p. 240, used in a laudatory sense. ↑

35 According to the Ma'āṣir and Blochmann, 465, it was the second son who attained the highest rank. ↑

36 *dah duwāzdah*, "10, 12"—*i.e.*, it is one-fifth larger. The *sāras* is the Ardea Antigone of naturalists. ↑

37 Two boundaries. The name signifies that it is on the borders of Mālwa and Gujaru, I. G. XI. 366. ↑

38 *pāk sākht.* Lit. cleaned it, which may mean also that he disembowelled it, or even that he cooked it. Probably the gunner left the body or part of it there, and it was this that the male circumambulated. ↑

39 Apparently this should be Pāvan. It was one of those caught in the elephant hunt. It is written Bāvan in the MSS. ↑

40 For meaning of *ḍara*, "yard," see text (15th year), pp. 298 and 303. For 3½ quarters (*pāo*) the text wrongly has 3½ feet (*pā*). ↑

41 MSS. has 17. Text has 7. According to Elliot, Supplement II., 177, the *Ilāhī gaz* was one of 41 fingers. ↑

42 This was not the son who died in the following year. See text, p. 282. That son was the eldest son, and probably was the one born in the 9th year. See Tūzuk, p. 137. ↑

43 The Zamindar of Cutch, whose residence was at Bhūj. See Jarrett, II. 250, where it is said that the Jām left his original country 60 years ago. ↑

44 Jahāngīr is referring to his visit to Gujarat in the 12th year of his reign. ↑

45 MSS. have this 70 or 80. ↑

46 Elliot, VI. 359. ↑

47 Text "of Merv," but the MSS. have Herat. ↑

48 Manṣūr Naqqās͟h is one of the illustrators to the Bābar-nāma in the British Museum. Rieu Supplement, p. 52. There is also a Ḥusain Naqqās͟h mentioned in the MS. there described. ↑

49 Apparently there were 32 days in this Tīr. ↑

50 The Sābarmatī rises in the hills of Mewār. ↑

51 I cannot find this Kokra or Gogra. The Sābarmatī falls into the Gulf of Cambay. Possibly Kokra thereby means "mountains." ↑

52 Apparently the Mairpūr of Bayley's map. ↑

53 Blochmann, 339. ↑

54 Perhaps this is the Bīrāgam of the Ā'īn A. (Jarrett, II. 230). Panjū Zamīndār may be the Bab-jīū, Zamindar of the Gond tribe, whom Abū-l-Faẓl mentions. The word Barākar is omitted in text. ↑

55 See Blochmann, 480 n., Elliot, VI. 344, and the Tūzuk, annals of 10th year. ↑

56 Probably the meaning is that the four mines occur within a space of 50 *koss*. Tavernier, vol. II., may be consulted. ↑

57 *Puk͟hta* in text, but the MSS. have not this word. Instead, they have a word which seems to be *taḥsina*, "beautiful." The R.A.S. MS. also seems to have *taḥsina*. ↑

58 *māhagī*? Probably it means that they were caught when a month old, and Elliot's translator so took it. ↑

59 This was the garden which ʿAbdu-r-Raḥīm made after his victory over Muzaffar Gujarātī. In Price's Jahāngīr, pp. 115–16, there is an account of an entertainment given there to Jahāngīr by ʿAbdu-r-Raḥīm's daughter. ↑

60 Or 22 Ramaẓān, 1027 = September 2, 1618. ↑

61 *Cf.* Iqbāl-nāma, 117. ↑

62 In MSS. written Marhāna or Sarhāna. Perhaps Harhāna in the Bet Jālandhar Dūʾāb, Jarrett, II. 317. Though the text says 22 lakhs of dams, the MSS. only say 22 lakhs, and possibly rupees are meant. ↑

63 *Khūd bi-inʿām iltimās namūd.* "As a favour to himself." It is not likely that Shāh Jahān would ask for the pargana for Bikramājīt if it was already his own. I presume the meaning is that Shāh Jahān asked that this pargana should be given to Bikramājīt as a favour to himself. But perhaps the meaning is "which he (Shāh Jahān) had asked for, for himself." ↑

64 In the MSS. the word *khūd* follows *inʿām* instead of preceding it. Perhaps the meaning is, "which was his own appanage," "and he requested," etc. ↑

65 Text wrongly has Muʿtamid. ↑

66 The saint who is buried at Gwalior. He died September 14, 1562. ↑

67 Elliot, VI. 360. ↑

68 The 8th Shahrīwar = August 20, 1618. The departure had been fixed for the 21st, and having mentioned this, Jahāngīr goes on to describe what occurred between the 7th and the 21st. ↑

69 So in text, but MSS. give Jahanda as the name of the brother of Balūch. ↑

70 Elliot, VI. 361. ↑

71 Text wrongly has Maghribī, who was a much later poet, for he died in 809 A.H. = 1416. Sulṭān Sanjar belonged to the sixth century of the Hijra, and Muʿizzī, who is the poet meant by Jahāngīr, died in 542 A.H. (1147–48), having been accidentally killed with an arrow by Sulṭān Sanjar. See Rieu, II. 552b. The ode quoted by Jahāngīr is to be found at p. 138b of British Museum MS. Add. 10588. ↑

72 *hamwār* used here in a favourable sense, though some pages farther back, 233 of Persian text, it seems to be used, when speaking of Jāmī, in disparagement. ↑

73 See Beale art. Saʿīdā-i-Gīlānī. He was styled Bī-badal. The date 1116 in Beale is manifestly wrong. He is the Mullā Shaidā of Rieu, III., 1083e. See

also Sprenger's Catalogue, 124; there is a notice of him in the Ma'āṣiru-l-Umarā, I. 405. He was the artist of the Peacock-throne. ↑

74 *Turunj*, rendered by Vullers as "citron." Probably the reference is to the colour of the sky, which is often spoken of by Orientals as green. The concluding lines play upon Jahāngīr's title of Nūru-d-dīn, on his son's title of S͟hāh-Jahān, and his name of K͟hurram. ↑

75 *Bārī* is a Hindu word meaning garden. ↑

76 *ayyām-i-jawānī.* The MSS. have *qazzāqī*, "raids." The name of the Mullā there seems to be Asīrī. ↑

77 *dar k͟halā wa-malā maḥram būda.* ↑

78 MS. 305. "On every side there are Būlsarī-trees." Both I.O. MSS. have Būlsarī, for which see Blochmann, 70. Apparently there was only one tree. ↑

79 Elliot, VI. 361. ↑

80 This was not the ʿId, for the month was not over. It was the feasting after nightfall usual in the Ramaẓān. ↑

81 *k͟hudāwandi-gār.* For which word see Vullers and the Bahār-i-ʿAjam. Perhaps it means here a locum-tenens or officiating master. ↑

82 Apparently this should be thirty-two. The egg was laid on 21 Amurdād, see p. 237, and the interval between the hatching of the two chicks was three or four days. ↑

83 Text *dah yāzdah*, ten to eleven. But MS. 305 has *dah pānzdah*, ten to fifteen, which is more likely. The meaning then would be that the young of the sāras were 50 per cent., or one-half, larger than goslings. The common expression for one-tenth is *dah yak.* ↑

84 Ganj in No. 181. Perhaps it should be Gajna, see I.G., 17, p. 11. ↑

85 MSS. Atrak. It is the Wātrak of Bayley's Gujarat, p. 201, and the Vātrak of I.G., XXI. 344. ↑

86 Sulṭān Maḥmūd III., killed by Burhān in February, 1554. Bayley's Gujarat, pp. 449 and 453. Jahāngīr calls him the last Sulṭān of Gujarat, because Aḥmad II. and Muẓaffar III. were regarded as spurious. See Āyīn-i-Akbarī, Jarrett, II. 261. ↑

87 Probably great-grandson, for S͟hāh ʿĀlam died in 880 (1475–76), as Jahāngīr tells us supra, and he says that he questioned Sayyid Muḥammad about S͟hāh ʿĀlam's raising the dead, and that Sayyid Muḥammad said he had

the story from his father and grandfather. The Ma᾽āṣiru-l-Umarā, III. 447, says Sayyid Muḥammad was *five* removes from Sẖāh ʽĀlam. ↑

88 For Yāqūt, see Blochmann, 99–100. He was a famous calligrapher, and lived in the thirteenth century. It appears, however, that Yāqūtī is also the name of a particular kind of writing. ↑

89 *Ba-qiṯaʽ-i-maṯbūʽa-i-mukẖtaṣar. Maṯbūʽa* is used in modern times to mean "printed," but here, I think, it means "elegant." It is so used in the annals of the 12th year, p. 208, line 18, where it is applied to a building. *Qiṯaʽ* probably refers to the shape of the volume, and *mukẖtaṣar* to its small size, or to the minuteness of the writing. ↑

90 Sayyid Muḥammad, the Mīr referred to by Jahāngīr, lived into Sẖāh-Jahān's reign, not dying till 1045 (1635–36). See Pādsẖāh-nāma, I., Part II., p. 329. But we do not hear anything more of his translation. Perhaps his ill-health prevented him. It is also the fact that orthodox Muhammadans object to translations of the Qoran, regarding it as an impossible task. The Mīr's son became chief ecclesiastical officer (Ṣadr) under Sẖāh-Jahān. See Ma᾽āṣiru-l-Umarā, III. 447, and Pādsẖāh-nāma, I., Part II., p. 328. ↑

91 Elliot, V. 361. ↑

92 There were twelve māsẖas in a tola; the six cups, then, of 6 tolas and a quarter came to 37½ tolas. ↑

93 Jahāngīr visited his father's tomb in the following year (the 14th). The passage describing the renunciation of shooting (not of hunting) is translated in Elliot, VI. 362. ↑

94 The version of the last two lines is by Sir William Jones, and is given by him in his Tenth Anniversary Discourse, delivered on February 28, 1793. As my friend Mr Whinfield has pointed out to me, the quotation comes from the story of Sẖiblī and the ant in the second chapter of the Būstān. It occurs in the sixth story of the second book and p. 161 of Graf's edition. Sir William Jones's remark is: "Nor shall I ever forget the couplet of Firdausi, for which Sadi, who cites it with applause, pours blessings on his departed spirit." The quotation from Firdūsī occurs on p. 67 of Vol. I. in Macan's edition of the Sẖāh-nāma. ↑

95 Ūrvasī is the name of a celestial nymph. It is also stated by Forbes to be the name of an ornament worn on the breast. ↑

96 Text *bā naqsẖ* by mistake for banafsẖa. ↑

97 I.O. MS. 181 has "thirty *surkẖ*." ↑

98 Perhaps the Moondah of Bayley's map, east of Maḥmūdābād. ↑

99 The text has خادا *k͟hāda*, “an oar,” but the word is perhaps *k͟hārwa*, “a sailor.” I.O. MS. 181, has *k͟hārwa.* ↑

100 The I.O. MSS. have Albatta. ↑

101 The youth who was afterwards drowned in the Jhelam. ↑

102 I.O., No. 181, has G͟hairat K. ↑

103 *gām* sometimes means a step, but here it seems to mean one foot-length. The distance mentioned by Jarrett appears to be 90 feet. ↑

104 No. 181 has “in three days.” ↑

105 Compare account in Akbar-nāma, II. 150. Akbar was then twenty years old. There is a picture of the two elephants crossing the bridge with Akbar on the elephant Hawāʾī in the Clarke MS. in the Victoria and Albert Museum, South Kensington. ↑

106 Presumably the other side of the tank; it was the wild male sāras that Jahāngīr put rings upon. ↑

107 The hunting of deer with decoys is described in Blochmann’s Āyīn, 291. ↑

108 Apparently a metaphorical expression, “fought with fire and water.” ↑

109 *sūʾu-l-qinya*, “Bad state of the body, cachexy” (Steingass). ↑

110 I do not know of any poet with the *tak͟hallus̤* Ustād. Possibly Jāmī is referred to. The lines are obscure, and I am not certain of the meaning. The I.O. MSS. omit the negatives in the first two lines. ↑

111 Not identified. I.O. MS. 305, seems to have Pānib. Can it be the Mānchan or Majham? Possibly we should read Banās. ↑

112 The I.O. MSS. have not the words *Nau Rūz*, “New Year,” and I am not sure what New Year’s day is meant. The time was October. Perhaps it was the first day of Ẕī-l-Qaʿda that was celebrated, or it may be what is described in Richardson as the New Year’s day of the Balance—viz., the entry of the Sun into the Sign of the Balance. Jahāngīr may have had special regard to that Sign as he was born under it. Perhaps all that is meant is that the feast of 1 Ābān was celebrated. Ābān was a sacred month because Akbar was born in it, and it may be that the feast was celebrated on Thursday the 2nd because the previous day, Wednesday, was regarded by Jahāngīr as unlucky, and was always spoken of as *Kam-s͟hamba.* But most probably Nau Rūz is simply a mistake of the text. ↑

113 I.O. MS. has 600. ↑

114 The name of the stage is not given. ↑

115 Literally the mother of children, but explained as meaning a female demon (larva) who torments children. See Lane's Dictionary, 1650, where it is described as "flatulence." ↑

116 See above, p. 243 of text. ↑

117 Apparently the vow applied only to shooting. Jahāngīr was not at that time fifty-one years of age by solar computation. ↑

118 The natural term of life, which some Orientals regarded as being 120 years. ↑

119 The name ʿĀlī is omitted in text. ↑

120 *qand-i-siyāh* (? treacle). ↑

121 We are not told what was the result of this experiment. ↑

122 MSS., as before, have G͟hairat instead of ʿĪzzat. ↑

123 This son was Aurangzīb. See K͟hāfī K., I. 296. K͟hāfī K. has 11th instead of 15th Ẕī-l-Qaʿda. The 11th Ẕī-l-Qaʿda corresponds to 20th October, 1618. ↑

124 Text has Sunday, but Wednesday must be the correct day, for immediately after Friday is spoken of as the 17th (Ābān). ↑

125 Perhaps the Samarnī of Jarrett, II. 207. The I.O. MSS. have Tamarna. ↑

126 I have been assisted by the translation in Elliot, VI. 363. See also Iqbāl-nāma, 117. The author there expatiates on the calamities which followed these celestial appearances. Elliot, *loc. cit.*, p. 364, has eight *years*, but the text of the Tūzuk and all the MSS. have "eight *nights*." The Iqbāl-nāma has Dai instead of Ābān, but probably Dai is a mistake for Ẕī-l-(qāʿda). Perhaps the first phenomenon was the Zodiacal Light. ↑

127 The MSS. have Sambhalkhera. ↑

128 MSS. have Badhnūr. Perhaps it is the Badhnāwar of Jarrett, II. ↑

129 Pargana Nūlāʾī in MSS., and this seems right as Nolāʾī, is mentioned in Jarrett, II. 198, as having a brick fort and as being on the Chambal. ↑

130 It seems to be Gambhīr in the MSS. ↑

131 There seems to be an omission in the recital. We are not told of the first half, but evidently the meaning is that the mice (or rats) ate half the crop on the field, and half of what was brought into the threshing floor. See also Iqbāl-nāma, p. 118. ↑

132 Elliot, VI. 364. ↑

133 The word *maʿnī*, "spiritual," does not occur in the I.O. MSS., and does not appear to be wanted. ↑

134 Also a weight = two barley-grains. Blochmann, 36. ↑

135 The line is wanting in some MSS. In I.O. MS. 181, the conjunction *wa* is omitted (p. 145*b*). ↑

136 So in text, but Sunday was either the 10th or the 17th. Apparently Sunday is a mistake for Wednesday, as, later on, Thursday is mentioned as the 14th. ↑

137 Iqbāl-nāma, 119, "Three sons." ↑

138 Apparently the meaning is that he carried them off as prisoners. ↑

139 Text *jāda-dūstī* by mistake for *jān-dūstī*. ↑

140 *Namak*, "salt." See for a similar expression, p. 149, in the account of Chīn Qilīj. Perhaps the phrase is a reminiscence of the answer given by Muḥammad Ḥusain M. when asked who had captured him. "The king's salt," was his reply. ↑

141 The Sind is mentioned in Tieffenthaler, I. 184. See also I.G., new ed., XXII., p. 432. It is one of the chief rivers of Central India. ↑

142 The word is *s̲h̲ikār*. Either the ducks were caught in nets and not shot, or the shooting was done by others, for Jahāngīr had vowed to give up shooting from the time of S̲h̲ujāʿ's illness. ↑

143 Akbar really took it in the 14th year of his reign (March, 1569). The siege lasted a month, according to Abū-l-Faẓl. Akbar-nāma, II. 339. ↑

144 Elliot, VI. 366. ↑

145 For notes about the meaning of the word *chaukandī*, "four-cornered," see Elliot, V. 347 and 503. ↑

146 Text Rustam, but it is Dastam in MS. 181, and it appears from Blochmann that Dastam or Dostam is the proper spelling. See pp. 398 and 620. ↑

147 Apparently Jahāngīr spent the night in this summer-house. ↑

148 *K̲h̲ilaʿāt*, surely used here on account of the alliteration *k̲h̲arjī u K̲h̲ilaʿāt*. At p. 10 of Price's "Jahangir" it is stated that he released 7,000 prisoners from Gwalior Fort! ↑

149 *durnā*, or *turnā*, a crane. It is a Turki word. ↑

150 The words *dīwān-i-buyūtāt* are repeated. It looks as if the word *buyūtāt* in the second place was a mistake, or if some word implying that Las̲h̲kar K. had been appointed director of buildings (*dīwān-i-buyūtāt*) had been omitted. Apparently ʿĀbid K. went to the Deccan as Dīwān, and not as Dīwān-i-buyūtāt. Compare Iqbāl-nāma, 122. ↑

151 No. 181 has no conjunction, and makes the meaning "porcelain from Tartary." ↑

152 See Blochmann, 140 and 233. Abū-l-Faẓl says the *mujannas* horses resemble Persian horses, and are mostly Turkī or Persian geldings. ↑

153 So in text, but evidently Māndū, or at least Māndū in Malwa cannot be correct. The MSS. seem to have Hindaun, and possibly this is the place meant. Or it may be the place called Mandawar or Hindaun Road (see I.G., new ed., XIII. 135). The position of Hindaun agrees fairly well with Jahāngīr's itinerary, for Tieffenthaler, I., 172, says that Hindaun is 12 leagues—*i.e.*, koss—S.S.-W. from Biāna, and Jahāngīr gives the distance from Māndū or Hindaun to the neighbourhood of Bayānā as 8¼ koss. Bayānā is in the Bhartpur State, and apparently about 21 miles from Hindaun. ↑

154 The quatrain which Jahāngīr describes as that of someone (*s̲h̲ak̲h̲sī*) is included in ʿUmar K̲h̲ayyām's poems, and is thus translated by Whinfield:

"My comrades all are gone, Death, deadly foe,

Hath caught them one by one, and trampled low;

They shared life's feast, and drank its wine with me,

But lost their heads and dropped a while ago."

(Quatrain 219, p. 148.)

FitzGerald has it as Quatrain XXII., and his version is:

"For some we loved, the loveliest and the best

That from his Vintage rolling Time hath prest,

Have drunk their Cup a Round or two before,

And one by one crept silently to rest."

The quatrain is also quoted by Badayūnī, Lowe's translation, p. 192. The phrase *tang-s̲h̲arāb* in the third line means "poor drinkers." Whinfield has *ba-yak s̲h̲arāb*. But *tang-s̲h̲arāb* is given in Johnson's dictionary with the meaning of being easily made drunk, unable to carry much liquor. ↑

155 Bayānā (Biāna) is described in I.G., new ed., VII. 137. It is stated there that it used to have a fort with a very high tower. Bahlūl's tomb still exists. It

was his brother, M. G̱hauṣ, who was most known for his skill in incantations, and who wrote a book on the subject. ↑

156 The story is told in the Akbar-nāma, Vol. I. Jahāngīr is not correct in saying that Humāyūn had ordered Hindāl to remain in Agra. Hindāl went there without permission, and doubtless in order to rebel. See also Gul-badan Begam's "Memoirs," who, naturally, tries to excuse her brother. ↑

157 This must be the Barmadh Mata mentioned by Beale (see Proceedings A.S.B. for August, 1873, p. 159). Beale says there is a place of worship of the Hindus about 1½ koss from Biana in the district of Bhartpur called Barmadh Mata. In the 7th year of Jahāngīr, 1022, 1613, Jahāngīr's mother Maryam-zamānī made a garden and a *bā'olī* (step-well) here at a cost of Rs. 20,000. The garden has disappeared, but the building which is over the *bā'olī* still exists. Beale gives the inscription. William Finch (Hakluyt Society) speaks of a place called Menhapur, near Biana, where there was a garden made by the Queen-Mother. It was a great *sarāy*. The pargana Jūsat of the text is no doubt the Chausath of Jarrett, II. 183, and of Elliot's Supp. Gloss., II., p. 83. Barah may be the Parath or Berath of Jarrett, II. 181. ↑

158 Apparently this is the Dā'ir or Dābar of Badayūnī, II. 171, and Akbar-nāma, III. 145. It is described by Badayūnī as being 4 koss from Fatḥpūr. Dā'ir may also be read Dābar in MSS., and it is Dābar in the map. It is in the Bhartpur State. ↑

159 So in the MSS. and the text, but must be a mistake for Aḥmadābād, which Jahāngīr left on 21 S̱hahrīwar or 22 Ramaẓān. See also Iqbāl-nāma, 117. He arrived at the environs of Fatḥpūr on 19 Dai, or about 22 Muḥarram, 1028 (end of December, 1618). Apparently he considered that he arrived at Fatḥpūr on 20 Dai. He remained on the outskirts and did not enter the town till the 28th (apparently should be 26th or 27th). The Iqbāl-nāma 122 makes Jahāngīr arrive at the outskirts of Fatḥpūr on 20 Dai, and it gives the date of his entering the town as 26 Dai or 1 Ṣafar, 1028 (January 8, 1619). See p. 123. ↑

160 Viz., the propitious hour of the 28th Dai, which had been fixed for the entry into Agra, but was now made the time for entering Fatḥpūr. ↑

161 The lake was to the north of the city, and is now dried up. It had been made by damming up a stream. ↑

162 Apparently this lady was relating what had occurred in Agra, for Jahāngīr has just told us that the plague did not come to Fatḥpūr. Her father was the Āṣaf K., known also as Ja'far K. The ladies seem to have come out from Agra to welcome Jahāngīr. His mother came later from Agra, *see infra*. ↑

163 *Tiryāq-i-Fārūq*. See Lane's Dict., p. 304, col. 3. ↑

164 I.O. MSS. have *az bālā radd u az pāyān iṭlāq shud*, "there was vomiting from above and evacuations from below." The text misses out the words az *bālā radd*. ↑

165 4,000 in No. 181. ↑

166 Certainly Thursday was the 27th according to Jahāngīr. The 28th must be a copyist's mistake here and previously. ↑

167 Jahāngīr says four *gharī* are nearly equal to two sidereal hours. According to Abū-l-Fażl, a *gharī* is the sixteenth part of a nychthemeron, or 360 out of the 21,600 breathings which make up a nychthemeron—*i.e.*, 24 hours. See Jarrett, III. 16 and 17, and II. 16, n. 4. According to the Bahār-i-ʿajam, 2½ *gharī* = one sidereal hour, so that, correctly speaking, five *gharī* = two sidereal hours. Each *gharī* is 24 minutes (Jarrett, II. 16, n. 4). Here it should be noted that there is a mistake in the translation at p. 17, line 2, of Jarrett, vol. III., due to a faulty reading in the Bib. Ind. edition of the text. Instead of *yakī* we should read *palī*, as in two MSS. in my possession. Abū-l-Fażl's meaning then becomes clear. What he says is, a *gharī* is 360 breathings, consequently (*pas*) every *pal* (already defined as the sixtieth part of a *gharī*) is 360 divided by 60, and equal to six breathings (*nafas*). Jahāngīr's line, however, is obscure. In two I.O. MSS. we have *ba-ṭālaʿī* instead of *ba-sāʿatī*. I think the meaning probably is that the same day which marked Jahāngīr's arrival at Fatḥpūr also marked Shāh-Jahān's birthday.

*Tawallā* is defined in the Bahār-i-ʿajam as meaning to have friendship with anyone. It also says that it is used in the sense of *taqarrub*—*i.e.*, nearness. It may be therefore that Jahāngīr's line means "At a moment which nearly corresponded to two (hours)." *Taqwīm* would then mean established or fixed, and not a calendar. *Taqwīm kardan* is a phrase which means "to adjust, to arrange." ↑

168 Shāh-Jahān was born on January 5, 1592, so that in January, 1619, he began to be in his 28th year—*i.e.*, he was 27 complete. ↑

169 That is, 120 according to Muhammadan idea. ↑

170 Afterwards drowned in the Jhelam. ↑

171 Text *darʿa*, MSS. *zirāʿ*. See text 298, account of fifteenth year, where a *darʿa* is defined. The *Ilāhī gaz* or *daraʿ* consisted of 40 digits (fingerbreadths), according to Jahāngīr. If the Kapūr tank be the one described in the Archæological Survey Reports, Vol. XVIII., for 1894, yards seem to be required here, for the tank is mentioned in the Report as being 95 feet 7 inches square. According to Jahāngīr, 34 krors odd of dams—*i.e.*, I presume,

*fulūs*, in copper money, and 16 lakhs and 80,000 rupees in silver were poured into the tank, making a total of 1 kror and 3 lakhs of rupees, or 3 lakhs 43,000 *tūmāns*. Apparently the *tūmān*, which was a gold coin, was, in Jahāngīr's time, reckoned as worth 30 rupees, and Wollaston, in his Dictionary, says it was worth £3 in S͟hāh ʿAbbās I.'s time. Jahāngīr's account of the tank should be compared with that given in the Akbar-nāma, III. 246 and 257, where the tank is called the Anūp-talāo, or the "Unequalled Tank."

In the text, difficulty has, I think, been made by the introduction of the word *kih* in p. 260, six lines from foot, and *bās͟had* in the fifth line from the foot. These words make the sense to be that 34 krors odd of dams were only equal to 16 lakhs odd of rupees. But this cannot be, for the dam was the fortieth part of a rupee, and so 34 krors of dams would be not far short of one kror—*i.e.*, 100 lakhs of rupees. The MSS. have not the *kih* and *bās͟had* in question, and have only a conjunction after the word *dām*. Thirty-four krors odd of copper and 16 lakhs of silver were poured into the tank, making a total, in round numbers, of 1 kror, 3 lakhs of rupees. According to Abū-l-Faẓl gold was also thrown in. ↑

172 Text Yād ʿAlī, but the MSS. have Nād. See also Blochmann, 508. ↑

173 This name is Bairām or Sirām in MSS. Chikanī may be a trade designation, and mean embroiderer, or worker in gold thread. ↑

174 *Kūh-damān*, "hill-subduing." ↑

175 *dībācha*. Here meaning the early part of the Memoirs. ↑

176 The text has *bā* by mistake for *yā*. ↑

177 *ʿaurāt-i-mustaḥaqqa*. Perhaps "pensioned women." ↑

178 These are the opening lines of Jāmī's Yūsuf and Zulaik͟hā (note by Mr. Rogers). ↑

179 Salīm Chis͟htī died on 29 Ramaẓān 979, or February 15, 1572. Jahāngīr was born on 17 Rabīʿ 1st, 977; and so he would be about two years and seven months old at the time of Salīm's death. See Beale and K͟hazīnatu-l-asfiyā, I. p. 435. ↑

180 The conjunction *wa* in text, p. 262, line 16, is a mistake. ↑

181 This is the Buland Darwāza. It was built many years after the mosque. For an account of it, see Mr. Edmund Smith's Fatḥpūr Sīkrī. The gateway is there said to be 134 feet high from the pavement and 176 feet from the roadway. The thirty-two steps mentioned in text must be those from the roadway to the gate. There are two flights of steps, and the total number, up to the top, is 123. The quadrangle or court is stated by Keene to be 433 feet

by 366. Another statement (in the Archæological Report) is 438–9 by 359–10 feet. Salīm's tomb was erected in 1581 (988). It is 47 feet 11 inches each way. ↑

182 4½, Iqbāl-nāma, 124. ↑

183 Text *aiwān*, but should be *alwān*, "coloured." See Iqbāl-nāma, 124. ↑

184 Finch says: "Under the courtyard is a good tank of excellent water." He also speaks of the lake and of its being covered with the *singāra (Trapa bicornis)*. ↑

185 That is, Bāyazīd, a grandson of the saint. Ikrām K. is another name for Hūshang. His mother was Abū-l-Fazl's sister. According to the Ma'āṣir, I. 120, he was a tyrant. According to local tradition, Quṭbu-d-dīn is buried in Bardwān near Shīr-afgan. ↑

186 So in text, but ought to be the 17th. ↑

187 Mau was a Himalayan fort. Blochmann, 345. The text has *Mau u shahrī*, and so have the MSS. The Iqbāl-nāma has *Maud u Mahrī*, p. 124, and so has the Ma'āṣir U., II. 178. Evidently from what follows there were two places, unless one was the fort and the other the city. See also Tūzuk, 304, l. 10, which has pargana Maud Mahrī. In the Āyīn, Jarrett, II. 319, we have Mau and Nabah, and the next name in the list is Mahror. Gladwin has Mowd, and possibly we should translate "Mowd, a city on which he relied." ↑

188 The Iqbāl-nāma, 125, says Rs. 20,000 which would be 40,000 *darbs*. ↑

189 Jagat Singh afterwards became a rebel, joining Shāh-Jahān, as also did Rāja Bikramājīt, or Sundar. He rebelled also in Shāh-Jahān's reign, but was pardoned, and did good service in Kabul and Badakhshan. He died in Peshawar in 1055 (1645). See Ma'āṣir U., II. 238, and Pādishāh-nāma, II. 481. ↑

190 It is *ḥaṣr* in text, but surely this is a mistake for *ḥafr*, and the meaning is that a new pit or well should be made in the middle of the garden. It appears to be *ḥafr* in MSS. The Nūr-manzil garden is the same as the Bāgh Dahra, and was near Agra. Blochmann, 499. ↑

# The Fourteenth New Year's Feast from the Auspicious Accession

On the morning of Thursday, the 4th of the month of Rabīʿu-l-āk͟hir, Hijrī 1028 (March 10, 1619), the world-enlightening sun entered his house of honour in Aries, and the fourteenth year of the reign of this suppliant commenced in all prosperity and happiness. On Thursday, the 1st of the New Year, my prosperous son, S͟hāh-Jahān, who is the star of the forehead of accomplished desires, and the brilliancy of the brow of prosperity, prepared a grand entertainment, and presented me as offerings with a selection of the precious things of the age, and rareties and curiosities of every country. One of these is a ruby, weighing 22 *surk͟hs*, of good colour, and water, and shape. The jewellers have valued it at Rs. 40,000. Another is a *Quṭbī*1 (?) ruby, in weight 3 *tānks*, and very delicate, valued at Rs. 40,000. Further, six pearls, one of them 1 *tānk* and 8 *surk͟hs* in weight. The Vakils of my son had bought it in Gujarat for Rs. 25,000, and the five others for Rs. 33,000. Also one diamond, the price of which was Rs. 18,000. Also a jewelled *parda* (sash), a sword-hilt made in his own goldsmith's shop; most of the jewels he had himself set and cut. He had brought great dexterity to bear on the design. Its value was fixed as Rs. 50,000. The designs2 were his own; no one else had up to this day thought of them. Undoubtedly it was a fine piece of workmanship. There was also a pair of drums made of gold for playing the *mursal* (overture?) with a whole orchestra—viz., *kuwarga*, *naqqāra*, *karanā*, *surnā*, etc.—whatever was required for the *naqqāra-k͟hāna* (music-hall) of great princes, and all made of silver. At the auspicious hour at which I had seated myself on the throne of success these were all sounded. The whole of them came to a value of Rs. 65,000. Another was a seat for riding an elephant, called by moderns a howdah (*hauda*), made of gold, worth Rs. 30,000. Beside this there were two large elephants and five elephant-trappings of the offerings of Quṭbu-l-mulk, ruler of Golconda. The first elephant was named Dād-i-Ilāhī (the gift of God). As it entered the private elephant-house on New Year's Day, I gave it the name of *Nūr-i-Naurūz* (the Light of New Year's Day). In truth he is a grand elephant, and lacks nothing of size, beauty, and dignity. As he looked well to my eye, I mounted him and rode him into the courtyard of the palace. His value was fixed at Rs. 80,000, and the value of six3 others at Rs. 20,000. Its golden trappings, consisting of golden chains, etc., my son had had made for the elephant Nūr-i-Naurūz, were worth Rs. 30,000. The second elephant, with silver housings, was also presented, with Rs. 10,000 more in various choice jewels. The *kurkarāqs*4 of my son had also prepared and sent delicate cloths from Gujarat. If all details were to be written, it would take too long. Briefly, the whole of his offerings was of the value of Rs. 450,000. It is hoped that he will eat the fruit of long life and prosperity.

On Friday, the 2nd, S̲hajā'at K. 'Arab, and Nūru-d-dīn Qulī, the kotwal, laid their offerings before me. On Saturday, the 3rd, Dārāb K., son of the K̲hān-k̲hānān, and on Sunday, the 4th, K̲hān Jahān, prayed to be allowed to entertain me. Out of the latter's offerings I accepted one pearl, bought for Rs. 20,000, with other rareties, altogether of the value of Rs. 130,000, and presented him with the rest. On Monday, the 5th, Rāja Kis̲han Dās and Ḥakīm K., on Tuesday, the 6th, Sardār K., and on Wednesday, the 7th, Muṣṭạfā K. and Amānat K., presented their offerings. From each of these I took a trifle in order to dignify them. On Thursday, the 8th, I'timādu-d-daula, *Madār-ul-mulk* (the pivot of the country), having prepared a royal entertainment, begged to be allowed to receive me. In accepting this request his standing was raised. In fact, in decorating the assembly and the largeness of his offering, he had exceeded himself, and made many decorations, and illuminated all sides of the lake as far as the eye could reach, and decorated the streets both near and far with all kinds of lights and coloured lanterns. Among the offerings of that *Madār-us-saltana* there was a throne of gold and silver, much ornamented and decorated, the supports of which were in the form of tigers. It had been completed with great assiduity in the space of three years, and was made at the cost of Rs. 450,000. This throne had been made by a skilful European of the name of Hunarmand (skilful), who had no rival in the arts of a goldsmith and a jeweller, and in all sorts of skill (*hunarmandi*). He had made it very well, and I gave him this name. In addition to the offerings he had brought for me, he offered the value of Rs. 100,000 in jewelled ornaments and cloths to the Begams and other ladies of the Palace. Without exaggeration, from the beginning of the reign of the late king (may the light of Allah be his testimony!) until now, which is the fourteenth year of the rule of this suppliant, not one of the great Amirs has presented such offerings. In fact, what comparison is there between him and others?

On this day Ikrām K., s. Islām K. was honoured with the mansab, original and increased, of 2,000 personal and 1,000 horse, and Anīrā'ī Singh-dalan with that of 2,000 personal and 1,600 horse, original and increased. On Friday, the 9th, I'tibār K. presented his offering, and on the same day K̲hān Daurān, having been presented with a horse and an elephant, took leave to go to the government of Patna.5 His mansab, according to a previous rule, was fixed at 6,000 personal and 5,000 horse. On Saturday, the 10th, Fāẓil K., on Sunday, the 11th, Mīr Mīrān, on Monday, the 12th, I'tiqād K. on Tuesday, the 13th, Tātār K. and Anīrā'ī Singh-dalan, and on Wednesday, the 14th, Mīrzā Rāja Bhāo Singh, presented their offerings. Selecting from them what was delicate and new, I gave the remainder to them. On Thursday, the 15th, Āṣaf K̲hān prepared a grand assembly and a royal entertainment in his own house, which is a very fine and pleasant place, and begged to be allowed to receive me. At his request, giving him the dignity of acceptance, I went there with the ladies. That pillar of the kingdom looked on this as a bounty from the secret Giver, and in the increase of his offering and preparation of the entertainment displayed great magnificence. Of jewels of great price and delicate gold brocades and all sorts of gifts, that which was approved was selected, and I presented him with the remainder. Among the offerings was a ruby weighing 12½ *tānks*, which was bought for Rs. 125,000. The value of the offerings that were accepted was Rs. 167,000. On this day K͟hwāja Jahān was raised to the mansab of 5,000 personal and 2,500 horse.

Las͟hkar K., having come, by order, from the Deccan, had the honour of waiting on me. As I had determined, after the rainy season had passed and in the beginning of the good weather, to go to the perpetual spring garden of Kashmīr under the favour of Almighty God, it seemed right to me that the guardianship and administration of the fort and city of Agra and the faujdārship of the district, after the manner in which they had been held by K͟hān Jahān, should be entrusted to Las͟hkar K., and I honoured him with the good news. Amānat K. was entrusted with the duty of superintendent of branding (of horses) and of parading the troopers.[6] On Friday, the 16th, K͟hwāja Abū-l-Ḥasan, Chief Bak͟hs͟hī, on Saturday, the 17th, Ṣādiq K. Bak͟hs͟hī, on Sunday, the 18th, Irādat K., Chief Butler, and on Monday, the 19th, which was the day of the sun's culmination, ʿAẓudu-d-daula K., presented offerings, and I accepted from each of them, by way of exalting their dignity, what I approved. At this New Year the value of the accepted offerings of the servants of the Court came to Rs. 2,000,000. On the day of culmination I conferred on my auspicious son Sulṭān Parwīz[7] the mansab of 20,000 personal and 10,000 horse, original and increased. Iʿtimādu-d-daula was promoted to that of 7,000 personal and horse. I selected ʿAẓudu-d-daula for the duty of tutor to the pupil of the eye of the Sultanate, S͟hāh S͟hujāʿ. I hope that he (the latter) may endure for his natural term of life and may be one of the prosperous ones. Qāsim K. was raised to the mansab of 1,500 personal and 500 horse, and Bāqir K. to that of 1,000 personal and 400 horse. As Mahābat K. had asked for reinforcements, I appointed 500 *Aḥadī* horse to Bangash, and presented ʿIzzat K., who had done approved service in that province, with a horse and a jewelled *khapwa*. At this time ʿAbdu-s-Sattār[8] presented as an offering a compendium in the handwriting of the late king Humāyūn (may the lights of Allah be his testimony!), containing some prayers, an introduction to the science of astronomy, and other marvellous things, most of which he had studied and carried into practice. After reverently inspecting his auspicious handwriting, I felt a joy such as I had seldom experienced. I was exceedingly rejoiced, for, by God, no precious thing I have can be compared with this. In return I increased his mansab beyond what he had imagined possible, and gave him a present of Rs. 1,000. Hunarmand, the European who had made the jewelled throne, I presented with 3,000 *darb*, a horse and an elephant. I gave Rs. 1,000 to Khwāja Khāwand Maḥmūd, who is a pilgrim of the Path of the Khwājas, and is not void of dervishism and spirituality. Lashkar K. was promoted to the mansab of 3,000 personal and 2,000 horse, Maʿmūr K. to that of 900 personal and 450 horse, Khwājagī Ṭāhir to that of 800 personal and 300 horse, and Sayyid Aḥmad Qādirī to that of 800 and 60 horse. On Rāja Sārang Deo was conferred the mansab of 700 personal and 30 horse, on Mīr Khalīl-u-llah, s. ʿAẓudu-d-daula, that of 600 personal and 250 horse, on the eunuch Fīrūz K., that of 600 and 150 horse, on Khidmat Khān that of 550 and 130 horse, on Maḥram K. that of 500 and 120 horse, on ʿIzzat K. that of 600 personal and 100 horse, on Rāy Newālī Dās, the accountant of the elephant department, that of 600 personal and 120 horse, on Rāy Mānī Dās, the superintendent of the Palace, that of 600 personal and 100 horse, on Nathmal and Jagmal, sons of Kishan Singh, that of 500 and 225 horse each. If the increase of mansab given to those of less than 500 were to be written in full it would be too long. Rs. 2,000 were given to Khiẓr K., who belonged[9] to Khandesh.

On Wednesday, the 21st, I went to Amānābād for the purpose of sport. Some days before this, in accordance with orders, Khwāja Jahān, and Qiyām K., the head huntsman, had chosen a wide plain for a *qamargha* hunt, and drawn an enclosure round it, and driven within it many antelope from the neighbouring plains. As I had vowed that I would hereafter not kill any living thing with my own hand, it occurred to me to take them all alive, and place them within the Chaugān (polo-ground) of Fatḥpūr, so that I might both enjoy the pleasure of sport and that at the same time no harm should happen to them. I accordingly took 700 head and sent them to Fatḥpūr. As the hour for entering the capital was near, I ordered Rāy Mān, *khidmatiyya*,[10] to put up a screen on two sides, like a lane, from the hunting-place to the plain of Fatḥpūr, and to drive the antelope there. About 800 antelope were sent in this way, or altogether 1,500. On the night of Wednesday, the 28th, marching from Amānābād, I halted in Būstān Sarāy, and on the eve of Thursday, the 29th, I halted at the Nūr-manzil garden.

On Friday, the 30th, the mother[11] of Shāh-Jahān attained the mercy of God. The next day I myself went to the house of that precious son, and having condoled with him in every way, took him with me to the palace. On Sunday, the 1st Urdībihisht, at the auspicious hour chosen by the astrologers and astronomers, I mounted a special elephant of the name of Dilīr, and in all prosperity and happiness entered the city. A great crowd of people, men and women, had collected together in the streets and bazaars, and at the gates and walls, expecting me. According to custom, I went on, scattering money on the way, to inside the palace. From the date on which the army of prosperity started for this happily terminated journey until now, when I returned in happiness and good fortune, it was five years, seven months, and nine days. At this time I ordered my son Sulṭān Parwīz that, as a long time had passed during which he had been deprived of waiting on me personally, or had been fortunate enough to pay his respects, if he were desirous of meeting me, he should come to Court. On the arrival of the gracious farmān, that son, considering the manifestation of this favour a gift from the hidden world, turned the face of his hope towards the sphere-resembling Court. At this time I gave away, as a means of livelihood, to Faqirs and deserving people 44,786 bighas of land, and two entire villages, with 320 ass-loads (*kharwār*, a weight) of grain from Kashmir, and seven ploughs12 of land in Kabul. I hope that the Grace of the Bestower of desires and benevolence may be their daily lot.

One of the occurrences of this time is the revolt of Allāhdād, son of Jalāl, the Afghan. The details of this are that when Mahābat K. obtained leave to go and take possession of Bangash and overthrow the Afghans, from an idea that that wretch would do some service in return for the favours and kindness I had conferred on him, he prayed that he might take him with him. As the natural tendency of such ungrateful men who do not recognize what is right, tends to enmity and malevolence, by way of precaution it was decided to send his son and brother to the Court that they might be as hostages. After the arrival there of his son and brother, I, by way of comforting them, did them all kinds of kindness, but, as they have said:

"The blanket of fortune of anyone that has been woven black

Cannot be whitened even by the waters of Zamzam and Kauṣar."

From the day on which he arrived in that country the signs of rascality and want of recognition of the right began to be apparent on the cheeks of his affairs, and Mahābat K., in order to control matters, did not loose from his hand the rope of forbearance until, at this time, he sent a force under the leadership of his son against a band of Afghans, and sent Allāhdād with him. When they reached the purposed place, from the enmity and malevolence of the aforesaid, that attack did not succeed, and they returned with their aim uncompleted. The evil-dispositioned Allāhdād, from a suspicion lest this time Mahābat K. should abandon his method of conciliation, and ascertain the real state of affairs, and that he should be caught in recompense for his evil deeds, lifted up the veil of reverence, and betrayed involuntarily the faithlessness to his salt, which he had till then concealed. When I heard from Mahābat K.'s letter the true state of affairs, I ordered them to imprison his son and brother in the fort of Gwalior. As it had happened (Jalāl Tārīkī), the father of this wretch had also fled from the service of the late king, and for years passed his time in thieving and highway robbery, until he was caught in the recompense of his own evil deeds. It is hoped that this rascal will also soon obtain the reward of his bad actions.

On Thursday, the 5th, Mān Singh, s. Rāwat Sh̲ankar, who was one of the auxiliaries of Bihar, was promoted to the mansab of 1,000 personal and 600 horse. I sent off ʿĀqil K. to look after the cavalry,13 and inquire into the corps of the mansabdars who had been appointed for duty in Bangash, and gave him an elephant. I sent as a gift to Mahābat K. a private dagger made after the Māzandarān fashion, along with Dūst Beg. The offering of Monday was given as a present to Maḥmūd Āb-dār, who from the time when I was a prince and the days of my childhood had served me. Mīrān (not Bīzan,14 as in the printed book), son-in-law of Pāyanda K. Moghul, was promoted to the mansab of 700 personal and 450 horse. Muḥammad Ḥusain, brother of Kh̲wāja Jahān, who was Bakhshi of Kāngṛa, was promoted to the mansab of 600 personal and 450 horse. On this day Tarbiyat K., who is one of the hereditary houseborn ones of this Court, and had been enrolled among the Amirs by reason15 of his good disposition, died. He was not devoid of sluggishness (*nā-murādī*, literally want of desires) and self-indulgence (*salāmat-i-nafs*), and was a young man fond of pleasure (*ʿayyāsh̲-ṭabīʿat*). He wished to pass his whole life at ease, and was devoted to Hindu music and did not understand it badly. He was a man void of evil. Rāja Sūraj Singh was raised to the mansab of 2,000 personal and horse. To Karamu-llah, s. ʿAlī Mardān K. Bahādur, Bāqir K., Faujdār of Multan, Malik Muḥibb Afghan, and Maktūb K. were given elephants. Sayyid Bāyazīd Bhakkarī, to whom was entrusted the charge of the fort of Bhakkar and the faujdārship of that region, was also honoured with an elephant. Amānu-llah, s. Mahābat K. was distinguished with the gift of a jewelled dagger. I gave elephants to Sh̲aikh̲ Aḥmad Hānsī, Sh̲aikh̲ ʿAbdu-l-Laṭīf Sambhalī, the eunuch Firāsat K., and Rāy Kunwar Chand Mustaufī (auditor). Muḥammad Sh̲afīʿ Bakhshi of the Panjab, was raised to the mansab of 500 personal and 300 horse. The mansab of 500 personal and 150 horse was conferred on Mūnis, s. Mihtar16 K. He (Mūnis) had charge of the fort of Kālinjar.

On this day arrived the news of the death of Sh̲āh-nawāz K. s. the Commander-in-Chief Kh̲ān Kh̲ānān. It was the cause of distress of mind to me. At the time when that Ātālīq (Kh̲ān Kh̲ānān) took leave from waiting on me, it had been strictly impressed upon him that, as it had been repeatedly brought to my ear that Sh̲āh-nawāz K. had been maddened with wine and drank immoderately, if there was truth in this it was a pity that he should destroy himself at his age. It was necessary that he should not leave him to his own way, but look after his case properly. If he could not leave his charge himself, he should write a clear report, so that, having summoned him into my presence, I might give the best order practicable under the circumstances. When he arrived at Burhanpur, having found Sh̲āh-nawāz Kh̲ān very weak and low, he tried to make some remedy for him. After some days' confinement to bed (literally, lord of the carpet) he fell on the couch of powerlessness. Whatever remedies and plans the physicians employed were of no avail, and in the best time of his youth and prosperity, in the thirty-third year of his age, to the sorrow and grief of the world, he went to the place of the mercy and pardon of God. On hearing this unpleasant news I was greatly grieved, for in truth he was an intelligent youth and born in the house. He would have performed important services in this State, and left great traces behind him. Although this road is before all and there is no escape for anyone out of the command of destiny, yet it appears sad to depart in this fashion. It is hoped he will be among those who are pardoned. I sent Rāja Sārang Deo, who was one of my close attendants and is a tactful person, to the Ātālīq, and favoured and consoled him in every way. The mansab of 5,000 held by S͟hāh-nawāz I added on to those of his brothers and sons. To Dārāb, his younger brother, I gave the mansab of 5,000 personal, original and increased, and presented him with a dress of honour, an elephant, a horse, and a jewelled sword, and gave him leave to go to his father to fill, in place of S͟hāh-nawāz, the post of governor of Berar and Ahmadnagar. Raḥmān-dād, another brother, I promoted to the mansab of 2,000 and 800 horse. Manūchahr, s. S͟hāh-nawāz, was given the mansab of 2,000 personal and 1,000 horse. Ṭag͟hzal (Tog͟hril?), s. S͟hāh-nawāz17 K. was promoted to the mansab of 1,000 personal and 500 horse. On Thursday, the 12th, Qāsim K., son-in-law of I'timādu-d-daula, was honoured with the favour of a standard. Asadu-llah, s. Sayyid Ḥājī, who had come with the intention of obtaining service, had the mansab bestowed on him of 500 personal and 100 horse. Ṣadr Jahān, son-in-law of the deceased Murtaẓā K., received that of 700 personal and 600 horse, and was appointed to the faujdārship of Sambhal, and, having had an elephant bestowed on him, I gave him leave. Bhārat Bandīla was also presented with the mansab of 600 personal and 400 horse, and had an elephant given him, and an elephant was bestowed on Sangrām, the Raja of Jammu.

In Ahmadabad I had two male *mārk͟hūr* goats. As I had not a female in my establishment to pair with them, it occurred to me that if I could pair them with Barbary goats, which they bring from Arabia, especially from the port of the city of Darkhar,18 young of their form and qualities might be obtained. In short, I paired them with seven Barbary ewes, and after six months had elapsed each of the latter had a young one at Fatḥpūr: there were four females and three males, very pleasing in appearance, of good shape and good colour. In their colour, those (kids) which resembled the male (*taka*, not *baka*, as in the printed copy) were dun-coloured with black stripes on their backs. Red,19 indeed, appears to me a more pleasing colour than any other, and it is the mark of a better breed. Of their liveliness and laughable ways and their manner of gamboling and leaping, what can be written? Some of their ways are such that the mind derived uncontrolled pleasure from looking at them.

It is notorious that painters cannot draw properly the motions of a kid. Granting that they may chance to draw the movements of an ordinary kid after a fashion, they certainly would have to acknowledge themselves at a loss how to draw the motions of these kids. When one month, or even twenty days old, they would leap up upon high places and throw themselves on to the ground in a way that if any other but a kid were to do so, not one limb would be left whole. As it pleased me, I ordered them always to be kept near me, and I gave each of them an appropriate name. I am much delighted with them, and pay great attention to bringing together mārkhūr males and well-bred she-goats. I desire to have many young ones from them, and that they may become well known among men. After their young shall have paired, most probably more delicate ones will be obtained. One of their peculiarities is that ordinary kids immediately they are born, and until they begin to suck, make a great bleating, whilst these, on the contrary, make no sound, and stand quite contented and without wailing. Perhaps their flesh would be very pleasant to the taste.

Before this, an order had been given that Muqarrab K., having been appointed to Bihar, should hasten off there. He came to Court in order to pay his respects before he repaired to his destination, and accordingly, on Thursday, the 2nd Khūrdād, an elephant with trappings, two horses, and a jewelled *khapwa* were conferred on him, and he took leave. Rs. 50,000 were given him as an advance of pay. On the same day Sardār Khān received a dress of honour, an elephant, and a horse, and obtained the Sarkar of Monghyr, which is in the province of Bihar and Bengal, and took leave. Mīr Sharīf,[20] the Vakīl of Quṭbu-l-mulk, who was at Court, took leave. My fortunate son, Shāh-Jahān, sent with him the brother of Afẓal K., his Diwan. As Quṭbu-l-mulk had shown attachment and desire to please, and repeatedly importuned me for a portrait, I presented him, at his request, with my likeness, a jewelled *khapwa*, and a *phūl kaṭāra*. 24,000 *darb*, a jewelled dagger, a horse, and a dress of honour were also given to the aforesaid Mīr Sharīf. Fāẓil K., director of buildings, was advanced to the mansab of 1,000 personal and 500 horse, and Ḥakīm Rāgho Nāth to that of 600 personal and 60 horse. As at this time the anniversary of the late king (Akbar) occurred, Rs. 5,000 were handed over to some of my chief servants to divide among poor and deserving people. Ḥasan ʿAlī K., jagirdar of the Sarkar of Monghyr, was honoured with the mansab of 2,500 personal and horse, and sent to the assistance of Ibrāhīm K. Fatḥ-jang, governor of the province of Bengal, and he was presented with a sword. As Mīrzā Sharafu-d-dīn Ḥusain Kāshgharī sacrificed his life on duty in Bangash, I promoted his son Ibrāhīm Ḥusain to the mansab of 1,000 personal and 500 horse. At this time Ibrāhīm K. constructed two boats,[21] which in the language of the country they call *Kosha*, one of gold and the other of silver, and sent them to me by way of offering.

Undoubtedly, of their own kind they are the finest. One of these I gave to my son S͟hāh-Jahān. On Thursday, the 9th, Sādāt K. was granted the mansab of 1,000 personal and 60 horse. On this day ʿAẓudu-d-daula and S͟hajāʿat K. ʿArab took leave for their jagirs. On this Thursday I presented Āṣaf K. with a jewelled *khapwa* and a *phūl katāra.* As my fortunate son Sulṭān Parwīz proposed to come to Court, he asked for a special *nādirī* dress of honour, a *chīra*, and a *fota*, so that he might wear them and be distinguished on the day of meeting me and of having the good fortune to pay his respects. According to his request, I sent by the hand of his Vakil, S͟harīf, a sumptuous dress of honour with a *chīra* and a special sash. On Thursday, the 23rd, Mīrzā Wālī, son of the aunt of this suppliant, came by order from the Deccan, and had the good fortune to kiss the threshold. His father, K͟hwāja Ḥasan K͟hāldār (the freckled?), was one of the Naqs͟hbandī K͟hwājas. My uncle, Mīrzā Muḥammad Ḥakīm, gave his sister in marriage to the K͟hwāja. I heard much praise of the K͟hwāja from people: he had both good family and got on well with every one, and for a long time the management of the affairs of my uncle Mīrzā Muḥammad Ḥakīm had been in his hands, and he was on very good terms with him. Before the Mīrzā's death he had himself delivered22 over the deposit of his life. Two sons survived him—viz., Mīrzā Badīʿu-z-zamān and Mīrzā Wālī. M. Badīʿu-z-zamān, after the death of the Mīrzā, ran away, and went to Mā-warāʾa-n-nahr (Transoxania), and in that exile became a traveller on the road of non-existence. The Begam and Mīrzā Wālī came to the glorious Court, and H.M. (Akbar) behaved very kindly to the Begam. The Mīrzā also is a steady and sedate young man, not devoid of reasonableness and understanding. He is very skilled in the science of music. At this time it occurred to me to marry the daughter of the deceased Prince Dāniyāl to the Mīrzā, and my reason for sending for the Mīrzā to Court was this. This girl (Bulāqī Begam) is the offspring of the daughter of Qilīj Muḥammad K. It is hoped that the grace of striving to please and to serve, which is the means of good fortune and prosperity, may be his (M. Wālī's) lot and fortune.

On this day Sarbuland Rāy, who had been sent on duty to the Deccan, was promoted to the mansab of 2,500 personal and 1,500 horse.

At this time it was reported to me that a *Shayyād* (a loud talker, a cheat) of the name of S͟haik͟h23 Aḥmad had spread the net of hypocrisy and deceit in Sirhind, and caught in it many of the apparent worshippers without spirituality, and had sent into every city and country one of his disciples, whom he called his deputy (k͟halīfa), and whom he considered more skilled than others in the adorning of shops (of deceit) and selling of religious knowledge, and in deceiving men. He had also written a number of idle tales to his disciples and his believers, and had made them into a book which he called *Maktūbāt* (letters). In that album (*Jung*) of absurdities many unprofitable things had been written that drag (people) into infidelity and impiety. Amongst these he had written in a letter as follows: "In the course of my travels I had come to the dwelling of the Two Lights (the Sun and Moon), and saw a very lofty and very splendid building. From there I passed to the abode of Discrimination (Fārūq), and from there I passed to the abode of Truth (Ṣiddīq), and to each I wrote a suitable explanation (or perhaps, of each I wrote a suitable description). From there I reached the abode of Love, and I beheld a brilliant dwelling. It had divers colours and lights and reflected glories. That is to say (God forgive us!—an exclamation of Jahāngīr's), I passed from the abode of the Vicegerents (k͟hulafā) and attained to the highest rank." There were other presumptuous expressions which it would be too long to write, and would be contrary to good manners. I accordingly gave an order that they should bring him to the Court that is based on justice. According to order he came to pay his respects. To all that I asked him he could give no reasonable answer, and appeared to me to be extremely proud and self-satisfied, with all his ignorance. I considered the best thing for him would be that he should remain some time in the prison of correction until the heat of his temperament and confusion of his brain were somewhat quenched, and the excitement of the people also should subside. He was accordingly handed over to Anīrā'ī Singh-dalan to be imprisoned in Gwalior fort.

On Saturday, the 25th K͟hūrdād, my fortunate son Sulṭān Parwīz came from Allahabad, and with prostration at the threshold of the Khalifate illuminated the forehead of sincerity. After he had performed the ceremony of kissing the ground and been honoured with special favour, I bade him sit. He presented 2,000 muhars and 2,000 rupees by way of *naẕr*, and made an offering of a diamond. As his elephants had not yet arrived, he would produce them on another occasion. He had brought with him to the Court, which is the asylum of the world, Rāja Kalyān, Zamindar of Ratanpūr, against whom this my son had by order sent an army, and had taken from him as an offering 80 elephants and Rs. 100,000. My son brought him with him, and he had the good fortune to kiss the threshold. Wazīr K., my son's Diwan who is one of the old servants of the Court, having had the good fortune to pay his respects to me, presented as offerings 28 elephants, male and female. Of these nine were accepted, and the rest bestowed on him.

As it had been represented to me that Muruwwat K., s. Iftik͟hār K., who was one born and bred up at this Court, had fought with a band of Maghs on the borders of Bengal and had sacrificed his life, I promoted Allāh-yār, his brother, to the mansab of 1,000 personal and 500 horse, and another brother to that of 400 personal and horse, so that those he had left behind should not be distressed. On Monday, the 3rd of the Divine month of Tīr, in the neighbourhood of the city four black bucks, a doe, and a fawn were taken.

As I passed by the house of my fortunate son, Sulṭān Parwīz, he presented two tusked elephants with their trappings by way of offering; both were ordered to be placed in the private elephant-stud.

On Thursday, the 13th, Sayyid Ḥasan, the ambassador of my happy brother, S̲h̲āh ʿAbbās, ruler of Persia, having had the good fortune to kiss the threshold, produced a letter, together with a crystal drinking-cup, on the cover of which was a ruby. As it was given from excessive friendship and sincerity it was the cause of the increase of amity and good fellowship. On this day Fidāʾī K. was promoted to the mansab of 1,000 personal and 500 horse, and Naṣru-llah, s. Fatḥu-llah, in whose charge was the fort of Ambar, that of 1,500 personal and 400 horse. On Thursday, the 20th, Amānu-llah, s. Mahābat K., was promoted to the mansab of 1,500 personal and 800 horse. Having conferred on Wazīr K. the Diwanship of Bengal, I gave him a horse, a dress of honour, and a jewelled dagger. Elephants were given to Mīr Ḥusāmu-d-dīn and Zabar-dast K. On this day Ḥāfiẓ Ḥasan, a servant of K̲h̲ān ʿĀlam, came to Court with a precious letter from my brother S̲h̲āh ʿAbbās, and a report from that pillar of the Sultanate (K̲h̲ān ʿĀlam). He laid before me a dagger the hilt of which was made of a fish's24 tooth spotted with black, that my brother had given to K̲h̲ān ʿĀlam. As it was a great rarity, he (K̲h̲ān ʿĀlam) had sent it to me. I greatly approved of it; in fact, it is a rare present. I had never seen a spotted one until now, and I was much pleased.

On Thursday, the 27th, M. Wālī was promoted to the mansab of 2,000 personal and 1,000 horse. On the 24th, I gave 1,000 darbs as a present to Sayyid Ḥasan, the ambassador, and an elephant to ʿAbdu-llah K. Bahādur Fīrūz-jang. On Thursday, the 2nd of the Divine month of Amurdād, a horse was presented to Iʿtibār K. ʿĀqil K. was promoted to the mansab of 1,000 personal and 800 horse.

On the night of Saturday, the 4th of the Ilāhī month of Amurdād, corresponding with 15 S̲h̲aʿbān, was the feast of the S̲h̲ab-i-barāt. By order, they decorated and brought before me on the river, boats with lamps and all kinds of fireworks. In truth, the lamps they had arranged appeared very pretty, and for a long time I enjoyed myself in going round and looking at them. On Tuesday, Mīrān,25 s. Nād ʿAlī Maidānī, who was one of the well-brought-up khanazads, was selected for the mansab of 700 personal and 500 horse, and K̲h̲wāja Zainu-d-dīn for that of 700 personal and 300 horse, and K̲h̲wāja Muḥsin for that of 700 personal and 100 horse. On Thursday, the 9th, I went to hunt at the village of Samūnagar. Passing my time pleasantly in going round and hunting on that pleasant plain until Monday, I returned on the eve of Tuesday to the palace. On Thursday, the 16th, Bis̲h̲ūtan, grandson of S̲h̲aik̲h̲ Abū-l-Faẓl (the author), was promoted to the mansab of 700 personal and 350 horse. On this day I went round to see the garden of Gul-afs<u>h</u>ān, which is on the bank of the Jumna. On the way rain fell heavily and filled the mead with freshness and greenness. Pineapples had arrived at perfection, and I made a thorough inspection. Of the buildings that overlooked the river none26 that I saw were without the charm of verdure and flowing water. These verses of Anwarī appeared appropriate to the place:

VERSE.

"'Tis a day of mirth and jollity,

A daily market of flowers and odours;

The earth-heaps are suffused with ambergris,

The zephyr sheds rose-water from his skirt,

From contact with the morning breeze the pool

Is roughened and pointed, like the edge of a file."

As this garden is in the charge of K<u>h</u>wāja Jahān, he presented me as offerings with some pieces of brocade of a new fashion they had lately brought for him from ʻIrāq. Selecting what I approved of, I presented the remainder to him. He had arranged the garden well, and his mansab was ordered to be raised to 5,000 personal and 3,000 horse, original and increased.

A strange circumstance was that I was so much delighted with a jewelled dagger-hilt of piebald teeth which K<u>h</u>ān ʻĀlam had got from S<u>h</u>āh ʻAbbās and sent to me (see *ante*), that I appointed several skilful men to go to Īrān and Tūrān to look for them and to be consistently searching for them, and to bring some from anywhere and any person, anyhow, and at any price. Many of my servants who knew my disposition, and dignified Amīrs in the course of their duty, engaged in the search. It happened that in this city a stupid stranger bought in the open bazaar a coloured tooth of great beauty and delicacy for a trifle; he believed that some time or other it had fallen into the fire, and that the black on it was the mark of burning! After some time he showed it to one of the carpenters on the establishment of my prosperous son S<u>h</u>āh-Jahān, desiring that he should take off a piece of the tooth in order to make a ring (*<u>sh</u>ast*), and pointed out that he should remove the marks of burning and the blacknesses, being ignorant that the blackness enhanced the value and price of the whiteness. Those moles and patches were what the tirewoman of destiny had given as an adornment of its beauty. The carpenter at once went to the Superintendent of his workshop, and gave him the good news that such a rare and precious thing, in search of which people were wandering and going long distances, and hastening to all corners and in all directions in various countries, had fallen for nothing into the hands of an ignorant man, who did not know its value. It could be easily and cheaply obtained from him. The Superintendent went off with him and immediately procured it, and next day produced it before my son. When my son S̲h̲āh-Jahān came to wait on me, he at first showed great delight, and after his brain had become free from the intoxication of the wine of joy, produced it, and greatly pleased me—

VERSE.

"Thy Time is happy in that thou hast made mine happy."

I invoked so many blessings on him that if one of them out of a hundred obtain acceptance, it will suffice for his spiritual and material well-being.

On this day Bahlīm K., one of the chief servants of ʿĀdil K. came and waited on me. As he had chosen my service out of sincerity, I bestowed on him unstinted favours, and presented him with a dress of honour, a horse, a sword, and 10,000 darbs, with the mansab of 1,000 personal and 500 horse. At this time a petition came from K̲h̲ān Daurān, stating that: "Your Majesty, from the perfection of kindness and knowledge of his worth, had appointed to the government of Thatta (Sind) an old slave, notwithstanding his great age and weak sight. As this weak old man was exceedingly bent and decrepit, and had not in him the ability to exert himself or to ride, he prays that he may be excused military service, and that he may be enrolled in the army of prayer." At his request, I ordered the chief Diwans to confirm him in the pargana of Khushāb,27 with a revenue of 3,000,000 of dāms, and which he for a long time had held as a *tank̲h̲wāh* jagir, and which had become peopled and cultivated, by way of providing for his expenses, so that he might pass his time in easy circumstances. His eldest son, by name S̲h̲āh Muḥammad, was promoted to the mansab of 1,000 personal and 600 horse, his second son, Yaʿqūb Beg, obtaining that of 700 personal and 350 horse. The third son, Asad Beg, was promoted to the mansab of 300 personal and 50 horse.

On Saturday, the 1st of the Divine month of S̲h̲ahriwar, I sent dresses of honour for the rainy season to the Ātālīq Commander-in-Chief K̲h̲ān-k̲h̲ānān Jān-sipār and the other great Amīrs, who had been sent on duty to the Deccan, by the hand of Yazdān.28

As the purpose of visiting the eternal spring of the rose-garden of Kashmir was settled in my mind, I sent off Nūru-d-dīn Qulī to hasten on before, to repair as far as was possible the ups and downs of the Pūnch29 route to it, and to prepare it, so that the passage of laden beasts over difficult hilltops might be accomplished with ease, and that the men should not undergo labour and hardship. A large number of artificers, such as stone-cutters, carpenters, spadesmen, etc., were despatched with him, to whom an elephant was also given. On the eve of Thursday, the 13th, having gone to the garden of Nūr-manzil, I passed the time in enjoyment in that rose-garden of delight until Sunday, the 16th. Rāja Bikramājīt Baghela came from the fort of Māndpūr, which is his native place, and had the good fortune to kiss the threshold, and by way of offering presented an elephant and a jewelled plume. Maqṣūd K. was honoured with the mansab of 1,000 personal and 130 horse. On Thursday, the 20th, my son S͟hāh Parwīz produced two elephants as an offering, and they were ordered to be included in the private stud. On the 24th of the aforesaid month the feast of the solar weighing took place in the palace of Maryamu-z-zamānī, and my 51st year according to the solar months began in gladness and victory. It is hoped that the period of my life may be passed in obedience to God (to whom be glory!). To Sayyid Jalāl, s. Sayyid Muḥammad, the grandson (?) of S͟hāh ʿĀlam Buk͟hārī, an account of whom has been written among the events of my Gujarat expedition, I gave leave to return. I gave him a female elephant for his riding, as well as his expenses. On the eve of Sunday,30 the 30th, corresponding with the 14th S͟hawwāl, when the disk of the moon was perfect (at full moon) a moonlight feast was prepared in the buildings of the garden which overlook the River Jumna, and a very pleasant entertainment took place. On the 1st of the Divine month, out of the veined (*jauhar-dār*) spotted tooth (walrus) which my son S͟hāh-Jahān had given me as an offering, I ordered to be cut off sufficient for two dagger-hilts and a thumb-stall:31 it came out of a beautiful colour and was very choice. I ordered the *Ustāds* (masters) Pūran and Kalyān, who had no rivals in the art of engraving,32 to make dagger-hilts of a shape that was approved at this time, and has become known as the Jahāngīrī fashion. At the same time the blade and the sheath and fastenings were given to skilful men, each of whom was unique in his age in his art. Truly, it was all carried out according to my wish. One hilt came out coloured in such a way as to create astonishment. It turned out of all the seven colours, and some of the flowers looked as if a skilful painter33 had depicted them in black lines round it with a wonder-working pencil. In short, it was so delicate that I never wish it to be apart from me for a moment. Of all the gems of great price that are in the treasury I consider it the most precious. On Thursday I girded it auspiciously and with joy round my waist, and the masters who in their completion had exercised great skill and taken great pains were rewarded, Ustād Pūran with the gift of an elephant, a dress of honour, and a golden bracelet for the wrist, which the people of India call *Kara*,34 and Kalyān with the title of ʿAjāʾib-dast (wondrous hand), and increased mansab, a dress of honour, and a jewelled bracelet (*pahūnchī*), and in the same way every one according to his circumstances and skill received favours.

As it had been represented to me that Amānu-llah, s. Mahābat K., having fought with the rebel Aḥdād, had defeated his army, and had made many of the Afghans—who are black-faced and black-hearted—the harvest of his blood-drinking sword, I sent him a special sword in order to dignify him.

On Saturday the 5th, news came of the death of Rāja Sūraj Singh, who had died a natural death in the Deccan. He was the descendant of Māldeo, who was one of the principal Zamindars of Hindustan, and had a zamindari which equalled that of the Rānā, and he had even overcome him in one battle. There is a full account of him (Māldeo) in the Akbar-nāma. Rāja Sūraj Singh, through the advantage of his being brought up by the late king (Akbar), and this suppliant at the throne of God, reached high rank and great dignities. His territory surpassed that of his father or grandfather.35 He had a son called Gaj Singh,36 whom he entrusted with all his administrative affairs. As I knew him to be capable and worthy of favour, I promoted him to the mansab of 3,000 personal and 2,000 horse, with a standard and the title of Raja, and his younger brother to that of 500 personal and 250 horse, and gave him a jagir in his native country.

On Thursday, the 10th of Mihr, at the request of Āṣaf K., I went to his house built on the bank of the Jumna. He has erected a very fine bath-house (ḥammām), with which I was much delighted. After bathing, a feast of cups was held, and my private servants were made happy with cups of delight. Having chosen out of his offerings what I approved, I gave the remainder to him. What I took of his offering might be of the value of Rs. 30,000. Bāqir K., faujdār of Multan, was honoured with a standard.

Previously to this, according to order, they had planted trees on both sides from Agra as far as the River of Attock (the Indus), and had made an avenue, and in the same way from Agra to Bengal. I now ordered that from Agra to Lahore they should put up a pillar37 (*mīl*) at every koss, to be the sign of a koss, and at every three koss make a well, so that wayfarers might travel in ease and contentment, and not endure hardships from thirst or the heat of the sun.

On Thursday, the 24th of Mihr, the festival of the Dasahrā was held. After the custom of India, they decorated the horses and produced them before me. After I had seen the horses they brought some of the elephants. As Muʿtamid K. on last New Year's Day had not made any offering, at this festival he presented a golden tablet (*takht*), a ruby ring, a piece of coral (*bussad*), and other items. The tablet was beautifully made. The total value of the offering was Rs. 16,000. As he had brought the things from pure sincerity and loyalty, they were accepted. On this day Zabar-dast K. was promoted to the mansab of 1,000 personal and 400 horse. As the day of the Dasahrā had been fixed as the time of starting, I embarked on a boat with all happy omens and pleasure in the evening, and went on to my goal. I halted for eight days at the first stage that the men might come on, after making all preparations at leisure. Mahābat K. had sent apples from Bangash by runners (*dāk-chokī*). They arrived very fresh, and were of excellent flavour. I was greatly pleased in eating them. They cannot be compared with the *sīb-i-k͟hūb* ("the good38 apples"?) of Kabul which I ate there, or with the Samarkand apples that they bring every year. For sweetness and delicacy of flavour they cannot be compared with either of the latter (*i.e.*, the Bangash apples were far better). I had until now never seen such delicate and delicious apples. They say that in Upper Bangash, near Lashkar-dara,39 there is a village called Sīv Rām, in which there are three trees of this apple, and although they have made many trials, they have never found so good ones in any other place. I gave Sayyid Ḥasan, ambassador of my brother S͟hāh ʿAbbās, a dish of these apples in order that he might tell me if there were any better apples in ʿIrāq. He said: "In the whole of Persia the apples of Isfahan are preferred, and they are of the same quality as these."

On Thursday, the 1st of the Divine month of Ābān, I went on pilgrimage to the mausoleum of the late king (Akbar) (may the lights of Allah be his testimony!), and rubbed the head of supplication on the threshold, the abode of angels, and presented 100 muhars as nazar. All the Begams and other ladies, having sought the blessing of circulating round that shrine, which is the circling-place of angels, presented offerings. On the eve of Friday a lofty assembly was held of the holy men (*Mas͟hāʾik͟h*), the turbaned people (*arbāb-i-ʿamāʾim—i.e.*, ecclesiastics, etc.), *Ḥuffāẓ* (those who recite the Qoran), and singing people, assembled in numbers, and practised ecstasies and religious dancing (*wajd* and *samāʿ*), to each of whom, according to the circumstances of his merit and skill, I gave a dress of honour, a *farjī*, and a shawl. The buildings of this blessed mausoleum have been made very lofty. At this time the money expended satisfied me, and was far more than it had previously been. (The MS.40 here is clear, and the printed words wrong.)

On the 3rd, after four gharis of day had passed, I marched on from that stage, and having traversed 5½ koss by the river at four gharis of the day, arrived at the next stage. After midday I left the boat and caught seven partridges (*durrāj*). At the end of the day I gave Rs. 20,000 to Sayyid Ḥasan, the ambassador (of Persia), as a present, and a dress of honour of gold brocade with a jewelled *jīg͟ha* (turban-ornament), and an elephant, and gave him leave to return, and sent for my brother with him a jewelled jug made in the shape of a cock, which could hold my usual stint of wine. It is hoped that it may reach its destination in safety. I gave leave to Las͟hkar K., who had been appointed to the defence and government of Agra, with a gift of a dress of honour, a horse, an elephant, drums, and a jewelled dagger. Ikrām K. was promoted to the mansab of 2,000 personal and 1,500 horse, and to the duty of faujdār of the Sarkār of Mewāt. He is s. Islām K., who was the grandson of the venerable asylum of pardon Shaikh Salīm, whose excellency of person and approved disposition and connection in blessing with this illustrious family have been described in these pages with the pen of sincerity.

At this time I heard from a certain person whose words are adorned with the light of truth that at the time when I was sick and weak at Ajmir, before this evil news arrived in the province of Bengal, one day Islām K. was sitting in private, when he suddenly became unconscious. When he came to himself he said to one of his confidants, of the name of Bhīkan, that it had been shown him from the world of mysteries that the holy person of the Emperor had been attacked by sickness, and that the remedy for it was to sacrifice for him something that was exceedingly dear and precious to himself. It at first occurred to him to sacrifice for the head of the revered one his own son Hūshang, but as he was young in years and as yet had derived no profit from life, and not attained to the desire of his heart, he had compassion on him, and would sacrifice himself for his lord and master. He hoped that as this was from the bottom of his heart, and the sincerity of his being, it would be accepted at the throne of Allah. The arrow of prayer at once reached the target of acceptance, and he perceived himself afflicted with weakness and disease. Verily, verily, the disease increased till he reached the neighbourhood of the compassion of God (he died). The Great Physician bestowed from the hidden dispensary complete recovery on this suppliant. Although the late king (the lights of Allah be his testimony!), was much attached to the children and grandchildren of the Shaikhu-l-Islām, and bestowed favours on them all according to the capacity and aptitude of each, yet when the turn of rule came to this suppliant, they received great kindnesses in order to perform what was due to that revered one (Salīm Chishtī), and many of them attained to the high nobility, and were advanced to the posts of head of Subahs, as has been brought to record each in its own place.

As in this village the eunuch Hilāl K.,[41] who was one of my attendants from the time when I was prince, had built a *sarāy*, and made a garden, he made an offering to me. In order to dignify him I took a trifle from him. After marching four stages from this halting-place, the army of prosperity encamped outside Mathura. On Thursday, the 8th, I went to see Bindrāban and the idol temples of that place. Although[42] in the time of the late king the Rajput nobles had built temples after their fashion, and ornamented them highly on the outside, inside them bats and owls (*abābīl*) had made their abode to such an extent, that on account of the malodours one could not breathe.

VERSE.

"Outside, like an infidel's grave, full of cracks,[43]

Inside, the anger of God, the honoured and glorious."

On this day Mukhliṣ K., according to order, came from Bengal, and had the good fortune to kiss the threshold. He gave 100 muhars and 100 rupees as nazar, and by way of offering, a ruby and jewelled aigrette (ṭurra). On Friday, the 9th, Rs. 600,000 of treasure for the maintenance (*zakhīra*) of the fort of Āsīr were sent to the Commander-in-Chief, Khān-khānān.

In the foregoing pages, something has been written about Gosā'īn Jadrūp,44 who lived as a hermit in Ujain. At this time he changed his residence to Mathura, which is one of the greatest places of worship of the Hindus, and employed himself in the worship of the true God on the bank of the Jumna. As I valued his society, I hastened to wait on him, and for a long time enjoyed his company without the presence of any stranger. In truth, his existence is a great gain to me: one can be greatly benefited and delighted.

On Saturday, the 10th, the huntsmen represented that there was in that neighbourhood a tiger that greatly troubled and injured the ryots and wayfarers. I immediately ordered them to bring together a number of elephants and surround the forest and at the end of the day myself rode out with my ladies. As I had vowed that I would not injure any living thing with my own hand, I told Nūr-Jahān45 to shoot at him. An elephant is not at ease when it smells a tiger, and is continually in movement, and to hit with a gun from a litter (*'imārī*) is a very difficult matter, insomuch that Mīrzā Rustam, who, after me, is unequalled in shooting, has several times missed three or four shots from an elephant. Yet Nūr-Jahān B. so hit the tiger with one shot that it was immediately killed.

On Monday, the 12th, my desire to see the Gosā'īn Jadrūp again increased, and hastening to his hut, without ceremony, I enjoyed his society. Sublime words were spoken between us. God Almighty has granted him an unusual grace, a lofty understanding, an exalted nature, and sharp intellectual powers, with a God-given knowledge and a heart free from the attachments of the world, so that, putting behind his back the world and all that is in it, he sits content in the corner of solitude and without wants. He has chosen of worldly goods half a *gaz* of old cotton (*kirpās*) like a woman's veil, and a piece of earthenware from which to drink water, and in winter and summer and the rainy season lives naked and with his head and feet bare. He has made a hole in which he can turn round with a hundred difficulties and tortures, with a passage such that a suckling could hardly be put through it. These two or three couplets of Ḥakīm Sanā'ī (may God have mercy on him!) appeared appropriate:

VERSE.46

"Luqmān had a narrow hut,

Like the hollow of a flute or the bosom of a harp.

A noodle put the question to him—

'What is this house—two feet and a span?'

Hotly and with tears the sage replied—

'Ample for him who has to die.'"

On Wednesday, the 14th, I again went to visit the Gosā'īn and bade him good-bye. Undoubtedly parting from him weighed upon my mind, that desires the truth. On Thursday the 15th, I marched and pitched near Brindāban. At this stage my fortunate son Sulṭān Parwīz took leave of me for Allahabad, and went to his jagir. I had intended that he should accompany me on this expedition, but as he had already shown symptoms of distress, I could not avoid letting him go. I presented him with a tipchāq horse, a waist dagger with a veined (*jauhar-dār*) walrus-tooth (hilt), and a sword and special shield. I hope he will come again soon, and have the good fortune of my presence. As the period of K͟husrau's imprisonment had been a long one, it seemed to me that to keep him longer in confinement and deprive him of the good fortune of waiting on me, would be wanting in kindness. I accordingly sent47 for him and bade him salute me. Once again the marks of his offences were washed with the pure water of forgiveness, and the dust of disgrace and humiliation was rubbed off his brow. I hope that the blessing of pleasing me, and the grace of service may be his lot.

On Friday, the 16th, I gave leave to Muk͟hliṣ K., whom I had sent for to take up the duties of diwan to S͟hāh Parwīz, and I gave him the rank he had48 had in Bengal—viz., 2,000 with 700 horse. On Saturday I halted. At this stage Sayyid Niẓām s. Mīr Mīrān Ṣadr Jahān, who was faujdār of Kanauj, waited upon me, and presented two elephants, and some hawks. I accepted one elephant and a pair of hawks. On Sunday, the 18th, we marched. At this time the King of Persia had sent with Parī Beg Mīr S͟hikār (chief huntsman) one falcon (s͟hunqār) of good colour. There was another which had been given to the K͟hān ʿĀlam. This one was sent along with the S͟hāhī falcon (*i.e.*, the one intended for Jahāngīr), and it died on the road. The S͟hāhī falcon, too, got mauled by a cat owing to the carelessness of the Mīr S͟hikār. Though it was brought to Court, it did not live more than a week. What can I write49 of the beauty and colour of this falcon? There were many beautiful black markings on each wing, and back, and sides. As it was something out of the common, I ordered Ustād Manṣūr, who has the title of *Nādiru-l-ʿaṣr* (wonder of the age) to paint and preserve50 its likeness. I gave the Mīr S͟hikār Rs. 2,000 and dismissed him.

In my father's reign (the light of God be his testimony!) the weight of the seer was 30 dams.51 About this time it came into my mind: "Why should I act contrary to his rules?" It would be better to have it still of 30 dams. One day Gosā'īn Jadrūp said that in the book of the Vedas, which the lords of his faith had written, the weight of the *sīr* was 36 dams. "As from the coincidences of the hidden world your order has fallen in with what is laid down in our book, if it be fixed at 36 dams, it will be well." It was ordered that hereafter throughout the whole territory it should be 36 dams.

On Monday, the 19th, I marched. A horse and dress of honour were given to Rāja Bhāo Singh, who had been ordered to the support of the army of the Deccan. From this day, till Wednesday, the 28th, I made successive marches. On Thursday, the 29th, Delhi, the abode of blessings, was adorned by the alighting of the army of good fortune. At first I hastened with my children and the ladies on a visit to the enlightened shrine of Humāyūn (may the lights of God be his testimony!), and having made our offerings there, went off to circumambulate the blessed mausoleum of the king of holy men (S<u>h</u>aik<u>h</u> Niẓāmu-d-dīn Chis<u>h</u>tī), and strengthened my courage, and at the end of the day alighted at the palace, which had been got ready in Salīmgaṛh. On Friday, the 30th, I halted. As they had at this time preserved the hunting-place of the pargana of Pālam, according to order, it was represented that a great number of antelope had collected there. Accordingly, on the 1st of the Divine month of Āẕar I started to hunt52 with cheetahs. At the end of the day, during the hunt, much hail fell of the size of apples, and made the air very cold. On this day three antelope were caught. On Sunday, the 2nd, I hunted 46 antelope, and on Monday, the 3rd, 24 antelope were caught with cheetahs. My son S<u>h</u>āh-Jahān killed two antelope with his gun. On Tuesday, the 4th, five antelope were caught. On Wednesday, the 5th, 27 antelope were caught. On Thursday, the 6th, Sayyid Bahwa Buk<u>h</u>ārī, who was in charge of the government of Delhi, made an offering of three elephants and eighteen horses, and other things. One elephant and other things were accepted, and I gave the rest to him. Hās<u>h</u>im of K<u>h</u>ost, faujdār of some parganas in Mewāt, had the honour of kissing the threshold. I employed myself within the limits of Pālam until Thursday, the 13th, in hunting with cheetahs. In the space of twelve days 426 antelopes were caught, and I returned to Delhi. I had heard, when in attendance on my father, that it is impossible for an antelope that has escaped from the grasp of a cheetah to live, although it has not been injured by its claws. In this hunt I, in order to ascertain the fact, released several antelopes of handsome appearance and strong bodies, before they had received any wounds from teeth or claws, and ordered them to be kept in my presence, and that they should be taken the greatest care of. For a whole day and night they remained at ease in their natural conditions: on the second day a change was observed, and they threw about their legs as if they were drunk, without any reason, and fell down and rose up. However much *tiryāq-i-fārūqī* (preparation of opium) and other suitable medicines were administered to them, they had no effect, and when one watch had passed in this condition, they died.

On this day the bad news arrived that the eldest son of S͟hāh Parwīz had died at Agra. As he was somewhat grown-up,53 and was very attached and affectionate towards his father, the latter was exceedingly grieved and wounded at heart at this event, and great bewilderment and weakness manifested themselves in him. In order to console and please him, I sent him gracious letters, and covered over the deadly wound of his heart with the balm of affection and kindness. I hope that God, the great and glorious, may grant him patience and resignation, for in this kind of calamities there can be no better driver away of grief than endurance and resignation.

On Friday, the 14th, at the request of Āqā54 Āqāyān, I went to her house. On account of her previous service and her hereditary attachment to this illustrious family, when the late king made me a married man, he took her from my sister S͟hāh-zāda K͟hānam, and placed her in charge of my Zanana. It is 33 years from that date that she has been in my service, and I esteem her greatly, for she has served me with sincerity. In no journey or expedition had she of her own will remained absent from attendance on me. When she felt her increasing age, she requested me to order her to remain at Delhi, and to spend the remainder of her life in prayer for me, for she had no longer the power to move about, and found it a great hardship and trouble to come and go (as she used). One of her felicities was that she was of the same age55 as ʿArs͟h-ās͟hyānī (Akbar). In brief, with a view to giving her rest, I ordered her to remain at Delhi, and in that place she had made for herself a garden, a saray, and a tomb, in the constructing which she has employed herself for some time past. In short, to please this ancient servitor, I went to her house, and strictly ordered Sayyid Bahwa, the governor of the city, to serve and guard her in such a manner that no dust from any road of vexation might settle on the hem of her contentment.

On this day Rāja Kis͟han Dās was promoted to the mansab of 2,000 personal and 300 horse, original and increased. As Sayyid Bahwa56 had performed satisfactorily the duties of faujdār of Delhi, and the people of the place were much pleased with his excellent conduct, according to previous custom, the protection and administration of the city of Delhi and the faujdārship of the surrounding country were entrusted to him, and he was promoted to the mansab of 1,000 personal and 600 horse, original and increased, and he was presented with an elephant, and allowed to take leave. On Saturday, the 15th, I honoured Mīrzā Wālī with the mansab of 2,000 and 1,000 horse, and presenting him with a standard and an elephant, appointed him to the

Deccan. S̱ẖaikẖ ʿAbdu-l-Ḥaqq Dihlawī,57 who was a pious and estimable man, had the good fortune to pay his respects to me. He had composed a book containing the biographies of the S̱ẖaikẖs of India, and produced it to me. He had endured some hardships, and for a long time had lived in Delhi in seclusion, and the practice of reliance on God, and of asceticism. He is a very worthy man, and his company is not without pleasure (for me). Bestowing various kinds of kindnesses on him, I dismissed him.

On Sunday, the 16th, I marched from Delhi, and on Friday, the 21st, halted in the pargana of Kairāna.58 This pargana is the native place of Muqarrab K. Its climate is equable and its soil good. Muqarrab had made buildings and gardens there. As I had often heard praise of his garden, I wished much to see it. On Saturday, the 22nd, I and my ladies were much pleased in going round it. Truly, it is a very fine and enjoyable garden. Within a masonry (*pukẖta*, pucca) wall, flower-beds have been laid out to the extent of 140 bighas. In the middle of the garden he has constructed a pond, in length 220 yards, and in breadth 200 yards. In the middle of the pond is a *māh-tāb* terrace (for use in moonlight) 22 yards square. There is no kind of tree belonging to a warm or cold climate that is not to be found in it. Of fruit-bearing trees belonging to Persia I saw green pistachio-trees, and cypresses of graceful form, such as I have never seen before. I ordered the cypresses to be counted, and they came to 300. All round the pond suitable buildings have been begun and are in progress.

On Monday, the 24th, Ḵẖanjar K., in whose charge is the Fort of Ahmadnagar, was promoted to the mansab of 2,500 personal and 1,600 horse. On Wednesday, the 26th, the Giver of Bounties gave my son S̱ẖāh-Jahān a son by the daughter of Āṣaf Ḵẖān. He presented an offering of 1,000 muhars, and begged for a name for him. I gave him the name of Umīd-bakẖsẖ (bestower of hope). I hope his advent59 may be auspicious to this State. On Thursday, the 27th, I halted. In these few days I was delighted with hawking the *jarz*60 (bustard or florican) and *tūgẖ-dārī* (also a kind of bustard). I ordered the *jarz-i-būr* (the red bustard?) to be weighed. It came to $2\frac{1}{4}$ *Jahāngīrī* sirs, and the variegated (*ablaq*) one to $2\frac{1}{8}$ sirs. The large tūgẖ-dārī was $\frac{1}{4}$ sir heavier than the jarz-i-būr. On Thursday, the 5th of the Divine month of Day, I left the boat at Akbarpur, and the victorious army then marched by land. From Agra to this halting-place, which is situated within two koss of the pargana of Buriya,61 is by river 123 koss or 91 koss by road. I did it in 34 marches and 17 halts. In addition to this I delayed a week in leaving the city, and 12 days in sporting in Pālam: altogether (I took) 70 days. On this day Jahāngīr Qulī K. came from Bihār, and had the good fortune to pay his respects. He presented 100 muhars and Rs. 100. From the last Thursday to Wednesday, the 11th, I marched every day. On Thursday, the 12th, I was pleased with going round to see the garden of Sirhind. It is one of the old gardens, and has old trees in it. It has not the freshness it formerly had, but it is still valuable. Kh̲wāja Waisī, who is well acquainted with agriculture and buildings, was appointed the *karorī* of Sirhind for the purpose of keeping the garden in order. I had sent him off from Agra before I marched from the capital, and he had put it somewhat in order. I strictly enjoined him again that he should remove all the old trees that had no freshness in them, and put in fresh plants, to clean up the *ʿirqbandī*[62] (it is *ʿirāq-bandī* in the text. The word does not occur in the B.M. MS. but is in the I.O. MS.), and repair the old buildings, and erect other buildings in the shape of baths, etc., in fitting places. On this date Dūst Beg, who was one of the auxiliaries of ʿAbdu-llah K., was promoted to the mansab of 700 personal and 50 horse, Muẓaffar Ḥusain, s. Wazīr K., to that of 600 personal and 300 horse. Sh̲aikh̲ Qāsim was sent to duty in the Deccan. On Thursday, the 19th, at the request of my auspicious son Sh̲āh-Jahān, I went to his house. On account of the birth of the son that God Almighty had bestowed on him a grand entertainment was given, and he presented offerings. Among these was a short, broad sword[63] (*sh̲amsh̲īr-i-nīmcha*), which was of Venetian workmanship. The hilt and fastenings were made of a sapphire[64] cut in Europe: in short, it had been beautifully made. Another offering was an elephant which the Raja of Baglāna had presented to my son in Burhānpur. As that elephant was handsome and well-behaved, it was ordered to be included among the private elephants. The value of the offerings that were accepted was Rs. 130,000, and he offered about Rs. 4,000 to his mothers and benefactors. On this day Sayyid Bāyazīd Bukh̲ārī, faujdār of Bhakkar, sent as an offering a *rang* (ibex), which he had brought from the hills when it was small and brought up in his house. It pleased me greatly. Of *mār-kh̲ūr* and hill sheep I have seen many brought up in the house, but I never saw a *rang* (tame). I ordered them to keep it with the Barbary goats, in order that they might pair and produce young ones. Without doubt, it is not allied to the mār-kh̲ūr or the quchqār. Sayyid Bāyazīd was raised to the mansab of 1,000 personal and 700 horse. On Monday, the 23rd, having honoured Muqīm K. with a robe of honour, a horse, an elephant, and jewelled *khapwa*, I appointed him to Bihār. On Sunday, the 29th, a feast was prepared for my auspicious son Sh̲āh-Jahān on the bank of the Biya (Beas), and on the same day Rāja Bikramājīt, who was employed in the siege of Kāngṛa, came to Court, by order, to represent certain requirements, and had the good fortune to kiss the threshold. On Monday, the 30th, my son Sh̲āh-Jahān took ten days' leave, and hastened to Lahore in order to see the palace buildings lately erected. Rāja Bikramājīt was presented with a special dagger, a robe of honour, and a horse, and returned to duty on the siege of Kāngṛa. On Wednesday, the 2nd of the Divine month of Bahman, the garden of Kalānaur was honoured by my halting there. At this place my father had ascended the throne.

When the news of the speedy arrival of Khān ʻĀlam reached the Court, every day I sent one of my servants to meet him. I loaded him with all kinds of favours and kindnesses, and added to his rank and dignity, and I decked the headings of the farmans sent to him with an impromptu hemistich or couplet suitable to the occasion, and so filled him with favours. Once I sent him some *Jahāngīrī* (otto of roses), and this opening verse came on my tongue:

VERSE.65

"To thee I've sent the scent of myself.

That I may bring thee the more quickly to myself."

On Thursday, the 3rd (Bahman), at the garden of Kalānaur, Khān ʻĀlam was honoured by kissing the threshold. By way of nazar he brought 100 muhars and Rs. 1,000, and (stated that he) would present his offerings in due course. Zambīl Beg, the ambassador of my brother Shāh ʻAbbās, was following him with the royal letter and the rarities of that country (Persia), which he had sent as presents. Of the favours and kindness conferred by my brother on Khān ʻĀlam, if I were to write of them in detail, I should be accused of exaggeration. In conversation he always gave him the title of Khān ʻĀlam, and never had him out of his presence. If he ever voluntarily stayed in his own quarter, he (ʻAbbās) would go there without ceremony, and show him more and more favour. One day there was a *qamurgha* hunt at Farrukhābād, and he ordered Khān ʻĀlam to shoot with a bow. Out of good manners he brought a bow with two arrows (only). The Shah gave him 50 other arrows from his own quiver. It happened that 50 of these arrows struck the game, and two arrows missed. Then he ordered some of his attendants who had the entrée at feasts and assemblies to shoot with arrows. Most shot well. Among them Muḥammad Yūsuf (qarāwul), shot an arrow which went through two boars, and those who were standing by broke out without control into applause. At the time Khān ʻĀlam took his leave, he seized him in the embrace of honour, and showed him great affection. After he had left the city, he went to his halting-place, and made many apologies and bade him farewell. As for the beautiful and costly things that the Khān ʻĀlam brought, it was indeed the assistance of his destiny that gave such rare things into his hand. Among them was the picture of the fight of Ṣāhib Qirān (Tīmūr) with Tuqtamish K., and the likenesses of him and his glorious children and the great Amirs who had the good fortune to be with him in that fight, and near each figure was written whose portrait it was. In this picture there were 240 figures. The painter had written his name as Khalīl Mīrzā Shāhrukhī (in the MS. it is Savaj and not Shāhrukhī). The work was very complete and grand, and resembled greatly the paint-brush of Ustād Bihzād. If the name of the painter had not been written, the work would have been believed to be his.

As it was executed before Bihzād's date it is probable that the latter was one of Khalīl Mīrzā's pupils, and had adopted his style. This precious relic had been obtained from the illustrious library of Shāh Ismā'īl (the 1st), or had come to my brother Shāh 'Abbās from Shāh Ṭahmāsp. A person of the name of Ṣādiqī, a librarian of his, had stolen it, and sold it to someone. By chance (the painting) fell into the hands of Khān 'Ālam at Isfahan. The Shah heard that he had found such a rare prize, and asked it of him on the pretence of looking at it. Khān 'Ālam tried to evade this by artful stratagems, but when he repeatedly insisted on it, he sent it to him. The Shah recognized it immediately he saw it. He kept it by him for a day, but at last, as he knew how great was our liking for such rarities, he—God be praised—made no request66 whatever for it, but told the facts of the case (about its being stolen) to Khān 'Ālam, and made the picture over to him.

At the time when I sent Khān 'Ālam to Persia, I had sent with him a painter of the name of Bishan Dās, who was unequalled in his age for taking likenesses, to take the portraits of the Shah and the chief men of his State, and bring them. He had drawn the likenesses of most of them, and especially had taken that of my brother the Shah exceedingly well, so that when I showed it to any of his servants, they said it was exceedingly well drawn.

On the same day Qāsim K., with the Bakhshi and Diwan of Lahore, had the good fortune to do homage. Bishan Dās, the painter, was honoured with the gift of an elephant. Bābā Khwāja, who was one of the auxiliaries of Qandahar, was accorded the mansab of 1,000 personal and 550 horse. On Tuesday, the 3rd, *Madāru-l-mahāmmī* (centre of important affairs) I'timādu-d-daula made ready his army. Inasmuch as the charge of the Panjab is entrusted to his agents, and he has also various jagirs in Hindustan, he held a review of 5,000 horsemen. As the area of Kashmir is not such that its produce may suffice for the expenses of the force that is always on service with the servants of the army of prosperity, and as, in consequence of the report (of the approach) of the glorious and victorious standards, the price of grains and vegetables had risen very high, an order was given, for the comfort of the public, that those servants who were in attendance on the royal stirrup should arrange their retinues, and only taking with them those who were indispensable, should send the remainder to their jagirs, and in the same way should take every precaution to reduce as far as possible the number of their beasts and followers. On Thursday, the 10th, my fortunate son, Shāh-Jahān returned from Lahore, and had the good fortune to do homage. Having honoured Jahāngīr Qulī K. with a dress of honour, a horse and an elephant, I gave him leave to proceed with his brothers and sons to the Deccan. On this day Ṭālib Āmulī received the title of *Maliku-sh-shu'arā* (king of poets), and was clothed in a dress of honour. His origin was from Āmul. For some time he was with

Iʿtimādu-d-daula. As the merits of his style surpassed that of his contemporaries, he was enrolled among the poets of the throne. The following couplets are by him:

VERSE.67

"Spring longs to rifle thy parterre.

For the flowers in thy hand are fresher than those on his branch.

I've so closed my lips from speech that you'd say

'His mouth is but a scar on his face.'"68

VERSE.

"Both first and last, Love is aye music and joy—

A pleasant wine both when fresh and when mellow.

VERSE.

"Were I glass instead of body,

I'd reveal thee to thyself without thy unveiling.

Two lips have I; one for drinking,

And one to apologize for drunkenness."

On Monday, the 14th, Ḥusainī s. Sulṭān Qiwām produced this quatrain:

QUATRAIN.

"A speck of dust sprinkled on thee from thy skirt

Becomes Solomon's collyrium; from the moisture of thy face69

Were the earth at thy door examined,

The sweat of kings' brows would exude."

At this time Muʿtamid K. repeated a quatrain which greatly pleased me, and which I entered in my common-place book:

QUATRAIN.70

"You give me the poison of parting to taste, (and say) 'What matters it?'

You shed my blood and expel me (and say), 'What matters it?'

O, heedless of what your dividing sword can do,

Sift my dust and then you'll know."

Ṭālib (*i.e.*, Bābā Ṭālib) is by family an Iṣfahānī. In his early youth he went to Kashmir clothed as an ascetic and calendar, and from the beauty of the place and the pleasantness of the climate set his heart on the country and settled there. After the conquest of Kashmir he joined the service of the late king (Akbar), and became enrolled among the servants of the Presence. His age is now nearly 100 years, and he is now with his sons and dependants in Kashmir, engaged in praying for the everlasting State.

As it was reported to me that in Lahore one Miyān S̲h̲aik̲h̲ Muḥammad Mīr by name, who was a Darvish, a Sindī by origin, very eloquent, virtuous, austere, of auspicious temperament, a lord of ecstasy, had seated himself in the corner of reliance upon God and retirement, and was rich in his poverty and independent of the world, my truth-seeking mind was not at rest without meeting him, and my desire to see him increased. As it was impossible to go to Lahore, I wrote a note to him, and explained to him the desire of my heart, and that saint, notwithstanding his great age and weakness, took the trouble to come. I sate with him for a long time alone, and enjoyed a thorough interview with him. Truly he is a noble personage, and in this Age he is a great gain and a delightful existence. This suppliant for Grace was taken out of himself by companionship with him,71 and heard from him sublime words of truth and religious knowledge. Although I desired to make him some gift, I found that his spirit was too high for this, and so did not express my wish. I left him the skin of a white antelope to pray upon, and he immediately bade me farewell and went back to Lahore.

On Wednesday, the 23rd, I pitched my camp at Daulatābād. A daughter of a gardener was brought before me who had a moustache and a thick beard as big as the hilt of a sword. Her appearance was like that of a man. There was hair in the middle of her chest as well, but she had no breasts.72 I discovered by her appearance that she ought not to have children. I told some women to take her aside and examine her, as perhaps she might be a hermaphrodite. They found she was in no way different from other women. I have recorded this in this volume on account of its strangeness.

On Thursday, the 24th, Bāqir K., having come from Multan, had the good fortune to pay his respects. In the preceding pages it has been recorded that Allāh-dād, s. Jalālā Tārīkī, had deserted from the victorious army and taken the road to ruin. He now repented, and through Bāqir K. petitioned Iʿtimādu-d-daula for pardon. At the latter's request I ordered that if he repented of what he had done, and turned his face in hope towards the Court, his crimes would be forgiven. On this day Bāqir K. brought him to Court, and at the intercession of Iʿtimādu-d-daula, the traces of disgrace and the dust of sorrow were washed off his forehead with the pure water of pardon. Sangrām, Zamindar of Jammu, was honoured with the title of Raja and the mansab of 1,000 personal and 500 horse, and was exalted with the gift of an elephant and a dress of honour. G͟hairat K., faujdār of the Dū-āb, was promoted to the mansab of 800 personal and 500 horse. K͟hwāja Qāsim received the rank of 700 and 250 horse, and Taham-tan Beg, s. Qāsim Koka, received that of 500 personal and 300 horse. I gave K͟hān ʿĀlam a private elephant with trappings. From this stage, having given Bāqir K. the mansab of 1,500 personal and 500 horse, I dismissed him again to his Subadarship.

On Monday, the 28th, I pitched in the pargana of Karohī, which is on the bank of the Bihat (Jhelam). As this hilly country is one of the established hunting-places, the huntsmen, according to order, had come on in advance and prepared a *jarga* (ring in which game is enclosed). On Wednesday, the 1st of the Divine month of Isfandārmuz̤, they drove in the game from six koss. On Thursday, the 2nd, they brought them into the enclosure, where 101 head of mountain sheep and gazelles were taken. As Mahābat K. had been prevented from the good fortune of coming before me for a long time, I ordered, at his request, that if he was satisfied with the order of affairs, and was not troubled with regard to any occurrence, he should leave his forces at their posts (*thānas*), and come to Court unattended. On this day he had the good fortune to kiss the threshold, and presented 100 muhars as nazar. K͟hān ʿĀlam was promoted to the mansab of 5,000 personal and 3,000 horse. About this time a written report came from Nūru-d-dīn Qulī that he had repaired the Pūnch road, and levelled the defiles as far as possible, but that snow fell for some days and nights, and lay on the *kotāls* to the depth of three cubits. It was still falling, and if I would delay outside the hills for a month, I could cross by that route, otherwise it appeared difficult. As my intention in this undertaking was to see the spring and the sprouting of bloom, my chance of seeing this was lost by this delay, and I necessarily turned my rein, and the royal standards proceeded by the way of Paklī and Damtūr. On Friday, the 3rd, I crossed the River Bihat (Jhelam), although the water was waist-deep. As it was running very fast, and men crossed with great trouble, I ordered them to take 200 elephants to the fords, and cross the effects of the people over, and take across as well those who were weak and feeble, so that there might be no loss of life or goods.

On this day news arrived of the death of K͟hwāja Jahān. He was one of the old servants, and from the time when I was prince. Although at last he left my service, and was for some time in that of my father, yet as he had not gone to any strange place, this did not weigh heavily on my mind. Accordingly, after my accession, I did him such kindness as he had never conceived possible, and gave him the mansab of 5,000 personal and 3,000 horse. I take this opportunity to record in this volume an account of his idiosyncrasy. He became practised in great affairs and acquired a wonderful skill in business. His capabilities were the result of labour, and he was void of natural ability, and of the other qualities which are the adornment of men's nature. On this journey he suffered from heart-failure, but for some days, in spite of illness and breakdown, he kept up with the march. When his weakness increased, he was allowed to go back at Kalānaur, and went to Lahore, and there died a natural death.73

On Saturday, the 4th of the aforesaid month, the camp was pitched at the Fort of Rohtās (in the Panjab). I favoured Qāsim K. with a horse, a sword, and a special shawl (*parm-narm*, literally very soft, and Akbar's name for a shawl, see Blochmann, 90). I gave him leave to go to Lahore. There was a small garden by the roadside, and I inspected the blossoms.

At this stage *tīhū*74 were obtained. The flesh of the *tīhū* is better than that of the partridge (*kabak*).

On Sunday, the 5th, M. Ḥasan s. Mīrzā Rustam, was promoted to the rank of 1,000 with 400 horse, and was appointed to the Deccan. Khwāja ʿAbdu-l-Laṭīf, the chief fowler, also received the rank of 1,000 with 400 horse. At this place I saw a flower, white inside, and red outside, while some of them were red inside and yellow outside. In Persian they call it *Laʿla-i-bīgāna*, and in Hindī *thal kanal*. *Thal* means land, and as the lotus (kanal) is an aquatic plant, they have called this land-lotus.75

On Thursday, the 9th, a report came from Dilāwar K., Governor of Kashmir, containing the good news of the conquest of Kishtwār. Details will be recorded by the pen of the newswriter after he (Dilāwar) comes to the foot of the throne. I sent him a gracious farman with a special dress of honour and a jewelled dagger, and granted him the revenue of the conquered province for a year, as a reward for this acceptable service. On Tuesday, the 14th, I halted at Ḥasan Abdāl. As the occurrences on this road and particulars of the stages have been related in detail in the account of the expedition to Kabul, I shall not repeat them. From this place as far as Kashmir, they will be written stage by stage, please Almighty God. From the date on which, disembarking from a boat, I reached Akbarpur in safety and prosperity, up to Ḥasan Abdāl, a distance of 178 koss, I took 69 days in 48 marches and 21 halts.76 As at this place there is a spring full of water, and a cascade, and a very beautiful reservoir, I halted here two days, and on Thursday, the 16th (Isfandārmuẕ), the feast of my lunar weighing took place. The 53rd year, according to lunar calculation, of this suppliant at the throne commenced auspiciously. As beyond this stage, hills, passes, and many ups and downs were before us, the passage of the camp appeared a difficult matter, and it was settled that H. M. Maryamu-z-zamānī and the other Begams should delay for some days, and come on at leisure. Madāru-l-mulk Iʿtimādu-d-daula al-Khāqānī, Ṣādiq K. Bakhshī, and Irādat K. Mīr-Sāmān, with the directors of the buildings and other offices, should attend to their transit. At the same time Rustam Mīrzā Ṣafawī, Kh̲ān-Aʿẓam, and a number of other servants, obtained leave to go by the Pūnch road, while the royal retinue went on with some privileged courtiers (*manẓūrān-i-bisāṭ-i-qarb*) and the necessary servants. On Friday, the 17th, we marched 3½ koss, and halted at the village of Sultanpur.77 On this day came the news of the death of Rānā Amar Singh, who had died a natural death at Udaipur (become a traveller on the road of non-existence). Jagat Singh, his grandson, and Bhīm,78 his son, who were in attendance on me, were presented with dresses of honour, and an order was given that Rāja Kish̲an Dās should proceed with a gracious farman conferring the title of Rānā, a dress of honour, a horse, and a private elephant for Kunār Karan, to perform the dues of condolence and congratulation. I heard79 from people of this country that when it is not the rainy season, and there is no sign of a cloud or lightning, a noise like the voice of the clouds comes from this hill, which they called Garj (thunder). This noise is heard every year or at least every two years. I had repeatedly heard of this also when I was in attendance on the late king. I have written this as it is not devoid of strangeness,80 but wisdom is from Allah. On Saturday, the 18th, marching 4½ koss, I halted at the village of Sanjī. From this stage I entered the pargana of Hazāra Qārlugh̲.81 On Sunday, the 19th, marching 3¾ koss, I halted at the village of Naush̲ahra.82 From this place we entered Dhantūr. As far as the eye could reach there were green meadows83 interspersed with the *thal-kanwal* (hibiscus) and other flowers in bloom. It was a very beautiful sight. On Monday, the 20th, marching 3½ koss, the camp was pitched at the village of Salhar.84 Mahābat K. presented as offerings jewels and inlaid vessels to the value of Rs. 60,000. In this country I saw a flower of the redness of fire, of the shape of *gul-i-kh̲atmī*,85 but smaller, and several flowers blooming together in one place, looked from a distance as if they were one flower. Its stem is of the size of the apricot-tree. On the hill-slopes here there are many wild violets,86 with a very sweet scent, but paler than the violet. On Tuesday, the 21st, marching 3 koss, I halted at the village of Mālgallī.87 On this day I dismissed Mahābat K. to his duty in Bangash, and conferred on him a special elephant and dress of honour with a *pūstīn* (sheepskin coat). This day there was a drizzling rain till the end of the march. On the eve of Wednesday, the 22nd, also there was rain. In the morning snow fell, and as most of the roads had become very slippery, the weak animals fell in every place, and could not rise again, and 25 of my own elephants were lent to assist88 them. I halted for two days on account of the snow. On Thursday, the 23rd, Sulṭān Ḥusain, Zamindar of Pakli, had the good fortune to pay his respects: this is the entrance to the Pakli country. It is a strange thing that when H. M. Akbar came here it snowed at this stage, and it has now snowed as well. For many years no snow has fallen, and there has even been little rain. On Friday, the 24th, I marched 4 koss and pitched at the village of Sawādnagar.89 On this road, too there was much mud.[90] Apricot and peach trees were blooming on all sides, and fir-trees like cypresses rejoiced the eye. On Saturday, the 25th, having marched nearly 3½ koss, the camp was pitched near Pakli. On Sunday, the 26th, I rode out to hunt partridges (*kabak*), and at the end of the day, at the request of Sulṭān Ḥusain, went to his house, and increased his dignity among his equals and neighbours. H. M. Akbar had also gone to his house. He offered several kinds of horses, daggers, hawks, and falcons. I presented him with the horses and daggers. I ordered the hawks and falcons to be got ready[91] (*kamar bar basta*), and shown everything that might fly up. The Sarkar of Pakli is 35 koss in length and 25 in breadth. On the east, on two sides, is the hill country of Kashmir; on the west, Atak Benares (Atak); on the north, Kator; and on the south, the Gakkar country. At the time when Timur, after conquering Hindustan, turned his rein backwards towards the capital of Tūrān, they say that he placed in these regions this body of people, who were in attendance on the victorious stirrup. They say themselves that they are Qārlughs, but do not know for certain who was their leader at that time. In fact, they are pure Lāhaurīs, and speak the same language. The people of Dhantūr think the same thing. In the time of my father, one of the name of S<u>h</u>āhruk<u>h</u> was Zamindar of Dhantūr; now it is Bahādur, his son. Although they are all related to one another, there are always disputes, as is usual with Zamindars, about boundaries. They have always been loyal. Sulṭān Maḥmūd, the father of Sulṭān Ḥusain and S<u>h</u>āhruk<u>h</u>, both came to wait on me when I was prince. Although Sulṭān Ḥusain is seventy years old, to all outward appearance there is no diminution in his powers, and he can still ride and be as active as possible. In this country they make *būẓa* (a beverage) from bread and rice, which they call *sar*.[92] It is much stronger than *būẓa*, and the older it is the better. This *sar* is their chief sustenance. They put this *sar* into a jar, and fastening it up, keep it for two or three years in the house. Then they take off the scum and call the liquor *ăchhī*. The *ăchhī* can be kept for ten years, and according to them, the older it is the better, and the shortest time in which they use it is a year. Sulṭān Maḥmūd used to take cup after cup of this *sar*; nay! he would drink a jar of it. Sulṭān Ḥusain is also addicted to it, and brought me some of his choicest quality. I took some in order to try it. I had also drunk it before. Its intoxicating effects are aphrodisiac, but its taste is harsh. It appeared that they mix some *bhāng* (bang) with it, which increases its intoxicating power. If there were no wine, it could in case of necessity be used as a substitute. The fruits are apricots, peaches, and pears (?) (amrūd). As they do not cultivate them, but they spring up of themselves, they are harsh-flavoured and unpleasant. Their blossoms are a joy. Their houses are of wood, and are built after the Kashmiri fashion. They have hawks, and horses, camels, cattle, and buffaloes, and many goats and fowls. Their mules are small and are not fit for heavy loads. As it was represented to me that some stages farther on the cultivation was not such as to provide sufficient grain for the royal camp, I gave an order that they should only take a small advanced camp, sufficient for our needs and the necessary establishments, and diminish the number of elephants, and take with them provisions for three or four days; that they should take with them only some of the immediate attendants on the royal stirrup, and that the rest of the men should come on some stages behind under the command of K͟hwāja Abū-l-Ḥasan, the Bakhshi. In spite of precautions and injunctions, it was found necessary to have 700 elephants for the advanced camp and the establishments.

The mansab of Sulṭān Ḥusain was 400 personal and 300 horse; I now promoted him to 600 personal and 350 horse, and conferred on him a robe of honour, a jewelled dagger, and an elephant. Bahādur Dhantūrī was an auxiliary of the army of Bangash. An order was given that he should hold the mansab, original and increased, of 200 personal and 100 horse. On Wednesday, the 27th, having marched 5¼ koss, and crossing by bridges the Nainsukh,93 I chose a halting-place. This Nainsukh (repose of the eyes) flows from the North, and comes down from the hills of Dārd94 (?), which is between the country of Badakhshan and Tibet. As at this place it forms two branches, they had, according to order, prepared two wooden bridges for the crossing of the victorious army, one 18 cubits and the other 14 cubits in length, with a breadth each of 5 cubits. The way in which they make bridges in this country is to throw pine-trees95 on the surface of the water, and fasten the two ends strongly to rocks, and having thrown on to these thick planks of wood, make them firm with pegs and ropes, and these, with a little repair, last for years. Briefly, they made the elephants ford, whilst the horsemen and foot passed over by the bridge. Sulṭān Maḥmūd called this river Nainsukh—that is, "Repose of the eye." On Thursday, the 30th, having marched about 3½ koss, a halt was made on the bank of the Kis͟han Gangā. On this road there is a *kotal* of great height, the ascent being 1 koss, and the descent 1½ koss, which they call *Pīm darang*. The reason for this name is that in the language of Kashmir they call cotton (*pamba*) *pīm*. As the rulers of Kashmir had placed a superintendent there, who took duties from loads of cotton, and delay takes place here for the collection of the duty, it has become known as the *Pīm darang*96 (cotton delay). After traversing the pass, there is a very fine and clear waterfall. Having drunk my usual cups on the edge of the water in the shade of the trees, I went on to my halting-place in the evening. There was an old bridge over this river, 54 yards long and 1½ yards wide, which footmen crossed by. According to orders, another bridge was prepared parallel to this, in length 53 yards and breadth 3 yards. As the water was deep and swift, they took the elephants across without loads, and the footmen and horses crossed by the bridge. By order of my father, a very strong saray of stone and lime was erected on the top of the ridge overlooking the river. One day before New Year's Day we had sent Muʿtamid K. forward to select a spot for the placing of the throne and preparing the New Year's entertainment. This had to be lofty and choice. By chance, as he crossed the bridge, there was a ridge overlooking the water, green and pleasant. On the top of this was a flat place of 50 cubits which one might say the rulers of fate had specially prepared for such a day. The aforesaid officer had made ready everything necessary for the New Year's feast on the top of that ridge, which was much approved. Muʿtamid K. was much applauded for this. The river Kis̱ẖan Gangā comes from the south97 and flows northwards. The Bihat (Jhelam) comes from the East, and joining the Kis̱ẖan Gangā, flows to the North.

---

1 Egyptian. Hitherto this has been read Quṭbī, but it really is, I think, Qibṭī, "Egyptian." Chardin, IV. 70, ed. 1723, says that the Persians state that the ruby of the East comes from Egypt. The etymology, however, is doubtful. ↑

2 Possibly the praise of S̱ẖāh-Jahān's inventive powers refers to his arrangements for the orchestra. The *kuwarga* is defined in the Ain, Blochmann, 50, as a *damāma—i.e.*, a large drum. See illustration in Plate VIII. to Blochmann's Ain. The *karanā* and *surnā* are wind-instruments, and are also represented in Plate VIII. With regard to the *mursal*, Blochmann, p. 51, has: "The mursalī, which is the name of a tune played by the *mursil*." Apparently the *mursal* is the overture, or some introductory strain, and played only by a portion of the band. ↑

3 MS. No. 181 has ten instead of two as the number of elephants presented by Quṭbu-l-mulk, and this seems likely to be correct, else where do the six now mentioned come from? But six should probably be eight. ↑

4 *Kurkarāqs*. See Blochmann, 87, *n.* 2, and p. 616. *Kurk* means fur, and *kurkarāqān* may be translated furriers. ↑

5 So in text, but it should be Tatta—*i.e.*, Sind. See Blochmann, 378, *n.* 2, and also the Tūzuk, *infra*, p. 275. ↑

6 *Suwārān-i-ḵẖūd-maḥalla*. I do not know the exact force of the last two words. Possibly they are pleonastic. The word *maḥalla* is explained in Irvine A. of M. 46. ↑

7 The Iqbāl-nāma, 127, mentions that Parwīz came from Allahabad to pay his respects. See *infra*, Tūzuk, 268, and 273. ↑

8 Probably this is the friend of Father Jerome Xavier and the abridger of the Ẓafar-nāma. See Rieu, 177*b* and 1077*a*. ↑

9 He was of the royal house of Khandesh. ↑

10 See Blochmann, 252, and *n.* 1. Jahāngīr himself saw 700 antelope taken, and Rāy Mān afterwards made a drive of 800 more. ↑

11 This was Jodh Bā'ī, d. the Mota (fat) Rāja. See Blochmann, 619. ↑

12 *Qulba*, ploughs. Here apparently used as a measure of land. But the expression is obscure. In Wilson's Glossary ḵulba is stated to be a measure of land in Sylhet, and equal to 1,008 cubits by 144. The corresponding Sanskrit word Sīr ("a plough") is used to mean land held by the landholder in his own possession. ↑

13 *Maḥalla*. Here used apparently for musters. ↑

14 Mr. Rogers corrects this to Mīrān on the authority of R.A.S., MS. It is, however, Bīzẖan in I.O. MS., 181, and as Blochmann points out, Bīzan or Bīzẖan is twice referred to in the Tūzuk, pp. 307, 309. He was son of Nād 'Alī Maidānī. ↑

15 I.O. MS. has "by favour of my rearing" (tarbiyat) and probably the words in text rather mean that he was promoted by virtue of Jahāngīr's liking for him, than that he was of good disposition. His real name was 'Abdu-r-Raḥīm. He was the son of Qā'im K., and his sister Ṣāliḥa Bānū was one of Jahāngīr's wives, and had the title of Pādisẖāh-Maḥall. Blochmann, 371. Before Nūr-Jahān she was the chief wife. ↑

16 Mihtar K. was a very old servant, and died in the third year of Jahāngīr. Blochmann, 417. ↑

17 Text wrongly has Sẖāh Nūr. ↑

18 This is the ancient Dhafur or Dofar on the south coast of Arabia now known as Mirbāṭ. The proper spelling was Ẓafr. See Redhouse's Annotations to the History of Yemen, published by the Gibb Trust, Nos. 349, 578, and 836. See also d'Herbelot, 269, and Jarrett, III, 51. ↑

19 The description is rather obscure. Apparently Jahāngīr regards *bamand* (dun- or bay-coloured) as equal to red (surkẖ). ↑

20 Text has Musẖrif. ↑

21 *Dū manzil kisẖtī* must surely mean "tray" here; or perhaps they were models. *Kosha* is a well-known Bengali name for a swift boat. ↑

22 Apparently Khwāja Ḥasan died in Badakhshān. Ma'āṣir, III., 459. ↑

23 This S. Aḥmad is a well-known man. He is mentioned in Beale as Aḥmad Sirhindī (Sẖaikẖ), and as having had the title of Mujaddid-i-Alf-i-Ṣānī, because he believed that he was the man of the second millenium. In other words, he claimed to be a Mahdī. He was s. 'Abdu-l-Waḥid Fārūqī, and born

in 1503. He died 29 November, 1624, and is buried at Sirhind. The I.G. new edition, XXIII. 21., says there are two tombs in Sirhind known as those of the Master and the Disciple, and it may be that one of them is S. Aḥmad's, although the Gazetteer says they probably belong to the fourteenth century. There is also a reference to him in Rieu's Catalogue, III. 1058*a.*, fol. 16. He belonged to the Naqs͟hbandī order, and one of his writings is called Majmūʿatu-t-taṣawwuf. There is a very long account of him, and of his interviews with Jahāngīr in the K͟hazīnatu-l-Auliyā, I. 607, etc. It is said there that he was imprisoned for two years, and then released, and that he died on the last day of Ṣafar, 1035, November 20, 1625, at the age of sixty-three. Jahāngīr afterwards pardoned S. Aḥmad. See Tūzuk, 308, account of fifteenth year. ↑

24 *Dandān-i-māhī*, explained in dictionary as the canine tooth of the Walrus (*Trichechus rosmarus*). But there is nothing black or piebald about walrus-teeth, and Jahāngīr would surely not admire greatly a kind of ivory which was inferior to that of the elephant. I incline to think that what is here meant is tortoise-shell. *Jauhar-dār* has two meanings—it may mean jewelled and also "striated." See Vullers, 542*a.* ↑

25 Apparently Mīrān is a mistake for Bīz͟han. See *ante* and Blochmann, 508, and Tūzuk, 307. It is Bīzan in I.O. MS., 181. ↑

26 The buildings referred to are the garden-houses made by K͟hwāja Jahān in the Nūr-manzil garden. ↑

27 See Jarrett, II. 323; it was near the Jhelam. See also I.G., new edition, XV. 297. It is in the S͟hāhpūr district. The land-revenue of it was 24 lakhs of rupees in 1903–1904. 30 lakhs of dāms would be equal to Rs. 75,000. K͟hān Daurān's name was S͟hāh Beg K. The Maʾāṣir says his resignation was not altogether voluntary. See Blochmann, 378. ↑

28 In the MSS. the name is written Nardānī. ↑

29 The route from the South. See Jarrett, II. 347, n. 3. ↑

30 I.O. MSS. have Monday. ↑

31 The word in text is *s͟has͟hsat. S͟hast* is a thumbstall, but it may also mean a ring. See Blochmann, 166 and *n.* 1. ↑

32 *K͟hātam-bandī.* It also means "inlaying." ↑

33 *Bandu bān.* In I.O. MSS. it is *bandu bārān.* Perhaps "skilful painter" should be "the Painter of Creation." ↑

34 Should be *Karā.* See Herklots Qānūn-i-Islām, Appendix XXIV. ↑

35 *Nabīra* here cannot mean grandson, for Sūraj Singh, commonly called Sūr Singh, was fifth in descent from Māldeo (Blochmann, 359). Sūraj or Sūr was s. Rāy Rāy Singh of Bikaner. See Tod, who says Sūr Singh passed nearly all his life as an alien. ↑

36 Tod has much to say about Gaj Singh, but the account seems hardly trustworthy. ↑

37 The text, p. 277, has a representation of one of these milestones which was outside Delhi. ↑

38 Perhaps *sīb-i-k͟hūb* is the name of a kind of apple. ↑

39 I.O. MS. 181 has S͟hukr-darā and the name of the village as S͟hin-warān. The printed text has Sīwarān. ↑

40 Mr. Rogers here refers to the R.A.S. MS. The I.O. MSS. are not clear. Apparently what Jahāngīr says is: "On this occasion fresh items of expenditure occurred to me, and the former outlay was greatly increased." The word *taṣarrufāt* ("expenditure") is omitted in the printed copy. ↑

41 The village must be Hilalabad, near Rankatta (Blochmann, 332). ↑

42 Jahāngīr says nothing about the permission that he gave to Bīr Singh Deo—as a reward for murdering Abū-l-Faẓl—to build a very splendid temple at Mathura. It was destroyed by Aurangzīb. See Growse's "Mathura." ↑

43 Text *ḥalal*, which means "weakness," or *ḥulal* ("striped garments"). But according to the MSS., the true reading is *k͟halal*, which means "a crack" and also "corruption." ↑

44 The Iqbāl-nāma, 128, calls him Achadrūp, and says that the K͟hān Aʿẓam went privately to him and begged him to use his influence with Jahāngīr for the release of K͟husrau. Achadrūp spoke accordingly, and K͟husrau was released and allowed to pay his respects. See *infra* for account of his release. After Jadrūp removed to Mathura, he was cruelly beaten by Ḥakīm Beg. See Maʾāṣiru-l-Umarā, I. 576. ↑

45 Elliot, VI. 367. ↑

46 Luqmān is the Eastern Æsop, and there is much about him in D'Herbelot. In the second line the word translated "hollow" is *gulūgāh*, literally "throat place," and the word for bosom is *sīna*, the whole expression being *sīna-i-chang*. Chang is a harp or lyre, and apparently the expression refers to the narrowness of the space between the horns of a lyre (*chang*, which appears to be the Jew's harp), or the sides of a harp. The fourth line is obscure, and the version in text seems corrupt. The words *s͟has͟h bidast dū pāy* seem

unintelligible. They, however, occur in I.O. MS. 181, f. 161a, and in I.O. MS. 305, f. 225*a.* The only difference is that they have a conjunction after *bidast.* On the other hand, the Iqbāl-nāma, which inserts the lines into the record of the eleventh year, has, at p. 95, a different reading for the fourth line. The words there are *k͟hāna yak bidast u sih pay. Bidast* is given in Richardson, and the Farhang-i-Ras͟hīdī as meaning a span, so the line as given in the Iqbāl-nāma may mean 3 feet and 1 span. The author of the Iqbāl-nāma was so struck with the verse of Ḥakīm Sanā'ī and the appearance of Jadrūp's dwelling, that he composed a *maṣnavī* on the subject, which he gives at pp. 95, 96. There is a third version in Daulat S͟hāh's anthology, p. 97 of Professor Browne's edition. There, in the second line we have *ḥalqa* ("ring"), or perhaps "plectrum" instead of *sīna.* We have also two lines not given in the Tūzuk or the Iqbāl-nāma, and the line containing the noodle's question is given thus: "Kīn chih jāyast yak pūst u dū pay."

"What place is this, one skin (?) and two feet."

As if the meaning was that Luqmān lived in a tent propped up by two sticks. In the first line, also, we have *wiṣāqī* instead of *kurīchī.*

The lines may be versified thus:

"Luqmān's cell was small and narrow to boot,

Like the throat of a pipe, or the breast of a lute.

A foolish one said to the grand old man—

'What house is this—three feet and six span?'

With tears and emotion the sage made reply—

'Ample for him whose task is to die.'"

In the Nawalkishor edition of Ḥakīm Sanā'ī's poem the lines are entered as in the seventh book of the Ḥadīqa, but in two B.M. MSS. (Add. 25,329, f. 145*a*, and Or. 358, f. 172*b*), they are placed in the fifth book. Both of these MSS. have *bidast*, apparently, and Add. 25,329, has *s͟has͟h* ("six"), but Or. 358 has *s͟hass.* There is such a word, meaning hard ground. Both MSS. have *sih* ("three"). *Bidast* may properly be *bad-pus͟ht* ("bad-backed"), or it may be *bad-past* ("bad and mean"). The reference in verse may be rather to the curvature of the *chang* (Arabic, *ṣanj*) than to its narrowness, for Jamī speaks of the back "being bent like a harp." ↑

47 Compare Price, 123. ↑

48 Ba *dustūrī* kih dar Bangāla dās͟ht.

I think this must mean that his men were allowed the Bengal batta, or exceptional allowance, which used to be 50 p.c. of pay elsewhere. See A.N., III. 293, the eighth reason for the rebellion. ↑

49 This passage has been translated by Colonel Phillott in the A.S.B.J. for February, 1907, p. 113. There is something wrong in the text. K͟hān ʿĀlam certainly did not die on the road (see Blochmann, 513), for he waited upon Jahāngīr at Kalān ūr (Tūzuk, 284); nor did the Mīr S͟hikār, for Jahāngīr says he gave him a present and dismissed him. I presume, therefore, that the word "aforesaid" refers to K͟hān ʿĀlam's hawk. ↑

50 *Nigāh-dārad.* Perhaps this means that the painter was afterwards to stuff the bird. ↑

51 This is an obscure passage, and Jadrūp's reference to the mention of *dāms* in the Vedas is curious, for *dām* is said to be derived from the Greek drachma. However, it appears from the Āyīn (Blochmann, 31), that the dam, though in value only the fortieth part of a rupee, weighed 5 *tānks* or 1 *tolā*, 8 *mās͟has*, 7 *surk͟hs*. The rupee, we are told there, weighed 11½ mashas—*i.e.*, half a masha less than a tola. Consequently the dam weighed over 20 mashas, and so was not far from being equal in weight to 2 rupees. The weight of a seer varied, and it may be 30 or 36 copper dams were reckoned as equal to a seer. By dam Jahāngīr probably meant *paisā*, or double *paisā*. According to Gladwin, 3½ tanks are by jeweller's weights = one tolā, and a tank is 70·112 grs. Troy. ↑

52 As stated below, the antelope which were caught all eventually died. ↑

53 Text *gul-rang*, which seems unintelligible. No. 181 MS. has *kalānak* ("somewhat grown-up"). The child was presumably the Sultan Dūr-andīs͟h, born at the end of the ninth year (Tūzuk, 137), and so was now about five years old. Gul-rang occurs in B.M. MS., and may mean "ruddy." ↑

54 Text has Āg͟hā-i-Āg͟hāmān. The MSS. have Āqā Āqāyān ("Agha of Aghas"). ↑

55 Akbar was born in October, 1542, so she was now seventy-seven years old. ↑

56 Sayyid Bahwa is commonly known as Dīn-dār K. Buk͟hārī, and is described under that name in the Maʾāṣir, II. 23. ↑

57 Elliot, VI. 366, and Rieu, I. 14 and 355. The book is called Ak͟hbāru-l-Ak͟hyār, id. ↑

58 In Sarkār Sahāranpur. Elliot, Supp. Gloss., II. 129. I.G. new edition, XIV. 287. ↑

59 The child was born at Sirhind on Wednesday, 11 Muḥarram, 1029 (December 8, 1619), and died at Burhānpur in Rabīʻu-s̱-s̱anī, 1031 (February–March), 1622. Pādis͟hāh-nāma, I. 392.

60 See Erskine's Bābur, p. 321.

61 Perhaps this is Birū'ī in Sambhal, Jarrett, II. 200. Or it may be the Mīyānī Nūriya of Jarrett, II. 317.

62 To clear the roots? Or is it to let the sap flow? Or is ʻirāq-bandī right, meaning footpaths? Jahāngīr's order then would be to clear out the brick footpaths.

63 *Yak-āwīz̤*. Defined in Vullers as a short, broad sword, and also as a two-edged knife. See Vullers, 1519a. The weapon is described in text as *s͟hams͟hīr-i-nīmcha-i-yak-āwīz̤*.

64 *Az̤ nīlam-i-farang-tarās͟h*. It is difficult to suppose that the hilt was a sapphire. Possibly "nīlam" is the European artist's name, or *nīlam-i-farang* may be some kind of European work or material. Query niello?

65 *Būy-i-k͟hwīs͟h* ("my own scent"). The scent (otto of roses) was invented by Jahāngīr's mother-in-law (the mother of Nūr-Jahān). She called it after Jahāngīr's name.

66 The meaning of the clause is obscure.

67 The first line is obscure and the MSS. do not help. Possibly the meaning is Spring thanks thee for robbing his garden, or it may be, Spring is exhorted to rob thy garden. The quatrain is also given in the Iqbāl-nāma, 132.

68 Meaning that the lips were so closed that the mouth looked like a thin scar.

69 The collyrium of Solomon was something which enabled one to see hidden treasures.

70 This quatrain is stated in the Iqbāl-nāma, 133, to be by Bābā Ṭālib Iṣfahānī. He is a quite different person from Ṭālib Āmulī. The same quatrain is given by Abū-l-Faẓl, and I am indebted to Mr. Blochmann, p. 607, for being able to understand it. Bābā

Ṭālib Iṣfahānī is not mentioned by Dr. Rieu. At Vol. II., 679b, of his Catalogue, there is an account of Ṭālib Āmulī, who, it is said, died young. Bābā Ṭālib died somewhat later, and at the age of over 100. See Iqbāl-nāma, *loc. cit.*, and Badayūnī, III. 265.

71 A Muḥammad S̲h̲aik̲h̲ is mentioned in Beale as the author of two books (see p. 273, col. 2). One of them was the Jām-i-Jahān-numā, and is perhaps the work mentioned in Rieu, II. 866a, V.

72 Some unnecessary details have been omitted here.

73 K̲h̲wāja Jahān's real name was Dūst Muḥ., and he was from Kabul. See Blochmann, 424. Jahāngīr's characterization of him is rather obscure, and I am not sure if my translation is correct. Jahāngīr had married his daughter. Blochmann, 477, *n.* 2.

74 This is the seesee partridge or *Ammoperdrix Bonhami* of Jerdon, p. 567 of first edition. Jerdon states that in Afghanistan it is called the teehoo, and that its flesh is said to be delicious.

75 Apparently this is the *Hibiscus mutabilis*, for which the Bengali name is *thal padma* ("land lotus").

76 The word for twenty is omitted in text, and also in Elliot, VI. 367.

77 "On the southern bank of the Harroh River," Elliot, VI. 367.

78 Bhīm was the younger brother of Karan (Tod). The passage is translated in Elliot, VI. 367.

79 Elliot, VI. 368 and n. 1.

80 Elliot, VI. 368, and note.

81 Elliot has Hazāra Fārig̲h̲.

82 On the eastern bank of the Dhor. Elliot, *loc. cit.*

83 Elliot has: "As far as the eye could reach, the blossoms of the thal kanwal, and other flowers were glowing between the green foliage. It was a beautiful scene."

84 Salhar in text, but Sālhar in Elliot.

85 Marsh-mallow of Steingass and Elliot. Query Hollyhock?

86 The word violets occurs in MS. 181 and also in Elliot.

87 The Bib. Ind. edition, Iqbāl-nāma, p. 135, changes this into Pakli. MS. 181 has Bankli (?) apparently. Pakli is probably not right, for the entrance to it is mentioned lower down.

88 *Taṣadduq s̲h̲ud.* This is how Mr. Rogers has translated the passage, and this seems to me to be right. Elliot has "lost," but surely Jahāngīr would not pass over so lightly the loss of 25 elephants. *Taṣadduq* is often used in the sense of almsgiving, or of granting a favour. The text 290, line 2, has *aks̲ar-i-rāh basta*

*būd.* The word *basta* seems unintelligible, and in the corresponding passage of the Iqbāl-nāma, 135, the words are *akṣar-i-rāh ajama būd.* This word perhaps means "muddy," and this would fit the sense. ↑

89 Elliot has Tawādkar. ↑

90 *Achamba.* But MS. 305 has ajamat, and this may mean forest, or woods. Perhaps Elliot's "mud" is a clerical error for wood, but *ajamat* means pools as well as woods. Perhaps this is the same word as occurs in the Iqbāl-nāma, 135, and means "muddy." ↑

91 So in text, but the MSS. *ba garaẓ basta* ("loosely tied"), so that they could be thrown off if any game appeared. ↑

92 Elliot has *sīr.* ↑

93 Now known as the Kunhār. It rises in Lake Lohusur at the head of the Kāgān glen. See I.G., old edition, VIII. 365, and ditto new edition, XIV. 272, for Kāgān Valley. ↑

94 Text Wārū. Iqbāl-nāma 136 has Kūh-i-Wāzūh. MS. 181 seems to have Dārd. ↑

95 Text *shākhdār* ("with branches"), but the true reading seems to be *nāj* ("pine"). Elliot has "sāl." ↑

96 This is a fanciful derivation. The word is not darang, but drang, which means a watch-station. See Stein, A.S.B.J., for 1899, p. 84. The Pamba-drang, however, was near the Kishan Gangā, and so is not the drang mentioned by Stein. ↑

97 A mistake. See Elliot, VI. 373, note. ↑

# The Fifteenth New Year's Feast after the Auspicious Accession

The transit of the sun, that fulfils the hopes of the world, into his house of honour in Aries, took place on Friday, the 15th of the month of Rabīʿu-ṣ-ṣānī in the Hijrī year 1029, (10 March), 1620, after 12½ gharis, or 5 sidereal hours,1 had passed, and the 15th year of the reign of this suppliant at the throne of Allah commenced happily and auspiciously. On Saturday, the 2nd (Farwardīn), having marched 4½ koss, I halted at the village of Bakkar. On this road there was no hill-pass (*kotal*), but it was rather stony. I saw peacocks, black partridges, and monkeys (*langūr*), such as exist in the Garmsīr country (Afghanistan). It is evident that these can also exist in cold countries. From this place to Kashmir the road is along the bank of the river Bihat. There are hills on both sides, and in the bottom of the valley the water flows with great force, boiling and raging. However large an elephant may be, he cannot hold his feet firmly in it, but immediately rolls over, and is carried away. There are also water-dogs2 in the river. On Sunday, the 3rd, marching 4½ koss, I pitched at Mūsarān. On the eve of Friday the merchants who live in the pargana of Bāra Mūla came and paid their respects. I asked the reason of the name of Bāra mūla, and they represented that in the Hindi language they call a boar *Bārāh* (*Varaha*) and mūla a place—that is, the boars' place. Among the incarnations that belong to the religion of the Hindus, one is the boar incarnation, and Bārāh mūla by constant use has become Bāra mūla. On Monday, the 4th, marching 2½ koss, I pitched at Bhūlbās. As they said these hills were very narrow and difficult (to pass), and they could be crossed by a crowd of men only with great trouble, I gave orders to Muʿtamid K. that, with the exception of Āṣaf K. and a few of the necessary attendants, no one should be allowed to march along with the prosperous stirrup (with the king personally), and the camp should be kept one stage behind. By chance, before this order was given, he had sent on his own tent. After this he wrote to his men that this order had been given with regard to him, and they should halt at whatever spot they had reached. His brothers heard this at the foot of the kotal of Bhūlbās,3 and pitched their own tent there. When the royal host reached the place, snow and rain began to fall. One plain of the road had not been crossed when his tent became visible. Looking on this as a gift from the hidden world, I and the ladies alighted, and remained protected from the cold and snow and rain. His brothers, according to orders, sent someone in haste to summon him. When the news reached him that the elephants and the advance camp had arrived at the top of the *kotal*, and blocked up the road, as it was impossible to ride, *with great zeal*, he, not knowing his head from his feet, traversed a distance of 2½ koss on foot in two hours, and came to wait on me, and repeated this couplet with the tongue of gesture.4

VERSE.

"At midnight came the thought of thee. I was ashamed and resigned my life.

The poor man was abashed when suddenly the guest arrived."

All that was in his store (*bisāṭ*) in the way of money and goods, of live stock or dead, he offered for me to tread upon. I gave them all back, and said: "What do worldly goods appear worth to the eye of our magnanimity? We buy the jewel of loyalty at a high figure. Such an event arising out of his devotion should be reckoned as the rising of his good star, in that a king like me with the people of his harem should remain in his house in comfort and at ease for a night and a day. It would be a cause of honour to him among his contemporaries and comrades." On Tuesday, the 5th, having traversed 2 koss, I alighted at the village of Kahā'ī.5 I presented the dress (*sar u pāy*) I had on to Mu'tamid K., and an order was given assigning him the mansab of 1,500 personal and 1,5006 horse. From this stage we entered within the boundary of Kashmīr. In the same kotal of Bhūlbās, Ya'qūb, s. Yūsuf K. Kas<u>h</u>mīrī, fought with the victorious army of my father, of which Rāja Bhagwān Dās, father of Rāja Mān Singh, was the leader.

On this day, the news came that Suhrāb K., s. Rustam Mīrzā, had been drowned in the Jhelam. The details are as follows: He, according to orders, was coming up one stage in the rear, and on the road it came into his mind that he would have a bathe in the river, though warm water was ready. The people forbade him, and said that when the air was so cold, unnecessarily to get into a river so agitated and bloodthirsty that it would roll over a war-elephant, was contrary to the dictates of caution. He was not restrained by their words, and as the unavoidable destined time had arrived, got in. From excessive self-will and pride and carelessness, in reliance on his powers of swimming, in which art he was unequalled, he was more determined than ever, and with a *k<u>h</u>idmatīyya* (Blochmann 252) and another servant, both of whom could swim, mounted a rock on the river bank and threw himself in. Immediately he fell, from the violent movement of the waves, he could not pull himself together or try to swim; to fall in and go were the same thing, and Suhrāb K.7 and the *k<u>h</u>idmatīyya* thus gave away the goods of their lives to the flood of destruction. The boatman,8 with a hundred difficulties, brought the boat of his being (himself) in safety to the shore. Mīrzā Rustam was much attached to this son. On hearing of this fatal news on the Pūnch road, he rent the robe of patience, and showed great agitation. With all his dependants, clothed in mourning garments, with head and feet bare, he came to wait on me. What shall I write of the grief of the mother? Although the Mīrzā has other sons, his heart was bound up in this one. His age was twenty-six years. In shooting with a gun he was an excellent pupil of his father, and knew well how to drive elephants and carriages. On the expedition to Gujarat he was often ordered to ride on the front part of my private elephant, and he was an active soldier.9

On Wednesday, the 6th, marching 3 koss, I pitched at the village of Rīwand. On Thursday, the 7th, crossing the *kotal* of Kuwārmat,10 which is the most difficult on this road (MS.), I alighted at the village of Wachaha (MS. and print differ). The distance of this stage is 4¼ koss. The *kotal* of Kuwārmat (Kulāmat in the MS.) is a difficult one, and is the last of the *kotals* on the road. On Friday, the 8th, having traversed nearly 4 koss, I halted at the village of Baltār.11 There was no *kotal* on this road. It was broad, and plain after plain, and mead after mead, of flowers. Sweet-smelling plants of narcissus, violet, and strange flowers that grow in this country, came to view. Among these flowers I saw (noticed especially) one extraordinary one. It had five or six orange flowers blooming with their heads downwards. From the middle of the flowers there came out some green leaves, as in the case12 of the pineapple (?). This is the *būlānīk*13 flower. There is another flower like the *pūy* (?), round which are small flowers of the shape and colour of the jessamine, some blue in colour and some red, with yellow points in the middle, exceedingly pretty in appearance: its name is "*ladar pus̱ẖ.*" They call it *pus̱ẖ-i-'aliyyu-l-'umūm*14 (the common *pus̱ẖ*?). There are many yellow *arg̱ẖawān* (Judas-trees) on the road as well. The flowers of Kashmīr are beyond counting and calculation. Which shall I write of? And how many can I describe? I have only mentioned the most remarkable. There is a waterfall on this road, very high and fine. It flows down from a high place. No other waterfall of such beauty was seen on the road. I delayed a moment at it, and filled my eye and heart with gazing on it from a high spot. On Saturday, the 9th, I marched 4¾ koss, and crossed over at Bāramūla.15 It is one of the noted towns of Kashmīr, and 14 koss16 distant from the city, situated on the bank of the Bihat. A number of the merchants of Kashmir live in it, and have built houses and mosques on the bank of the river, and spend their days in ease and contentment. According to orders, before the arrival of the host of prosperity, they had prepared decorated boats at the place. As17 the hour for entry (into Srinagar) had been fixed for Monday, when two watches of the day had passed, on Sunday, the 10th, I entered S̱ẖihābu-d-dīn-pūr. On this day Dilāwar K. Kākar, the Governor of Kashmir, came from Kis̱ẖtwār,18 and had the good fortune to kiss the threshold. He was exalted with various royal favours and all kinds of imperial gratifications. He had done his duty here in an acceptable manner, and it is hoped that the great Giver of favours may light up the foreheads of all my servants with honour.

Kis̱ẖtwār is to the south of Kashmir. From the city of Kashmir (Srinagar) to the stage of Alkah (?),19 which is the capital of Kis̱ẖtwār, the distance is 60 koss by measurement. On the 10th of the Ilāhī month of S͟hahriwar, in my 14th year, Dilāwar K., with 10,000 horse and foot, determined to conquer Kis͟htwār. He appointed his son, Ḥasan by name, with Gird ʿAlī *Mīr-baḥr* (admiral) to guard the city and administer the territory. And as Gohar Chak and Aiba Chak laid claim to Kashmir as heirs, and were stirring up strife in Kis͟htwār, and were wandering in the valley of confusion and ruin, he left Haibat, one of his brothers, with a force at Desū, which is near the *kotal* of Pīr Panjāl, by way of caution, and, dividing his forces at that place, he himself hastened with a force by the road of Sangīnpūr, sending his son Jalāl, with Naṣru-llah ʿArab, and ʿAlī Malik Kas͟hmīrī, and a band of Jahāngīrī servants by another road, and his elder son Jamāl with a band of zealous young men as an advanced guard to his own force. At the same time he placed two other forces to move forward on his right and left. As no horses could go on the road, by way of precaution he took some with him, but left nearly20 all his sipahis' horses behind, and sent them to Kashmir (*i.e.*, Srinagar). The young men girded the belt of duty on their waists, and went up the hills on foot. The *g͟hāzīs* of the army of Islam fought from post to post with the ill-fated unbelievers as far as Narkot, which was one of the enemy's strongholds. There the corps of Jalāl and Jamāl, which had been sent by different roads, met, and the enemy, not having the power to oppose them, took to flight. The brave ones who offered their lives traversed many ups and downs with the courage of determination, and hastened on to the Mārū river. On the bank of that river the fire of slaughter was lighted, and the *g͟hāzīs* of the army of Islam displayed approved activity. The ill-fated Aiba Chak, with many of the people of ruin, were slain. By the death of Aiba the Raja became powerless and without heart, and took the road of flight, and, crossing by the bridge, stopped at Bhandarkoṭ, which is on the other side. A band of the brave ones (*bahādurān*) quickly advanced, wishing to cross the bridge. A great fight took place at its head, and some of the young men attained to martyrdom. In this way for twenty days and nights the servants of the Court tried to cross the river, and the unbelievers of darkened fortune did not fail to attack and try to drive them back, until Dilāwar K., after establishing *thānas* and arranging for the commissariat, arrived with his army. The Raja, by way of stratagem and vulpine trickery, sent his Vakils to Dilāwar K., and begged that he might send his brother with offerings to the Court, so that when his offences obtained pardon, and his mind were freed from fear and trouble, he could also himself proceed to the Court, the refuge of the world, and kiss the threshold. Dilāwar K. did not lend his ear to these deceitful words, and did not throw away from his hand the coin of opportunity. He dismissed the envoys of the Raja without the attainment of their object, and made every exertion to cross the bridge. His eldest son Jamāl, with a band of the crocodiles of the sea of bravery and valour, went up the river, and by bravely swimming it although swollen crossed over, and engaged in a fierce battle with the enemy. The devoted servants of the Court made an attack from the other side, and made matters tight for these ruined people. These, when they found they had no longer the strength to oppose them, broke down the planking of the bridge, and took to flight. The victorious servants made the bridge strong again, and transported the remainder of the army. Dilāwar K͟hān drew up his forces at Bhandarkoṭ. From the aforesaid river (the Mārū) to the Chenāb, which is a strong support of these unfortunate people, is a distance of two bow-shots, and on the bank of the Chenāb there is a lofty hill. The crossing of the water is a difficult matter, and, with a view to the coming and going of people on foot, they attach strong ropes, and place planks of the width of a cubit between two ropes, and fasten one rope's end to the top of the hill, and the other on the other side of the water. Then they attach two other ropes a *gaz* higher than these, that foot-passengers may place their feet on the planks, and, taking hold of the upper ropes, may descend from the top of the hill to the bottom, and so cross the river. This bridge they call *zampa*, in the language of the people of the hill country. Wherever they apprehended that a rope bridge might be constructed, they stationed musketeers and archers and men-at-arms, and so felt secure. Dilāwar K. made rafts (*jhāla*), and, placing on them eighty of his valiant young men, sent them across the river at night. As the water was flowing with great violence, the rafts were carried down by the flood of destruction, and sixty-eight of these gallant men were drowned in the sea of non-existence, and obtained the renown of martyrdom, whilst ten, by the aid of swimming, reached the shore of safety (*i.e.*, returned), and two on the other side became prisoners in the hands of the infidels. In short, for four months and ten days Dilāwar K͟hān, having planted the foot of courage at Bhandarkoṭ, made endeavours to cross over; but the arrow of stratagem did not reach the target of intent until a Zamindar pointed out a place which the enemy had no idea of. There, having constructed a *zampah*, in the heart of night, Jalāl, Dilāwar K.'s son, with some of the servants of the Court and a band of Afghans, about 200 in number, crossed over in safety, made unawares in the morning an attack on the Raja, and blew loudly the trumpets of victory. A few who were around and before the Raja rushed out, bewildered, half asleep and half awake, and most of them became the harvest of the blood-drinking sword, while the rest quickly withdrew themselves from that whirlpool of calamity. In that encounter one of the soldiers came upon the Raja, and wished to finish him with a sword. He called out: "I am the Raja; take me alive to Dilāwar K͟hān." The men rushed on him and made him prisoner. After the Raja was made prisoner, his people all fled. When Dilāwar K͟hān heard this good news of victory, he prostrated himself in thankfulness to Allah, and, having crossed the river with the victorious army, came to Mandal Badr,21 which was the capital of the country, and is 3 koss from the river. The daughter22 of Sangrām Raja of Jammu, and the daughter of the abandoned Sūraj Mal, s. Rāja Bāso, were in the Raja's house (*i.e.*, married to him). By Sangrām's daughter he had children. Before the victory he had, by way of caution, sent his family for refuge to the Raja of Jaswāl and other Zamindars. When my victorious retinue approached, Dilāwar K͟hān, according to order, took the Raja with him, and came to kiss the threshold, leaving Naṣru-llah ʿArab with a body of horse and foot to guard the country.

In Kis͟htwār there are produced much wheat, barley, lentils, millet, and pulse. Differing from Kashmir, it produces little rice. Its saffron is finer than that of Kashmir. About a hundred hawks and falcons are caught there (annually). Oranges, citrons, and water-melons of the finest kind are obtained. Its melons are of the same kind as those of Kashmir, and other fruits, such as grapes, apricots, peaches, and sour pears, are grown. If they were cultivated, it is possible they would improve. A coin23 of the name of *sanhasī*24 is a relic of the old rulers of Kashmir, one and a half of which equal a rupee. In their business transactions they reckon fifteen *sanhasī*, or ten rupees, as one *pāds͟hāhī* muhar. They call two seers of Hindustani weight a *man* (maund). It is not the custom for the Raja to take revenue from cultivation; he takes annually six *sanhasī*—that is, four rupees—from each house. All the saffron is assigned, as pay, to a body of Rajputs and to 700 musketeers (*tūpchī*) who are old retainers. When the saffron is sold, four rupees per maund, or two seers, are taken from the purchaser. The whole income of the Raja consists of fines, and for a small offence he takes a heavy sum. From whomsoever is wealthy and in comfortable circumstances the Raja, on some pretext, clears out all that he has. From all sources his income is about Rs. 100,000. In time of war 6,000 or 7,000 men on foot collect together; there are but few horses among them. The Raja and the chief men have about fifty between them. I bestowed a year's revenue on Dilāwar K. by way of reward. By conjecture, his jagir was worth about 1,000 personal and 1,000 horse, according to the *Jahāngīrī* rules. When the chief diwans calculate the allowances to the jagirdars, the exact amount will be ascertained.

On Monday, the 11th, after two watches and four gharis had passed, the royal cortege alighted auspiciously and happily at the buildings lately erected on the bank of the lake (the Dal lake). By order of my father, a very strong fort of stone and lime had been built. It is not quite completed, one side being unfinished. It is hoped that hereafter it will be completed. From Ḥasan Abdāl to Kashmir by the road I came is a distance of 75 koss; this was accomplished in nineteen marches and six halts—that is, in twenty-five days. From Agra to Kashmir, in the space of 168 days, a distance of 376 koss was traversed in 102 marches and 63 halts. By land25 and the ordinary route the distance is 304½ koss.

On Tuesday, the 12th, Dilāwar K., according to order, brought the Raja26 of Kis<u>h</u>twār, chained, into my presence, and did homage. He (the Raja) is not wanting in dignity. His dress is after the Indian fashion, and he knows both the Hindi and the Kashmiri languages. Contrary to other Zamindars of these regions, he looked like the inhabitant of a town. I told him that, notwithstanding his offences, if he would bring his sons to Court, he should be released from confinement, and might live at ease under the shadow of the eternal State, or else he would be imprisoned in one of the forts of Hindustan. He said that he would bring his people, his family, and his sons to wait on me, and was hopeful of my clemency.

I shall now give a brief account of the country of Kashmir and of its peculiarities.

Kashmir27 belongs to the fourth climate. Its latitude is 35° N., and its longitude, from the White Islands, 105°. In old times the country was in the possession of Rajas. Their dynasty lasted for 4,000 years. An account of them, and a list of their names, are given in the Rāja-tarang, which, by my father's order, was translated28 from the Sanskrit (Hindi in text) into Persian. In the Hijrī year 712 (1312–13) Kashmir was illumined by the religion of Islam. Thirty-two Muhammadan princes reigned over it for 282 years, until, in 994 (1586), my father conquered it. From that date till now, being a period of thirty-five years, the country has been in the possession of the Crown. Kashmir, from the Pass of Būlīyāsa29 to Qambarbar, is 56 *Jahāngīrī* koss long, and its breadth is never more than 27 koss, or less than 10 koss. S<u>h</u>aik<u>h</u> Abū-l-Faẓl has, in the Akbar-nāma, stated, by guess and conjecture, that the length of Kashmir from the Kis<u>h</u>an Gangā to Qambarbar is 120 koss, and its breadth from 10 to 25 koss. I, out of prudence and caution, appointed a number of trustworthy and intelligent men to measure the length and breadth with ropes (*ṭanāb)*. The result was that what the S<u>h</u>aik<u>h</u> wrote as 120 koss came out as 67. As it is agreed that the boundary of a country is the place up to which people speak the language of that country, it follows that the boundary of Kashmir is Būlīyāsa, which is 11 koss on this side (*i.e.*, east) of the Kis<u>h</u>an Gangā. So, according to the preceding figures, the length of Kashmir is 56 (67 - 11) koss. The variations in breadth were found to be not more than 2 koss. The koss30 which is in use during my reign is that prescribed by my father. That is, a koss is 5,000 yards, and the yard is 2 *s<u>h</u>arʿī* yards, each of the latter (yards) being 24 digits31 (*angus<u>h</u>t*). Wherever the koss or *gaz* is mentioned, the reference is to the above koss and the above *gaz*. The name of the city is Srīnagar, and the Bihat river flows through the midst of it. They call its fountain-head Vīr-nāg.32 It is 14 koss to the south. By my order they have made a building and a garden at that source. There have been built in the city four very strong stone and wooden bridges, over which people come and go. They call a bridge in the language of this country *kadal.*

There is a very lofty mosque in the city, one of the marks of Sulṭān Sikandar,33 made in 795 (1393). After a time it was burnt, but was rebuilt by Sulṭān Ḥusain. It had not been completed when the mansion of his life fell down. In 909 (1503–04) Ibrāhīm Māqrī, Vizier of Sulṭān Ḥusain, finished it handsomely. From that day till now it is 120 years since it has been in existence. From the *Miḥrāb* to the eastern wall it is 145 yards, and its breadth is 144 yards, containing four (*ṭāq*) alcoves. On all sides of the hall they have erected beautiful cloisters and pillars. In short, no better memorial of the rulers of Kashmir has been left than this. Mīr Sayyid ʿAlī of Hamadan (may his grave be sanctified!) was for some time in this city. There is a monastery34 to his memory. Near the city there are two35 large lakes full of water all the year round. Their flavour36 does not vary; they are the means for coming and going of the people, and for the conveyance of grain and firewood on boats. In the city and parganas there are 5,700 boats, with 7,40037 boatmen. The country of Kashmir has thirty-eight parganas. It is divided into two provinces; the territory on the upper part of the river they call *Marrāj*, and that on the lower *Kāmrāj*. It is not the custom to use gold and silver for payment of the revenue from land or in commerce, except for a portion of the cesses (*sāʾir-jihāt*).38 They reckon the value of things in *kharwārs* of rice, each *kharwār* being three maunds and eight seers of the current weight. The Kashmiris reckon two seers as one maund, and four maunds, or eight seers, make one *tark*. The revenue of Kashmir is 30,63,050 *kharwārs* and 11 *tarks*, which in cash represents 7,46,70,000 *dāms*. Ordinarily it maintains 8,500 horse. It is very difficult to enter Kashmir. The routes by Bhimbhar39 and Paklī are the best. Though that by Bhimbhar is the shorter, yet if one wishes to find spring in Kashmir, he is confined to the road by Paklī, for the other roads at this season are blocked with snow. If one were to take to praise Kashmir, whole books would have to be written. Accordingly a mere summary will be recorded.

Kashmir is a garden40 of eternal spring, or an iron fort to a palace of kings—a delightful flower-bed, and a heart-expanding heritage for dervishes. Its pleasant meads and enchanting cascades are beyond all description. There are running streams and fountains beyond count. Wherever the eye reaches, there are verdure and running water. The red rose, the violet, and the narcissus grow of themselves; in the fields, there are all kinds of flowers and all sorts of sweet-scented herbs more than can be calculated. In the soul-enchanting spring the hills and plains are filled with blossoms; the gates, the walls, the courts, the roofs, are lighted up by the torches of banquet-adorning tulips. What shall we say of these things or of the wide meadows (*julgahā*) and the fragrant trefoil?

VERSE.

"The garden-nymphs41 were brilliant,

Their cheeks shone like lamps;

There were fragrant buds on their stems (or 'under their rind'),

Like dark amulets on the arms of the beloved.

The wakeful, ode-rehearsing nightingale

Whetted the desires of wine-drinkers;

At each fountain the duck dipped his beak

Like golden scissors cutting silk;

There were flower-carpets and fresh rosebuds,

The wind fanned the lamps of the roses,

The violet braided her locks,

The buds tied a knot in the heart."

The finest inflorescence is that of the almond and the peach. Outside the hill-country the commencement of blossoming is the 1st Isfandārmuẕ (February 10). In the territory of Kashmir it is 1st Farwardīn (March 10), and in the city gardens it is the 9th and 10th of that month, and the end of their blooming joins on to the commencement of that of the blue jessamine. In attendance on my revered father I frequently went round the saffron fields, and beheld the spectacle of the autumn. Thank God that on this occasion I beheld the beauties42 of the spring. The beauties of the autumn shall be described in their place. The buildings of Kashmir are all of wood; they make them two-, three-, and four-storied, and covering the roofs with earth, they plant bulbs of the *chaug͟hās͟hī*43 tulip, which blooms year after year in the spring season, and is exceedingly beautiful. This custom is peculiar to the people of Kashmir. This year, in the little garden44 of the palace and on the roof of the chief mosque, the tulips blossomed luxuriantly. There are many blue jessamines in the gardens, and the white jessamines that the people of India call *chambīlī* are sweet-scented. Another kind is of the colour of sandal-wood, and this is also very sweet-scented. This is special to Kashmir. I saw several sorts of red roses: one is specially sweet-scented, and another is a flower of the colour of sandal (light yellow), with an exceedingly delicate scent. It (the scent?) is of the nature of (that of) the red rose, and its stem is like that of the red rose. There are two kinds of lilies. That which is grown in gardens is vigorous *(bālīda)* and fresh (lit. green) coloured, the other is a wild kind. Although the latter has less colour it is very sweet-scented. The flower of the *Ja'farī*45 (a yellow flower) is large and sweet-scented; its stem is above a man's height, but in some years, when it has grown large and has flowered, a worm is produced, and spreads over the flower a kind of spider's web, and destroys it and dries up its stem. This year it has so happened. The flowers that are seen in the territories of Kashmir are beyond all calculation. Those that Nādiru-l-ʿaṣrī Ustād Manṣūr,46 has painted are more than 100. Before my father's time there were no *s͟hāh-ālū* (cherries).47 Muḥammad48 Qulī Afs͟hār brought them from Kabul and planted them, and there are now ten or fifteen fruit-bearing trees. There were also some apricot-trees. The aforesaid made them known in this country, and now there are many of them. In fact, the apricot49 of Kashmir is good. There was a tree in the S͟hahr-ārā garden at Kabul, called *Mīrzāʾī*, better fruit than which I had not eaten, but in Kashmir there are trees equal to this in the gardens. There are pears (*nās͟hpātī*) of the best kind, better than those of Kabul, or Badakhshan, and nearly equal to those of Samarkand. The apples of Kashmir are celebrated for their goodness. The guavas (*amrūd*) are middling. Grapes are plentiful, but most of them are harsh and inferior, and the pomegranates are not worth much. Water-melons of the best kind can be obtained. The melons are very sweet and creased, (? *s͟hikananda*)50, but for the most part when they become ripe a worm is found in them that spoils them. If by chance they are preserved from this misfortune they are very delicate. There are no *s͟hāh-tūt*51 (some kind of large mulberry), but there are other (*tūt*) mulberries everywhere. From the foot of every mulberry-tree a vine-creeper grows52 up. In fact, the mulberries of Kashmir are not fit to eat, with the exception of some on trees grown in gardens, but the leaves are used to feed the silkworm. They bring the silkworms' eggs from Gilgit and Tibet. There is plenty of wine and vinegar, but the wine is sour and inferior, and in the Kashmir language is called *mas*. After they take cups of it some heat of head ensues. They make various pickles with the vinegar. As the garlic of Kashmir is good, the best pickle is that of garlic. There are all kinds of crops except peas. If they sow peas, they give a crop the first year, in the second they are inferior, and in the third year they are like *mus͟hang*.53 Rice is the principal crop. Probably there are three parts under rice and one under all other grains. The chief food of the people of Kashmir is rice, but it is inferior. They boil it fresh,54 and allow it to get cold, and then eat it, and call it *batha*. It is not usual to take their food warm, but people of small means keep a portion of the *batha* for a night, and eat it next day. Salt is brought from India. It is not the custom to put salt into the *batha*. They boil vegetables in water, and throw in a little salt in order to alter the flavour, and then eat them along with the *batha*. Those who want to have something tasty put a little walnut-oil into the vegetables. Walnut-oil soon becomes bitter and evil-flavoured. They also use cow-oil (*raug͟han—i.e.*, *ghī*), but this is taken fresh, and fresh from newly-made butter (*maska*). They throw this into the food, and call it "sadā-pāk" in the Kashmiri language. As the atmosphere is cold and damp, it becomes altered by being kept for three or four days. There are no buffaloes, and the cattle are small and inferior. The wheat55 is small and of little substance (*kam maghz*). It is not the custom to eat bread (*nān*). There are tailless sheep, resembling the *kadī*56 (or *gaddī*) of India. They are called *handū*, and their flesh is not without flavour. Fowls, geese, and ducks (*murghābī*)—golden and others—are plentiful. There are all kinds of fish, both with and without scales, but they are inferior. The woollen cloths are well known. Men and women wear a woollen tunic (*kurtā*), and call it *paṭṭū*. If they do not put on a tunic, they believe that the air affects them, and even that it is impossible to digest their food without it. The shawls of Kashmir, to which my father gave the name of *parm-narm*, are very famous: there is no need to praise them. Another kind is *taharma* (*naharma* in the printed version); it is thicker than a shawl, and soft.57 Another is called *darma*. It is like a *jul-i-khirsak*,58 and is put over carpets. With the exception of shawls they make other woollen materials better in Tibet. Though they bring the wool for the shawls from Tibet they do not make them there. The wool for shawls comes from a goat which is peculiar to Tibet. In Kashmir they weave the *paṭṭū* shawl from wool, and sewing two shawls together they smooth them into a kind of *saqarlāt* (broad-cloth), which is not bad for a rain-coat. The men of Kashmir shave the head and put on a round turban, and the common women do not wear clean, washed clothes. They use a tunic of *paṭṭū* for three or four years; they bring it unwashed from the house of the weaver, and sew it into a tunic, and it does not reach the water till it falls to pieces. It is considered wrong to wear drawers (*izār*); they wear the tunic long and ample as far as the head and falling down to the feet, and they also wear59 a belt. Although most of the houses are on the river-bank not a drop of water touches their bodies. In short, they are as dirty outside as inside, without any cleanliness. In the time of Mīrzā Ḥaidar there were many skilled people there. They were skilled in music, and their lutes, dulcimers, harps, drums, and flutes were celebrated. In former times they had a musical instrument like a lute, and used to sing in the Kashmīrī language compositions according to Hindi musical modes, there being even two or three modes combined together. Moreover, many sing together in chorus. In fact, Kashmir is much indebted to Mīrzā Ḥaidar for its excellencies. Before the reign of my father the chief method by which the people of these parts rode was on *gūnts* (ponies). They had no large horses, but used to bring ʿIrāq and Turki horses by way of rare gifts for their rulers. *Gūnt* means a *yābū*60 (pony). They have thick shoulders, and are low in the body. They are common in other of the hill-countries of India. For the most part they are vicious61 and hard-mouthed. When this God-created flower-garden acquired eternal beauty under the auspices of the State, and by the blessing of the teaching of the Alexander-minded Khāqān, many of the Aimāqs (cavalry) were presented with jagirs in this Subah, and herds of ʿIrāqī and Turkī horses were given them to breed from (*kih kurra bagīrand*). The soldiers also brought horses62 on their own account, and in a short time horses were obtainable, so that many Kashmiri horses were bought and sold for 200 and Rs. 300, and even for Rs. 1,000.

The merchants and artificers of this country are mostly Sunnis, while the soldiers are Imāmiyya Shias. There is also the sect of Nūr-bakhshīs.63 There is also a body of Faqirs whom they call *Rīshīs*.64 Though they have not religious knowledge or learning of any sort, yet they possess simplicity, and are without pretence. They abuse no one, they restrain the tongue of desire, and the foot of seeking; they eat no flesh, they have no wives, and always plant fruit-bearing trees in the fields, so that men may benefit by them, themselves deriving no advantage. There are about 2,000 of these people. There is also a body of brahmans living from of old in this country, who still remain there and talk in the Kashmiri tongue. Outwardly one cannot distinguish them from Mussulmans. They have, however, books in the Sanskrit language, and read them. They carry into practice whatever relates to the worship of idols. Sanskrit is a language in which the learned of India have composed books, and esteem them greatly. The lofty idol temples which were built before the manifestation of Islam are still in existence, and are all built of stones, which from foundation to roof are large, and weigh 30 or 40 maunds, placed one on the other. Near the city there is a small hill which they call Kūh-i-Mārān65 ("The Wicked Hill," Lawrence, 298), as well as Harī Parbat. On the east side of the hill there is the Dal Lake, which measures round a little more than 6½ koss.66 My father (may the lights of Allah be his testimony!) gave an order that they should build in this place a very strong fort of stone and lime; this has been nearly completed during the reign of this suppliant, so that the little hill has been brought into the midst of the fortifications, and the wall of the fort built round it. The lake is close to the fort, and the palace overlooks the water. In the palace there was a little garden, with a small building in it in which my revered father used constantly to sit. At this period it appeared to me to be very much out of order and ruinous. As it was the place where that veritable *qibla* (place turned towards in prayer) and visible Deity used to sit, and it is really a place of prostration for this suppliant, therefore its neglected state did not appear right to me. I ordered Muʿtamid K., who is a servant who knows my temperament, to make every effort to put the little garden in order and repair the buildings. In a short space of time, through his great assiduity, it acquired new beauty. In the garden he put up a lofty terrace 32 yards square, in three divisions (*qiṭʿa*), and having repaired the building he adorned it with pictures by masterhands, and so made it the envy of the picture gallery of China. I called this garden *Nūr-afzā* (light increasing).

On Friday, the 15th of the Divine month of Farwardīn, two *quṭās* oxen, out of the offerings of the Zamindar of Tibet, were brought before me. In form and appearance they closely resemble the buffalo. All the limbs are covered with wool which properly belongs to animals in a cold country. For instance, the *rang* goats (ibex), which they brought from the country of Bhakkar (Sind) and the hill-country of the Garmsīr (in Afghanistan) were very handsome, and had but little wool, and those that are met with in these hills, on account of the excessive cold and snow, are covered with hair and ugly. The Kashmiris call the rang *kapal*.67 On this day they brought a musk deer as an offering. As I had not tasted its flesh, I ordered it to be cooked; it appeared very tasteless and bad for food. The flesh of no other wild animal is so inferior. The musk-bag when fresh has no scent, but when it is left for some days and becomes dry, it is sweet-scented. The female has no musk-bag. In these two or three days I frequently embarked in a boat, and was delighted to go68 round and look at the flowers of Phāk and S͟hālamār. Phāk is the name of a pargana situated on the other side of the lake. S͟hālamār is near the lake. It has a pleasant stream, which comes down from the hills, and flows into the Dal Lake. I bade my son K͟hurram dam it up and make a waterfall, which it would be a pleasure to behold. This place is one of the sights of Kashmir.

On Sunday, the 17th, a strange affair took place. S͟hāh S͟hujāʿ was playing in the buildings of the palace. By chance there was a window with a screen in front of it looking towards the river. They had put a screen in front, but had not fastened the door, and the prince in play went towards the window to look out. As soon as he arrived there he fell headlong. By chance they had laid down a carpet below the wall, and a farrās͟h (carpet-spreader) was sitting near it. The child's head fell on this carpet, and his feet on the back and shoulders of the farrās͟h, and so came to the ground. Though the height was 7 yards69 (*daraʿ*), the compassion of God, the Great and Glorious, came to his aid, and the carpet and the farrās͟h became the means of saving his life. God forbid, but if it had not been so it would have been a serious matter for him. At the time Rāy Mān, the head of the K͟hidmatiyya70 piyādas, was standing below the *jharoka*. He immediately ran and picked him up, and holding him in his arms, was taking him upstairs. In that condition he asked: "Whither are you carrying me?" He replied: "Into the presence of His Majesty." Then weakness overcame him, and he could speak no more. I was lying down when this alarming news reached me, and ran out in a state of bewilderment. When I saw him in this state my senses forsook me, and for a long time holding him in my affectionate embrace I was distracted with this favour from Allah. When a child of four years of age falls headlong from a place ten ordinary (*s͟harʿī*) gaz in height, and no harm happens to his limbs, it is a cause for amazement. Having performed my prostrations for this fresh act of goodness, I distributed alms, and ordered that deserving people and the poor who lived in the city should be brought before me in order that I might assure them their means of livelihood. A strange thing was that three or four months before this event Jotik Rāy, the astrologer, who is one of the most skilled of the class in astrology, had represented to me, without any intermediary, that it was predicted from the Prince's horoscope that these three or four months were unpropitious to him, and it was possible he might fall down from some high place, but that the dust of calamity would not settle on the skirt of his life. As his prognostications had repeatedly proved correct, this dread dwelt in my mind, and on these dangerous roads and difficult mountain passes I was never for a moment forgetful of that nursling of the *parterre* of Fortune. I continually kept him in sight, and took the greatest precautions with regard to him. When I arrived in Kashmir this unavoidable71 catastrophe occurred. His nurses (*anagahā*) and wet-nurses must have been very careless. God be praised that it ended well!

In the garden of ʿAishābād72 (abode of pleasure) I saw a tree which had numerous73 blossoms. They were very large and beautiful, but the apples that the tree produced were bitter.

As excellent service had been done by Dilāwar K. Kākar, I promoted him to the mansab of 4,000 personal and 3,000 horse, and also conferred mansabs on his sons. Shaikh Farīd, s. Quṭbu-d-dīn K. was raised to the mansab of 1,000 personal and 400 horse. The mansab of Sar-barāh K. was ordered to be 700 personal and 250 horse, and I promoted Nūru-llah Kurkīrāq (in charge of furriery?) to that of 600 personal and 100 horse, bestowing on him the title of Tashrīf K. The offerings of Thursday, the 21st, were handed over as a reward to Qiyām K., the chief huntsman. As Allah-dād Afghan, s. the Tārīkī,74 had repented of his evil deeds and come to Court at the request of Iʿtmādu-d-daula I pardoned his offences; the signs of disgrace and shame were evident on his forehead and, according to the previous arrangement, I bestowed on him the mansab of 2,500 and 200 horse. Mīrak Jalāyir, one of the auxiliaries of Bengal, was promoted to the mansab of 1,000 personal and 400 horse.

As it was reported that the *jūghāsī* (*i.e.*, black) tulips were in good bloom on the roof of the Jāmiʿ mosque, on Saturday, the 23rd, I went to see them. In truth, one side of that flower-garden was very beautiful. The parganas of Mau75 and Mihrī (?) (text has Maud Mihrī), which previously to this had been granted to Rāja Bāso, and afterwards continued to his rebel son Sūraj Mal, were now bestowed on Jagat Singh, his brother, who had not obtained the *tīka* (mark of royal succession), and I gave the pargana of Jammū to Rāja Sangrām. On Monday, the 1st of Urdībihisht, I went to the house of Khurram, and entered his bath-house, and when I came out he presented his offerings. Of these I accepted a trifle in order to please him. On Thursday, the 4th, Mīr Jumla was promoted to the mansab of 2,000 personal and 300 horse. On Sunday, the 7th, I rode to the village of Chārdara,76 which is the native country of Ḥaidar Malik, to hunt partridges. In truth this is a very pleasant spot of ground, and has flowing streams and lofty plane-trees. At his request I gave it the name of Nūrpūr77 (city of light). On the road there was a tree78 called *halthal*; when one takes one of the branches and shakes it, the whole of the tree comes into movement. The common people believe that this movement is peculiar to that tree. By chance in the said village I saw another tree of the same kind, which was in similar movement, and I ascertained that it was common to that species of tree, and not confined to one tree. In the village of Rāwalpūr, 2½ koss from the city towards Hindustan, there is a plane-tree, burnt in the inside. Twenty-five years before this, when I myself was riding on a horse, with five other saddled horses and two eunuchs, we went inside it. Whenever I had chanced to mention this people were surprised. This time I again ordered some of the men to go inside, and what I had in my mind came to pass in the same manner. It has been noted in the Akbar-nāma that my father took79 thirty-four people inside and made them stand close to each other.

On this day it was represented to me that Prithī-chand, s. Rāy Manohar, who was one of the auxiliaries of the army against Kāngṛa, had sacrificed his life in a useless (*bī-ṣarfa*80) battle with the enemy.

On Thursday, the 11th, certain servants of the State were promoted in the following manner: Tātār K. to 2,000 personal and 500 horse; ʿAbdu-l-ʿAzīz K. to 2,000 personal and 1,000 horse; Debī Chand of Gwalior to 1,500 personal and 500 horse; Mīr K͟hān, s. Abū-l-Qāsim K. Namakīn to 1,000 personal and 600 horse; Mīrzā Muḥammad to 700 personal and 300 horse; Luṭfu-llah to 300 personal and 500 horse; Naṣru-llah ʿArab to 500 personal and 250 horse; and Tahawwur K. was appointed to the faujdārship of Mewāt. On Thursday, the 25th, Sayyid Bāyazīd Buk͟hārī, faujdār of Bhakkar, raised his head of honour with the Subadarship of Sind, and his mansab, original and increased, was fixed at 2,000 personal and 1,500 horse, and he was also presented with a standard. S͟hajāʿat K. ʿArab obtained the honour of exaltation to the mansab of 2,500 personal and 2,000 horse. Anīrāʾī Singh-dalan, at the request of Mahābat K., was appointed to Bangash. Jān-sipār K. was promoted to the mansab of 2,000 personal and 1,500 horse.

At this time, on the representation of the Commander-in-Chief, K͟hān-K͟hānān, and all the loyal people, it was shown to me that ʿAmbar, the black-fated one (he was an Abyssinian), had again placed his foot beyond the bounds of good behaviour, and had, according to his nature, laid a foundation for trouble and sedition, and as the victorious army had proceeded to a distant part of the country, he, considering it a good opportunity, had broken the pledges he had given to the servants of the Court, and had stretched out his hand to take possession of royal territory. It is hoped that he will soon be entangled in the disgrace of his deeds. As he (the Commander-in-Chief) had asked for treasure, it was ordered that the diwans of Agra should send Rs. 20,00,000 to the Commander-in-Chief. Close upon this news came that the Amirs had left their posts, and come together to Dārāb K., and that the *Bargīs*81 (the Mahrattas) were surrounding his camp, and that K͟hanjar K. had taken refuge in Aḥmadnagar. Two or three battles had already taken place between the rebels and the servants of the Court, and each time the enemy had been defeated, and many of them killed. On the last occasion Dārāb K., taking with him well-mounted young men, attacked the rebels' camp. A fierce battle ensued, and the enemy being defeated turned the face of ruin towards the valley of flight. Their camp had been plundered, and the victorious army had returned in safety to their camp. As difficulty and distress had fallen on the victorious army, those who were loyal came to the conclusion that they should go down by the Pass of Rohangaṛh82 and remain below the *ghāt*, so that forage and grain might be easily obtained, and the men not incur any labour or distress. Having no choice, they prepared the army of prosperity at Bālāpūr, and the rebels of black fortune, with impertinence and importunity, appeared near Bālāpūr. Rāja Bīr Singh Deo, with some of the devoted servants, plucking up courage in order to beat back the enemy, slew many of them. An Abyssinian of the name of Manṣūr, who was in the rebel army, fell into their hands, and although they wished to put him on an elephant (see Iqbāl-nāma 161, the text wrongly has *zīr* "under"), he would not agree, and was insolent.83 Rāja Bīr Singh Deo ordered them to separate his head from his body. It is hoped that the circling sphere will lay the recompense of improper deeds on the skirt of life of all who do not recognize the right.

On the 3rd Urdībihis͟ht I rode to see the Sukh Nāg.84 It is a beautiful summer residence (īlāq). This waterfall is in the midst of a valley, and flows down from a lofty place. There was still ice on its sides. The entertainment of Thursday was arranged for in that flower-land, and I was delighted at drinking my usual cups on the edge of the water. In this stream I saw a bird like a *sāj*.85 A *sāj* is of a black colour and has white spots, while this bird is of the same colour as a *bulbul* with white spots, and it dives and remains for a long time underneath, and then comes up from a different place. I ordered them to catch and bring two or three of these birds, that I might ascertain whether they were waterfowl and were web-footed, or had open feet like land birds. They caught two and brought them. One died immediately, and the other lived for a day. Its feet were not webbed like a duck's. I ordered Nādiru-l-ʿaṣr Ustād Manṣūr to draw its likeness. The Kashmiris call it *galkar*86—that is, "water sāj."

On this day the Qāẓī and the Chief Justice represented to me that ʿAbdu-l-Wahhāb, the son of Ḥakīm ʿAlī, claimed Rs. 80,000 from the Sayyids of

Lahore, and produced a bond with the seal of Qāẓī Nūru-llah. He said that his father had placed that sum in deposit with Sayyid Walī, the father of these men, who denied it.[87] If an order were given, the Ḥakīm's son, by way of caution,[88] would swear an oath on the Qoran, and would take what was his due from them. I told them to do whatever was right by the Divine Law. The next day Muʿtamid Khān represented that the Sayyids showed great humility and submissiveness. The matter was a complicated[89] one. The greater reflection shown in ascertaining the truth in the matter the better. I accordingly ordered that Āṣaf K. should take exceeding trouble and forethought in ascertaining the truth of this quarrel, and point out such a way (of unravelling it) that no doubt whatever should remain. With all this, if it could not be cleared up, I would examine them in my own presence. Immediately he heard these words, the Ḥakīm's son lost both his hands and his heart in the affair, and made a number of his friends intercessors, and proposed a withdrawal. His representation was that if the Sayyids would not[90] refer the matter to Āṣaf K. he would give a release, and that hereafter he would have no right against nor claim from them. Whenever Āṣaf K. sent to fetch him, as he was a low deceiver, he passed his time in making excuses, and did not appear until he handed over the deed of release to one of his friends, and the true state of affairs became evident to Āṣaf K. They brought him by force into the place of examination, and, having no choice, he confessed that the deed had been prepared by one of his servants, who himself witnessed it, and had misled him. He gave a writing to this effect. When Āṣaf K. informed me of the real state of matters, I took away his mansab and jagir, and cast him out of my presence, and gave the Sayyids leave to return to Lahore in all honour and respect.

On Mubārak-shamba (Thursday), the 8th of Khūrdād, Iʿtiqād Khān was promoted to the mansab of 4,000 personal and 1,500 horse, and Ṣādiq Khān to that of 2,500 personal and 1,400 horse. Zainu-l-ʿābidīn, son of the deceased Āṣaf Khān (Jaʿfar), was promoted to be Bakhshi of *Aḥadīs*. Rāja Bīr Singh Deo Bandīla raised his head of honour with the high mansab of 5,000 personal and horse.

In Kashmir the most juicy(?) fruit is the *ashkan*(?) (*askamī* in the MSS.). It is subacid (*mai-khūsh*), smaller than the *ālū bālū* (sour cherry), much better flavoured, and more delicate. When drinking wine, one cannot eat more than three or four *ālū bālū*, but of these one can take as many as a hundred in twenty-four hours, especially of the *paiwandī*(?) sort. I ordered that the *ashkan* should hereafter be called the *khūshkan*. It grows in the hills of Badakhshan and in Khurasan; the people there call it *jamdamī*. The largest of them weigh ½ *misqāl*. The *shāh-ālū* (cherry), on the 4th Urdībihisht, appeared of the size of a grain of pulse; on the 27th it reddened, and on the 15th Khūrdād it was ripe, and new fruit (*nau-bar*) had formed(?). The *shāh-ālū* (cherry), to my taste, is better than most fruits. Four trees had borne fruit in the Nūr-afzā garden. I called one of these *Shīrīn-bār*, the second *Khūsh-guwār*, the third, which bore the most fruit, *Pur-bār*, and the fourth, which had less, *Kam-bār*. One tree in Khurram's garden had also borne fruit, and I called it *Shāhwār*. There was a young plant in the little garden of *ʿIshrat-afzā* (joy enhancing), and this I called *Nau-bār* (new fruit). Every day I plucked with my own hand sufficient to give a flavour to my cups. Although they sent them by runners from Kabul as well, yet to pick them oneself from one's home garden gave additional sweetness. The *shāh-ālū* of Kashmir is not inferior to that of Kabul; it is even better grown. The largest of them weighed one *tānk*, five *surkhs*.

On Tuesday, the 21st, Pādshāh[91] Bānū Begam died (became a sitter in the bridal chamber of the permanent world), and grief for this heart-rending event laid a heavy load on my mind. I hope that Almighty God may give her a place near his own forgiveness. A strange thing is—that Jotik Rāy, the astrologer, two months before this, had informed some of my servants that one of the chief sitters in the harem of chastity would hasten to the hidden abode of non-existence. He had discovered this from the horoscope of my destiny, and it fell out accordingly.

One of the events (that now took place) was the martyrdom of Sayyid ʿIzzat[92] K. and of Jalāl K. Gakhar in the army of Bangash. The particulars of this are that when the season for the collection of revenue arrived, Mahābat K. appointed a force to go into the hill-country to eat up the crops of the Afghans, and not omit one tittle of raiding and plundering, and killing and binding. When the servants of the Court arrived at the foot of the Pass the ill-fated Afghans attacked them from all sides, and took the head of the Pass, and fortified it. Jalāl K., who was an experienced man, and an old man that had undergone labours, thought it better to delay for a few days, so that the Afghans might expend the few days' provisions they had brought with them on their backs, and necessarily disperse of their own accord; that then his men would be able to cross with ease over the head of the difficult Pass. When he once passed the head of the defile they would be unable to do any more, and would be punished. ʿIzzat K., who was a battle-lighting flame and a foe-burning lightning, did not fall in with Jalāl K.'s idea, and excited the steed of courage of some of the Sayyids of Bārha. The Afghans, swarming round on all sides, like ants and locusts, attacked him, and caught him in their midst. Though the battlefield was not fit for cavalry, yet wherever the forehead of his wrath shone, he consumed many with the fire of his sword. In the midst of the fighting they hamstringed his horse, but he fought on foot and as long as he had breath, and at last fell bravely. At the time when ʿIzzat K. made his attack, Jalāl K. Gakhar[93] and Masʿūd, s. Aḥmad Beg K., and

Bīzan (or Bīzhan), s. Nād ʿAlī Maidānī, and other servants, lost restraint, and rushed on from all sides of the pass, and the rebels seized the tops of the hills, and fought with stones and arrows. The devoted young men, both of the servants of the Court and the retainers of Mahābat K., performed the duties of valour, and slaughtered many of the Afghans. In this contest Jalāl K. and Masʿūd, with many other brave men, sacrificed their lives. Owing to the rashness of ʿIzzat K. such a disaster as this befell the Imperial army.

When Mahābat K. heard this fearful news, he sent a fresh body of men to assist, and strengthened the posts. Wherever they found a trace of those ill-fortuned ones, they did not fail to slay or bind them. When I heard this news, I summoned Akbar Qulī, s. Jalāl K. who had been told off for duty in the conquest of the fort of Kāngṛa, to my presence, and gave him the mansab of 1,000 personal and 1,000 horse, and confirmed to him, according to custom, his hereditary territory (the Gakhar country) in jagir, presented him with a dress of honour and a horse, and sent him to the support of the army of Bangash. As ʿIzzat K. had left a son of very tender years, keeping before my eyes, that discerned the truth, his life-sacrifice, I gave him (the child) a mansab and a jagir, so that those left behind should not be scattered abroad, and others might have increased hope.

On this day S̲h̲aik̲h̲ Aḥmad of Sirhind, who had for some time been placed in the prison of correction on account of his pretentiousness (literally, adorning his shop and selling himself) and immoderate language, was summoned to my presence, and I released him, giving him a dress of honour and Rs. 1,000 for expenses, and making him free to go or remain. He justly represented that his punishment had really been a valuable lesson to him, and that his desire was to wait on me.

On the 27th K̲h̲ūrdād apricots arrived94 (from Kabul). The picture-gallery in the garden had been ordered to be repaired; it was now adorned with pictures by master hands. In the most honoured positions were the likenesses of Humāyūn and of my father opposite to my own, and that of my brother S̲h̲āh ʿAbbās. After them were the likenesses of Mīrzā Kāmrān, Mīrzā Muḥammad Ḥakīm, S̲h̲āh Murād, and Sulṭān Dāniyāl. On the second storey (row?) were the likenesses of the Amirs and special servants. On walls of the outer hall the stages of the road to Kashmir were recorded in the order in which I had come to them. A poet fixed the date by this hemistich:

Pictures of kings of Solomon-like glory.95

On Thursday, the 4th of the Ilāhī month of Tīr, the Feast of *būriyā-kūbī*96 took place. On this day the Kashmir cherries came to an end. From the four trees of the Nūr-afzā garden, 1,500, and from other trees 500 had been plucked. I strictly ordered the officials of Kashmir to plant *s̲h̲āh-ālū* (cherry) trees in all the gardens. On this day Bhīm, s. Rānā Amar Singh, was honoured with the title of Raja, and Dilīr K., brother of the brave ʿIzzat K., was promoted to the mansab of 1,000 personal and 800 horse, Muḥammad Saʿīd, s. Aḥmad Beg K., to that of 600 personal and 400 horse, and Mukẖliṣ-ullah, his brother, to that of 500 personal and 250 horse. On Sayyid Aḥmad Ṣadr the mansab of 1,000, and on Mīrzā Ḥusain, s. Mīrzā Rustam Ṣafawī, that of 1,000 personal and 500 horse, were bestowed, and the last-named was despatched for duty to the Deccan. On Sunday, the 14th of the Divine month of Tīr, Ḥasan ʿAlī Turkmān was made Governor of Orissa, and his personal and horse mansab was raised to 3,000. On this day Bahādur K., Governor of Qandahar, sent offerings of nine Iraq horses, some nine pieces of gold brocade, some brocaded satin, and some marten97 skins, and other things; these were laid before me.

On Monday, the 15th, I rode to see the summer quarters of Tūsī-marg98 (?). Arriving in two matches at the foot of the *kotal*, on Wednesday, the 17th, I reached the top of the pass. For a distance of 2 koss very elevated ground was crossed with difficulty. From the top of the *kotal* to the *Īlāq* (summer quarters) was another koss of high and low land. Although here and there flowers of various colours had bloomed, yet I did not see so many as they had represented to me, and as I had expected. I heard that in this neighbourhood there was a very beautiful valley, and on Thursday, the 18th, I went to see it. Undoubtedly, whatever praise they might use in speaking of that flowery land would be permissible. As far as the eye reached flowers of all colours were blooming. There were picked fifty kinds of flowers in my presence. Probably there were others that I did not see. At the end of the day I turned my reins in order to return. That night an account was given in my presence of the siege of Ahmadnagar. Kẖān-Jahān told a strange tale, which I had also heard before, and it is written on account of its strangeness. At the time when my brother Dāniyāl was besieging the fort of Ahmadnagar, one day the garrison laid the gun *Malik-maidān*99 (king of the plain) against the Prince's camp, and fired it. The ball reached nearly to the Prince's tent; from that place it bounded (ricocheted), and went to the lodging of Qāẓī Bāyazīd, who was one of the Prince's companions, and fell there. They had tied up the Qāẓī's horse at a distance of 3 or 4 gaz. As the ball touched the ground, the horse's tongue100 was torn out by the root and fell on the ground. The ball was of stone, weighing 10 maunds as current in Hindustan, or 80 Khurasar maunds. The said gun is so large that a man can sit comfortably in it.

On this day I promoted Abū-l-Ḥasan, the chief Bakshi, to the mansab of 5,000 personal and 2,000 horse, Mubāriz K. to that of 2,000 personal and 1,700 horse. Bīzan (or Bīzhan) s. Nād ʿAlī, to that of 1,000 personal and 500 horse, and Amānat K. to that of 2,000 personal and 400 horse. On Thursday, the 25th, I gave Nawāzish K., s. Saʿīd K., the mansab of 3,000 personal and 2,000 horse, Himmat K. that of 2,000 personal and 1,500 horse, and Sayyid Yaʿqūb K., s. Sayyid Kamāl Bukhārī, that of 800 personal and 500 horse. Mīr ʿAlī ʿAskar,[101] s. Mīr ʿAlī Akbar Mūsawī, was dignified with the title of Mūsawī K. As I had repeatedly heard praise of the *Īlāq* of Kūrī-marg,[102] I felt much disposed to visit it at this time, and on Tuesday, the 7th Amurdād, rode in that direction. How shall I write its praise? As far as the eye could reach flowers of various hue were blooming, and in the midst of the flowers and verdure beautiful streams of water were flowing: one might say it was a page that the painter of destiny had drawn with the pencil of creation. The buds of hearts break into flower from beholding it. Undoubtedly there is no comparison between this and other *Īlāqs*, and it may be said to be the place most worth seeing in Kashmir.

In Hindustan (*i.e.*, Upper India) there is a bird called *Papīhā*,[103] of a sweet voice, which in the rainy season utters soul-piercing (*jān-sūz*, lit. soul-burning) laments. As the *koyal* lays its egg in the nest of the crow, and the latter brings up its young, so I have seen in Kashmir that the *papīhā* lays its egg in the nest of the *ghaughāʾī*[104] (ring-dove?) and the *ghaughāʾī* brings up its young.

On Thursday, the 17th, Fidāʾī K. was promoted to the mansab of 1,500 personal and 700 horse. On this day the ambassador of ʿIzzat[105] K., ruler of Ūrganj, by name Muḥammad Zāhid, came to the Court, and presented a petition, accompanied with some trifling presents, and recalled the existence of hereditary relations (lit., shook the chain of hereditary connection). I distinguished him with the eye of kindness, and on the spur of the moment gave the ambassador 10,000 darbs (Rs. 5,000) as a present, and ordered the officials of the buyūtāt (household) to prepare and send (by him) such things as he might ask for.

At this time a strange act of grace occurred to my son[106] Khān-Jahān (Lodī). He had become very ill from the madness of wine, and from the overpowering of this man-destroying intoxication things had come to such a pass that it threatened his precious life. Suddenly he reformed, and God directed him, and he made a vow that thereafter he would not defile the fringe of his lip with wine. Although I warned him that it was not good to give it up all at once, and that he should leave it off gradually, he would not consent, but gave it up manfully.

On the 25th of Amurdād Bahādur K., Governor of Qandahar, was promoted to the mansab of 5,000 personal and 4,000 horse, and on the 2nd of the Divine month of Shahrīwar, Mān Singh, s. Rāwat Shankar, to that of 1,500 and 800 horse, Mīr Ḥusāmu-d-dīn to that of 1,500 and 500 horse, and Karamu-llah, s. ʿAlī Mardān K.[107] to that of 600 with 300 horse.

As at this time I was much inclined to parti-coloured108 veined teeth, the great Amirs exerted themselves greatly in looking out for them. Of these, ʿAbdu-l-ʿAzīz K. Naqs͟hbandī sent a servant of the name of ʿAbdu-llah with a letter to K͟hwāja Ḥasan and K͟hwāja ʿAbdu-r-Raḥīm, ss. K͟hwāja Kalān Jūybārī, who are to-day the leading holy men of Transoxiana, containing a request for these things. By chance, K͟hwāja Ḥasan had a perfect tooth, exceedingly delicate, and immediately sent it with the aforesaid (servant) to the Court, which it reached this day. I was greatly pleased, and ordered them to send the value of Rs. 30,000 in choice goods to the K͟hwājas, a service for which Mīr Baraka Buk͟hārī was fixed upon. On Thursday, the 12th S͟hahrīwar, Mīr Mīrān obtained leave to take up the faujdārship of Mewāt, and his mansab, original and increased, was fixed at 2,000 with 1,500 horse. I gave him a special horse, with a dress of honour and a sword.

At this time it was made clear from a report of Sundar109 that Jauhar Mal, the rebel, had delivered his soul to the lords of hell (had died). It was also reported that a force sent against one of the Zamindars had abandoned the path of caution, and without fortifying the way of entrance and exit, or taking possession of the hill-tops, had entered into the fastnesses of the hills, and had fought without any good result. As the day drew towards its close, they had turned their reins with their object unaccomplished, and in turning back, had made every haste. Many people had been killed, especially those who would not put up with the disgrace of flight. They purchased martyrdom with their lives. Out of them S͟hāh-bāz K. Dalūmānī110 (?), which is a tribe of Lodī Afghans, sacrificed his life with a band of his servants and tribesmen. In truth he was a good servant, and had intelligence combined with modesty. Another report was that Jamāl Afg͟hān, Rustam, his brother, Sayyid Naṣīb Bārha, and some others had come in wounded. It was also reported that the siege (of Kāngṛa) had become a close one, and the affair was going hard with the besieged. They had sent (literally thrown out) men as mediators, and had asked for quarter. It was hoped that by the blessing of increasing fortune the fort would be subdued.

On Wednesday, the 18th of the same month (S͟hahrīwar), Dilāwar K. Kākar died a natural death. Beyond all the other Amirs of high rank, he combined valour with leadership and knowledge of affairs, and from the time when I was a prince carried away from all the ball of superiority in my service. He acted constantly with the perfection of sincerity and the jewel of doing right, and had thus arrived at the dignity of Amirship. In the end of his life God Almighty bestowed grace upon him, and the conquest of Kis͟htwār, which was an exemplary service, was accomplished by his courage. It is hoped he may be one of the pardoned. His sons and the others that he left behind him I exalted with all kinds of favours and patronage, and enrolled those of his people who were fit for mansabs amongst the servants of the Court. I ordered the rest, to remain as usual with his sons, so that his company might not be split up.

On this day Qūr Yasāwul came with a diamond that Ibrāhīm K. Fatḥ-jang had obtained from the Bengal mine, and waited on me. Wazīr K., dīwān of Bengal, who was an old servant of the Court, died a natural death.

On the night of Thursday, the 19th, the Kashmiris had lined with lamps both sides of the Bihat. It is an ancient custom that every year on this day everyone, whether rich or poor, whoever has a house on the bank of the river, should light lamps as on the Shab-i-barāt. I asked the brahmans the reason of this, and they said that on this day the fountain-head of the Jhelam was disclosed, and the custom had come down from old days that on this date must take place the feast of *Veth tarwāh*.[111] Veth means the Jhelam, and they call thirteen *tarwāh*; as this day is the 13th of Shawwāl, they light lamps. In this way they call it the *Veth tarwāh*. Undoubtedly the lamp-lighting was good. I sate in a boat and went round to see it. On this day the feast of my solar weighing took place, and according to the usual custom, I weighed myself against gold and other things, which I distributed among deserving people. The 51st year of the age of this suppliant at the throne of Allah came to an end; the 52nd year lit up the face of expectation. It is hoped that the period of my life will be spent in pleasing God. The entertainment of Thursday, the 26th, was held in the lodging of Āṣaf K. (Nūr-Jahān's brother), and that pillar of the Sultanate fulfilled the duties of homage, and of offerings, and thereby acquired eternal bliss.

On 1 Shahrīwar (about 11 August) ducks (*murghābi*) appeared on the Wular lake, and on the 24th of that month they appeared on the Dal lake. The following is the list of birds which are *not* met with in Kashmir:

LIST.

| | | | | |
|---|---|---|---|---|
| 1. | Crane[112] (*kulang*). | | 16. | Goose (*qāz*). |
| 2. | Sāras (*grus Antigone*). | | 17. | Konkla (*kokilā*, the black cuckoo?). |
| 3. | Peacock. | | 18. | Partridge (*durrāj*). |
| 4. | Bustard (*jarz or charz*). | | 19. | Shāvak (starling). |
| 5. | Stork (*laglag*). | | 20. | Nol-i-surkh (redbeak, [parrot]?). |

| | | | | |
|---|---|---|---|---|
| 6. | Bustard (*tughdarī*). | | 21. | Mūsīcha (wood-pigeon?). |
| 7. | Bustard (*tughdāgh*). | | 22. | Hariyal (green pigeon?). |
| 8. | Karwānak (kind of crane?). | | 23. | Dhīng (adjutant). |
| 9. | Zard-tilak (golden oriole?). | | 24. | Koyal (*Eudynamys Orientalis*). |
| 10. | Nuqra-pāy (silver-foot). | | 25. | Shakar-khwāra (sugar-eater, [parrot]?). |
| 11. | ʿAzam-pāy. | | 26. | Mahokhā (*cuculus castaneus*?). |
| 12. | Boza laglag (royal curlew). | | 27. | Mahirlāt (?). |
| 13. | Pelican (*hawāsil*). | | 28. | Dhanesh (hornbill). |
| 14. | Makisa (Ardea indica?). | | 29. | Gulchaṛī (quail?). |
| 15. | Baghlā (paddy-bird). | | 30. | Ṭaṭīrī, which the Turks call (blank in MSS.) and I have named *bad-āwāz*, "evil-voiced." (It is perhaps the sandpiper.) |

As the Persian names of some of these are not known, or rather, these birds don't exist in Persia (*Wilāyat*), I have written the Hindi names.[113] The names of the carnivorous and herbivorous animals that are *not* in Kashmir are as follows: The tiger, the panther (*yūz*), the rhinoceros,[114] the wild buffalo, the black antelope, the gazelle, the *kotāh pācha* (hog-deer), the *nīl-gāw*, the wild ass, the hare, the lynx, the wild cat, the *mūshak-i-karbalāʾī* (?),[115] the porpoise, and the porcupine.

On this day peaches came from Kabul by runners. The largest of these weighed 26 *tolas*,[116] or 65 *miṣqāls*. As long as their season lasted, such a number came that I gave them to most of the Amirs, and to the private servants fed from the royal table.

On Friday,117 the 27th, I went out to see Vīrnāg,118 the source of the Bihat. Going up the river 5 koss in a boat, I alighted at the village of Pāmpūr.

On this day unpleasant news came from Kis<u>h</u>twār. The details of this are that when Dilāwar K. conquered it and returned to Court, he left Naṣru-llah ʿArab, with some of the mansabdars to guard it. Naṣru-llah made two mistakes. One was that he treated the Zamindars and the people of the place harshly, and did not observe a conciliatory demeanour towards them. The second was that the forces sent as auxiliaries to him, in expectation of increase of mansab, asked him for leave to go to Court and transact their affairs. He yielded to their representations,119 and gave them leave one after the other. When only a small force was left with him, the Zamindars, whose hearts had been wounded by him, and were on the look out for a disturbance, found their opportunity and made an attack from all quarters. Having burnt the bridge by which the army had crossed, and by which assistance could come, they lighted the fire of disturbance and sedition. Naṣru-llah shut himself up, and for two or three days defended himself with the greatest difficulty (literally, with a thousand life-extractions). As he had no provisions, and they had closed the road, he determined to accept martyrdom, and manfully, with some of those who were with him, performed the dues of bravery and valour until most of his men were killed, and some became captives in the hands of destiny.

When this news reached my ear, I appointed Jalāl, s. Dilāwar K., on whose forehead the traces of bravery and ambition were manifest, and who had done good service in the conquest of Kis<u>h</u>twār, with the mansab of 1,000 personal and 600 horse, giving him the attendants of his father who were enrolled among the servants of the Court, and an army of the soldiers of Kashmir, with many of the Zamindars and men on foot with muskets, to assist him in overcoming that mob, doomed to a vile end. An order was also given that Rāja Sangrām, the Zamindar of Jammu, with his own men, should come in by the hill-road from Jammu. It is hoped that the rebels will quickly obtain the recompense for their deeds.

On Saturday, the 28th, I marched 4½ koss. Passing one koss beyond Kākāpūr, I came to the bank of the river. The *bang*120 (*bhang*) of Kākāpūr is well-known. It grows wild on the bank of the river in quantities. On Sunday, the 29th, I halted at the village of Panj Brāra.121 This village122 has been bestowed on my fortunate son S<u>h</u>āh Parwīz. His Vakils had prepared a small building and a little garden overlooking the river. In the neighbourhood of Panj Brāra there is a meadow (*julga*)123 exceedingly clean and pleasant, with seven lofty plane-trees in the middle of it, and a stream of the river flowing round it. The Kashmiris call it *Sathā Bhūlī*(?)124 It is one of the great resorts of Kashmir.

On this day arrived the news of the death of Khān Daurān,125 who died a natural death at Lahore. He had nearly reached ninety years of age. He was one of the brave men of the age and valiant in the battlefield. He combined bravery with leadership. He performed great services for the dynasty. It is hoped that he will be among the pardoned ones. He left four sons, but none of them was worthy to be his son. He left about Rs. 400,000 in cash and goods, which were given to his sons.

On Monday, the 30th, I first visited the fountain of Inch. This village had been given by my father to Rām Dās Kachhwāha,126 and he had erected buildings and basins at the spring. Undoubtedly, it is an exceedingly sweet and delightful place. Its water is perfectly clear and pure, and many fish swim in it.

VERSE.

So clear the water that the grains of sand at bottom

Could be counted at midnight by a blind man.

As I gave127 the village to my son Khān Jahān, he prepared an entertainment there, and presented offerings. I chose a trifle in order to please him. Half a koss from this spring, there is a fountain that they call Machhī Bhawan,128 above which Rāy Bihārī Chand, one of the servants of my father, built an idol-temple. The beauty of this spring is more than one can describe, and large trees of ancient years, planes, white and black poplars, have grown up round it. I passed the night at this place, and on Tuesday, the 31st, pitched at the fountain of Achval.129 The water of this spring is more plentiful than that of the other, and it has a fine waterfall. Around it lofty plane-trees and graceful white poplars, bringing their heads together, have made enchanting places to sit in. As far as one could see, in a beautiful garden, *Ja'farī* flowers had bloomed, so that one might say it was a piece of Paradise. On Wednesday, the 1st of Mihr, marching from Achval, I pitched camp near the fountain of Vīrnāg.130 On Thursday, the 2nd, the feast of cups was prepared at the spring. I gave my private attendants permission to sit down. Filling brimming cups, I gave them Kabul peaches as a relish, and in the evening they returned drunk (*mastān*, exhilarated?) to their abodes. This spring is the source of the River Bihat, and is situated at the foot of a hill, the soil of which, from the abundance of trees and the extent of green and grass, is not seen. When I was a prince, I had given an order that they should erect a building at this spring suitable to the place. It was now completed. There was a reservoir of an octagonal shape, forty-two yards in area and fourteen131 gaz in depth. Its water, from the reflection of the grass and plants on the hill, had assumed a hue of verdure. Many fish swam in it, round it halls with domes had been erected, and there was a garden in front of them. From the edge of the pond to the gate132 of the garden there was a canal 1 gaz in width and

180133 gaz in length, and 2 gaz in depth. Round the reservoir was a stone walk (*k͟hiyābān-i-sang*). The water of the reservoir was so clear that, notwithstanding its 4 gaz of depth, if a pea had fallen into it, it could have been seen. Of the trimness of the canal and the verdure of the grass that grew below the fountain, what can one write? Various134 sorts of plants and sweet-smelling herbs grew there in profusion, and among them was seen a stem (*būṭā*), which had exactly the appearance of the variegated tail of a peacock. It waved about in the ripple, and bore flowers here and there. In short, in the whole of Kashmir there is no sight of such beauty and enchanting character. It appears to me that what is upstream135 in Kashmir bears no comparison with (*i.e.*, is far superior to) what is downstream. One should stay some days in these regions, and go round them so as to enjoy oneself thoroughly. As the hour for marching was near, and snow was beginning to fall at the head of the passes, I had not the leisure to linger there, and was obliged to turn my rein towards the city. I gave an order that plane-trees should be planted on both sides, on the banks of the canal above mentioned. On Saturday, the 4th, I encamped at the spring of Loka Bhawan.136 This spring is also a pleasant spot. Although at present it is not equal to the others, if it were to be repaired it would be very good. I ordered them to construct a building worthy of the place, and to repair the reservoir in front of it. On the road I passed by a spring which they call Andha Nāg137 (blind fountain. *See* Iqbāl-nāma, 166). It is well known that the fish in this fountain are blind. I delayed a while near this spring, and threw in a net and caught twelve of the fish. Of these, three were blind and nine had eyes. Evidently the water of this spring has the effect of making them blind. Certainly this is not devoid of strangeness. On Sunday, the 5th, I again passed by the springs of Machhī Bhawan and Inch, and went to the city.

On Wednesday, the 8th, news arrived of the death of Hās͟him, s. Qāsim K. On Thursday, the 9th, Irādat K. was promoted to the governorship of Kashmir. Mīr Jumla in his place was chosen for the duty of *K͟hānsāmān*, and Muʿtamid138 K. to that of *ʿArẓ-muqarrir*. The mansab of 2,000 personal and 500 horse was ordered for Mīr Jumla. On the night of Saturday, the 11th, I entered the city. Āṣaf K. was appointed to the duty of Diwan of Gujarat. Sangrām, Raja of Jammu, was promoted to the mansab of 1,500 personal and 1,000 horse.

On this day I saw an unusual kind of fishing on the part of the fishermen of Kashmir. In a place where the water was up to a man's chest, they propelled two boats that were side by side, and so that at one end they were in contact, and at the other end they were 14 or 15 yards apart. Two boatmen held long poles in their hands, and sate on the outside edge of each boat (?) so as to regulate the space between each boat, and that they should proceed equally. Then ten or twelve boatmen got down into the water, and laying hold of the ends of the two boats that were joined139 together with their hands, trampled the bottom with their feet, and moved on. The fish which were between the boats wanted to get out of the narrow space, and came against the feet of the boatmen. Immediately one of the boatmen dived, and another one pressed upon his back, and with his two hands kept him from coming to the surface. The latter caught a fish and produced it. Some who are skilful in the art catch two fish with their hands, and bring them to the surface. Among them was an old boatman, who generally at each dive brought up two fish. This kind of fishing occurs at Panj Brāra,140 and is peculiar to the Jhelam. It is not used in ponds or in other streams. It also only takes place in the spring when the water is not cold or impetuous (*gazanda*, "biting"?).

On Monday, the 13th, the feast of the Dasahrā took place. According to the annual custom, they decorated the horses in the special stables, and those that had been entrusted to Amirs, and brought them out. At this time I experienced in myself a shortness of breath and difficulty in breathing. I hope that in the end, please God, it may all go well.

On Wednesday, the 15th, I went to make an autumn tour in the direction of Ṣafāpūr and the valley of Lār, situated downstream of the Kashmir River. In Ṣafāpūr there is a fine tank, and on the north side of it a hill full of trees. It being the beginning of autumn, it had a wonderful appearance, with trees of all colours, such as the planes, the apricot, and others, reflected in the middle of the tank, and very beautiful. Undoubtedly the beauties of autumn are not less than those of spring.

VERSE.

There's no exhilaration in decay, but to the eye

The glory of autumn is more brilliant than the Spring.

As the time was short and the hour of marching near, I took a short circuit and returned. These few days I passed pleasantly in catching141 ducks. One day, in the midst of the sport, a boatman caught and brought me a young *qarqara* (the demoiselle crane, *Ardea virgo*). It was very thin and miserable. It did not live longer than one night. The *qarqara* does not live in Kashmir. This had become ill and thin at the time of coming from, or going to, Hindustan, and fallen there.

On Friday news came of the death of Mīrzā Raḥmāndād, s. the K͟hān-k͟hānān. He died a natural death at Bālāpūr. It appears that he had been suffering from fever for some days. When he was recovering, the Deccanis one day appeared with an army. His elder brother, Dārāb K., mounted with the intention of fighting. When the news reached Raḥmān-dād, with great bravery, notwithstanding his weakness and failing health, he went to his brother. After he had beaten the enemy, he returned and in taking off his *jubba* (quilted waistcoat) was not sufficiently careful. The wind immediately caught him, and he was seized with convulsions, and his tongue became powerless to speak. He remained two or three days in this state and died. He was a good and brave youth, was fond of sword-play, and was very zealous. In every place it was his idea to display his skill with the sword. Although fire burns equally what is green and what is dry, yet it appeared very grievous to me, and what must it have been to his broken-hearted old father? Hardly had the wound from the calamity of Shāh-nawāz K. healed, when he received this fresh wound. I trust that God Almighty may give him patience and resignation.

On Thursday, the 16th, Khanjar K. was promoted to the mansab of 3,000 personal and horse, Qāsim K. to that of 2,000 personal and 1,000 horse, and Muḥammad Ḥusain, brother of Khwāja Jahān, who held the post of Bakhshī to the army of Kāngṛa, that of 800 personal and horse. On the night142 of Monday, the 27th of the Divine month of Mihr, after one watch and seven gharis had passed, the royal standards were raised auspiciously and happily to return towards Hindustan. As the saffron had blossomed, a march was made from the neighbourhood of the city to the village of Pāmpūr.143 In the whole country of Kashmir there is saffron only in this place. On Thursday, the 30th, the feast of cups was held in a saffron field. Groves on groves, and plains on plains were in bloom. The breeze in that place scented one's brain. The stem is attached (close?) to the ground. The flower has four petals, and its colour is that of a violet. It is of the size of a *champa* flower, and from the middle of it three stigmas of saffron grow. They plant the bulbs, and in a good year obtain 400 maunds of the current weight or 3,002144 Khurasan maunds. The custom is for half to go to the government, and half to the cultivators. A seer is bought and sold for Rs. 10. Occasionally its market price is more or less, and it is an established custom that they bring the saffron flowers plucked, and according to the plan they have adopted from of old, they take half its weight in salt as wages. There is no salt in Kashmir, and they bring it from Hindustan. Again, among the excellencies of Kashmir are the plumes of feathers (*kalgi*) and the hawks (*jānwar-i-shikāri*). As much as 10,700 feathers are yearly obtained. Hawks and falcons are taken in nets to the number of 260. It has also nest sparrow-hawks (*bāsha*),145 and the nest sparrow-hawk is not bad. On Friday, the 1st of the divine month of Ābān, marching from Pāmpūr, I pitched my camp at Khānpūr. As it was reported to me that Zambīl146 Beg, ambassador from my brother Shāh 'Abbās, had reached the neighbourhood of Lahore, a dress of honour and Rs. 30,000 for expenses were sent to him by Mīr Ḥusāmu-d-dīn s. 'Aẓudu-d-daula Injū.147 I ordered that whatever he might expend on entertaining the ambassador should be sent to him to the extent of Rs. 5,000.148 Before this I had directed that from Kashmir to the end of the hilly country buildings should be erected at each stage for the accommodation of myself and the ladies, for in the cold weather one should not be in tents. Although the buildings at this stage had been completed, as they were still damp and there was a smell of lime, we put up in tents. On Saturday, the 2nd, I halted at Kalampūr. As it had repeatedly been represented to me that in the neighbourhood of Hīrāpūr there was a waterfall[149] very high and wonderful, as it was 3 or 4 koss off on the left of the road, I hastened there to see it. What can be written in its praise? The water pours down in three or four gradations(?). I had never seen such a beautiful waterfall. Without hesitation, it is a sight to be seen, very strange and wonderful. I passed the time there in enjoyment till the third watch of the day, and filled my eye and heart with the sight; but in the cloudy and rainy season it is not devoid of wildness. After the third watch had passed, in the evening I rode back to Hīrāpūr,[150] and passed the night at that stage. On Monday, the 4th, crossing over the *kotal* of Bārī Brārī,[151] I chose Pīrpanjal, at the head of the *kotal*, for a halting-place. Of the roughnesses of the pass and the difficulties of this road what shall I write? It is difficult for thought even to cross it. In these last few days snow had repeatedly fallen, the hills had become white, and in the middle of the path in some places ice had formed, so that the hoof of a horse had no hold, and a rider could only pass with difficulty. God Almighty bestowed upon us His mercy, for it did not snow on this day. The advantage was for those who went on in front. Those who followed came in for snow. On Tuesday, the 5th, going by the pass of Pīrpanjal the camp was pitched at Poshāna. Although on this side there is a descent, yet as it is high, most of the people passed it on foot. On Wednesday, the 6th, we pitched at Bahramgalla. Near this village there is a waterfall and a very fine spring. According to orders, they had made a terrace for me to sit upon; indeed, this is a sight to be seen. I ordered that they should engrave on a stone tablet the date of the crossing, and place it on the top of the terrace (*ṣuffa*). Bī-badal K.[152] composed some couplets, and this mark of my fortune remains on the path of poetry as a memorial on the tablet of Time(?). There are two Zamindars on this road in whose charge are the arrangements for the traffic on it, and they are in reality the keys of the country of Kashmir. They call one Mahdī Nāyak and the other Ḥusain Nāyak. The charge of the road from Hīrāpūr to Bahramgalla is in their hands. Bahrām Nāyak, the father of Mahdī Nāyak, during the Kashmiri government, was an important person. When the authority passed to the imperial servants, Mīrzā Yūsuf K., during his government, made Bahrām Nāyak a traveller to the country of non-existence. It is now equally in the possession and charge of the two.[153] Although outwardly they are on good terms, they really bear great enmity towards each other. On this day Shaikh Ibn Yamīn, who was one of the old trusted servants, went to the neighbourhood of God's mercy (died).[154] On account of my great reliance on him, my opium and drinking water[155] were in his charge. On the night when we were encamped above the *kotal* of

Pīrpanjal, the tents and furniture had not arrived. He was rather infirm and the cold affected him, and he became cramped so that he could not speak. He remained alive for two days in this state and then died. I gave over the private opium to Khawāṣṣ K., and the *āb-dār-khāna* (the water department) to Mūsawī K. On Thursday, the 7th, the village of Thāna156 became the encamping place. Many monkeys (*maimūn*) were seen in Bahramgalla, and from that stage a great difference was apparent in the climate, the language, the clothing, the animals, and whatever properly belongs to a warm country. The people here speak both Persian and Hindi. Evidently Hindi is their real language, and they have acquired Kashmiri on account of the proximity of Kashmir. Briefly, one enters India at this place. The women do not wear woollen clothing, and like Indian women, they wear nose-rings.

On Friday, the 8th, Rājaur was the camping-ground. The people of this country were in old times Hindus, and the landholders are called Rajas. Sulṭān Fīrūz made them Muhammadans, but they are still called Rajas. They still have the marks of the times of ignorance. One of these is that just as some Hindu women burn themselves along with their husbands (bodies), so these women (the Rājaur women) are put into the grave along with their (dead) husbands. I heard that recently they put alive into the grave a girl of ten or twelve along with her (dead) husband, who was of the same age. Also, when a daughter is born to a man without means, they put her to death by strangulation.157 They ally themselves with Hindus, and both give and take girls. Taking them is good, but giving them, God forbid! I gave an order that hereafter they should not do such things, and whoever was guilty of them, should be capitally punished. There is a river at Rājaur. Its water during the rainy season becomes much poisoned. Many of the people there get a swelling (*būghma*) under the throat, and are yellow and weak. The rice of Rājaur is much158 better than the rice of Kashmir. There are self-grown and sweet-scented violets in this skirt of the hills.

On Sunday, the 10th, I encamped at Naushahra. At this place, by order of my father, they had built a stone fort, and there is constantly here, by way of a station (*thāna*), a body of men from the governor of Kashmir. On Monday the camp was at Chaukī Hattī. A *chela* named Murād had exerted himself to complete the buildings at this place, and had done it well. In the middle of the royal abode there was a fine terrace, superior to those of other stages. I increased his mansab. On Tuesday, the 12th, I halted at Bhīmbar. Passing this day out of *kotals* and hills, we entered the broad plains of Hindustan. The hunters had previously been dispatched to form *qamurghas*, so as to prepare *jirgas* (hunting rings) in Bhīmbar and Girjhāk159 and Makhiyāla. On Wednesday and Thursday they drove in the game. On Friday I rejoiced in a hunt. Hill *qūchqār*,160 etc., to the number of 56 head were taken. On this day Rāja Sārang Deo, who was one of the intimate attendants, was promoted to the mansab of 800 personal and 400 horse. On Saturday, the 16th, I went towards Girjhāk, and in five marches encamped on the bank of the Bihat. On Thursday, the 21st, I hunted in the hunting-ring of Girjhāk. Less game than usual was taken, and I was not satisfied. On Monday, the 25th, I hunted with much enjoyment in the hunting-ring of Makhiyāla,161 thence in ten stages I encamped at the stage of the hunting-place of Jahāngīrābād. When I was prince, this was my hunting-place. Afterwards, I founded a village with my own name, and erecting a small building, placed it in charge of Sikandar Muʿīn, who was one of my best huntsmen. After I came to the throne I made a pargana of it, and bestowed it as a jagir on him. I gave an order that they should construct there a building as a royal residence, with a tank and a minaret162 (manāra). After his death this pargana was given in jagir to Irādat K., and the charge of the buildings was given to him. It has now been handsomely completed. Undoubtedly the tank was very broad,163 and in the middle there is a delightful building. Altogether the buildings here cost Rs. 1,50,000. Really it is a kingly hunting-place. On Thursday and Friday, having halted, I enjoyed myself with various kinds of sport. Qāsim K., who was honoured with the charge of Lahore, had the good fortune to pay his respects to me, and presented 50 muhars.

In one march after this stage I encamped at the garden of Mūmin ʿIsẖq-bāz,164 which is on the bank of the Lahore River (the Ravi), and has some lofty plane-trees and handsome cypresses. It is certainly a rare garden. On Monday, the 9th of the Divine month of Āẕar, corresponding with the 5th Muḥarram of A.H. 1030165 (20 November, 1620), mounting an elephant of the name of Indra, I went towards the city, scattering coin as I proceeded. After three watches and two gharis of day had passed, at the selected auspicious hour, having entered the royal residence, I alighted happily and auspiciously at the building recently brought to completion and finished handsomely by the exertions of Maʿmūr K. Without exaggeration, charming residences and soul-exciting sitting places had been erected in great beauty and delicacy, adorned and embellished with paintings by rare artists. Pleasant green gardens with all kinds of flowers and sweet-scented herbs deceived the sight.

VERSE.166

From head to foot, wherever I look,

A glance plucks at the heart's skirt (saying),

"This is the place" (to stop at).

Altogether, there had been expended on these buildings the sum of Rs. 700,000 or 23,000 current tumans of Persia.167

On this day the joy-enhancing news of the conquest of the fort of Kāngṛa rejoiced our mind. In thankfulness for this great boon and important victory, which was one of the renewed favours of the Bestower of Gifts, I bowed the head of humility at the throne of the merciful Creator, and beat with loud sounds the drum of gladness and pleasure. Kāngṛa is an ancient fort to the North of Lahore, situated in the midst of the hill country, famous for its strength and the difficulty of conquering it. Who was the founder of this fort God only knows. The belief of the Zamindars of the province of the Panjab is that, during this period the said fort has never passed to any other tribe, and no stranger has stretched out to it the hand of dominion. Wisdom is from Allah! But certainly from the time when the voice of Islam and the sound of the established religion of Muḥammad reached Hindustan, not one of the Sultans of lofty dignity has obtained the victory over it. Sulṭān Fīrūz-s͟hāh, with all his power and might, himself went to conquer it, and besieged it for a long time. As he knew that the strength of the fort was such that as long as the means for holding it and provisions were with the besieged, victory over them was unattainable, *nolens volens* he was contented with the coming of the Raja to pay his respects to him, and withheld his hand. They say that the Raja prepared an offering and an entertainment, and at his request took the Sultan inside the fort. The Sultan, after going round and inspecting it, said to the Raja that to bring a king like him inside the fort was not according to the dictates of caution. What could he do if the body of men who were in attendance were to attack him and take possession of the fort? The Raja made a sign to his men, and instantaneously an army of valiant men armed and accoutred, came out from a concealed place and saluted the Sultan. The Sultan became suspicious and anxious about an attack from these men, and suspected some stratagem. The Raja came forward and kissed the ground of service, and said: "I have no thought but that of service and obedience, but as has been spoken by the auspicious tongue, I observe far-sighted caution, for all times are not the same." The Sultan applauded him. The Raja, having accompanied him for some stages, obtained leave to return. After this, whoever sat on the throne of Delhi sent an army to subdue Kāngṛa, but the thing went no further. My revered father also sent a large army once under the leadership of Ḥusain Qulī K., who, after approved service, was honoured with the title of K͟hān Jahān. Whilst the siege was in progress, the outbreak of Ibrāhīm Ḥusain Mīrzā took place. That ingrate fled from Gujarat, and raised the flag of rebellion and calamity towards the Panjab. K͟hān Jahān was compelled to raise the siege, and to turn to extinguish the flame of his sedition. Thus the acquisition of the fort fell into the knot of delay. The thought was continually lurking in the royal mind: "The longed-for Fair one does not show her face from the secret place of Destiny." When by the Grace of the Glorious God the throne of the State was adorned by the existence of this suppliant, this was one of the holy wars which I considered incumbent on me. In the first instance I dispatched Murtaẕā K., who was governor of the Panjab, with a force of brave men skilled in war, to conquer the fort. This important matter had not been completed when Murtaẕā K. attained to the mercy of God (died). After this Jauhar Mal,168 s. Rāja Bāso, undertook this duty. I sent him, giving him the command of the army. That wicked one, taking to evil revolt and ingratitude, committed sin, and dispersion found its way into that army, and the acquisition of the fort fell into the knot of delay. No long time elapsed before that ingrate received the recompense of his deeds and went to hell, as has been described in its own place.169 In fine, at this time K͟hurram undertook that duty, and sent his own servant Sundar170 with all haste, and many of the royal servants obtained leave to go to his support. On the 16th S͟hawwāl, A.H. 1029, (5 September, 1620), the armies, having invested the fort, erected batteries. Looking to the ways of entrance into and exit from the fort with the eye of caution, they closed the road for the entrance of provisions. By degrees the besieged became straitened, and when there remained in the fort no grain that they could eat, for four months more they boiled dry grasses171 with salt and ate it. When destruction was imminent, and no hope of escape was left, they asked for quarter and surrendered the fort.

On Thursday, the 1st Muḥarram, A.H. 1030,172 Hijrī (16 November, 1620), the victory unattainable by all preceding Sultans of lofty dignity, and which appeared distant to the short-sighted, God Almighty of His own grace and mercy granted to this suppliant. The troops, who had displayed praiseworthy activity in this service, were exalted according to their exertions and fitness by increase of mansab and dignities.

On Thursday, the 11th, I went, at the request of K͟hurram, to his newly-built house. I took those of his offerings that pleased me. Three elephants were placed in the private stud. On the same day I appointed ʿAbdu-l-ʿAzīz K. Naqs͟hbandī to the faujdārship of the district of Kāngṛa, and his mansab was fixed at 2,000 personal and 1,500 horse. I gave a private elephant to Iʿtiqād K. Alf K. Qiyām-k͟hānī K. obtained leave to take charge of the fort of Kāngṛa, and his mansab, original and increased, was fixed at 1,500 personal and 1,000 horse. S͟haik͟h Faiẕu-llah, son-in-law of Murtaẕā K., was appointed in company with him to stay at the top of the fort (*bālā-i-qilʿa*).

On the night of Saturday, the 13th of the same month, a lunar eclipse took place. Having performed the dues of humility at the throne of the highest and most powerful God, cash and goods were distributed by way of charity among the faqīrs and poor, and deserving people. On this day Zambīl Beg, ambassador of the ruler of Persia, had the good fortune to kiss the threshold. After performing salutation, he laid before me the gracious letter of that brother of high degree, containing expressions of sincerity and perfect friendship. He presented 12 *'Abbāsī*[173] (coin) as *naẕar*, four horses with trappings, three *tūyg͟hūn* (white) falcons, five mules, five camels, nine bows, and nine scimitars. The Shah had given him leave, in company with K͟hān 'Ālam, but for certain necessary matters he could not come with him. On this day he arrived at Court. I presented him with a superb dress of honour, with a plume and a jewelled turban fringe, and a jewelled dagger. Wiṣāl Beg and Ḥājī Ni'mat, who had come with him, were honoured by waiting on me. Amānu-llah, s. Mahābat K., was promoted to the mansab, original and increased, of 2,000 and 1,500 horse. At the request of Mahābat K., I added 300 horse to the mansab of Mubāriz K. Afg͟hān, and brought it up to 2,000 personal and 1,700 horse. One hundred horse were also added to the mansab of Kabak[174] (?). I sent winter dresses of honour to 'Abdu-llah K. and Las͟hkar K. At the request of Qāsim K. I went to his garden in the neighbourhood of the city, and in the course of the procession, scattered 10,000 *charans* (4-anna pieces). Out of his offerings I selected one ruby and one diamond, and some cloths.

On the night of Sunday, the 21st, the advanced camp proceeded auspiciously and happily towards Agra. Barq-andāz K. was appointed superintendent of artillery with the army of the Deccan. S͟haik͟h Isḥāq (Isaac) was appointed to duty at Kāngṛa. The brother of Allah-dād, the Afghan, I released from prison, and made him a present of Rs. 10,000. I gave also a *tūyg͟hūn* falcon to K͟hurram. On Thursday, the 26th, the usual entertainment took place. The presents from the ruler of Persia, which had been sent by Zambīl Beg, were laid before me. I gave an elephant to Sulṭān Ḥusain, and made a present of Rs. 1,000 to Mullā Muḥammad Kas͟hmīrī.[175] The mansab of Sardār Afg͟hān, at the request of Mahābat K., was fixed at 1,000 personal and 400 horse. As Rāja Rūp Chand of Gwalior[176] had been very active in his service at Kāngṛa, an order was given to the chief diwans to hand over half of his native place to him in free gift, and the remaining half as a *tank͟hwāh* jagir.

On the 3rd I demanded in marriage for my son S͟hahriyār the daughter's daughter[177] of Madāru-l-mulk I'timādu-d-daula, and sent Rs. 100,000 in cash and goods by way of *sāchaq* (dowry given as part of the marriage rites). Most of the Amirs and the chief servants went to his house with gifts. He prepared a grand entertainment with much ceremony. It is hoped that it may be auspicious to him. As that Chief of the State had erected lofty buildings, and highly decorated bowers in his house, he invited me to an entertainment. I went there with the ladies. He had prepared a great feast, and laid before me appropriate offerings of all kinds. In order to please him, I took such as I approved of. On this day Rs. 50,000 were presented to Zambīl Beg, the ambassador. The mansab of Zabar-dast K. was fixed at 1,000 personal and

500 horse, original and increased. Maqṣūd, brother of Qāsim K., was promoted to the mansab of 500 personal and 300 horse, and Mīrzā Dakhanī, s. Mīrzā Rustam, to that of 500 personal and 200 horse.

At this auspicious time[178] when the standards of victory and conquest were in Kashmir, the province of eternal spring, happily employed in sight-seeing and sport, representations constantly came from the officials in the Southern territories to the effect that when the victorious standards went to a distance from the centre of the Khalifate, the rulers of the Deccan, owing to their wickedness, broke their promises and raised their heads by giving trouble and exciting sedition, and placing their feet beyond their own boundary, took possession of many of the districts of Ahmadnagar and Berar. It was constantly reported that the chief object of these evil-fortuned ones was to plunder and ruin the cultivated fields and the grazing-lands. When at the first time the world-opening standards had proceeded to the conquest of the regions of the south and the overthrow of that band, and K̲h̲urram, with the vanguard, had gone to Burhanpur, they, by feline tricks suitable to such seditious people, made him their intercessor and evacuated the royal dominions. They also sent by way of tribute large sums in cash and goods, and promised that they would not let loose from their hands the rope of service, and would not place their feet beyond the boundary of respect, as has been recorded in the preceding pages. At the request of K̲h̲urram, I had halted for a few days at the Fort of S̲h̲ādī'ābād Māndū, and at his intercession, and on their humiliation and bewailing, they were pardoned.

As they had now broken their agreement through evil disposition and quarrelsomeness, and had turned back from the way of obedience and service, I sent off the hosts of good fortune again under his leadership, that they might receive retribution for their evil deeds, and be an example to all those of crooked fortune and turned heads. But as the important business of Kāngṛa had been entrusted to him, he had sent most of his experienced men there. For some days, accordingly, he could not arrange the matter. At last, report followed on report one after another, that the enemy had gathered strength, and that nearly 60,000 vagabond horsemen had collected together and taken possession of royal territory, and wherever there were posts, had removed them, and joined together in the town of Mahakar. For three months the imperialists had passed their days in strife and fighting with their rascally enemies, and during this time three pitched battles had taken place, and each time the self-sacrificing servants (of the State) had proved superior to the evil-fortuned rebels. As grain and provisions could not reach the camp by any road, and the enemy was plundering on all sides of the army of good fortune, a great scarcity of grain resulted, and the animals were in bad plight. Having no choice, they came down from the Bālāg̲h̲āt, and took up their position at Bālāpūr. The rebels, waxing valiant in their pursuit, engaged in plundering in the neighbourhood of Bālāpūr. Of the servants of the Court 6,000 or 7,000 horsemen, well mounted, were selected, and they made an attack on the enemy's camp. They (the enemy) numbered about 60,000 cavalry. Briefly, a great fight took place, and their camp was plundered. Having killed and taken prisoners many of them, they returned in safety and with plunder. When they turned back those wretches again attacked them from all sides, and they came on, fighting as far as the camp. On both sides about 1,000 were killed. After this fight they (the imperialists) remained about four months at Bālāpūr. When the scarcity of grain became excessive, many of the qulaqchīs (servants) ran away and joined the enemy, and constantly bands of them, taking to the road of disloyalty, were enrolled among the rebels. On this account, not considering it advisable to delay any longer, they (the imperialists) came to Burhanpur. Again, those wretches followed them and besieged Burhanpur, and they were six months shut up there. Many parganas of the provinces of Berar and Khandesh passed into their possession, and they stretched out the hand of oppression over the cultivators and poor, and engaged in collecting the revenues. As the army had undergone great hardships and the animals had fallen into bad condition, they could not leave the city to inflict substantial punishment. Thus the pride and conceit of those short-sighted ones became greater. Just at this time the royal standards returned to the capital, and by the grace of God Kāngṛa was conquered.

Accordingly, on Friday, the 4th of Dai, I despatched K͟hurram in that direction, bestowing on him a dress of honour, a sword, and an elephant. Nūr Jahān Begam also gave him an elephant. I told him after he had conquered the province of the Deccan he should take as a reward two179 crores of dams from the conquered country. 650 mansabdars, 1,000 *Aḥadīs*, 1,000 Turkish musketeers, and 1,000180 gunners on foot, in addition to the 31,000 horse already in that quarter, and a large force of artillery, and many elephants, were appointed to accompany him. I also gave him a crore of rupees for the expenses of the victorious army. The servants (of the Court) who were appointed on this duty received each, according to his standing as a reward, horses, elephants, and dresses of honour.

At the same auspicious hour and favourable time, the standards of the expedition were turned toward Agra, and a halt was made at Naus͟hahr.181 Muḥammad Riẓā Jābirī was appointed Diwan to Bengal, and K͟hwāja Mulkī to the post of Bakhshi in the same, and were promoted in mansab. Jagat Singh, s. Rānā Karan, came from his native place, and had the good fortune to kiss the threshold. On the 6th of the same month the open space on the bank of Rāja Todar Mal's tank182 became the alighting place of the Court of good fortune. Here I halted for four days. On this day some of the mansabdars who had obtained leave to go to the conquest of the Deccan were promoted as follows: Zāhid K. held the mansab of 1,000 and 400 horse; he received that of 1,000 and 500 horse; Hardī Narāyan Hāḍā I promoted to 900 and 600 horse, original and increased; Ya'qūb, s. Khān Daurān, was given that of 800 and 400 horse, and in the same manner a great number of the servants of the State received increase of mansab according to their capabilities. Mu'tamid K. was appointed to the post of Bakhshi and newswriter to the royal army, and was honoured with a *tūgh*. The offering of Lachmī Chand, Raja of Kumaon, consisting of hawks and falcons and other hunting animals, was brought before me. Jagat Singh, s. Rānā Karan, obtained leave to proceed as an auxiliary to the army of the Deccan, being presented with a private horse and saddle. Rāja Rūp Chand, having been honoured with the gift of an elephant and a horse, took leave to go to his jagir. On the 12th my son Khān Jahān (Lodī) was made governor of Multan, and was given leave. There were conferred on him a complete dress together with a *nādirī* (a robe of Jahāngīr's invention), a jewelled dagger, a special elephant with trappings, a female elephant, a special horse of the name of Khadang (*i.e.*, Arrow), and a pair of hawks. Sayyid Hizabr K. held the mansab of 1,000 and 400 horse. Increasing these by 500 and 200 horse, I gave him leave to accompany Khān Jahān. Muḥammad Shafī' was appointed Bakhshi and newswriter to the Subah of Multan. Bhawāl (or Bahwāl), who was one of the old servants, was made *Ashraf-i-tūp-khāna* (head of the artillery?), and received the title of Rāy. On the 13th the bank of the river Gobindwāl became the camp of the army of prosperity, and a halt of four days was made. A special elephant called Jai Singh, with a female, were given to Mahābat K., and sent to him by Ṣafiyyā his servant. Robes of honour were also forwarded to the Amirs of the Subah of Bangash by 'Isā Beg.

On the 17th[183] the feast of my lunar weighing took place. As Mu'tamid K. had been appointed Bakhshi to the army of the Deccan and given leave, the post of 'Arẓ-muqarrir was given to Khwāja Qāsim. Mīr Sharaf was made Bakhshi of the Aḥadīs, and Fāẓil Beg made Bakhshi of the Panjab. As Bahādur K., governor of Qandahar, in consequence of a disease in his eyes, had requested to be allowed to kiss the threshold, entrusting the government of Qandahar this day to 'Abdu-l-'Azīz K., an order was issued to Bahādur K., that when he arrived he should hand over the fort to him and come himself to Court. On the 21st of the same month I took up my quarters at Nūr-sarāy.[184] At this spot the Vakils of Nūr Jahān Begam had built a lofty house, and made a royal garden. It was now completed. On this account the Begam, having begged for an entertainment, prepared a grand feast, and by way of offering, with great pains produced all kinds of delicate and rare things. In order to please her, I took what I approved. I halted two days at this place. It was settled that the officials of the Panjab should send Rs. 200,000, in addition to the Rs. 60,000 already ordered for provisions for the fort of Qandahar. Mīr Qiwāmu-d-dīn, the diwan of the Panjab, obtained leave to go to Lahore, and received a dress of honour. Qāsim K., with a view to punish the seditious in the neighbourhood of Kāngṛa, and to preserve order in those regions, was given leave to go, and I presented him with a special *nādirī*, a horse, a dagger, and an elephant. His mansab, original and increased, was fixed at 2,000 personal and 500 horse. At his request, I allowed Rāja Sangrām (of Jammu) to proceed to that region, conferring on him a robe of honour, a horse, and an elephant.

On Thursday the camp was pitched outside the town of Sihrind. I halted one day, and amused myself with going round the garden. On Sunday, the 4th, Abū-l-Ḥasan was sent on service for the conquest of the Deccan. A dress of honour, with a *nādirī*, a special shawl, an elephant named Ṣubḥ-dam (breath of morn), a horsetail banner, and drums, being given him. I gave leave to Mu'tamid K., presenting him with a dress of honour, and a special horse called Ṣubḥ-i-ṣādiq (the true dawn). On the 7th of the same month the bank of the river Sarasatī (Saraswatī) was the place of encampment of good fortune in the neighbourhood of the *qaṣba* of muṣṭafā'ābād. The next day I encamped at Akbarpūr,185 whence I sat in a boat on the river Jumna, to reach my object. On this day 'Izzat K. Chāchī,186 with the faujdār of that region, had the good fortune to kiss the threshold. Giving Muḥammad S̲h̲afī' leave to proceed to Multan, I presented him with a horse, a dress of honour, and a *nūr-s̲h̲āhī muhar*, and sent by him a special turban (*chīra*) to K̲h̲ān Jahān, my son (*farzand*).

Thence, in five marches, I reached the pargana of Kirāna, the native country of Muqarrab K., and the Court encamped there. By way of offering, his Vakils laid before me 91 rubies187 and 4 diamonds, 1,000 gaz of *mik̲h̲mal* (satin) as a *pā-andāz* (foot-carpet), with a petition from him, presenting also 100 camels as charity. I ordered them to be distributed among deserving people. From this place, in five marches Delhi became the halting-place of the standards of good fortune I sent It'imādu-d-daula to my fortunate son S̲h̲āh Parwīz with a special *farjī* (a dress), for him, and it was settled that he should return in the space of one month and wait on me. Having halted for two days at Salīmgaṛh, on Thursday, the 23rd, I passed through the district of Delhi with the intention of hunting in the pargana of Pālam, and halted on the bank of the S̲h̲amsī tank. On the road I scattered 4,000 *charans* (Rs. 1,000) with my own hand. Twenty-two elephants, male and female, had arrived from Bengal as an offering from Allah-yār, s. Iftik̲h̲ār K., and were passed before me.

Ẕū-l-Qarnain188 obtained leave to proceed to the faujdārship of Sambhar. He is the son of Iskandar, the Armenian, and his father had the good fortune to be in the service of 'Ars̲h̲-ās̲h̲yānī (Akbar), who gave him in marriage the daughter of ʿAbdu-l-Ḥayy,[189] the Armenian, who was in service in the royal harem. By her he had two sons. One was Ẕū-l-Qarnain, who was intelligent and fond of work, and to him, during my reign, the chief diwans had entrusted the charge of the government salt works at Sambhar, a duty which he performed efficiently. He was now appointed to the faudjarship of that region. He is an accomplished composer of Hindi songs. His method in this art was correct, and his compositions were frequently brought to my notice and were approved. Laʿl Beg[190] was selected for the daroghahship of the records in the place of Nūru-d-dīn Qulī. I passed four days pleasantly in sporting in the neighbourhood of Pālam and returned to Salīmgaṛh. On the 29th, 19 elephants, 2 eunuchs,[191] 1 slave, 41[192] fighting cocks, 12 bullocks, and 7 buffaloes were brought before me as offerings from Ibrāhīm K. Fatḥ-jang. On Thursday, the 30th, corresponding with the 25th Rabīʿu-l-awwal, the ceremony of my lunar weighing[193] was performed. I had sent Koka K. to the K͟hān-k͟hānān, and forwarded some messages by him. On this day a petition from him arrived. Mīr Mīrān, who had been appointed to the faujdārship of Mewāt, on this day came and paid his respects, and was dignified with the governorship of Delhi, in the room of Sayyid Bahwa.

On this day Āqā Beg and Muḥibb ʿAlī, the envoys of the ruler of Persia, paid their respects, and presented a loving letter from that noble brother, together with a black and white plume (*kalgī-i-ablaq*), valued by the jewellers at Rs. 50,000. My brother also sent me a ruby weighing 12 tānks,[194] which had belonged to the jewel-chamber of M. Ulug͟h Beg, the successor of M. S͟hāh-ruk͟h. In the course of time, and by the revolutions of fate, it had come into the hands of the Ṣafawī family. On this ruby there were engraved in the Nask͟h[195] character the words: "Ulug͟h Beg b. M. S͟hāh-ruk͟h Bahādur b. Mīr Tīmūr Gūrgān." My brother, S͟hāh ʿAbbās, directed that in another corner they should cut the words:

Banda-i-S͟hāh-i-Wilāyat[196] ʿAbbās

"The slave of the King of Holiness, ʿAbbās."

in the *Nastaʿlīq* character. He had this ruby inserted in a *jīg͟ha* (turban ornament), and sent to me as a souvenir. As the ruby bore the names of my ancestors, I took it as a blessing for myself, and bade Saʿīdā, the superintendent of the goldsmith's department, engrave in another corner the words "Jahāngīr S͟hāh b. Akbar S͟hāh," and the current date. After some days, when the news of the conquest of the Deccan arrived, I gave that ruby to K͟hurram, and sent it to him.

On Saturday, the 1st of Isfandārmuẕ, I marched from Salīmgaṛh, and going first to the glorious mausoleum of Humāyūn (may the lights of Allah be his testimony!), performed the dues of humility, and presented 2,000 quarter rupees (*charan*) to those who sat in seclusion in that pure cemetery. I encamped twice on the bank of the Jumna in the environs of the city. Sayyid Hizabr K.,[197] who had been appointed an auxiliary to Kh̲ān Jahān, was sent off with the distinction of a dress of honour, a sword, a dagger, a horse, and a standard. Sayyids ʿĀlim and ʿAbdu-l-Hādī, his brothers, were also each honoured with a horse and a dress of honour. Mīr Baraka Bukh̲ārī was allowed to go to Transoxiana. I entrusted Rs. 10,000 to him, 5,000 of them to be conveyed to Kh̲wāja Ṣāliḥ Dihbīdī, who from his fathers was one of the well-wishers of this State, and the other 5,000 to be divided among the *mujāwirs* (custodians) attached to the tomb of Tīmūr (may the lights of Allah be his testimony!). I also gave a special turban (*chīra*) to Mahābat K., and sent it to him by Mīr Baraka. I also ordered Mīr Baraka to make every effort to procure mottled fish-teeth, and to procure them from any possible quarter, and at any price.

I went by boat from Delhi, and in six stages reached the plain of Brindāban. I gave an elephant to Mīr Mīrān, and permitted him to go to Delhi. Zabardast K. was selected to be Mīr Tūzuk (master of ceremonies) in the place of Fidāʾī K., and I presented him with a special shawl (*parm-narm*). Next day, Gokul[198] was the place of encampment. At this stage, Lash̲kar K., the governor of Agra, ʿAbdu-l-Wahhāb Dīwān, Rāja Nath Mal, Kh̲iẓr K. Fārūqī, ruler (deposed) of Āsīr and Burhanpur, Aḥmad K., his brother, the Qāẓī, the Muftī, and other chief men of the city (of Agra), had the good fortune to wait[199] on me. On the 11th I halted auspiciously at the Nūr-afsh̲ān[200] garden, which is on the opposite side of the Jumna. As the auspicious hour for entering the city had been fixed for the 14th, I halted here, and at the selected auspicious hour proceeded to the fort, and entered the palace happily and victoriously. The propitious journey from Lahore to Agra was accomplished in the period of two months and two[201] days, with 49 marches and 21 halts. No day either of marching or halting, on land or water, passed without sport. 114 deer, 51 duck, 4 heron (*kārwānak*), 10 black partridge (*durrāj*), and 200 *bodna*[202] were taken on the way.

As Lash̲kar K. had satisfactorily performed his duties at Agra, I increased his mansab by 1,000 personal and 500 horse, and made it 4,000 personal and 2,500 horse, and sent him as an auxiliary to the army of the Deccan. Saʿīdā, superintendent of the goldsmith's department, was dignified with the title of Bī-badal K. Four horses, some silver ornaments and cloths, which the ruler of Persia had sent me by Āqā Beg and Muḥammad Muḥibb ʿAlī, were produced before me on this day. The entertainment of Thursday, the 20th, took place in the Nūr-manzil garden. I gave a present of Rs. 1,00,000 to my son Sh̲ahriyār. Muẓaffar K., according to order, came from Thatta, and had the good fortune to wait on me. He offered 100 muhars and Rs. 100. Lashkar K. produced a ruby as an offering. It was valued at Rs. 4,000. A special horse of the name of Muṣāḥib (companion) was given to ʿAbdu-llah K. ʿAbdu-s-Salām, s. Muʿaẓẓam K., having arrived from Orissa, had the good fortune to wait on me: 100 muhars and Rs. 100 were laid before me as his *naẓar*. The mansab of Dūst Beg, s. Tūlak K., was fixed at 900 personal and 400 horse. The entertainment of Thursday, the 27th, was held in the Nūr-afshān garden. A special dress of honour was given to M. Rustam, and a horse to his son, who was called Dakhanī, and a special horse and an elephant to Lashkar K.

On Friday, the 28th, I went to hunt to the village of Samonagar, and returned at night. Seven Persian horses, with their trappings, were laid before me as an offering from Āqā Beg and Muḥibb ʿAlī. I presented Zambīl Beg, the ambassador, with a Nūr-jahānī muhar of the weight of 100 *tolas*, and gave a jewelled penholder to Ṣādiq K., the chief Bakhshi. I also gave a village[203] in Agra, by way of *inʿām*, to Khiẓr K. Fārūqī. In this year 85,000 *bīghās* of land, 3,325 *khar-wārs* (of rice), 4 villages, 2 ploughs (of land), and a garden, Rs. 2,327, 1 *muhar*, 6,200 *darbs* (half rupees), 7,880 quarter rupees (*charan*), 1,512 *tolas* of gold and silver, and 10,000 dams from the treasury were given, in my presence, as alms to faqīrs and necessitous people. Thirty-eight elephants, of the value of Rs. 2,41,000,[204] were presented as offerings, and were placed in the special elephant house, whilst 51 were presented by me to the great Amirs and the servants of the Court.

---

1 Each sidereal hour being equal to 2½ gharis. ↑

2 *Sag-i-ābī*. Probably otters are meant, as a name for them is *pānī kuttā* ("water-dogs"). But in the dictionaries *sag-i-ābī* is given as meaning the beaver. The otter occurs in Kashmir, and is known as *wudar*. Lawrence, Valley of Kashmir, 111. ↑

3 Properly Būlīyāsa. See Stein, A.S.B.J., for 1899, p. 85. It is the Peliasa of the maps. Later on, Jahāngīr indicates its position by saying that it is 11 koss on the Kashmir side of the Kishan Gangā. ↑

4 That is, I presume, he did not really utter the words, but his appearance represented them. The Iqbāl-nāma has, p. 138, *mihmān chū Bīga* ("a guest such as a Begam"). MS. 181 has *nāgah chū Sulṭān*. I.O. MS. 305 has *nāgah chū mihmān*. The reading Bega or Begam certainly seems preferable. The text is wrong as usual, and has *mihān* ("the great"), unless it is to be read *mahān*, and taken in the sense of Moons—*i.e.*, ladies. ↑

5 The Iqbāl-nāma, 139, has Kahtāʾī. ↑

6 The Iqbāl-nāma, 139, has 500 horse. ↑

7 The name of M. Rustam's son, who was drowned. ↑

8 *Kushtīgīr*, which means a wrestler. But Jahāngīr puns on the word as if it were *kishtīgīr* ("a boatman"). Perhaps kushtīgīr was his name. I presume that the person meant is the other servant. There was no boat there. The Iqbāl-nāma has either kishtīgīr, or kushtīgīr. ↑

9 There is an extraordinary account of the Mīrzā's death in Price's "Jahangir" which quite differs from the story told here. See Price, p. 138. It is also stated there that he had been married six months before to a daughter of I'timādu-d-daula. There is also an account of the accident in the Iqbāl-nāma, p. 139. ↑

10 Or Kuwārmast. ↑

11 Perhaps we should read Būniyār. See Stein, *loc. cit.*, p. 87. Jahāngīr seems to have crossed over to the left bank of the Jhelam in the course ot his march. Perhaps he did so at Ooriu of the map (Ūrī). Būniyār seems to be the Bhaniar of the map. I.O. MS. 181 has Butiyār. ↑

12 The allusion may be to the tuft of leaves at the top of a pineapple. ↑

13 Perhaps *būlā nīk*. ↑

14 Pūsh means flower in Kashmiri. Does the name mean "flower of 'Alī the Perfect"? ↑

15 Bāramūla is on the left bank of the Jhelam according to the I.G., new edition. But maps and travellers seem to place it on the right bank. ↑

16 Fourteen koss seem too little. The distance to Srinagar seems to be 31 miles by the road. The old city Vāramūla was on the right bank. Stein, 201. It is 32 miles from Srinagar. ↑

17 There is an omission in the text here. The MSS. have: "As Monday had been fixed for entering Srinagar, I did not think it advisable to halt at this stage, but immediately entered boats with the ladies and proceeded on with blessings towards the goal. On Sunday, the 10th, when two watches of the day had passed, I arrived at Shihābu-d-dīn-pūr." ↑

18 See Jarrett, II. 310, *n.* 7. ↑

19 The MSS. have Lā? Apparently the kah of text is a relative pronoun and not part of the name. Perhaps Lah in Ladakh is the place meant. ↑

20 *Dar kull* ("in general, in bulk") (?). ↑

21 The MSS. have also Mandal Badr. They have not Mulk after Badr as in text. ↑

22 Sister in MSS.

23 *Zar* here does not, I think, mean gold.

24 The silver *sāsnū* of Jarrett, II. 354, and *n.* 2.

25 Jahāngīr went part of the way by water.

26 Perhaps he is the Raja Bhagwān Singh mentioned by Drew in his book on Kashmir, p. 119.

27 Abū-l-Faẓl, Jarrett, II. 347, puts Kashmir into the third and fourth climates, but at Vol. III., p. 89, he puts Kashmir into the fourth climate. Probably both he and Jahāngīr mean by Kashmir Srinagar. The appellation "White Islands" is probably a mistake for "The Fortunate Islands," *safīd* (white) being written instead of *saʿāda*, which is the word in the Iqbāl-nāma. *Jazāʾir-i-Saʿāda* ("The Fortunate Isles") is also the expression used in the Ẓafar-nāma, II. 178, which is probably the source of the Āyīn and the Tūzuk. In the extract from the Ẓafar-nāma given in the T. Rashīdī translation, 430, the longitude is given as 105° from the "Fortunate Islands." The *text* of the Āyīn, Bib. Ind. edition, II. 42, gives 105.40° as the longitude.

28 See Rieu, I. 296. The translator was Mullā Shāh Muḥ. of Shāhābād. See also Blochmann, 106.

29 The Peliasa of the maps and the Bolvasaka of Stein. Qambarbar is Farūtar in text. The Iqbāl-nāma, 147, has Qambarbar. It is evidently the Qambarber of Jarrett, II. 347 and 361. It lies in the south-east of Kashmir. Measured by the compass, Jahāngīr's 67 is much more correct than Abū-l-Faẓl's 120. The I.G. new edition gives the area of Kashmir and Jammu as 80,900 square miles. Lawrence states the approximate length of the valley as 84 miles, and the breadth as from 20 to 25 miles.

30 The word used by Jahāngīr is *daraʿ*, which is given by Steingass as Arabic, and as meaning a yard. *Ẓaraʿ* again, is given as equal to a cubit. Clearly Jahāngīr uses the word here as equivalent to a *gaz* or yard, for he says that there are 5,000 *daraʿ* in the koss adopted by himself and his father, and Abū-l-Faẓl in the Āyīn (Jarrett, II. 414) says the koss is 5,000 *gaz*. The word *daraʿ* is also rendered *gaz* in the Hindustani translation of the Memoirs. There is an important discrepancy between the two I.O. MSS. and the printed text of the Memoirs. The former, instead of saying that the *daraʿ* or yard is = 2 *sharʿī daraʿ*, say that 1¼ *daraʿ* are = 2 *sharʿī daraʿ*. In the Āyīn (Jarrett, II. 417) the *gaz* is given as equal to 24 digits. See later on, p. 303 of text, where, in describing Shāh Shujāʾs accident, 7 *daraʿ* are said to be equal to 10 *sharʿī*, or ordinary, *gaz*.

31 See text (thirteenth year), p. 234, where it is stated that the *Ilāhī* gaz is 40 finger-breadths. ↑

32 Vīr is willow, so Vīr-nāg means Willow-fountain. ↑

33 Jarrett, II. 387. The I.G., XXIII. 100, says it was built by Zainu-l-ʿābidīn. The inscription shows that Zainu-l-ʿābidīn built it (Lawrence, 290). It is stated there that it was also burnt in 1029. A.H.—*i.e.*, in the year of Jahāngīr's visit. ↑

34 *K͟hānaqāhī.* Lawrence, 292. ↑

35 So in text and MSS., but perhaps *dū* is a mistake for Dal. However, the I.G. speaks of two lakes, the Dal and the Anchar (north of Srīnagar). See also Lawrence, 20 and 36. ↑

36 Probably the meaning is that the water never causes indigestion. Abū-l-Faẓl speaks of the streams being kh͟ūsh͟-guwār—*i.e.*, their water is digestible. ↑

37 The number of boatmen, when compared with the number of boats, seems very small, but the figures are the same in the I.O. MSS. and in the Iqbāl-nāma, 149. Perhaps the word *bīst*, 20, has been omitted, and we should read 27,400 boatmen. Lawrence states the number of boatmen at 33,870, and the boats, exclusive of private ones, at 2,417. The revenue of Kashmir, as stated by Jahāngīr, is that mentioned in the Āyīn, Jarrett, II. 366, and is according to the assessment of Qāẓī ʾĀlī. In the two I.O. MSS. the corresponding number of dāms is given as 7,46,70,400 (Rs. 1,866,760), being only 11 less than that given in Jarrett, II. 367, line 3. The figures given in Lawrence, 234, are taken apparently from the Persian text (compare Bib. Ind. edition, I. 571), corresponding to Jarrett, II. 368. The pargana Der, which Lawrence failed to trace, is a mistake for the well-known Ver, *dal* having been written or read by mistake for *wa.* ↑

38 Compare Jarrett, II. 366. "Some part of the Sair Jihat cesses are taken in cash." ↑

39 Jarrett, II. 347. ↑

40 Compare Jarrett, II. 348, where we have "the country is enchanting, and might be fittingly called a garden of perpetual spring surrounding a citadel terraced to the skies." ↑

41 That is, the flowers. ↑

42 Text *jawānībā*, but I.O. MSS. have *k͟hūbībā.* ↑

43 Apparently the proper spelling is jūg͟hās͟hī. See Vullers' s. v. and Bahār-i-ʿajam, 368, col. a. It is a black tulip. Sir George King thought it might be the *Fritillaria imperialis*. See Jarrett, 349, and *n.* 1. ↑

44 Nūr-afzā garden. See *infra.* ↑

45 *Tagetes patula.* The genda of Bengal? ↑

46 Compare text, p. 235. ↑

47 Compare Jarrett, II. 349, where the words "Besides plums and mulberries" should be "except cherries (shāh-ālū) and shāh-tūt" (a large mulberry). ↑

48 Blochmann, 411. Abū-l-Fazl, Āyīn, Blochmann, 65, speaks of cherries coming from Kabul. But cherries both sweet and sour are mentioned in the T. Rashīdī as growing in Kashmir (Translation, p. 425). ↑

49 Zard-ālū-i-paiwandī. ↑

50 *Shikananda*, query, melting. The word occurs also in Iqbāl-nāma, 152. Possibly it means "with good markings." ↑

51 But see I.G., XV. 124, where shāh-tūt is mentioned. See also Lawrence, 348. ↑

52 Compare Jarrett, II. 349. ↑

53 *Mushang* or *mushanj*, a small pea ("pisum arvense"). ↑

54 Text *khushka-tar.* MSS. have *khushka narm.* Perhaps we should translate "it is inferior and dry. They boil till it is soft, etc." The Iqbāl-nāma has *khushka narm mī-pazand.* ↑

55 The sentence about wheat is omitted in the text. ↑

56 Text kūhī ("hill"); but this is opposed to the MSS. and also to the Āyīn-i-Akbarī which Jahāngīr is evidently copying. See Jarrett II. 350, and *n.* 3, and Persian text, I. 563. The I.O. MSS. of Tūzuk have *kaddī* or *gaddī. Gaddī* is the name of a pastoral tribe (see Lawrence, 12), and there is a Turkish word *kedī* meaning a cat, and a word *gaddī* which means "horned." The Iqbāl-nāma, 153, has "*kadī-i-Hindustān.*" Jarrett, *loc. cit.* states that *handū* in Kashmiri means a domestic ram. The word for tailless is *bī-dumba*, and perhaps means that the sheep have not the enormously thick tails of some kinds of hill sheep. ↑

57 Possibly *nahrma* ("like a river"), is right, for the garment is said to be *mauj-dār* ("having waves"). The word *mauj-dār* occurs in the Iqbāl-nāma, 153, and in the two I.O. MSS. ↑

58 *Jul* is a coverlet, and *khirsak* means a little bear, but is applied to a rough woollen coverlet—a drugget. *Darma* is a name in Bengal for a reed mat. ↑

59 Perhaps "tie it at the waist." But see Lawrence, 252: "The Panditana wears a girdle, but no drawers." ↑

60 The MSS. have *ṭaṭṭū*. Both they and the text have also the words *chahār shāna ba-zamīn nazdīk*. *Chahār shāna* means a dwarf. Literally it means "four shoulders," and Vullers following, the Bahār-i-ʿAjam, defines it as a man of small stature with thick shoulders. Evidently the words *ba-zamīn nazdīk* are meant as an explanation or addition to *Chahār-shāna*, and signify that the *yābū* or *ṭaṭṭū* has his withers near the ground. The words also occur in the Iqbāl-nāma, 154. ↑

61 *Jangrah u shakh-jilau*. *Jangrah*, however, may refer to their gait, and may mean that they don't go straight, and very likely we should read *changrah* "going crookedly." *Shakh-jilau* is not in the dictionaries, and I only guess at the meaning. The phrase is also in the Iqbāl-nāma, 154. ↑

62 Text *īlchī-i-sāmān*. The real word is *īlkhī*, which is also spelt *īlqī* and *īlghī*, and is a Turki word meaning a horse, and also a troop of horses. See Pavet de Courteille Dictionary, p. 132, and Vullers I. 149b, who refers to the Burhān-i-qāṭiʿ, Appendix. See also Zenker, p. 152. The Iqbāl-nāma, p. 155, top line, wrongly has *balkhhā* (from Balkh?). ↑

63 Jarrett, II. 352, and *n.* 1, also T. Rashīdī, translation, 435. But perhaps all that is meant is the followers of the national saint Shaikh Nūru-d-dīn. Lawrence, 287. ↑

64 Taken from the Āyīn, see Jarrett, II. 353. There they are called brahmans, but this seems to be an error of the Bib. Ind. text. Gladwin has "Rishi." The Rīshīs were Muhammadans. See Jarrett, II. 359, where mention is made of Bābā Zainu-d-dīn Rīshī. See also Colonel Newall's paper on the Rīshīs or Hermits of Kashmir, A.S.B.J., 1870, p. 265. ↑

65 Text Bārān. MSS. have Mārān, and Eastwick has Koh-i-Mahran. He calls it an isolated hill 250 feet high. It is on the north outskirts of the city. See also Lawrence, 184, and *n.* 2, and Stein, 147–48. ↑

66 The Dal Lake is 3.87 miles long and 2.58 broad, the Ānchar Dal is 3.51 miles long and 2.15 broad. Lawrence, 20. ↑

67 MSS. have *kīl*, and so has the Iqbāl-nāma. *Kīl* is given in Lawrence, 114, as the Kashmir name for the ibex. ↑

68 Jarrett, II. 360. ↑

69 This is the *Ilāhī gaz*. ↑

70 Blochmann, 252, and note. ↑

71 So called because in Shujāʿ's horoscope. ↑

72 A village called ʿAis<u>h</u>-maqām is mentioned in Jarrett, II. 359, *n.* 1, but it is probably not the ʿAis<u>h</u>ābād here mentioned, for ʿAis<u>h</u>-maqām was on the Lidar and a long way S.S.E. Srinagar. ↑

73 *S<u>h</u>igūfa-i-sad-barg* ("the blossoms of the hundred-leaved rose"?). ↑

74 Allah-dād was s. Jalālu-d-dīn Tārīkī, also called Raus<u>h</u>ānī, and he became a distinguished officer of S<u>h</u>āh-Jahān under the title of Ras<u>h</u>īd K. See Maʾāṣir, II. 248, and Dabistān, 390. ↑

75 There are different readings. No. 181 has Maud and Mihrī. Apparently it is the Mau and Nabah of Jarrett, II. 319, where also there are various readings. See also Tūzuk, 263, where the text has Mau u s<u>h</u>ahra. ↑

76 Or Chārvara. See Rieu Catalogue, I. 297. Ḥaidar Malik wrote a history of Kashmir. It was he who protected Nūr-Jahān after her first husband's murder. Stein has Cadura, *recte* Isādur p. 43; it is 10 miles south of Srinagar. ↑

77 An allusion to Nūr-Jahān and to Nūru-d-dīn Jahāngīr. ↑

78 See Akbar-nāma, III. 542, and Ṭabaqāt-i-Akbarī extract in Appendix, translation of Tārīk<u>h</u>-i-Ras<u>h</u>īdī, p. 490. The place was K<u>h</u>ānpūr or near it. Perhaps the tree is the Adansonīa. See also Jarrett, II. 363. According to Stein, 191, Halthal is the name of the village, and is a corruption of Salasthala. This agrees with the Āyīn I. 569, but not with Akbar-nāma III. 542, where *halthal* is given as the name of the tree. ↑

79 I have not found this passage in the Akbar-nāma. The Iqbāl-nāma, 159, says that 70 people stood erect inside of the trunk. Rāwal-pūr is marked on the map of Kashmir, a little to the south of Srinagar. Niẓāmu-d-dīn, in his chapter on Kashmir in the Ṭabaqāt-i-Akbarī, speaks of a tree under the shade of which 200 horsemen could stand. ↑

80 Possibly *bī-ṣarfa* only means "unsuccessful." But it is used lower down (text 308, line 8), in the sense of immoderate or unprofitable. ↑

81 Text has Turks (Turkiyān). ↑

82 Apparently the Rohankhed of I.G., XXI. 304. ↑

83 Literally, "raised the foot of ignorance." ↑

84 Perhaps Sukh Nāg is the Shakar Nāg of Jarrett, II. 361. The Sukh Nāg River is mentioned in Lawrence, 16. It may also be the waterfall mentioned by Bernier, which he says Jahāngīr visited and levelled a rock in order to see properly. ↑

85 From Dr. Scully's list it appears that this is the sāch, the rose-coloured starling, *Pastor roseus*. See also Vullers, Dictionary, s. v. The bird seen by Jahāngīr may have been a dipper, Lawrence, 153. ↑

86 The MSS. have *kulhai*. ↑

87 According to the two I.O. MSS.—which are corroborated by the Iqbāl-nāma—the text has here omitted an important part of the report—presumably a written one—submitted by the Qāẓī and the Mīr ʿAdl. After the words "denied it," there comes in the MSS. the statement: "The Ḥakīm-zāda (Ḥakīm's son) produced two witnesses in court. The Sayyids invalidated (or impeached) the testimony of one of them, and the Ḥakīm-zāda brought a third witness and proved his case according to law." The Iqbāl-nāma, p. 161, has not the whole of this, and it has *kh̲ārij* instead of *jāriḥ*, but it has the words *guwāh-i-s̤āliṣ̤* ("a third witness"). ↑

88 The meaning seems to be that he would in corroboration and *ex cautela* take the oath. He had already proved his claim in the ordinary way by witnesses and the production of the bond. See the account in the Iqbāl-nāma, 160–63, which is fuller than that in text. ↑

89 *Muʿāmala-i-kullī ast*. "The case was involved" (like a bud?), or perhaps "the case was important." ↑

90 The text wrongly omits the negative. See Iqbāl-nāma, I. 62. ↑

91 Apparently this was Ṣāliḥa Bānū d. Qāʾim K. Blochmann, 371, and 477, *n*. 2. She had the name of Pādsh̲āh-maḥall. See Hawkins' account in Purchas, IV. 31, and Kh̲āfī K. I. 259. He calls the father Qāsim. ↑

92 It is Gh̲airat K. in I.O. MS., 181. ↑

93 For Jalāl K., see Blochmann, 455 and 486. He was grandson of Sulṭān Ādam. ↑

94 *Rasīd*. See lower down text 308, where it is noted that the cherries came to an end. ↑

95 This represents A.H. 1029, or 1620. ↑

96 Mat-treading or beating = house-warming. This was in honour of the new picture-gallery. ↑

97 *Dānahā-kīsh̲*. See Vullers, s.v. Kesh. The *kīsh̲* is a marten of whose skin neckcloths, etc., are made. This note corrects the one at p. 321 of translation, as also the text there. ↑

98 It is Būsī-marg in the I.O. MSS. But perhaps the text is right, and the place is the Tosh Maidān of Lawrence, 16. ↑

99 The gun is now at Bijapur, I.G., VIII. 186. ↑

100 Compare Iqbāl-nāma, 163–64. The text has *rān* ("thigh") instead of *ẓabān*. ↑

101 Blochmann, 382. The name of the son is given in the MSS. as Mīr 'Alī Aṣghar. ↑

102 Perhaps this is the Gurais Valley of Lawrence, 16, for Kūrī may be read Gūrī. ↑

103 See Jarrett, III. 121 and n. 5. The bird is either the common hawk-cuckoo of Jerdon (*Hierococcyx varius*) or his *Coccystes melanoleucos*—*i.e.*, the pied-crested cuckoo, for both birds seem to have the native name of *Papīhā*. The *Hierococcyx varius* is the "brain-fever" bird of the Anglo-Indian, I.G., I. 250. The pied-crested cuckoo occurs in Kashmir, and so also apparently does a bird of the genus *Hierococcyx*. Lawrence, pp. 138, 139. ↑

104 I am not sure what bird this is. *G͟haug͟hā'ī* means a turtle dove in Bengal, but I doubt if this be the bird meant by Jahāngīr. *G͟haug͟hā'ī* would mean a noisy bird, and perhaps is the Bengal Babbler of Jerdon, or the *Sāt Bhā'ī* (seven brothers) of the Indians. It belongs to the *Malacocircus* genus, and Jerdon, I. 340, states that the pied-crested cuckoo generally lays her egg in the nest of the *Malacocirci*. The babbling thrushes occur in Kashmir. In Blochmann, 296, there is an account of how *g͟haug͟hā'īs* are caught. ↑

105 MS. 305 has G͟hairat K., but No. 181 has 'Arab K., and this agrees with Stanley Lane Poole's Muhammadan dynasties (p. 279), which has 'Arab Muḥammad as ruling down to 1623. Ūrganj is in K͟hīva. ↑

106 Jahāngīr called K͟hān-Jahān his *farzand* (son). ↑

107 Not the famous 'Alī Mardān, but 'Alī Mardān, who was killed in the Deccan. Blochmann, 496. ↑

108 *Dandān-i-ablaq-i-jauhar-dār. Jauhar-dār* here does not mean "jewelled," but veined or striped. See Vullers, I. 542*a*. Walrus-teeth may be meant by Jahāngīr, but tortoise-shell is more likely. ↑

109 Sundar is another name for Rāja Bikramājīt, and the reference must be to the Siege of Kāngṛa. Jauhar Mal was a son of Rāja Bāso, and appears to be the same person as Sūraj Mal. It is Jauhar in I.O. MS., 181. ↑

110 Deotānī in No. 181. Blochmann has the name Dutānī, apparently as a tribal name (p. 504), and Elphinstone speaks in vol. II., p. 82, of a small tribe called Dumtauny. ↑

111 Veth is the Kashmiri name for the Jhelam (Lawrence, 18). It is contracted from Vitasta. It is curious that the date of the festival should be given

according to a Muhammadan month (Shawwāl), which must recur at different seasons. Apparently the meaning is that the birth of the Jhelam took place on that day.

Apparently the festival is not much celebrated nowadays, for it is not mentioned by Lawrence (264–266), except that in a note to p. 266 the Vathtrwah is mentioned as a day on which daughters receive presents. The 19th Shahrīwar, the corresponding date mentioned by Jahāngīr, would answer to the end of August or beginning of September, and to the Hindu month of Āsin. 13 Shawwāl, 1029, would correspond to 1 September, 1620. Possibly the Shawwāl of text is a mistake for the Hindu month Sāwan—*i.e.*, Srāvan. The legend of the birth of the Jhelam is told in Stein, 97. Possibly Shawwāl does not here mean the month, and we should read *shaghal-i-chirāghān*, "the business of lamps." ↑

112 The crane visits Kashmir in winter, but Jahāngīr was never there in that season. ↑

113 The text wrongly gives this as a list of birds which are found in Kashmir. The Iqbāl-nāma 159 and the MSS. show that the text has omitted a negative, and that the list consists of Indian birds which are *not* met with in Kashmir. Several of the names do not occur in the dictionaries. No 2 (the sāras) is described in Babur's Memoirs, 321. No. 4 is the florikan, or *Otis Bengalensis*. For Nos. 5–7 see Babur's Memoirs, 321. Karawān is a crane in Arabic, apparently, and so Karwānak should be a little crane. It is also described as a kind of partridge. Perhaps the Karwānak is the demoiselle crane. No. 9 may be the oriole, or mango-bird, but that, too, is common in Kashmīr. For No. 12, which may be the ibis, see Babur's Memoirs, 322. For No. 14 see Babur's Memoirs, p. 321, and for No. 18 Babur's Memoirs, 320. For the Shārak (No. 19), see Babur's Memoirs, 319. No 22 may possibly be the bee-eater (*Merops viridis*). For No. 23 see Babur's Memoirs, 267 and 321. No. 25 may be one of the parrots, as Ḥāfiẓ. called the Indian parrots and poets *ṭuṭiyān-i-shakar-shikan*. See Āyīn-i-Akbarī, Persian text, I. 415, and Jarrett, II. 150. The ṭaṭīrī, No. 30, is apparently the black partridge *Francolinus vulgaris*. The names of the birds seem to be often wrong in the text, and so I have followed the I.O. MSS. ↑

114 Kurg, but perhaps Gurg, "the wolf," is meant. The wolf is very rare in Kashmīr (Lawrence, 109). ↑

115 Query, mūshak-i-kūr—*i.e.*, mole. ↑

116 According to Wilson's Glossary, the tola is = 180 grains Troy, and the misqāl = 63½ grains Troy. ↑

117 Elliot, VI. 373, and Iqbāl-nāma 165. ↑

118 Vernag of Lawrence, 23. ↑

119 Text *u ān*; in MSS. ū. ↑

120 Lawrence, 67. ↑

121 Jarrett, II. 356, where it is written Vej Brára. ↑

122 Iqbāl-nāma, 164. ↑

123 This must be the Nandīmarg of Jarrett II. 357 and of Akbar-nāma III. 551. In the Āyīn (Jarrett II. 356), mention is made of a place where there are seven *fountains*. Stein, 182, speaks of a spring sacred to the seven Rīs̲h̲īs. Is it possible that *c̲h̲as̲h̲ma* in the A.N. (Persian text, I. 565) is a mistake for *c̲h̲inār*? ↑

124 Satha phūlī? Seven fountains? ↑

125 K̲h̲ān Daurān is the S̲h̲āh-Beg K. Arg̲h̲ūn of Blochmann, 377. ↑

126 See Ma'āṣir, II. 155, and Blochmann, 483, for an account of Rām Dās. Inch is mentioned in Jarrett, II. 356. Perhaps Inch is the Yech pargana of Stein, 190–191. ↑

127 Rām Dās had died eight years before this. ↑

128 Akbar-nāma, III. 725, last line; Lawrence, 298; Stein, *loc. cit.*, 176, 177. ↑

129 The Achh Dal of Jarrett, II. 358, and the Achabal of Lawrence, 22. ↑

130 Jarrett, II. 361. The Dīr Nāg of Iqbāl-nāma, 165. See also Jarrett, II. 361. The Vernag of Lawrence, 23. Jahāngīr interpolates an account of Vīrnāg into the annals of the second year. See p. 92 of translation. ↑

131 So in text, but a few lines lower down the depth is spoken of as four gaz. The Ibqāl-nāma has "fourteen yards." ↑

132 The Iqbāl-nāma has "to the end of the garden." ↑

133 Iqbāl-nāma, 165, has "186 yards." ↑

134 Compare Iqbāl-nāma, 166. ↑

135 The meaning is that the Marāj (or Marrāj), the upper part of Kashmir, is superior to the lower part, or Kāmrāj. See Tūzuk, 298. ↑

136 Iqbāl-nāma, 166. Perhaps the Bawan Send of Jarrett, II. 361. Loka Bhavan (bhavan means "abode") is mentioned in Stein, 180. It is the Lokapūnya of the Rājataranginī. It is five miles south of Achbal. ↑

137 Is this a corruption of Ānantanāg—*i.e.*, Islāmābād? ↑

138 Author of Iqbāl-nāma, 166. The appointment was that of examiner of petitions. ↑

139 I presume that the ends laid hold of by the boatmen were the disengaged ends—*i.e.*, the ends 14 or 15 yards apart. But see Iqbāl-nāma, 166–167. ↑

140 Text Panj Hazāra. The MSS. are not clear. It may be the Sendbrary of Bernier. ↑

141 The word is *s͟hikār*, but, as he had renounced shooting, netting is probably what is meant. ↑

142 Iqbāl-nāma, 169. ↑

143 Or Pāmpar, the ancient Padmapūra. See Stein, J.A.S.B. for 1899, p. 167; Elliot, VI. 375. But the passage, as in Elliot, does not come directly from the Tūzuk or the Iqbāl-nāma. ↑

144 MSS. have 3,200. ↑

145 *I.e.*, hawks taken from the nest, and not born in captivity. ↑

146 Iqbāl-nāma, 169. ↑

147 This is Mīr Jamālu-d-dīn, the dictionary-maker and friend of Sir Thomas Roe. ↑

148 The sentence appears obscure, but probably it was an order to the authorities at Lahore to supply Ḥusāmu-d-dīn with the cost of entertaining the ambassador up to the amount of Rs. 5,000. ↑

149 Perhaps the waterfall described by Bernier in his ninth letter, and mentioned as having been admired by Jahāngīr. ↑

150 Hīrāpūr is Hūrapūr and the ancient Sūrapūra. ↑

151 Marī or Nārī Brāra in the MSS. ↑

152 Bī-badal K. is the name given by Jahāngīr to Saʿīdā or S͟haidā who was chief goldsmith. See end of 15th year, p. 326 of text. For S͟haidā, who died in Kashmir in 1080 (A.D. 1669–70), see Rieu, III. 1083*a*, and I. 251, and Supp. Catalogue, p. 207, and Sprenger's Catalogue 124. ↑

153 Text calls them brothers, but the MSS. show that *birādar* is a mistake for *barābar*, "equally." ↑

154 The MSS. add: "He was a good youth (*jawān*) and without guile." ↑

155 Āb-i-ḥayāt, "water of life," a name given by Akbar to his āb-dār-k͟hāna, or supply of drinking-water, etc. See Blochmann, 51. ↑

156 Text wrongly has Thaṭṭa. ↑

157 Elliott, VI. 376. Apparently *Satī* was not practised by burning, but by burying. ↑

158 Bisyār bihtar, MS., 181. ↑

159 Girjhāk is said to be the Hindu name for Jalālpūr, and the probable site of Bukephala, Jarrett, II. 324. Makhiyāla is also mentioned there. It seems that Mūkhyāla is the famous Mānikiyāla, where the Buddhist tope is which was first described by Elphinstone. Abū-l-Faẓl says in the Āyīn that it was a place of worship. See I.G., new ed., XVII. 182. ↑

160 Mountain-sheep. Apparently three rings were made. ↑

161 The I.O. MSS. add here 76 head of *mārk͟hwur*, etc., were taken. ↑

162 Perhaps the reference is to the tomb he formerly put up over a favourite deer. ↑

163 MSS. have "is very noble." ↑

164 Pigeon-fancier. He belonged to Herat, and is mentioned in Blochmann, 302. ↑

165 Text wrongly has 1031. It should be 1030, as in the Iqbāl-nāma, 171. ↑

166 The couplet is given in Iqbāl-nāma, 171, with some verbal differences. ↑

167 Elliott, VI. 374. ↑

168 Jauhar Mal is mentioned at p. 310. Perhaps he was not Sūraj Mal, but it looks as if he was the same person. *Cf.* corresponding passage in Iqbāl-nāma, 173, where he is called Sūraj Mal. ↑

169 P. 310 of text. ↑

170 Rāja Bikramājīt. See *ante*, p. 310. ↑

171 Text wrongly has *g͟halla* grain, instead of *'alafhā* fodder, grasses, etc. See MSS. and Iqbāl-nāma, 174. ↑

172 Text wrongly has 1031, but it is 1031 in the MSS. and in Elliot, VI., 375. See, however, Elliot, VI. 378, and text, 326, which shew that the 16th year began in 1030. ↑

173 The *'Abbāsī* is also the name of a dress. The MSS. have fourteen, instead of four, horses. Apparently the presents were Zambil's own offering, not that of his master. See below. ↑

174 *Mansab-i-kabak*. Perhaps we should read *katak*, and regard the increase as made to the office of guarding the palace. It is *katak*, apparently, in I.O. MSS. It may, however, be *Kang* or *Gang* and a man's name. ↑

175 Apparently the translator of the Rājataranginī. ↑

176 Doubtless the Gwalior in the Panjab. ↑

177 Nūr Jahān's daughter by S͟hīr-afgan. The date of the asking is given in the text as the third, but should be the 30th, as in the I.O. MSS. ↑

178 Elliot, VI. 376. ↑

179 The Iqbāl-nāma, 176, has "ten crores." ↑

180 The MSS. have 5,000. The word for "gunners" is *tūpchī.* ↑

181 The MSS., instead of Naus͟hahr, have *sawād-i-s͟hahr*, "the environs of the city" (*cf.* Lahore?). ↑

182 It was in the vicinity of Lahore. Akbar-nāma, III. 569. ↑

183 But the next page of text records another feast of the lunar weighment. Can it be that the lunar weighment refers to Nūr Jahān's birthday, not to Jahāngīr's? The 17th here mentioned is the 17th of the solar month of Dai, and corresponded to about December 28, 1620. In the following page (324) we are told that the lunar weighment took place on 30 Bahman, corresponding to 25 Rabīʿu-l-awwal—*i.e.*, February 8, 1621: Jahāngīr's birthday was on Rabīʿu-l-awwal 17, so the anniversary fell this year on 22 Bahman. Consequently, if he celebrated it, as stated on p. 323, on 17 Dai, he did so more than a month too soon! Evidently there is a mistake somewhere. ↑

184 This place is mentioned again in the account of the 16th year, p. 338. It evidently received its name from Nūr Jahān. ↑

185 Akbarpūr, twelve miles N.W. Mathurā. J. Sarkar's India of Aurangzeb, 171. ↑

186 That is, of Chāch in Transoxiana, but according to I.O. MS. 181, the word is K͟hāfī—*i.e.*, from K͟hāf or K͟hwāf. ↑

187 Ninety-one rubies is surely a mistake. The Iqbāl-nāma, 177, only speaks of one. It is, however, 91 *yāqūt* in I.O. MS., 181. ↑

188 This is the Armenian of whom so much is said by Father Botelho and other missionaries. It is mentioned in M. Wāriṡ's continuation of the Pādis͟hāh-nāma, p. 392, of B.M. MS., that Ẕū-l-Qarnain Farangī came from Bengal and presented poems which he had composed on S͟hāh Jahān's name, and got a present of Rs. 4,000. He it was, probably, who entertained Coryat. The passage in the text seems to show that Akbar had an Armenian wife. ↑

189 He is mentioned in some MSS. of the Akbar-nāma, vol. III., as taking part in the religious discussions. ↑

190 Probably this is the Laʿl Beg who wrote a book about the Naqs͟hbandī order. See Maʾāṣiru-l-Umarā, II., 382. ↑

191 The Iqbāl-nāma has "42 eunuchs." ↑

192 The MSS. have 40 cocks, 12 buffaloes, and 7 buffalo-horns. The text also has *shākh*, horns, but this has been taken as a pleonasm. ↑

193 But there was such a ceremony a few days before (see p. 323 of text). ↑

194 For *tānk* see Blochmann, 16 *n.* The Iqbāl-nāma, 178, has "twelve misqāls." ↑

195 For the *Naskh* character see Blochmann, 99–100, and for the *Nasta'līq*, 101. See also the elaborate article on Writing in Hughes' Dictionary of Islam. ↑

196 By Shāh-i-Wilāyat is meant the Caliph 'Alī b. Abī Ṭālib. ↑

197 The Houshabarchan of Hawkins. ↑

198 Mahāban, five or six miles from Mathura. ↑

199 They had made an *istiqbāl*, or visit of welcome, from Agra. ↑

200 This was Bābar's garden. It was on the opposite side of the Jumna to Agra. ↑

201 So in text, but two (*dū*) must be a mistake for "ten," as 2 months, 2 days = 62, and the marches and halts 49 + 21 amount to 70, or 8 more. It is 10 in I.O. MSS. ↑

202 The *būdna*, or *bodna*, is a species of quail. See Bābar's Memoirs, Erskine, p. 320, where it is spelt *budinah*. There is a description in the Āyīn, Blochmann, 296, of the mode of catching them. ↑

203 The word "village" is omitted in both the I.O. MSS. ↑

204 This gives an average of Rs. 6,342 for each animal. ↑

## THE SIXTEENTH NEW YEAR'S FEAST AFTER THE AUSPICIOUS ACCESSION

On Monday,1 the 27th Rabī'u-l-ākhir, A.H. 1030 (10 March, 1621), the sun that bestows bounty on the world lit up the abode of fortune of Aries with his world-illuminating light, and gladdened the world and its inhabitants. The sixteenth year of the reign of this suppliant at the throne of Allah commenced with gladness and victory, and at the auspicious hour and blessed time I sat on the throne of success in the capital of Agra. On this joy-enhancing day my fortunate son Shahriyār lifted up his head with the honour of the mansab of 8,000 and 4,000 horse. My revered father bestowed, for the first time, this mansab2 on my brothers. It is hoped that in the shadow of my education and in carrying out my pleasure, he may reach the extreme of life and prosperity. On this day Bāqir K. arrayed his men and passed them before me in order. The great Bakhshis recorded (the number as) 1,000 horse and 2,000 foot, and reported to me. Having promoted him to the mansab of 2,000 personal and 1,000 horse, I entrusted the duties of faujdār of Agra to him.

On Wednesday, together with the ladies seated in a boat, I went to the Nūr-afshān garden, and rested there at night. As the garden belongs to the establishment of Nūr Jahān B., on Thursday, the 4th, she held the royal3 entertainment and presented great offerings. Of jewels, jewelled ornaments, and all sorts of precious goods, I selected what I approved of, of the value of Rs. 100,000. During these days, every day after midday I embarked in a boat, and went to Samonagar, 4 koss distant from the city, for sport, returning to the palace at night. Sending Rāja Sārang Deo to my prosperous son Shāh Parwīz, I sent with him a special dress of honour, with a jewelled belt, which contained a sapphire4 and several rubies. As I had given Behar to that son in the place of Muqarrab K., I started off a *sazāwul* to conduct him from Allahabad to Behar. Mīr Zāhid,5 son-in-law of Muẓaffar K., having come from Thatta, waited on me. As Mīr 'Aẓudu-d-daula6 had become very old and decrepit, he could not carry out the duties of the camp and his jagir. I released him from the trouble of service and active work. I ordered that he should receive Rs. 4,000 every month out of the public treasury, and living at ease and in comfort at Agra or Lahore, or wherever he wished, should employ himself in prayers for my increased life and welfare.

On the 9th Farwardīn the offering of I'tibār K. was laid before me. Of jewels, cloths, etc., the value of Rs. 70,000, was accepted, and I returned the remainder to him. Muḥibb 'Alī and Āqā Beg, envoys of the ruler of Persia, presented twenty-four horses, two mules, three camels, seven greyhounds (*sag-i-tāzī*), twenty-seven pieces (*ṭāq*) of brocade, a *shamāma*7 of ambergris, two pairs of carpets, and two *namad takya*8 (woollen coverlets). Two mares with foals that my brother had sent with them were also brought before me.

On Thursday, at the request of Āṣaf K., I went to his house with the ladies. Having prepared a grand entertainment, he submitted to me many delicate gems and wonders in cloths, and rare gifts. Choosing out of these to the value of Rs. 130,000, I gave the rest to him. Mukarram K., governor of Orissa, sent by way of offering thirty-two elephants, male and female, and these had the honour of being accepted. At this time I saw a wild ass9 (*gūr-k͟har*), exceedingly strange in appearance, exactly like a lion. From the tip of the nose to the end of the tail, and from the point of the ear to the top of the hoof, black markings, large or small, suitable to their position, were seen on it. Round the eyes there was an exceedingly fine black line. One might say the painter of fate, with a strange brush, had left it on the page of the world. As it was strange, some people imagined that it had been coloured. After minute inquiry into the truth, it became known that the Lord of the world was the Creator thereof. As it was a rarity, it was included among the royal gifts sent to my brother S͟hāh ʿAbbās. Bahādur K. Uzbeg had sent as an offering some tipchāq horses and cloth stuffs from ʿIrāq, and they were produced before me. Dresses of honour for the winter were sent for Ibrāhīm K. Fatḥ-jang and the Amirs of Bengal by Mūmin S͟hīrāzī. On the 15th the offering of Ṣādiq K. was produced. It was of all sorts. Having taken what was worth Rs. 15,000, I gave the remainder to him. Fāẓil K. on this day also gave an offering according to his condition. Of this a trifle was taken. On Thursday (19th Farwardīn) the feast of the culmination was held, and when two watches and one *g͟harī* of the day had passed, I took my seat on the throne. According to the request of Madār-ul-mulk Iʿtimādu-d-daula, the feast of the culmination was held in his house. He presented a remarkable offering of rare and choice things from all countries. Altogether I took the value of Rs. 138,000. On this day I gave Zambil Beg, the ambassador, a muhar10 equal to 200 *tolas* in weight. At this time Ibrāhīm K. had sent some eunuchs from Bengal. One of these was a hermaphrodite. Among the offerings of the above-mentioned were two boats made in Bengal, of a very pleasant shape, on the decoration of which a sum of Rs. 10,000 had been expended. They were really kingly boats. Having made S͟haik͟h Qāsim K. governor of Allahabad, I honoured him with the title of Muḥtas͟him K. and the mansab of 5,000, and gave an order that the Diwans should give him an increase to his jagir out of the unappropriated (*maḥāll-i-g͟hair-i-ʿamalī*) estates. Rāja S͟hyām Singh, Zamindar of Srīnagar (in Garhwāl) was given a horse and an elephant.

At this time it was reported to me that Yūsuf K., s. Ḥusain K.,11 had died in the victorious army of the Deccan a sudden death. The report said that when he was at his jagir he had become so fat that he got out of breath with the least exertion. One day when he was paying his respects to Khurram, in coming and going his breathing12 became difficult. When a dress of honour was given him, in putting it on and saluting he became helpless, and a trembling affected all his limbs, and with a hundred labours and exertions he saluted and stumbled out and fell under the shelter of the tent enclosure, and became unconscious. His servants placed him in a palanquin, and took him home, and as he arrived, the messenger of death came also. He received his command, and left his heavy lump of earth in the perishable dustbin. On 1st Urdībihisht, I gave a special dagger to Zambil Beg, the ambassador. On the 4th of the same month the feast of the *kār-i-khair* (consummation of marriage) of my son Shahriyār increased the joy of my heart. The Ḥinna-bandī (putting on henna) assembly took place in the palace of Maryamu-z-zamānī. The feast of the *nikāḥ* (marriage) was held in the house of I'timādu-d-daula. I myself went there with the ladies and adorned the feast of joy. After seven gharis of night had passed, on Friday13 the marriage took place with rejoicings. I hope that it will be propitious to this daily-increasing State. On Tuesday, the 19th, in the Nūr-afshān garden, I presented my son Shahriyār with a jewelled *chārqab* (coat), with a turban and waist-belt (*kamar-band*), and two horses, one an 'Irāqī, with a gold saddle, and the other a Turkī, with an embroidered saddle.

In these days Shāh Shujā' had an eruption so violent that water would not go down his throat, and his life was despaired of. As it had been recorded in his father's horoscope that his son would die this year, all the astrologers were unanimous that he would not live, but Jotik Rāy said, on the contrary, that the dust of calamity would not settle on the skirt of his life. I asked: "By what proof?" He said that in the horoscope of my destiny it was recorded that in this year no distress or trouble would find its way to the royal mind from any road, and as I had a great affection for the child, it behoved that no calamity should happen to him, and some other child would die. It came to pass as he said, and he carried his life out of this deadly place, and a son that he (Shāh Jahān) had by the daughter of Shāh-nawāz K., died at Burhanpur. Besides this, many of Jotik Rāy's judgments (aḥkām) turned out correct. This is not without strangeness, and it is therefore recorded in these memoirs. I accordingly ordered him (Jotik Rāy) to be weighed against money and the weight came to Rs. 6,500. This was given him as a reward.

Muḥammad Ḥusain Jābirī was appointed Bakhshi and newswriter of the Subah of Orissa. The mansab of Lāchīn Munajjim (astrologer) Qāqshāl, at the request of Mahābat K., was fixed, original and increased, at 1,000 personal and 500 horse. Muḥammad Ḥusain, brother of Khwāja Jahān, came from Kāngṛa and waited on me. Having presented an elephant to Bahādur K. Uzbeg, I sent it with his Vakil. Hurmuz and Hūshang, grandsons of the asylum of pardon Mīrzā Muḥammad Ḥakīm, by reason of the caution that is fitting to rulers, had been imprisoned in the fort of Gwalior. At this time, having summoned them into my presence, I ordered them to remain in Agra, and a daily allowance sufficient for their expenses was allowed for them. At this time a brahman of the name of Rūdar Bhattachāraj, who was one of the learned ones of this caste, and was engaged at Benares in teaching, had the good fortune to pay his respects to me. In truth, he has studied well, both in the rational and traditional sciences, and is perfect in his own line.

One of the strange events of this time14 was that on 30 Farwardīn (about 10 April, 1621) in the present year, in a certain village of the pargana of Jālandhar, in the morning, a terrible noise arose from the East, such that its inhabitants, from fright at that terror-increasing sound, nearly deserted their bodies. Whilst this noise and disturbance were going on, a light fell from above on the ground, and the people thought that fire was raining down from heaven. After a moment, when that noise ceased, and their troubled hearts recovered from their bewilderment and terror, they sent a quick runner to the collector (*ʿāmil*) Muḥammad Saʿīd, and informed him of what had occurred. He immediately rode there himself, and went to look at the spot. For ten or twelve yards in length and breadth the land was so burnt that no trace of any grass or green was left, and there were still signs of heat and burning. He ordered them to dig up the soil, and the more they dug the greater the heat appeared to be till they came to a place where a piece of heated iron appeared. It was as hot as if it had been taken out of a furnace. After a while it became cold, and taking it up, he conveyed it to his house, and placing it in a *k̲h̲arīṭa* (cover), which he sealed, he sent it to Court. I ordered them to weigh it in my presence, and it came to 160 *tolas*. I ordered Master (Ustād) Dāʾūd15 to make a sword, a dagger, and a knife of it, and bring them to me. He represented that it would not stand below the hammer, and fell to pieces. I told him in that case to mix it with other iron and make use of it. As I had told him, he mixed three parts of lightning-iron and one of other iron, and having made two swords, one dagger, and one knife, brought them to me. From the mixing of other iron he had brought out its quality (watering). According to the manner of the excellent swords of Yaman16 and the South, it could be bent, and became straight again. I ordered them to test it in my presence. It cut very well, equal to true swords. I called one the S̲h̲ams̲h̲īr-i-qāṭiʿ (keen sword) and the other Barq-siris̲h̲t (lightning-natured). Bī-badal K. composed a quatrain which demonstrated17 these particulars, and recited it:

By S̲h̲āh Jahāngīr the world acquired order.

There fell in his reign raw iron from lightning.

From that iron were made by his world-taking command,

A dagger, a knife, and two scimitars.

And "Spark of royal lightning" gave the date (A.H. 1030).

At this time Rāja Sārang Deo, who had gone to my fortunate son S̲h̲āh Parwīz, came and waited on me. Parwīz represented that he, according to order, had proceeded from Allahabad to Behar. I hope he will be prosperous (there). Qāsim K. was dignified with the gift of drums. On this day one ʻAlīmu-d-dīn, a servant of K̲h̲urram, brought a report from him containing the good news of the victory, with a jewelled thumbstall (*s̲h̲ast*, perhaps a ring), which he had sent as *naẕar.* I gave him leave, sending by him a dress of honour. Amīr Beg, brother of Fāẕil Beg. K., was appointed Diwan to my son S̲h̲ahriyār and Muḥammad Ḥusain, brother of K̲h̲wāja Jahān, was made Bakhshi, and Maʻṣūm was appointed *Mīr-Sāmān.* Sayyid Ḥājī obtained leave to go as an auxiliary to the army of the Deccan, and I gave him a horse. Muẓaffar K., was also promoted to the post of Bakhshi.

As at this time the mother18 of Imām-qulī K., the ruler of Tūrān, had sent to Nūr Jahān Begam a letter containing expressions of good will and the dues of acquaintanceship, and sent some rarities from that country. K̲h̲wāja Naṣīr, who was one of the old servants and one of my attendants from the time when I was a prince, was sent by way of embassy on the part of Nūr Jahān Begam with a letter, with choice gifts from this country. At the time when the ladies were staying in the Nūr-afs̲h̲ān garden, a *rang* (ibex) fawn eight days old, jumped down from the terrace of the palace, which is 8 gaz in height, on to the ground, and began to leap about, no sign of injury or pain being perceptible in it.

On the 4th of the Divine month19 of K̲h̲urdād, Afẕal K., K̲h̲urram's Diwan brought a letter from him containing the good news of his victory, and kissed the threshold. The details are as follows: When the victorious army reached Ujain, a band of the servants of the Court, who were in the fort of Māndū, sent a report that an army of the rebels, putting forward the foot of audacity, had crossed the Narbadā, and burning several villages that were under20 the fort, were busy with rapine and plunder. Madāru-l-mahāmm K̲h̲wāja Abū-l-Ḥasan, with 5,000 cavalry, were appointed to go in all haste and inflict punishment on that vain lot of people. The K̲h̲wāja made a night march, and at the dawn of day reached the bank of the Narbadā. When the enemy learnt this, they in one moment threw themselves into the river and reached the bank of safety. The brave cavalry galloped after them, and pursued them for nearly 4 koss,21 and with the sword of vengeance, made many of them travellers on the road of non-existence. The ill-fated rebels did not turn back the reins of haste till they reached Burhanpur. K̲h̲urram wrote to Abū-l-Ḥasan to remain on that (the South) side of the river till he came. Soon he, with his army, joined this advanced force, and hastened on, march by march, till he reached Burhanpur. The graceless rebels were still keeping[22] their ground, and were encamped round the city. As the imperial servants had been contending with the rebels for two years, they had suffered much hardship from want of land (*bī-jāgīrī*,[23] non-possession of fiefs, landlessness) and scarcity of corn, and their horses were worn out by continued service. Accordingly, they had to delay nine days in order to recruit. During this period, thirty lakhs of rupees and many cuirasses[24] were distributed among the soldiers, and *sazāwuls* had been sent out and had brought many men out of the city (Burhanpur). The gallant troops had not yet put their hands to the work, when the black-fated rebels felt that they could not resist, and scattered like "the daughters of the Bier" (the stars of the constellation of the Great Bear, which are dispersed over the heavens, instead of being clustered like the Pleiades). The brave and swift cavaliers followed them, and with the sword of vengeance cast many of them upon the earth of perdition. They gave them no rest, but smiting and slaying them, pursued them as far as Khirkī, which was the residence of the Niẓāmu-l-mulk and the other rebels. One day before this the ill-starred one (Malik ʿAmbar) had got information of the approach of the imperialists, and had removed the Niẓāmu-l-mulk and his family and effects to the fort of Daulatābād. There he had encamped, with his back resting on the fort, while in front of him there were marshes and quagmires.[25] Most of his men became scattered in all directions. The leaders of the victorious army, with their vengeance-seeking soldiers, halted three days in the town of Khirkī, and so destroyed a city which had taken twenty years to build, that it is not known if it will regain its splendour in other twenty years. In fine, after throwing down its buildings, all agreed in opinion that as an army of rebels was still besieging Ahmadnagar, they must at once go there, and inflict condign punishment on the originators of the disturbance, renew the supplies (of the Ahmadnagar garrison), and leave assistance there, and then return. With this view they set out, and came as far as the town of Paṭan (in Berar, Jarrett II. 233). Meanwhile, the crafty ʿAmbar[26] sent agents and officers, and said: "After this I will not drop the thread of service and loyalty from my hand, nor put out my foot beyond orders, and will regard whatever tribute and fine be commanded as a favour, and will send it to the government." It happened that just then there was great scarcity in the camp in consequence of the dearness of provisions, and also that news came that the rebel force which was besieging Ahmadnagar had withdrawn on hearing of the approach of the imperialists. Accordingly, a force was sent to help K͟hanjar K. (the governor of Fort Ahmadnagar), and a sum of money for his charges. Thereupon the imperialists were relieved from all anxiety and returned (across the Narbadā?). After much entreaty and lamentation (on the part of ʿAmbar) it was settled that in addition to the territory which of old had belonged to the empire, the rebels should surrender 14 koss of the adjoining country, and should pay into the public treasury fifty lakhs of rupees as tribute.

I gave Afẕal K. (S̲h̲āh Jahān's diwan) leave to return, and sent with him, for K̲h̲urram, the ruby plume (*kalgī-i-laʿlī*) which the King of Persia had sent to me, and which has been already described, and I gave to the aforesaid (Afẕal) a dress of honour, an elephant, an inkpot, and a jewelled pen. K̲h̲anjar K., who, when besieged in the Fort of Ahmadnagar, had performed approved services, and shown proper activity, was promoted to the mansab of 4,000 personal and 1,000 horse.

Mukarram K., having come by order from Orissa, had, with his brothers, the good fortune to wait upon me. He presented a string of pearls by way of offering. Muẕaffaru-l-mulk, s. Bahāduru-l-mulk, was honoured with the title of Nuṣrat K. A standard was conferred on Ūdā Rām, Dakhanī, and to ʿAzīzu-llah, s. Yūsuf K., was given the mansab of 1,000 personal and 500 horse. On Thursday, the 21st, Muqarrab K. arrived from Behar, and had the good fortune to wait upon me. At this time Āqā ʿAlī, Muḥibb ʿAlī Beg, Ḥājī Beg, and Fāẕil Beg, the envoys of the ruler of Persia, who had come at different times, were allowed to depart. To Āqā Beg I made a present of a dress of honour, a jewelled dagger, and Rs. 40,000 in cash; to Muḥibb ʿAlī Beg a dress of honour and Rs. 30,000; and to the others in the same way I presented gifts according to their positions. I also sent a suitable souvenir by them to my brother. On this day Mukarram K. was appointed Subahdar of Delhi, and faujdār of Mewāt. S̲h̲ajāʿat K. ʿArab was dignified with the mansab of 3,000 personal and 2,500 horse, original and increased; S̲h̲arza K. with that of 2,000 and 1,000 horse; Girdhar, s. Rāy Sāl Kachhwāha, with that of 1,200 and 900 horse.

On the 29th, Qāsim Beg, an envoy of the ruler of Persia, came and waited on me, bringing a letter from that brother of lofty dignity, containing expressions of sincerity and friendship. What he had sent by way of royal gifts was laid before me. On the 1st of Tīr, I sent a special elephant called Gaj Ratan, for my son (*farzand*) K̲h̲ān Jahān. Naẕar Beg, a servant of K̲h̲urram, laid before me a letter from him asking for the gift of horses. I ordered Rāja Kis̲h̲an Dās, the mus̲h̲rif (accountant) to prepare within fifteen days 1,000 horses from the royal stables, and to send them off with him. I sent to K̲h̲urram as a present a horse of the name of Rūm-ratan27 ("the jewel of Turkey"), which the ruler of Persia had sent me out of the spoils of the Turkish camp.

On this day a servant of Irādat K., of the name of G̲h̲iyāṣu-d-dīn, laid before me a report from him containing the good news of his victory. In the preceding pages there has been written with the pen of demonstration an account of the rebellion of the Zamindars of Kis̲h̲twār and of the despatch of Jalāl, s. Dilāwar K. As this important matter had not been properly managed by him, an order was given to Irādat K. to hasten to take up that duty, and to inflict severe punishment on the rebels, and make such arrangements in the hill-country that the dust of dispersion and calamity might not settle on its frontiers. He, as ordered, hastened there and did approved service, and the people of sedition and disturbance, having turned their heads towards the desert of exile, escaped half dead. Thus once more was the thorn of calamity and mischief rooted out of that country, and having established the officials and established posts, he returned to Kashmir. As a reward for this service I added 500 horse to his mansab.

As Kh̲wāja Abū-l-Ḥasan had done good service and shown proper activity in the affair of the Deccan, I increased his mansab by 1,000 horse. Aḥmad Beg, nephew of Ibrāhīm K. Fatḥ-jang, being exalted to the Subahdarship of Orissa, was dignified with the title of *Kh̲ān*, and had given him a standard and drums. His mansab also was raised to 2,000 with 500 horse.

As I had often heard of the virtues and good qualities of Qāẓī Naṣīr of Burhanpur, my truth-seeking mind had a desire for his society. At this time he came, according to summons, to the Court. Doing honour to his learning, I paid him great regard. The Qāẓī is one of the unique of the age for rational and traditional sciences, and there are few books that he has not read, but his exterior did not agree with his interior, and I could not be delighted with his company. As I found him much devoted to being a dervish and seclusion, I respected his feelings, and did not give him the trouble of serving me. I gave him Rs. 5,000, and dismissed him to his native country to pass his days in ease.

On the 1st of the Divine month of Amurdād Bāqir K. was promoted to the mansab of 2,000 personal and 1,200 horse, and of the Amirs and royal servants who had distinguished themselves in the conquest of the Deccan, thirty-two individuals were exalted by having their mansabs raised. ʿAbdu-l-ʿAzīz K. Naqsh̲bandī, who had been appointed to the governorship of Qandahar at the request of my son Kh̲ān Jahān, was promoted to that of 3,000 personal and 2,000 horse. On the 1st Sh̲ahrīwar I gave the ambassador Zambil Beg a jewelled sword, and also presented him with a village under the jurisdiction of the capital, the revenue of which was Rs. 16,000.

At this time, knowing that he was unfit for duty on account of his bad temper and want of knowledge, I dismissed Ḥakīm Ruknā,28 and told him he might go wherever he wished. As it was reported to me that Hūsh̲ang, the brother's son of Kh̲ān ʿĀlam, had committed an unjust murder, having summoned him to my presence, I investigated the charge, and after it was established, gave an order for his execution. God forbid that in such affairs I should consider princes, and far less that I should consider Amirs. I hope that the grace of God may support me in this. On 1st S͟hahrīwar, at the request of Āṣaf K., I went to his house and bathed in the bath-house that he has lately built. It is beautifully finished. After I had done bathing he laid before me offerings fit for a *naẕar.* I took what I approved of and gave him the rest. The *Waẕīfa* (pension) of K͟hiẓr K͟hān (late ruler) of Khandesh, was fixed at Rs. 30,000,29 original and increased.

At this time it was reported to me that a blacksmith of the name of Kalyān was much in love with a woman of his own caste, and was always laying his head at her feet, and showing symptoms of infatuation. The woman, though she was a widow, would in no way consent to accept him, and the love of this wretch who had given his heart to her made no impression on her. Having summoned both of them into my presence, I cross-examined them, and however much I advised her to unite herself to him, she did not agree. At this time the blacksmith said that if he could make sure that I would30 give her to him, he would throw himself down from the S͟hāh-burj of the fort. I said by way of jest: "Never mind the S͟hāh-burj; if your love be genuine, fling yourself from the roof of this house, and I'll make her submit herself to you." I had not ended before he ran like lightning and threw himself down. When he fell, blood began to flow from his eyes and mouth. I repented myself greatly of that jest, and was grieved in my mind, and bade Āṣaf K͟hān take him to his house and look after him. As the cup of his life was brimming over, he died from the injury.

VERSE.

The life-sacrificing lover who stood on that threshold

Gave up his life with joy and regarded death as a trifle.

At the request of Mahābat K. the mansab of Lāchīn Qāqs͟hāl, original and increased, was fixed at 1,000 personal and 500 horse.

It has been mentioned31 that on the day of the Dasahara festival in Kashmir, I had perceived in myself a catching and shortness of breath. Briefly, from excessive rain and the dampness of the air, a difficulty in drawing breath showed itself on my left side near the heart. This by degrees increased and became intensified. Of the physicians who were in waiting on me, Ḥakīm Rūḥu-llah first tried his remedies, and for some time warm, soothing medicines were of use, for there was evidently a slight diminution (of the symptoms). When I came down from the hills, they came on again violently. This time for some days I took goats' milk, and again camel's milk, but I found no profit whatever from them. About this time Ḥakīm Ruknā, who had been excused from the journey to Kashmir, and whom I had left at Agra, joined me, and confidently and with a show of power, undertook my cure, and relied on warm and dry medicines. From his remedies, too, I derived no advantage; on the contrary, they appeared to increase the heat and dryness of my brain and temperament, and I became very weak. The disease increased and the pain was prolonged. At such a time and in this state, at which a heart of stone would have burnt (been distressed) about me, Ṣadrā,[32] s. Ḥakīm Mīrzā Muḥammad, who was one of the chief physicians of Persia (was in attendance on me). He had come from Persia in the reign of my revered father, and after the throne of rule had been adorned by this suppliant, as he was distinguished above all others by natural skill and experience (*taṣarruf-i-ṭabīʿat*), I was attended to by him, and I distinguished him with the title of Masīḥu-z-zamān (Messiah of the Age). I made his position more honourable than that of the other Court-physicians, with the idea that at some crisis he would help me. That ungrateful man, in spite of the claims which I had on him, though he saw me in such a state, did not give me medicines or treat me. Notwithstanding that I distinguished him beyond all the physicians who were waiting on me, he would not undertake my cure. However great attention I showed him and troubled myself to soothe him, he became more obstinate (*ṣullab*), and said: "I have no such reliance on my knowledge that I can undertake the cure." It was the same with Ḥakīm Abū-l-Qāsim, s. Ḥakīmu-l-mulk, notwithstanding his being a k̲h̲ānazād, and what was due for his bringing up; he professed himself suspicious and afraid, and that considering the matter in his mind, he was terrified and vexed, and how, then, could he prescribe a remedy? As there was no help for it, I gave them all up, and weaning my heart from all visible remedies, gave myself up to the Supreme Physician. As drinking alleviated my sufferings, I took to it in the daytime, contrary to my habit, and gradually I carried this to excess. When the weather became hot, the evil effects of this increased, and my weakness and laboured breathing were augmented. Nūr Jahān Begam, whose skill and experience are greater than those of the physicians, especially as they are brought to bear through affection and sympathy, endeavoured to diminish the number of my cups, and to carry out the remedies that appeared appropriate to the time, and soothing to the condition. Although previously to this she had approved of the remedies made use of by the physicians, yet at this time I relied on her kindness. She, by degrees, lessened my wine, and kept me from things that did not suit me, and food that disagreed with me. I hope that the True Physician will grant me perfect recovery from the hospital of the hidden world.

On Monday, the 22nd[33] of the same month, corresponding with the 25th of S̲h̲awwāl, A.H. 1030 (2 September, 1621), the feast of my solar weighing took place auspiciously and happily. As in the past year (of my life) I had suffered from severe illness, I had passed it in continuous pain and trouble. In thankfulness that such a year ended well and in safety, and that in the commencement of the present year the signs of health became apparent, Nūr Jahān Begam begged that her Vakils might make the arrangements for the entertainment (of the solar weighment). In truth, they prepared one which increased the astonishment of beholders. From the date on which Nūr Jahān Begam entered into the bond of marriage with this suppliant, although in all weighing entertainments, both solar and lunar, she had made such arrangements as were becoming to the State, and knew what were the requirements of good fortune and prosperity; yet on this occasion she had paid greater attention than ever to adorn the assembly, and arrange the feast. All the servants of approved service and the domestics who knew my temperament, who in that time of weakness had constantly been present and been ready to sacrifice their lives, and had fluttered round my head like moths, were now honoured with suitable kindnesses, such as dresses of honour, jewelled sword-belts, jewelled daggers, horses, elephants, and trays full of money, each according to their positions. And though the physicians had not done good service, yet in consideration of the slight contempt34 with which they had been treated for two or three days, they received various favours, and on the occasion of this feast also, they received presents in jewels and cash.

After the conclusion of the weighment, trays of gold and silver were poured out by way of *niṣār* (coin-scattering) into the hope-skirts of the ministers of amusement (*ahl-i-nis̱hāṭ*), and of the poor. Jotik Rāy, astrologer, who had given the glad news of my recovery and restoration to health, I had weighed against muhars and rupees, and by this method a present was made35 him of 500 muhars and 7,000 rupees. At the end of the entertainment the offerings she (Nūr Jahān) had prepared for me were produced. Of the jewels, jewelled ornaments, cloths and various rarities I selected what I approved of. Altogether the cost of this great entertainment which Nūr Jahān Begam gave was recorded to be two lacs of rupees, exclusive of what she laid before me as offerings. In previous years, when I was in health, I weighed 3 maunds and 1 or 2 seers more or less, but this year, as a result of my weakness and leanness, I was only 2 maunds and 27 seers.

On Thursday, the 1st of the Divine month of Mihr, Iʿtiqād K., the Governor of Kashmir, was promoted to the mansab of 4,000 and 2,500 horse, and Rāja Gaj Singh to that of 4,000 and 3,000 horse. When the news of my illness reached my son, S̱hāh Parwīz, without waiting for a farman he came to see me, being unable to restrain himself. On the 14th36 of the same month (September 25, 1621), at an auspicious hour and propitious time, that fortunate son had the good fortune to kiss the threshold, and went three times round the couch (*tak̲h̲t*). However much I adjured him and forbade him to do so, he insisted the more in lamentation and importunity. I took him by the hand and drew him towards me, and by way of kindness and affection held him fast in an embrace, and displayed great love to him. I hope that he may enjoy a long life with prosperity.

At this time Rs. 20,00,000 were sent to K͟hurram for the expenses of the army of the Deccan by Allah-dād K., who was honoured with an elephant and a standard. On the 28th Qiyām K., chief huntsman, died a natural death. He was a confidential servant, and apart from his skill in hunting, looked over every trifling detail relating to it, and consulted my pleasure in it. In short, I was much grieved at this event. I hope that God may grant him forgiveness.

On the 29th the mother of Nūr Jahān Begam died. Of the amiable qualities of this matron (*Kad-bānū*) of the family of chastity what can I write? Without exaggeration, in purity of disposition and in wisdom and the excellencies that are the ornament of women no Mother of the Age[37] was ever born equal to her, and I did not value[38] her less than my own mother. With regard to the attachment that Iʿtimādu-d-daula bore towards her it is certain that no husband was equal to him. Here one must imagine what had happened to that grief-stricken old man. Also with regard to the attachment of Nūr Jahān Begam to her mother what can one write? A son like Āṣaf K., exceedingly intelligent and clever, rent in pieces his robe of patience and left off the dress of men of the social state (lit., men of dependence, or connection). At the sight of his dear son, the grief and sorrow of the father, wounded at heart, increased more and more. However much we admonished him, it had no result. On the day on which I went to condole with him, as the disturbance of his mind and grief of his heart had commenced, I spoke a few words of admonition by way of affection and kindness, but did not urge him. I left him until (the sense of) his calamity should abate. After some days I ministered to his inward wound the balm of kindness, and brought him back to the position of sociable beings. Although in order to please me and satisfy my mind he outwardly controlled himself, and made a show of resignation, yet with regard to his affection for her what resignation could there be?

On the 1st of the Divine month of Ābān, Sar-buland K., Jān-sipār K., and Bāqī K., were honoured with the gift of drums. ʿAbdu-llah K. had gone to his jagir without the leave of the Subahdar[39] of the Deccan: I accordingly told the Chief Diwans to deprive him of his jagir, and Iʿtimād Rāy was ordered to act as a *sazāwul*, and to send him back to the Deccan.

It has been recorded with regard to the case of Masīḥu-z-zamān (Ḥakīm Ṣadrā) that, notwithstanding what was due from him for his bringing-up and my kindness to him, he had not the grace to attend upon me in such an illness, and more strange still is it that he suddenly threw off the veil of modesty and asked for leave to undertake a journey to the Hijaz, and make a pilgrimage to the holy house. Inasmuch as at all times and under all circumstances the reliance of this suppliant is on the Lord, that needs no return, and the gracious Creator, I gave him leave with an open brow. Though he had all kinds of things (for the journey) I made him a present of Rs. 20,000 in aid of his expenses, and I hope that the Supreme Physician, without the assistance of physicians and the means of medicine, may grant this suppliant complete recovery from the Dispensary of His mercy.

As the air of Agra, in consequence of the increase of the temperature, did not agree with me, on Monday, the 13th of the Divine month of Ābān and 16th year (of my reign), the standards were raised to go towards the hill country of the North, so that if the air of that quarter should be equable, I might choose some spot of ground on the bank of the River Ganges, and found a city there, to make a permanent place of residence for the hot weather, or else turn the reins of purpose in the direction of Kashmir. Leaving Muz̤affar K. to guard and administer Agra, I dignified him with drums, a horse, and an elephant. Having appointed his nephew, M. Muḥammad faujdār of the city, I gave him the title of Asad K., and selected him for increase of mansab. Having exalted Bāqir K. to the duty of the Subah of Oudh, I dismissed him. On the 26th of the said month my prosperous son S̱ẖāh Parwīz obtained leave to proceed from Mathura to Bihar and his jagir. I gave him leave after presenting him with a special dress of honour, a *nādirī*, a jewelled dagger, a horse, and an elephant. I hope that he may enjoy long life. On 4 Āẕar, Mukarram K., governor of Delhi, was exalted with the good fortune of paying his respects. On the 6th I alighted at Delhi, and having halted two days in Salīmgaṛh I employed myself with the pleasure of sport. At this time it was reported to me that Jādo Rāy Kaitha (or Kathiya), who is one of the leading Sardars of the Deccan, by the guidance of good fortune and reliance on God, had elected for loyalty, and had been enrolled amongst the loyal servants. Bestowing on him a dress of honour and a jewelled dagger, I sent a gracious farman to him by the hand of Narāyan Dās Rāthor. On the 1st of the Divine month of Dai, corresponding with the 7th Ṣafar, A.H. 1031, Maqṣūd, brother of Qāsim K., was honoured with the title of Hās̱ẖim K. and Hās̱ẖim Beg K̲h̲ūs̱ẖī40 with that of Jān-niṣār K.

On the 7th of the same month the camp was pitched at Hardwār on the bank of the Ganges. It is one of the most famous places of worship of the Hindus, and many brahmans and recluses have chosen a corner of retirement in this place and worship God according to the rule of their religion. I gave alms in cash and goods to each of them according to his requirements. As the climate of this skirt of the hills was not approved by me, and I could not see a spot of ground on which to make a permanent residence, I proceeded towards the skirt of the hill country of Jammu and Kāngṛa.

At this time it was reported to me that Rāja Bhāo Singh had died in the Deccan (become a traveller on the road of non-existence). From excess of wine-drinking he had become very weak and low. Suddenly a faintness came over him. However much the physicians tried remedies for him and burnt scars on the top of his head, he did not come to his senses: for a night and a day he lay without perception, and died the next day. Two wives and eight concubines burnt themselves in the fire of fidelity for him. Jagat Singh, his elder brother, and Mahā Singh, his nephew, had spent the coin of their lives in the wine-business, and the aforesaid, not taking warning from them, sold sweet life for bitter fluid. He was of very good disposition and sedate. From the days when I was a prince he was constantly in my service, and by the blessing of my education had reached the high rank of 5,000. As he left no son, I dignified the grandson of his elder brother, though of tender years, with the title of Raja, and gave him the mansab of 2,000 personal and 1,000 horse. The pargana of Amber, his native place, was assigned to him as jagir, according to former custom, in order that his family might not be dispersed. Aṣālat K., s. K͟hān Jahān, was promoted to the mansab of 1,000 personal and 500 horse. On the 20th41 of the same month I halted at the saray of Alwātū.42 As I am constantly engaged in the pleasure of hunting, and the flesh of animals I have killed with my own hand is very much to my taste, in consequence of the suspicions and caution that I have in such matters, I order them to be cleaned in my presence, and myself inspect their stomachs to see what they have eaten and what the food of the animals is. If by chance I see anything to which I have a dislike I forbear from eating the flesh. Before this I was not inclined towards any kind of waterfowl except the *sona* (golden duck?). When I was at Ajmir I saw a tame *sona* duck eating horrible worms. From seeing this, my taste turned against it, and I gave up eating tame *sona* ducks until now, when a duck was caught, and I ordered them to clean it in my presence. From its crop there first came out a small43 fish: after this there appeared a bug44 so large that I could not believe till I saw it with my own eye that it could swallow a thing of such a size. Briefly I this day determined that I would not eat waterfowl. K͟hān ʿĀlam represented that the flesh of the white heron (*ʿuqāb-i-safīd*) was very delicious and tender. I accordingly sent for a white heron, and ordered them to clean it in my presence. By chance there came out of its crop ten bugs in a manner disgusting to me, at the remembrance of which I am distressed and disgusted.

On the 21st the garden of Sirhind brought joy to my senses, and on the day of halt there I delighted myself by going round and looking at it. At this time K͟hwāja Abū-l-Ḥasan came from the Deccan, and had the good fortune to wait on me. He had great favour shown him. On the 1st of the Divine month of Bahman I halted at Nūr-Sarāy.45 The mansab of Muʿʾtamid K., original and increased, was ordered to be 2,000 personal and 600 horse. K͟hān ʿĀlam was made governor of Allahabad,46 and having been presented with a horse, a dress of honour, and a jewelled sword, took his leave. Muqarrab K. was selected for the mansab of 5,000 personal and horse. On Thursday, when I was encamped on the bank of the Biyāh (Beās), Qāsim K. came from Lahore, and had the good fortune to wait on me. Hāshim K., his brother, with the Zamindars of the country bordering on the hills, had the honour of kissing the threshold.

Bāso'ī,47 the zamindar of Talwāra, brought me a bird, which the hill-people call *jān-bahan*. Its tail resembles the tail of the *qirqāwul* (pheasant), which is also called the *tazrū*, and its colour is exactly like that of the hen-pheasant, but it is half as large again. The circle round the eyes of this bird is red, while the orbit of the pheasant is white. The said Bāso'ī stated that this bird lived in the snow-mountains, and that its food was grass and other stuff. I have kept pheasants and have reared young ones, and have often eaten the flesh both of young birds and of mature ones. One may say that there is no comparison between the flesh of the pheasant and this bird. The flesh of the latter is much more delicate. Among the birds which I saw in the hill-country one was the *phūl-paikār*,48 which the Kashmiris call *sonlū*. It is one-eighth (*nīm sawā'ī*?) less than a pea-hen. The back, tail, and wings resemble those of the bustard, and are blackish, with white spots. The breast to the end of the bosom is black, with white spots, and some red ones. The ends of the feathers are fiery red, and very lustrous and beautiful. From the end of the back of the neck it is also brilliantly black. On the top of its head it has two fleshy horns of a turquoise colour. The skin of its orbits and round its mouth is red. Below its throat there is skin round it enough to cover the palms of two hands, and in the middle of this the skin is of a violet colour of the size of a hand, with blue spots in the middle. Around it each streak is of a blue colour, consisting of eight plumes; round the blue streak it is red to the breadth of two fingers, like the peach flower, and again round its neck is that blue-coloured streak: it has red legs also. The live bird, which was weighed, came to 152 tolahs. After it was killed and cleaned it weighed 139 tolahs. Another bird is of a golden colour: this the people of Lahore call *Shan*49 (?) and the Kashmiris *pūṭ*. Its colour is like that of a peacock's breast. Above its head is a tuft (*kākul*). Its tail of the width of five fingers is yellow, and is like the long feather (*shah-par*) of the peacock, and its body as large as that of a goose. The neck of the goose is long and shapeless: that of this one is short, and has a shape.

My brother, Shāh 'Abbās, had asked for golden birds,50 and I sent some to him by his ambassador. On Monday51 the ceremony of my lunar weighing took place. At this entertainment Nūr Jahān Begam gave dresses of honour to forty-five of the great Amirs and private servants. On the 14th of the same month the camp was pitched at the village of Bahlwan52 belonging to the Sībā district. As I constantly longed for the air of Kāngṛa and the hill-country above-mentioned, I left the large camp at this place, and proceeded to inspect the said fort with some of my special servants and attendants. As Iʿtimādu-d-daula was ill I left him in the camp, and kept Ṣādiq K., the chief Bakhshi, there to look after him and guard the camp. The next day news came that his state had undergone a change, and that the signs of hopelessness were apparent. I could not bear the agitation of Nūr Jahān Begam, and, considering the affection which I bore towards him, I returned to the camp. At the end of the day I went to see him. It was the hour of his death agony. Sometimes he became unconscious and sometimes came back to his senses. Nūr Jahān Begam indicated me, and said: "Do you recognise (him)?" At such a time he recited this couplet of Anwarī:

Were a mother-born blind man present

He'd recognise Majesty in the World-Adorner.

I was for two hours at his pillow. Whenever he was conscious, whatever he said was intelligent and rational. In fine, on the 17th of the said month (Bahman) (about the end of January, 1622), after three gharis had passed he attained to eternal mercy. What shall I say about my feelings through this terrible event? He was a wise and perfect Vizier, and a learned and affectionate companion.

VERSE.53

By the reckoning of the eye, there's one frame less:

By Wisdom's reckoning, the lessening is more than thousands.

Though the weight of such a kingdom was on his shoulders, and it is not possible for or within the power of a mortal to make everyone contented, yet no one ever went to Iʿtimādu-d-daula with a petition or on business who turned from him in an injured frame of mind. He showed loyalty to the sovereign, and yet left pleased and hopeful him who was in need. In fact, this was a speciality of his. From the day on which his companion (his wife) attained to the mercy of God he cared no longer for himself, but melted away from day to day. Although outwardly he looked after the affairs of the kingdom, and taking pains with the ordering of civil matters, did not withdraw his hand from business, yet in his heart he grieved at the separation, and at last, after three months and twenty days, he passed away. The next day I went to condole with his sons and sons-in-law, and, presenting 41 of his children and connections and 12 of his dependents with dresses of honour, I took them out of their mourning garments.

The next day I marched with the same purpose (as before), and went to see the fort of Kāngṛa. In four stages the camp was pitched at the river Bānganga. Alf K. and S̲h̲aik̲h̲ Faiẓu-llah, the guards of the fort, had the good fortune to pay their respects. At this stage the offering of the Raja of Chamba54 was laid before me. His country is 25 koss beyond Kāngṛa. There is no greater Zamindari in these hills than this. The country is the asylum of all the Zamindars of the country. It has passes (*'aqabahā*) difficult to cross. Until now he had not obeyed any king nor sent offerings. His brother also was honoured by paying his respects, and on his part performed the dues of service and loyalty. He seemed to me to be reasonable and intelligent and urbane. I exalted him with all kinds of patronage and favour.

On the 24th55 of the same month I went to see the fort of Kāngṛa, and gave an order that the Qāẓī, the Chief Justice (*Mīr 'Adl*), and other learned men of Islam should accompany me and carry out in the fort whatever was customary, according to the religion of Muḥammad. Briefly, having traversed about one koss, I went up to the top of the fort, and by the grace of God, the call to prayer and the reading of the *Khuṭba* and the slaughter of a bullock, which had not taken place from the commencement of the building of the fort till now, were carried out in my presence. I prostrated myself in thanksgiving for this great gift, which no king had hoped to receive, and ordered a lofty mosque to be built inside the fort. The fort of Kāngṛa is situated on a high hill, and is so strong that if furnished with provisions and the necessaries for a fort the hand of force cannot reach its skirt, and the noose of stratagem must fall short of it. Although there are heights (*sar-kūbhā*) in some places, and guns and muskets might reach (the fort) from them, yet no harm would accrue to the garrison, for they could move to another part of the fort,56 and be safe. It has 23 bastions and seven gates. Its inner circumference is 1 koss and 15 ropes, its length is ¼ koss and 2 ropes (*ṭanāb*), its breadth not more than 22 ropes nor less than 15. Its height is 114 cubits. There are two reservoirs inside the fort, one 2 ropes long and 1½ broad; the other is of the same length (?).57

After going round the fort I went to see the temple of Durgā, which is known as Bhawan.58 A world has here wandered in the desert of error. Setting aside the infidels whose custom is the worship of idols, crowds on crowds of the people of Islam, traversing long distances, bring their offerings and pray to the black stone (image). Near the temple, and on the slope of the hill there is a sulphur-mine (*kān*), and its heat causes flames to continually burst forth. They call it Jwālā Mukhī59 (Flame-Face or Burning Mouth), and regard it as one of the idol's miracles. In fact, Hindus, while knowing the truth,60 deceive the common people. Hindus say61 that when the life of Mahādeo's wife came to an end and she drank the draught of death, Mahādeo, in his great love and attachment to her, took her dead body on his back, and went about the world carrying her corpse. When some time had passed in this manner, her form dissolved and dropped asunder, and each limb fell in a different place: they give honour and dignity to the place according to the dignity and grace of the member. As the breast, which when compared with other members has the greatest dignity, fell in this place, they hold it more precious than any other. Some maintain that this stone, which is now a place of worship for the vile infidels, is not the stone which was there originally, but that a body of the people62 of Islam came and carried off the original stone, and threw it into the bottom of the river, with the intent that no one could get at it. For a long time the tumult of the infidels and idol-worshippers had died away in the world, till a lying brahman hid a stone for his own ends, and going to the Raja of the time said: "I saw Durgā in a dream, and she said to me: 'They have thrown me into a certain place: quickly go and take me up.'" The Raja, in the simplicity of his heart, and greedy for the offerings of gold that would come to him, accepted the tale of the brahman, and sent a number of people with him, and brought that stone, and kept it in this place with honour, and started again the shop of error and misleading. But God only knows!

From the temple I went to see the valley which is known as Kūh-i-Madār.63 It is a delightful place. From its climate, the freshness of its verdure, and its delightful position it is a place of pleasure worthy to be seen. There is a waterfall here which pours down water from the top of the hill. I ordered them to put up a symmetrical building there. On the 25th of the month the standards were turned back to return. Having presented Alf K. and S̲haik̲h̲ Faiẓu-llah with horses and elephants I left them to defend the fort. Next day I encamped at the fort of Nūrpūr.64 It was reported to me that in this neighbourhood there were many jungle fowl. As I had never yet caught these, I made a halt of another day, and enjoyed myself with the sport, having caught four. One cannot distinguish them in shape and colour from domestic fowls. One of the peculiarities of these birds is that if they are caught by the feet and turned upside down, wherever they are taken they make no sound, and remain silent, contrary to the domestic fowl, which makes an outcry. Until the domestic fowl is plunged into hot water its feathers do not come off easily. The jungle fowl, like the partridge and *podna*,65 can be plucked when dry. I ordered them to roast them. It was found that the flesh of the full-grown ones was very tasteless and dry. The chickens had some juiciness, but were not good to eat. They cannot fly farther than a bow-shot. The cock66 is chiefly red, and the hen black and yellow. There are many in this Nūrpūr jungle. The ancient name of Nūrpūr is Dhamerī.67 Since Rāja Bāso built the fort and made houses and gardens they call it Nūrpūr, after my name. About Rs. 30,000 were expended on the building. Certes, the buildings Hindus construct after their fashion, however much they decorate them, are not pleasant. As the place was fit and the locality enchanting, I ordered them to spend Rs. 1,00,000 out of the public treasury, and to erect buildings at it, and to make lofty edifices suited to the spot.

At this time it was reported to me that there was a *Sannyāsī Motī*68 in the neighbourhood who had entirely renounced control over himself. I ordered them to bring him that I might ascertain the real state of affairs. They call Hindu devotees *Sarb bāsī*.69 By usage the word has become *San-nyāsī* (laying down everything). There are many degrees among them, and there are several orders among the Sarb bāsī. Among them there is the *Motī* order. They put themselves into the figure of a cross (?) (*ṣalb ikhtiyār mīkunand*) and surrender themselves (*taslīm*70 *mīsāzand*). For instance, they never speak. If for ten days and nights they stand in one place, they do not move their feet forwards or backwards; in fact, make no movement at all, and remain like fossils. When he came into my presence I examined him, and found a wonderful state of persistence. It occurred to me that in a state of drunkenness and absence of mind and delirium, some change might be wrought in him. Accordingly I ordered them to give him some cups of spirit (*'araq*) of double strength. This was done in royal fashion (liberally?), but not the least change took place, and he remained in the same impassive state. At last his senses left him, and they carried him out like a corpse. God Almighty granted him mercy so that he did not lose his life. Certainly there was great persistence in his nature.

At this time Bī-badal K. presented me with the chronogram of the conquest of Kāngṛa, and that of the foundation of the mosque which I had ordered. As he had hit it off well, I here record it:

VERSE.

World-gripper, World-giver, World-holder, World-king,

With the sword of *ghāzī*-ship he conquered this fort.

Wisdom spoke the date "The Jahāngīrī Fortune opened this fort."

He composed the chronogram71 of the building of the mosque as follows:

VERSE.

Nūru-d-dīn Shāh Jahāngīr s. Shāh Akbar

Is a king who in the Age hath no equal.

He took Fort Kāngṛa by the aid of God.

A drop from the cloud of his sword is a tempest.

As by his order this illumined mosque was built,

May his forehead shine by his prostration.

A hidden messenger said: "In seeking for the date

(Say) The mosque of Shāh Jahāngīr was illumined."72

On the first of the Divine month of Isfandārmuz I gave the establishment and everything belonging to the government and Amirship of I'timādu-d-daula to Nūr Jahān Begam, and ordered that her drums and orchestra should be sounded after those of the king. On the 4th of the same month I pitched in the neighbourhood of the pargana of Kashhūna.73 On this day Khwāja Abū-l-Ḥasan was raised to the lofty dignity of supreme Diwan. I conferred dresses of honour on 32 individuals of the Deccan Amirs. Abū Sa'īd, grandson of I'timādu-d-daula, was raised to the mansab of 1,000 personal and 500 horse. At this time a report came from Khurram that Khusrau, on the 8th74 (20th) of the month, had died of the disease of colic pains (*qūlanj*), and gone to the mercy of God.

On the 19th of the month I pitched on the bank of the Bihat (Jhelam). Qāsim K. was raised to the mansab of 3,000 personal and 2,000 horse. Rāja Kishan Dās was selected for the duty of faujdār of Delhi, and his mansab was fixed at 2,000 personal and 500 horse, original and increased. Previously to this, huntsmen and *yasāwulān* (guards) had been ordered to prepare a *jarga* (hunting-ring) in the *shikār-gāh* (hunting-place of) Girjhāk. When it was reported to me that they had brought the game into the enclosure, on the 24th of the month I went out to hunt with some of my special servants. Of hill *quchqār* (rams?) and gazelles 12475 head were taken. On this day it was reported that Ẓafar K. s. Zain K., had died. I promoted Sa'ādat Umīd, his son, to the mansab of 800 personal and 400 horse.

---

1 The I.O. MSS. have "Saturday." But Monday seems right, as Thursday was 4 Farwardīn. ↑

2 In the Āyīn, which was composed in the 40th year of Akbar's reign, Salīm's rank is given as 10,000, Murād's as 8,000, and Dāniyāl's as 7,000 (p. 308). ↑

3 In celebration of the commencement of the 16th year of the reign. ↑

4 *Yāqūt-i-kabūd*, "a blue ruby." ↑

5 The I.O. MSS. have Mīrzā Muḥammad. ↑

6 Jamālu-d-dīn Ḥusain Injū. ↑

7 See Vullers, s.v. It is a smelling-bottle or case containing ambergris. ↑

8 Blochmann, 55. ↑

9 Apparently a zebra. See Iqbāl-nāma, 179, where it is stated that it was brought by sea. The text of the Tūzuk is wrong, as usual. What we should

read is: “It was like a tiger (MS. 181 and Iqbāl-nāma have *s͟hīr*, not *babar*), but the markings on a tiger are black and yellow, and these were black and white.” ↑

10 Perhaps this is the muhar now in Germany. ↑

11 Ḥusain K. Tukrīya. ↑

12 *Nafs mī-sūzad.* ↑

13 Thursday night or Friday eve is what is meant. ↑

14 Elliot, VI. 378. ↑

15 King David was said to be a maker of cuirasses. ↑

16 *Yamānī.* Elliot has *almāsī* (adamant-like). ↑

17 See Blochmann’s translation and remarks in Proceedings A.S.B. for 1869, p. 167. It is there stated that the date of the fall of the meteorite was Friday, April 10, 1621, O.S., and that the weight would be nearly 5.271 pounds troy. ↑

18 A widow of Bāqī Muḥammad. ↑

19 Elliot, VI. 379. ↑

20 Elliot, VI. 379, has “in sight of the fort.” Perhaps the meaning is that the villages were in the jurisdiction of the fort. ↑

21 The Iqbāl-nāma, 181, has “fourteen.” ↑

22 The account of S͟hāh Jahān’s spirited attack on the Deccanis is in some places rather obscurely worded, and the printed edition is not always correct. Help can be obtained from the Iqbāl-nāma, 181, etc., and from Elliot, VI. 379. The text has *firār*, “flight,” and this has been followed by Elliot, who has “on their approach the rebels took to flight, and removed to a distance from Burhanpur.” But the true reading, as shown by the Iqbāl-nāma, is *qarār*, “firmness,” not *firār*, and the words are *bar daur-i-s͟hahr*, “round the city,” not *bar dūr*, “far from.” The rebels were, as the Iqbāl-nāma states, “in the environs of the city,” “*dar sawād-i-s͟hahr*,” but apparently not in such force as to prevent S͟hāh Jahān’s *sazāwuls*—*i.e.*, his apparitors and summoners—from going into the city and bringing out recruits. ↑

23 In the I.O. MSS. the word looks like *bī-jāgarī* (want of settled home or residence?). ↑

24 Text has *chasa*. The word may be *jus͟hs͟ha*, given in Vullers, 516*b*, as meaning robes or garments, and this is the meaning given to it by Elliot, but the Iqbāl-nāma has *jubba*, “cuirasses,” and this I have adopted. It is *jubba* in I.O. No. 181. ↑

25 Text, *chihlā u k̲h̲amcha.* The last word should, I think, be *jamjama. Chihlā* in Hindustani means a "slimy place." It is *jamjama* in I.O. MS., No. 181. ↑

26 Text has *g̲h̲air* instead of ʿAmbar. ↑

27 Text wrongly has *Rūp-ratan.* ↑

28 Pādis̲h̲āh-nāma, I., Part II., p. 349. ↑

29 The text wrongly has 1,000. ↑

30 The Bib. Ind. ed. of Iqbāl-nāma, 184, inserts a negative here, but this seems wrong. In a MS. in my possession there is no negative. ↑

31 Elliot, VI. 380. ↑

32 Elliot, VI. 448, the Maʾāṣiru-l-Umarā, I. 577, and Pādis̲h̲āh-nāma I., Part II., 347. ↑

33 Text wrongly has 12th. Jahāngīr's birthday was on the 18th S̲h̲ahrīwar. ↑

34 *K̲h̲iffatī.* I am not sure of the reading. One B.M. MS. seems to have *ḥaqqī*, and perhaps the meaning is that the physicians had already been abundantly recompensed for their labour for two or three days, *ḥaqqī* being taken as equal to *ḥaqq-i-saʿī.* ↑

35 A little before his weight came only to Rs. 6,500 (p. 329 of text). But possibly Jahāngīr means that he had himself weighed for Jotik's benefit. ↑

36 Elliot, VI. 381. ↑

37 *Mādar-i-dahr.* ↑

38 Text and MSS. have *mādar-i-ūrā*, "her mother"(?) Perhaps we should read *mā ūrā*, "we (esteemed) her not less than our own mother." Or it may be that the "her" means Nūr Jahān, and that Jahāngīr means he esteemed his mother-in-law as much as his own mother. ↑

39 That is, S̲h̲āh Jahān (see Iqbāl-nāma, 186). ↑

40 The MSS. seem to have K̲h̲ostī—*i.e.*, of K̲h̲ost. ↑

41 Text 8th, but should be 20th. ↑

42 Alwanū in MSS. It appears to be Aluwa, 11m. S.-E. of Sirhind. ↑

43 Text *pahangī*, which seems unintelligible. The MSS. have *māhīki(?)-i-k̲h̲ūrd*, "a small fish." ↑

44 *Baqqa.* ↑

45 Founded by Nūr Jahān (see Cunningham, "Archæological Reports," XIV. 62). ↑

46 Spelt Ilah-bās. ↑

47 I have translated this passage from the MSS., which differ a good deal from the text. Talwāra was in the Bārī Dū'āb Sarkār (Jarrett, II. 318.) ↑

48 Apparently this is the *pulpaikar* of Bābar (Erskine, 320), though the two descriptions do not altogether agree. Perhaps it is a hornbill. ↑

49 The MSS. have *sal* and *lūt.* Is it the *s̲h̲ām* of Bābar? (Erskine, 320). ↑

50 *Murg̲h̲-i-zarīn*, goldfinch or golden oriole (?). ↑

51 The date and month are not mentioned, but it appears from the Iqbāl-nāma, which gives the next entry as 14 Bahman, that the month was Bahman, and that the date was probably about 20 January, 1622. ↑

52 The Bhalon of Jarrett, II. 316. Sībah is mentioned at p. 317, *ibid.* The text has Sītā. ↑

53 The couplet comes from Budags's elegy on Abū-l-Ḥasan Nahid Balk̲h̲i. See Aufi's *Lababu-l-Albab*. Browne's ed., Part II., p. 3. ↑

54 Text wrongly has Chītā. Chamba is N.-W. of Kāngṛa. ↑

55 Elliot, VI. 382. ↑

56 The fort was destroyed by the earthquake of 1905 (I.G., XIV. 397). Presumably Jahāngīr's mosque was also destroyed then. ↑

57 The breadth of the second tank is not mentioned in the MSS. ↑

58 "The present temple of Bajreswari Devi is at Bhawan, a suburb of Kāngṛa" (I.G., XIV. 386). ↑

59 See I.G., XIV. 86, and Jarrett, II. 314 and n. 1. Jarrett states that Jwālā Mukhī is two days' journey from Kāngṛa. Apparently Jahāngīr took his statement from the Āyīn, which has the words "in the vicinity" (Jarrett, *ibid.*). Jarrett's statement that Jwālā Mukhī is two days' journey from Kāngṛa is taken from Tieffenthaler, I. 108. Tieffenthaler adds that the distance is 14 to 15 *milles* (leagues, or kosses). He speaks of the Fort of Kāngṛa as being only one-fourth of a *mille* in circumference. The image, he states, was that of Bhowani, and represented the lower part of the goddess's body. The head was alleged to be at Jwālā Mukhī. ↑

60 *I.e.*, know the physical cause of the flame. The MSS. do not mention Hindus in this clause. ↑

61 See Jarrett, II. 313, and note 2. ↑

62 The temple was sacked by Maḥmūd of G͟haznīn. ↑

63 This might be Koh-i-Mandār, the hill which was used as a churning-stick by the gods. There is a hill of this name in Bhagalpur district which is known as Mandārgirī. But probably Kūh-i-Madār here means the centre-hill, for in the Bib. Ind. text of the Āyīn-i-Akbarī, I. 538, two lines from foot, it is said that the place is called Jālandharī, and a note (7) gives the various reading, "this spot is regarded as the centre," "*sar-i-ẕamīn-rā madār pindārand.*" Apparently it is regarded as the central place because the breast fell here, Jarrett, II. 314, n. According to the list given there the right breast fell at Jālandhara and the tongue at Jwālā Mukhī. ↑

64 I.G., new ed., XIX. 232. ↑

65 *Podna*, or *būdana.* The quail. ↑

66 Text *k͟hirdas͟h*, which I presume is a mistake for *k͟hurūs.* ↑

67 Dhameri. See I.G., XIX. 232. ↑

68 *Mautī* might mean "dead," but probably the word means "Pearl," and was the title assumed by a tribe or family among the Sannyāsīs. See *infra.* The statement that this order put themselves into the figure of a cross doubtless means that they belong to the Urdu bāhū (arms-aloft) sect—*i.e.*, the sect who raise their arms above their heads, in the figure of a cross. In Tavernier, II. 378, of ed. of 1676, this is the 8th posture of ascetics, and at that page and at 376 there are figures of such ascetics. The I.O. MSS. have *salab*, "mourning," instead of *ṣalb.* ↑

69 *Sarva vāsī* means "all-abiding." Perhaps the word should be *Sarva nāsī*, "all-destroying." ↑

70 For *taslīm*, see Hughes' Dict. of Islam. Possibly we should read *taṣlīb*, "make the sign of the cross." ↑

71 The chronogram of the taking of the fort yields 1029, and that of the building of the mosque 1031. ↑

72 *Nūrānī*, "illumined," an allusion to Jahāngīr's name. ↑

73 The MSS. have Kahtūma apparently. ? Kahūta in Rāwalpindī district. ↑

74 This should be, I think, the 20th, and though the name of the month is not given, it should be Bahman. See MSS. and Iqbālnāma, 191. K͟husrau died in the Deccan, and presumably at Burhanpur or Āsīr. 20 Bahman, 1031, corresponds to January 29, 1622, O.S. But the date of his death has not been quite determined. See J.R.A.S. for 1907, p. 601. ↑

75 The I.O. MSS. have 121 instead of 124, and they add to the information about Ẓafar K. that he died in Ghaznin. They also give his son's name as Sa'ādatu-llah. The Iqbāl-nāma, p. 191, has 121 hill sheep, mārkẖūr and deer. ↑

# THE SEVENTEENTH NEW YEAR'S FEAST AFTER THE AUSPICIOUS ACCESSION

On the eve of Monday, the ——,1 of the month of Jumāda-l-awwal, A.H. 1031, March 10–12, 1622, after one watch, five gharis and a fraction had passed, the sun that illuminates the world lighted the mansion of Aries, and the 17th year of the reign of this suppliant began auspiciously and happily. On this joy-increasing day Āṣaf K. was promoted to the mansab of 6,000 personal and horse. Having given Qāsim K. leave to proceed to the government of the Panjab, I presented him with a horse, an elephant, and a dress of honour. Eighty thousand darbs were given to Zambil Beg, ambassador of the ruler of Persia. On the 6th of the same month (Farwardīn) the royal camp was at Rāwalpindī. Fāẓil K. was promoted to the post of Bakhshi. Zambīl Beg was ordered to remain at ease in Lahore until the return of the victorious army from Kashmir. An elephant was conferred on Akbarqulī K. Gakkar.

At this time I frequently heard that the ruler of Persia had hastened from Khurasan for the purpose of conquering Qandahar. Although looking to our previous and present connections, it appeared very unlikely, and beyond all calculation, that such a great king should entertain such light and crude ideas, and himself come against one of my humble slaves who was in Qandahar with 300 or 4002 servants, yet as caution is one of the duties of a ruler and becoming to a king, I sent Zainu-l-ʿĀbidīn, Bakhshi of *Aḥadīs*, with a gracious farman to K͟hurram to come and wait on me with all possible speed with a victorious host, and elephants of mountain hugeness, and the numerous artillery that were assigned for his support in that Subah. So that, if these words should be near the truth, he might come and be despatched with an innumerable army and countless treasure, in order that he (the king of Persia) might discover the result of breaking faith and of wrong-doing.

On the 8th I halted at the fountain of Ḥasan Abdāl. Fidāʾī K. was promoted to the mansab of 2,000 personal and 1,000 horse, and Badīʿu-z-zamān was appointed Bakhshi of the Aḥadīs. On Friday, the 12th, Mahābat K., having come from Kabul, waited on me and had the good fortune to pay his respects, and became the recipient of daily-increasing favours. He presented 100 muhrs as a present and Rs. 10,000 as alms. K͟hwāja Abū-l-Ḥasan passed his followers before me in review; 2,500 well-horsed cavalry were enrolled of whom 400 were matchlock men. At this stage a *qamurg͟ha* hunt was arranged, and I shot3 33 hill *qūchqār* (mountain sheep), etc. At this time Ḥakīm Mūminā, at the recommendation of the pillar of the State, Mahābat K., had the good fortune to wait on me. With power and courage he undertook my cure, and I hope that his coming may prove auspicious to me. The mansab of Amānu-llah, s. Mahābat K., was fixed at 2,000 personal and 1,800 horse. On the 19th I encamped near Pakhlī, and the feast of the culmination was held there. Having given Mahābat K. leave to return to Kabul, I gave him a horse, an elephant, and a dress of honour. The mansab of I'tibār K. was ordered to be 5,000 personal and 4,000 horse. As he was an old servant, and had become very weak and old, I promoted him to the Subah of Agra, and entrusted to him the defence of the fort and the treasury, and, presenting him with an elephant, a horse, and a dress of honour, dismissed him. At the Pass of Kunwar4 Mast, Irādat K. came from Kashmir, and had the good fortune to kiss the threshold. On the 2nd of the Divine month of Urdībihisht, I entered the enchanting region of Kashmir. Mīr Mīrān was promoted to the mansab of 2,500 personal and 1,400 horse. At this time, in order to ease the condition of the ryots and soldiery, I did away with the faujdāri cess, and gave an order that in the whole of my dominions they should not impose anything on account of faujdāri. Zabar-dast K., Master of the Ceremonies (Mīr Tūzuk), was promoted to the mansab of 2,000 personal and 700 horse. On the 13th, by the advice of the physicians, and especially of Ḥakīm Mūminā, I was lightened by being bled from my left leg. A present of a dress of honour was made to Muqarrab K., and one of 1,000 darbs to Ḥakīm Mūminā. At the request of Khurram the mansab of 'Abdu-llah K. was fixed at 6,000. Sarfarāz5 K. was honoured with the gift of drums. Bahādur K. Uzbeg, having come from Qandahar, had the good fortune to pay his respects: by way of nazar he gave 100 muhrs, and by way of charity offered Rs. 4,000. Muṣṭafā K., governor of Thatta, had sent as an offering a Shāh-nāma and a Khamsa (quintet) of Shaikh Niẓāmī illustrated by masters (of painting), along with other presents: these were laid before me. On the 1st of the Divine month of Khurdād Lashkar K. was exalted to the mansab of 4,000 personal and 3,000 horse, and to Mīr Jumla was given that of 2,500 personal and 1,000 horse. Some of the Amirs of the Deccan were similarly honoured with an increase of mansab. Promotion was also given as follows: Sardār K., 3,000 and 2,500 horse; Sar-buland K., 2,500 personal and 2,200 horse; Bāqī K., 2,500 and 2,000 horse; Sharza K., 2,500 and 1,200 horse; Jān-sipār K., 2,000 personal and 2,000 horse; Mīrzā Wālī, 2,500 and 1,000 horse; Mīrzā Badī'u-z-zamān s. Mīrzā Shāhrukh, 1,500 personal and horse; Zāhid K., 1,500 and 700 horse; 'Aqīdat K., 1,200 and 300 horse; Ibrāhīm Ḥusain Kāshgharī, 1,200 and 600 horse; and Ẕū-l-faqār K., 1,000 personal and 500 horse. Rāja Gaj Singh and Himmat K. were selected for drums. On the 2nd of the Divine month of Tīr, Sayyid Bāyazīd was honoured with the title of Muṣṭafā K., and was also presented with drums. At this time Tahawwur K., who is one of the personal servants, was despatched with a gracious farman to summon my fortunate son Shāh Parwīz.

Some days before this, petitions came from the officials in Qandahar reporting the intention of the ruler of Persia to conquer Qandahar, but my mind, which is actuated by sincerity, looking to past and present relations, placed no reliance on the truth of this until the report of my son Khān Jahān arrived that Shāh ʿAbbās, with the armies of Iraq and Khurasan, had come and besieged Qandahar. I ordered them to fix an hour for leaving Kashmir. Khwāja Abū-l-Ḥasan, the Diwan, and Bakhshī Ṣādiq K. hastened to Lahore in advance of the victorious army to expedite the arrival of the princes of high degree with the armies of the Deccan, Gujarat, Bengal, and Behar, and to send on the Amirs who were present with the victorious stirrups, and those who one after another should come in from the districts of their jagirs to my son Khān Jahān at Multan. At the same time the artillery, with the strings of warlike elephants, and the armoury[6] were to be prepared and forwarded. As there was little cultivation between Multan and Qandahar, the despatch of a large army without provisions was not to be thought of. It was therefore decided to encourage the grain-sellers, who in the language of India are called *banjārā*, and, providing them with money, to take them along with the victorious army, so that there might be no difficulty about supplies. The Banjārās[7] are a tribe. Some of them have 1,000 bullocks, and some more or less. They take grain from different districts (*bulūkāt*) into the towns and sell it. They go along with the armies, and with such an army there would be 100,000 bullocks or more. It is hoped that by the grace of the Creator, the army will be furnished with numbers and arms so that there may be no delay or hesitation until it reaches Isfāhan, which is his (the Shah's) capital. A farman was sent to Khān Jahān to beware and not start in that direction (Qandahar) from Multan before the arrival of the victorious army, and not be disturbed, but attend to orders. Bahādur K. Uzbeg was selected to go as an auxiliary to the army of Qandahar, and favoured with a horse and dress of honour. Fāẓil K. was given the mansab of 2,000 personal and 750 horse.

As it had been brought to notice that the poor of Kashmir suffer hardships in the winter from the excessive cold, and live with difficulty, I ordered that a village of the rental of Rs. 3,000 or Rs. 4,000 should be entrusted to Mullā Ṭālib Iṣfahānī,[8] to be expended in providing clothes for the poor, and for warming water, for purposes of ablution, in the mosques.

As it was reported that the Zamindars of Kishtwār had again raised their heads in disobedience and sin, and engaged in sedition and disturbance, Irādat K. was ordered to proceed hot-foot, before they had time to establish themselves firmly, and having inflicted condign punishment on them to tear up the root of sedition. On this day Zainu-l-ʿĀbidīn, who had been sent to summon Khurram, came and waited on me, and reported that the stipulation he made was that he should pass the rainy season in the fort of Māndū, and then come to Court. His report was read. I9 did not like the style of its purport nor the request he made, and, on the contrary, the traces of disloyalty (*bī-daulati*) were apparent. There being no remedy, an order was given that as he proposed to come after the rains, he should despatch the great Amirs, the servants of the Court who were employed in assisting him, and especially the Sayyids of Bārha and Bukhara, the S͟haik͟h-zādas, the Afghans, and the Rajputs. Mīrzā Rustam and I'tiqād K. were ordered to go to Lahore in advance, and assist the army of Qandahar. Rs. 1,00,000 were given them as advance of pay, and I also granted drums to 'Ināyat K. and I'timād K. Irādat K., who had hastened to punish the rebels of Kis͟htwār, having killed many of them and regained the mastery and established himself firmly, returned to duty. Mu'tamid K. had been appointed Bak͟hs͟hī to the army of the Deccan. As that matter was over10 he was sent for at his own request. He came on this day, and on his arrival kissed the threshold.

It is a strange thing that when a pearl of the value of Rs. 14,000 or 15,000 was lost in the harem, Jotik Rāy, the astrologer, represented that it would be found in two or three days. Ṣādiq K. Rammāl (soothsayer) represented that in the same two or three days it would come from a place which was perfectly clean and pure, such as the place of worship or oratory. A female soothsayer represented that it would soon be found, and that a woman with white skin would bring it in a state of ecstasy, and give it into the hand of the Ḥaẓrat (the king). It happened that on the third day one of the Turkish girls found it in the oratory, and all in smiles and in a happy frame of mind gave it to me. As the words of all three came true each one was favoured with an acceptable reward. This is written because it is not devoid of strangeness.

At this time I appointed Kaukab and K͟hidmatgār K., and others to the number of twelve in all, of the familiar servants to be *saẓāwuls* of the Amirs in the Deccan in order that they might exert themselves and send them forward as soon as possible to Court, so that they (the Amīrs) might be sent to the victorious army at Qandahar.11 At this time it was frequently reported to me that K͟hurram had taken into his possession some of the estates of the jagir of Nūr Jahān Begam and S͟hahriyār, and especially the pargana of Dholpur, which had by the High Diwan been assigned to S͟hahriyār, and had sent there an Afghan of the name of Daryā, one of his own servants, with a body of men. Daryā fought with S͟harīfu-l-mulk, a servant of S͟hahriyār, who had been appointed to the faujdāri of that region, and many were killed on both sides. Although in consequence of his (K͟hurram's) remaining in the fort of Māndū, and the unreasonable requests made in his letter it appeared that his reason was turned, yet from hearing this news it became clear that he was unworthy of all the favours and cherishing I had bestowed on him, and that his brain had gone wrong. Accordingly I sent Rāja Rūz-afzūn, who was a confidential servant, to him, and made inquiries as to the cause of this boldness. He was ordered hereafter to behave properly, and not place his foot beyond the path of reasonableness and the high road of politeness, and content himself with the districts of his own jagir that he had obtained from the High Diwan. He must also beware not to form any intention of coming to wait upon me, but to send the body of the servants of the State I had requisitioned on account of the disturbance at Qandahar to the Court. If anything contrary to this order should come to notice, he would repent it.

At this time Mīr Ẓahīru-d-dīn, the grandson of Mīr Mīrān, s. the famous S̲h̲āh Niʿmatu-llah, came from Persia and waited on me, and received as a present a dress of honour and 8,000 darbs. Ujālā Dakhanī obtained leave to go to Rāja Bīr Singh Deo with a gracious farman in order that he should act as *saẓāwul* and collect the men. Previously to this, on account of the great regard and abundant affection I bore to K̲h̲urram and his sons, at the time when his son (S̲h̲ujāʿ) was very ill, I had determined that if God Almighty would grant him to me I would not again sport with a gun, and would inflict no injury on a living thing with my own hand. Notwithstanding my inclination and love for hunting, especially with a gun, I had given it up for five years. At this time, when I was greatly distressed at his unkind behaviour, I took again to sporting with a gun, and gave orders that nobody should remain in the palace without one. In a short time most of the servants took a liking to shooting with guns, and the archers,12 in order to perform their duties, became cavalry soldiers.

On the 25th of the month, corresponding with the 7th S̲h̲awwāl, at the favourable hour that had been chosen, I turned towards Lahore from Kashmir (apparently means Srinagar, the capital). I sent Bihārī Dās Brahman with a gracious farman to Rānā Karan to the effect that he should bring his son with a body of men to pay his respects to me. Mīr Ẓahīru-d-dīn was promoted to the mansab of 1,000 personal and 400 horse. As he represented to me that he was in debt, I made him a present of Rs. 10,000. On the 1st of S̲h̲ahrīwar I encamped at the fountain of Achbal,13 and on Thursday I had a feast of cups beside the fountain.14 On this auspicious day my fortunate son S̲h̲ahriyār was appointed to the Qandahar expedition, and was promoted to the mansab of 12,000 personal and 8,000 horse. A special dress of honour, with a *nādirī* with pearl buttons, was also given him. At this time a merchant had brought two large pearls from the country of Turkey, one of them weighing 1¼ *misqāls*, and the second 1 *surk̲h̲* less. Nūr Jahān Begam bought the two for Rs. 60,000, and presented them to me as an offering on the same day. On Friday, the 10th, by the advice of Ḥakīm Mūminā,15 I was relieved by bleeding from the arm. Muqarrab K., who has great skill in this art, always used to bleed me, and possibly never failed before, but now failed twice. Afterwards Qāsim, his nephew, bled me. I gave him a dress of honour and

Rs. 2,000, and gave 1,000 darbs to Ḥakīm Mūminā. Mīr Khān, at the request of Khān Jahān, was promoted to the mansab of 1,500 and 900 horse.

On the 21st of the month the feast of my solar weighing took place, and the 54th year of the age of this suppliant at the throne of God began auspiciously and happily. I hope that the whole of my life will be spent in fulfilling the will of God. On the 28th, I went to see the waterfall of Ashar16 (?). As this spring is famous for its sweetness and agreeable flavour, I weighed it in my presence against Ganges water, and that17 of the valley of Lār. The water of Ashar was 3 *māsha* heavier than that of the Ganges, and the latter was ½ *māsha* lighter than that of the valley of Lār. On the 30th the camp was at Hīrāpūr. Though Irādat K. had done his duty in Kishtwār well, yet as the ryots and inhabitants of Kashmir complained of his treatment of them, I promoted I'tiqād K. to the governorship of Kashmir. I bestowed on him a horse, a dress of honour, and a special enemy-piercing18 sword, and appointed Irādat K. to do duty with the army of Qandahar. Having brought Kunwar Singh, the Raja of Kishtwār, out of the fortress of Gwalior, where he was imprisoned, I bestowed Kishtwār on him, and gave him a horse and a dress of honour, with the title of Raja. I sent Ḥaidar Malik to Kashmir (*i.e.*, Srinagar) to bring a canal from the valley of Lār to the Nūr-afzā garden, giving him Rs. 30,000 for the materials and labour. On the 12th of the month I came down from the hill country of Jammū, and pitched at Bhimbhar. The next day I had a *qamurqha* hunt. To Dāwar-bakhsh, s. Khusrau, I gave the mansab of 5,000 personal and 2,000 horse. On the 24th I crossed the Chenāb.19 Mīrzā Rustam came from Lahore, and waited on me. On the same day Afẓal20 K., Khurram's Diwan, bringing a petition from him, waited on me. He had clothed his immoderate acts in the garment of apology, and had sent him with the idea that perhaps he might carry his point by flattery and smooth speeches, and so correct his improprieties. I21 paid no attention, and did not listen to him. The Diwan Khwāja Abū-l-Ḥasan and Ṣādiq K. Bakhshī, who had hastened to Lahore to make provision for the army of Qandahar, had the good fortune to kiss the threshold. On the 1st of the Divine month of Ābān, Amānu-llah, s. Mahābat K., was promoted to the mansab of 3,000 personal and 1,700 horse. A gracious farman was sent to summon Mahābat K. At this time 'Abdu-llah K., whom I had sent for for service at Qandahar, having come from the district of his jagir, paid his respects. On the 4th of the same month I entered the city of Lahore auspiciously and happily. Alf K. was promoted to the mansab of 2,000 and 1,500 horse. I gave22 an order to the chief Diwans to levy the pay of the force of servants of the State who had been appointed for service at Qandahar out of the jagirs of Khurram, which were in the Sarkar of Ḥiṣār, and in the Dū-āb and those regions. In the place of these he might take possession of districts from the Subah of Malwa and the Deccan, and Gujarat and Khandesh, wherever he wished. Presenting

Afẕal K. with a dress of honour I gave him leave to go. An order was passed that the Subahs of Gujarat, Malwa, the Deccan and Khandesh should be handed over to him (K̲h̲urram), and he might take up a permanent residence wherever he might wish, and employ himself in the administration of those regions. He was to send quickly the sazāwuls who had been appointed to bring the servants of the State who had been summoned to my presence on account of the disturbance at Qandahar. After that he was to look after his own charge, and not depart from order: otherwise, he would repent. On this day I gave the best *tipchāq* horse that was in my private stable to ʿAbdu-llah K. On the 26th Ḥaidar Beg and Walī Beg, envoys of the ruler of Persia, had an audience. After performing the ceremony of salutation they produced a letter from the Shah. My son K̲h̲ān Jahān, according to order, having come post from Multan, waited on me. He presented as offerings 1,000 muhrs, 1,000 rupees, and 18 horses. Mahābat K. was promoted to the mansab of 6,000 personal and 5,000 horse. I gave an elephant to Mīrzā Rustam. Rāja Sārang Deo was appointed sazāwul to Rāja Bīr Singh Deo. I told him to produce him at Court as quickly as possible. On23 the 7th of the Divine month of Āẕar the ambassadors of S̲h̲āh ʿAbbās, who had come at different times, were presented with dresses of honour and their expenses, and given leave to go. The letter he had sent by Ḥaidar Beg making excuses in the matter of Qandahar has been given in this record of good fortune (Iqbāl-nāma) along with my reply.

LETTER OF THE KING OF PERSIA.

(After compliments, and good wishes for that "brother dear as life" the letter proceeds as follows):

"You will be aware that after the death of the Nawāb S̲h̲āh Jannat-makān (S̲h̲āh Ṭahmāsp) great misfortunes befell Persia. Many territories which belonged to our saintly family passed out of possession, but when this suppliant at the throne of Grace became sovereign, he, by God's help, and the excellent measures of friends, recovered the hereditary lands which were in the possession of enemies. As Qandahar was held by the agents of your lofty family, I regarded you as myself, and did not make any objection. From feelings of unity and brotherhood we waited, thinking that you would, after the manner of your ancestors24 who are in Paradise, voluntarily take the matter into your consideration. When you neglected to do this, I repeatedly, by writing and verbal messages, directly and indirectly, asked for the disposal of the question, thinking that perhaps that petty country (Qandahar) was not regarded as worthy of your notice. You said several times that by making over the territory to our family, the notions of enemies and censurers would be disposed of, and praters, enviers, and fault-finders would be put to silence. A faction25 formerly delayed the settlement of this matter. As the truth of the affair was known to friends and enemies, and as no clear answer, either of refusal or concession, came from you, it occurred to me that I would go to Qandahar to see it, and to hunt. In this way the agents of my distinguished brother, in accordance with the ties of friendship which exist between us, might welcome us and wait upon us. By this means the relationship of union would be renewed, and would be made evident to the world, and the tongues of the envious and the evil-speaking be shortened. With this view, I set off without apparatus for taking forts, and when I came to Farāh I sent a rescript to the governor of Qandahar, mentioning that I intended to see the place and hunt there. I did this in order that he might treat me as a guest. We also called the honourable K͟hwāja Bāqī Kurkarāq, and sent a message to the governor and the other officers in the fort to the effect that there was no difference between Your Majesty and ourselves, and that we were aware of each other's territories, and that we were coming to see the country. Therefore they were not to act in such a way as to give umbrage or to vex anyone. They did not receive the conciliatory order and message in the proper way, but showed obstinacy and a rebellious spirit. When I came to the fort I again called the honourable aforesaid (K. Bāqī), and sent him with the message that I had directed my troops not to invest the fort till the lapse of ten days. They did not receive the wholesome advice, and were stubborn in their opposition. As there was nothing more to be done, the Persian army set about taking the fort, though it was in want of appliances, and soon levelled the walls and bastions with the ground. The garrison became straitened, and asked for quarter. We, too, maintained the ties of love which had existed from of old between the two exalted dynasties, and the brotherly relation which was formed between you and me when you were prince (Mīrzā), and which was an object of envy to contemporary sovereigns, and from my innate kindness forgave their errors and offences. Encompassing them with favours, I sent them safe and sound to your Court along with Ḥaidar Beg Qūrbāsh͟ī, who is one of the sincere Ṣūfīs of this family. Of a truth, the foundation of love and union, both inherited and acquired, on the part of this seeker after affection, has not grown old or decayed, and is strong so that no rupture in it can take place on account of any things which may have transpired owing to the action of Fate.

VERSE.

Between us and you there cannot be trouble,

There can be naught but love and trust.

"It is hoped that you, too, will preserve your affection for us, and that you will not approve of certain strange actions, and that if any suspicion about friendship arise you will endeavour by your innate goodness and continual love to efface it. May the ever-vernal flower of union and cordiality remain in bloom, and every effort be made to strengthen the foundations of concord, and to cleanse the fountains of agreement which regulate temperaments and territories. You will regard all our dominions as belonging to you, and will extend your friendship to everyone (in them?), and will proclaim that it (Qandahar) has been given up to him (ʿAbbās) without any objection, and that such trifles are of no importance, and that though the governor and officers who were in the fort did some things which were obstacles to friendship, yet what took place was done by you and me. They performed the duties of service and life devotion. It is certain, too, that Your Majesty will be gracious to them, and will treat them with royal kindness, and will not shame me before them. What more need I write? May thy star-brushing standards ever be associated with the Divine aids!" REPLY TO THE LETTER OF SHAH ʿABBĀS.

"Unfeigned thanks, and pure thanksgivings are due to the sole object of worship (God) for that the maintenance of the compacts and treaties of great princes is the cause of the order of Creation and the repose of mankind. A proof of this is the harmony and unity which existed between us and the exalted family (of Persia), and which were increased during our time. These things were the envy of contemporary sovereigns. The glorious Shah—the star of heaven's army, the ruler of the nations, the adorner of the Kayānī tiara, the fitting occupant of the throne of Chosroes, the fruitful tree of the gardens of sovereignty, the splendid nursling of the parterres of prophecy and saintship, the cream of the Ṣafawī dynasty—hath without ground or reason, engaged in disturbing the rose-garden of love and friendship and brotherhood in which for long periods there has been no possibility of a breath of confusion. Clearly the methods of union and concord among princes require that they make oaths of friendship to one another, and that there should be perfect spiritual agreement between them. There should be no need of physical contact, and still less should there be any necessity for visiting one another's countries for 'shooting and spectacle' (*sair u shikār*).

VERSE.

Alas, a hundred times for the love passing thought!

"By the arrival of your loving letter apologizing for the 'spectacle and shooting' (*sair u shikār*) of Qandahar, which came with the honourable Ḥaidar Beg and Walī Beg, I became apprised of the bodily health of your angelic personality, and the flowers of joy were scattered over the world. Let it not be hidden from the world-adorning mind of my exalted and prosperous brother that until the arrival of the letter and messages brought by Zambīl Beg no mention had been made by you in letters or verbal messages of your wish for Qandahar. At the time when we were engaged in visiting the delightful land of Kashmir, the Deccan lords, in their shortsightedness, extended their feet beyond the limits of obedience, and trod the path of rebellion. Accordingly it became necessary for me to chastise them. I moved my standards to Lahore, and appointed my worthy26 son S͟hāh Jahān to proceed against them with a victorious army. I myself was proceeding to Agra when Zambīl Beg arrived, and produced your loving letter. I took it as a good omen, and went off to Agra to put down the enemies and the rebels. In the jewelled and pearl-dropping letter there was no mention of a wish for Qandahar. It was mentioned verbally by Zambīl Beg. In reply, I said to him that I made no difficulty with regard to anything that my brother wished. Please God, after settling the Deccan affair, I would send him back in a manner suitable to my sovereignty. I also said that as he had made long marches he should repose for some days in Lahore, and that I would afterwards send for him. After coming to Agra, I sent for him and gave him leave to depart. As the favour of God attaches to this suppliant, I withdrew my mind from victories and proceeded to the Panjab. My intention was to send him away, but after disposing of some necessary matters I went to Kashmir on account of the hot weather. After coming there I sent for Zambīl Beg in order to give him his leave. I also wished to show him something of that delightful country. Meanwhile news came that my prosperous brother had come to take Qandahar. This idea had never entered my mind, and I was entirely astonished. What could there be in a petty village that he should set out to take it, and that he should shut his eyes to so much friendship and brotherly feeling? Though truthful reporters sent the news, I could not credit it! When it became certain I immediately gave orders to ʿAbdu-l-ʿAzīz K. not to transgress in any way the good pleasure of that prosperous brother. Up to now the relationship of brotherhood stands firm, and I do not value the world in comparison therewith, nor do I consider any gift equal to it. But it would have been right and brotherly that he should have waited till the arrival of the ambassador. Perhaps he would be successful in the object27 and claim for which he had come. When he (ʿAbbās) takes such steps before the return of the ambassador, to whom will mankind ascribe the merit of keeping compacts and of preserving the capital of humanity and liberality! May God preserve you at all times!"

---

After I had given leave to the ambassadors, I devoted all my energy to urging on the Qandahar force, and presented my son K͟hān Jahān, who had been sent for for certain matters, with an elephant, a special horse, a jewelled sword and dagger, and a dress of honour. I sent him on as an advance guard, and directed him to remain in Multan until the arrival of Prince S͟hahriyār with the victorious army. Bāqir K., who was faujdār of Multan, was summoned to Court, and I appointed ʿAlī-qulī Beg Darman to assist him (K͟hān Jahān), and raised him to the mansab of 1,500. In the same manner, having raised M.

Rustam to the mansab of 5,000, I appointed him to the duty of assisting that son with the (Qandahar) army. Lashkar K. came from the Deccan, and waited on me, and was also attached to that army. Allah-dād K. Afghān, M. ʿĪsā Tarkhān, Mukarram K., Ikrām K., and other Amirs, who had come from the Deccan and from their fiefs, after being presented with horses and dresses of honour, were sent with Khān Jahān. ʿUmdatu-s-salṭana Āṣaf K. was sent to Agra to bring to Court the whole of the treasure in muhrs and rupees which had accumulated from the beginning of the reign of my father. Aṣālat K., s. Khān Jahān, was promoted to the mansab of 2,000 and 1,000 horse. Muḥammad Shafīʿā, Bakhshi of Multan, had the title of Khān conferred on him. I gave leave to Sharīf, Vakil of my fortunate son Shāh Parwīz, to go with all possible haste, and bring my son to wait on me with the army of Behar, and writing a gracious farman with my own hand I urged him to come.

On this day Mīr Mīrān, the grandson of Shāh Niʿmatu-llah, died suddenly. I hope that he will be among the pardoned. A raging elephant threw down the huntsman Mīrzā Beg and killed him: I assigned his duties to Imām-wirdī.

As in consequence of the weakness that came over me two years ago and still continues, heart and brain do not accord. I cannot[28] make notes of events and occurrences. Now that Muʿtamid K. has come from the Deccan, and has had the good fortune to kiss the threshold, as he is a servant who knows my temperament and understands my words, and was also formerly entrusted with this duty, I gave an order that from the date which I have written he shall hereafter write them with his own hand, and attach them to my Memoranda. Whatever events may occur hereafter he should note after the manner of a diary, and submit them for my verification, and then they should be copied into a book.

### From This Place the Notes Are Written by Muʿtamid Khān.[29]

As the whole of my world-opening mind was taken up with the preparation of the Qandahar army, and the remedy for that business, the unpleasant news that reached me of a change in the condition of Khurram, and his want of moderation, became a cause for aversion and dissension. I accordingly sent Mūsawī K., who is one of the sincere servants who knows my temperament, to that wretch (*bī-daulat*) to lay before him the threatening messages and my wishes, and to give admonitions that might sharpen his intelligence, so that by the guidance of good fortune he might awake from the dream of carelessness and pride, and that he (Mūsawī) having gained a (true) knowledge of his futile ideas and aims might hasten to my presence, and carry out whatever appeared to be necessary. On the 1st of the Divine month of Bahman the feast of my lunar weighing took place. At this auspicious ceremony Mahābat K., having come from Kabul, paid his respects, and was the recipient of special favours. I appointed Ya'qūb K. Badakhshī to Kabul, exalting him with the gift of drums. About this time report came from I'tibār K. from Agra that Khurram, with the army of adversity, had left Māndū and started in that direction. He had evidently heard the news that the treasure had been sent for, and fire had fallen into his mind, and having let fall from his hand the reins of self-control, had started (with the idea) that on the road he might lay hold of the treasure. Accordingly I thought it best to proceed for a tour, and in order to hunt to the bank of the river of Sulṭān-pūr (the Beas). If that wretch by the guidance of error should place his foot in the desert of audacity, I might hasten farther forward and place the punishment of his unbecoming behaviour in the skirt of his fortune. If matters turned out in any other way I might take steps accordingly. With this purpose, on the 17th of the same month, at an auspicious hour, I marched. Mahābat K. was dignified with a dress of honour. Rs. 1,00,000 were ordered to be given to Mīrzā Rustam and Rs. 2,00,000 to 'Abdu-llah K. by way of advance of pay. I sent Mīrzā Khān, s. Zain K., with a gracious farman to my fortunate son Shāh Parwīz, and renewed my urgency for his attendance. Rāja Sārang Deo had gone to summon Rāja Bīr Singh Deo: he came, and having paid his respects, reported that the Rāja, with a proper force and an equipped army, would join me at Thanesar. At this time constant reports30 came from I'tibār K. and other servants of the State from Agra that Khurram in revolt and disloyalty (*bī-daulati*) had changed what was due by him for rearing into undutifulnesses,31 and having placed the foot of ruin in the valley of ignorance and error, had started in that direction. They therefore did not consider it advisable to bring the treasure, and were engaged in strengthening the towers and gates, and providing things necessary for the defence of the fort. Similarly a report came from Āṣaf K. that the wretch had torn off the veil of respect, and turned his face towards the valley of ruin, and that the odour of good came not from the manner of his approach. As it was not for the advantage of the State to bring the treasure, he had entrusted it to God, and was himself on the way to wait on me. Accordingly, having crossed the river at Sulṭānpūr, by successive marches I proceeded to punish that one of dark fortune, and gave an order that henceforth they should call him *Bī-daulat* (wretch). Wherever in this record of fortune "Bī-daulat" is mentioned it will refer to him. From the kindnesses and favours bestowed upon him I can say that up till the present time no king has conferred such on his son. What my reverend father did for my brothers I have done for his servants, giving them titles, standards, and drums, as has been recorded in the preceding pages. It will not be hidden from the readers of this record of prosperity what affection and interest I have bestowed on him. My pen's tongue fails in ability to set them forth. What shall I say of my own sufferings? In pain and weakness, in a warm atmosphere that is extremely unsuited to my health, I must still ride and be active, and in this state must proceed against such an undutiful son. Many servants cherished by me for long years and raised to the dignity of nobility, whom I ought to employ to-day in war against the Uzbeg or the Persian, I must punish32 for his vileness and destroy with my own hand. Thank God that he has given me such capacity to bear my burdens that I can put up with all this, and go on in the same path, and reckon them as light. But that which weighs heavily on my heart, and places my eager temperament in sorrow is this, that at such a time when my prosperous sons and loyal officers should be vying with each other in the service against Qandahar and Khurasan, which would be to the renown of the Sultanate, this inauspicious one has struck with an axe the foot of his own dominion, and become a stumbling-block in the path of the enterprise. The momentous affair of Qandahar must now be postponed, but I trust that Almighty God will remove these griefs from my heart.

At this time it was reported to me that Muḥtarim K., the eunuch, K̲h̲alīl Beg Z̲ū-l-qadr, and Fidā᾽ī K., the Master of the Ceremonies, had allied themselves with Bī-daulat, and opened the gates of correspondence with him. As it was no time for mildness and winking at matters, I imprisoned all three, and as, after making inquiry into the circumstances, no doubt remained as to their falseness to their salt, and about the evil designs and malevolence of K̲h̲alīl and Muḥtarim, and as Amirs like Mīrzā Rustam swore to the insincerity and malevolence of K̲h̲alīl, having no remedy I punished them33 capitally. Fidā᾽ī K., the dust of whose sincerity was free of suspicion and pure, I brought out of confinement and promoted. I sent Rāja Rūz-afzūn by post (*dāk-chauki*) to my son S̲h̲āh Parwīz that he might bring him with all haste to wait on me; so that Bī-daulat might be brought to punishment for his improper conduct. Jawāhir K., the eunuch, was appointed to the post of *Ihtimām-i-darbār-i-maḥall* (superintendent of the harem).

On the 1st of Isfandārmuz̲ the royal army arrived at Nūr-sarāy. On this day a report came from Iʿtibār K., that Bī-daulat had arrived in all haste in the neighbourhood of Agra, in the hope that before the fort was strengthened, the gates of strife and mischief might be opened, and he might attain his end. When he arrived at Fatḥpūr, he found the gates closed against him, and, being struck with the disgrace of ruin, he had halted. The K̲h̲ān-k̲h̲ānān and his son and many of the royal Amirs attached to the Deccan and Gujarat had come with him as companions on the road of rebellion and ingratitude. Mūsawī K. saw him at Fatḥpūr, and showed him the royal orders, and it was settled that he should send his servant Qāẓī ʿAbdu-l-ʿAzīz with him to Court to put his requests before me. He sent to Agra his servant Sundar,34 who was the ringleader of the people of error and the chief of the seditious, to take possession of the treasures and hidden wealth of those servants of the State who were at Agra. Amongst35 others he entered the house of Las_h_kar K., and seized Rs. 9,00,000. In the same manner, wherever he suspected there was property in the houses of other servants (of the Court), he stretched out his hand to seize it, and took possession of all that he found. When nobles like K_h_ān-k_h_ānān, who had been distinguished with the rank of Ātālīk and arrived at the age of seventy years, made their faces black with rebellion and ingratitude, how could one complain of others? It may be said that his very nature was seditious and ungrateful. His father (Bairam K.) at the end of his life behaved in the same unbecoming way towards my reverend father. He, following the example of his father, at his age made himself accursed and rejected to all eternity.

In the end a wolf's cub becomes a wolf

Although he grow up with man. (Sa'dī.)

On this day Mūsawī K. arrived with 'Abdu-l-'Azīz, the envoy of Bī-daulat. As his requests were unreasonable, I did not allow him to speak, but handed him over to Mahābat to be kept in prison. On the 5th of the month I pitched on the bank of the river of Lūdiyāna (the Sutlej). I promoted K_h_ān A'ẓạm to the mansab of 7,000 with 5,000 horse. Rāja Bhārat, the Bandīla, from the Deccan, and Dayānat K. from Agra, came and waited on me. I pardoned the offences of Dayānat K., and gave him the same mansab that he had previously held. Rāja Bhārat was raised to the mansab of 1,500 and 1,000 horse, and Mūsawī K. to that of 1,000 and 300 horse. On Thursday, the 12th, in the pargana of Thānesar, Rāja Bīr Singh Deo, having waited on me, reviewed his army and elicited great praise. Rāja Sārang Deo was promoted to the mansab of 1,500 with 600 horse. In Karnāl Āṣaf K., coming from Agra, lifted up the head of honour in kissing my stirrup. His coming at this time was the herald of victory. Nawāzis_h_ K., s. Sa'īd K., having arrived from Gujarat, paid his respects. When Bī-daulat was at Burhanpur, at his request I had appointed Bāqī K. to Jūnāgaṛh. He had been ordered to come to Court, and now came and shared in my service. As my march from Lahore took place without previous notice, and time did not admit of delay or reflection, I came with the few Amirs who were in attendance. Until I arrived at Sihrind only a few men had the good fortune to accompany me, but after passing beyond it, great numbers of the army came in from all sides and quarters. Before arrival at Delhi such a force had come together that in any direction in which one looked the whole plain was occupied by troops.

As it was reported that Bī-daulat had left Fatḥpūr and was coming in this direction, and making continuous marches towards Delhi, I gave the victorious army orders to put on their *chiltas* (quilted coats). In this disturbance the pivot of the management of affairs and the arrangement of the army were entrusted to Mahābat K. The command of the vanguard was given to ʻAbdu-llah K. Of the selected young men and experienced *sipāhīs*, whoever was asked for by him was enrolled in his corps. I ordered him to march a koss ahead of the other forces. He was also entrusted with the intelligence department and the control of the routes. I was ignorant of the fact that he was in league with Bī-daulat, and that the real object of that evil-natured one was to send news from my army to him. Previously to this he used to bring long written slips of true and false news, saying that his spies had sent them from that place. The purport was that they (the spies) suspected some of my servants of being in league with Bī-daulat, and of sending him news. Had I been led away by his intrigues and become alarmed at this time when the wind of disturbance was blowing strongly I would have been obliged to destroy many of my servants. Although some faithful servants suspected his evil intentions and untruthfulness, the time was not one for removing the veil openly from the face of his deeds. I guarded my eye and tongue from doing anything which might carry terror into his evil mind, and showed him more attention and favour than before, with the idea that possibly he would be struck with shame, and might turn away from his evil deeds, and give up his evil nature and sedition. That rejected one to all eternity, in whom a tendency to vileness and falsity was natural, did not fail to do what was in accordance with himself, as will be related hereafter.

The tree36 that is bitter in its nature

If you plant it in the garden of Paradise,

And water it from the eternal stream thereof,

If you pour on its root pure honey,

In the end it shows its natural quality,

And it bears the same bitter fruit.

In fine, when I was near Delhi, Sayyid Bahwa Bukhārī, Ṣadr K., and Rāja Kishan Dās came out of the city, and had the good fortune to kiss my stirrup. Bāqir K., faujdār of Oudh, also on this day came to the victorious camp. On the 25th of the month, passing by Delhi, I pitched my camp on the bank of the Jumna. Girdhar, s. Rāy Sāl Darbārī, having come from the Deccan, had the honour to pay his respects. He was promoted to the mansab of 2,000 and 1,500 horse, and obtained the title of Raja, and was clothed in a dress of honour. Zabar-dast K., Master of the Ceremonies, was honoured with a standard.

---

1 Date not given. The Iqbāl-nāma, 191, has "the 8th." ↑

2 The Iqbāl-nāma, p. 192, speaks of a report of K͟hān Jahān that K͟hwāja ʿAbdu-l-ʿAzīz Naqs͟hbandī, the governor of Qandahar, had a garrison of 3,000 men. ↑

3 Jahāngīr appears on this occasion to have forgotten the vow he made in the 13th year. See Elliot, VI. 362. Jahāngīr's words are clear: "*ba tīr u tufang andāk͟htam.*" ↑

4 Apparently this is the Barahmūla Pass. It is mentioned in the Akbar-nāma, III. 480–81 and 558, but does not appear on modern maps. Jahāngīr refers to it in the account of the 15th year, p. 204, and says it is the last of the passes. ↑

5 Sar-afrāz in No. 181. ↑

6 The I.O. MS., No. 181, adds "and treasure." ↑

7 "Wilson" Glossary, p. 60. Elliot, Supp. Glossary, I. 52. The word seems connected with *barinj*, "rice." ↑

8 This is the poet Bābā Ṭālib Iṣfahānī of Blochmann, 607. ↑

9 Elliot, VI. 383. ↑

10 Not that the question of the Deccan had been settled, but that S͟hāh Jahān had left Burhanpur and come to Māndū. See Iqbāl-nāma, 193. ↑

11 Elliot, VI. 383. ↑

12 *Tarkas͟h-bandān*, literally quiver-holders. Apparently the meaning is that the archers who were footmen (see Blochmann, 254, about *Dāk͟hilī* troops) lost their vocation when guns came into use, and became cavalry soldiers. But the meaning in text may be that the archers took to practising with bows and arrows on horseback. It appears from a Dastūru-l-ʿamal in the I.O., No. 1,855 (E. 2736) that the *tarkas͟h-bands* were an inferior order of servants receiving 1,000 dams or less a year. They probably were not necessarily archers. ↑

13 The Achh Dal of the Āyīn, Jarrett, II. 358. ↑

14 No. 181 has "at Vīrnāg." ↑

15 Pāds͟hāh-nāma, I., Part II., p. 349. ↑

16 May also be read Uhar and Adhar. It is Adhar or Udhar in I.O. MSS. ↑

17 The Sind River of Kashmir is meant. Jarrett, II. 364. ↑

18 This seems a translation of Akbar's word *arīnās* (enemy-destroying). ↑

19 Elliot, VI. 384, where Jhelam is a mistake. ↑

20 Pādsh̲āh-nāma, I., Part II., p. 339. His name was Mullā Sh̲ukru-llah, and he was from Shiraz. He is the Mirza Sorocolla of Roe. ↑

21 Compare Iqbāl-nāma, 194 and 196. It is stated there that Nūr Jahān would not allow Afẓal K. to have an audience, and that he was dismissed without gaining his object. ↑

22 See Iqbāl-nāma, 196, where it is said that these orders were not really given by Jahāngīr, but were Nūr Jahān's. ↑

23 Elliot, VI. 280. ↑

24 This alludes to the facts that Humāyūn promised Sh̲āh Ṭahmāsp that he would restore the fort after he had conquered India, and that Akbar had acknowledged the justice of Persia's claim. ↑

25 The clause is very obscure. Perhaps it is part of what Jahāngīr had said. ↑

26 *Farẓand-i-barkh̲ūrdār.* ↑

27 It is noteworthy that Jahāngīr does not attempt to controvert the statement of Sh̲āh ʿAbbās that Qandahar rightfully belonged to Persia. There is a very long account in the ʿĀlam-ārāʾī of the claims of Persia to Qandahar, and of the various attempts made to realize them, until at last it was taken by Sh̲āh ʿAbbās. See the account of the 35th year in the Teheran lithograph, p. 682, etc. The fort of Qandahar surrendered on 11 Sh̲aʿbān, 1031, or June 11, 1622. The Shah's letter announcing the fact and explaining his procedure was presented by Ḥaidar Beg on 26 Ābān, 1031—*i.e.*, early in November, 1622. He brought the officers of the garrison with him. See ʿĀlam-ārāʾī and the Tūzuk text, 348 (annals of the 17th year). ↑

28 Elliot, VI. 280. ↑

29 These words do not appear in the I.O. MSS. And what is written in this chapter about the fates of Kh̲alīl and Muḥtarim, etc., does not agree with Muʿtamid's writing in Iqbāl-nāma. ↑

30 Elliot, VI. 384. ↑

31 *Ḥuqūq ba-ʿuqūq*, "rights into wrongs." ↑

32 I rather think the meaning is "he by his baseness and illfatedness has capitally punished them, and has (as it were) slain them by his own hand," the meaning being that they will fall in the civil war about to take place. ↑

33 Compare Iqbāl-nāma, 199. ↑

34 This is the man whom Jahāngīr had made Rāja Bikramājīt. ↑

35 Elliot, VI. 385. ↑

36 The lines come from Firdūsī's satire on Maḥmūd of Ghazni. ↑

# The Eighteenth New Year's Feast after the Auspicious Accession

On the eve of Tuesday, the 20th of Jumādā-l-awwal, A.H. 1032 (March 10, 1623), the sun that lights the world entered his house of honour in Aries, and the eighteenth year from the beginning of my reign commenced auspiciously and happily. On this day I heard that Bī-daulat, having gone to the neighbourhood of Mathura, had encamped the army tainted with ruin in the pargana of S̲h̲āhpūr, and reviewed 27,000 cavalry. It is hoped that they will soon be subdued and miserable. Rāja Jay Singh, grandson1 of Rāja Mān Singh, came from his native country, and had the good fortune to kiss my stirrup. I dignified Rāja Bīr Singh Deo, than whom in the Rajput caste there is no greater Amir, with the title of Maharaja, and promoted his son Jogrāj to the mansab of 2,000 with 1,000 horse. Sayyid Bahwa was presented with an elephant. As it was reported to me that Bī-daulat was coming by the bank of the Jumna, the march of the victorious army in that direction was also decided on. The array of the army that resembled the waves of the sea was divided into the van, the right and left wings, the *altmis̲h̲*, the *ṭaraḥ* (reserve), the *chandāwul* (rear), etc., and arranged in a manner suitable to the circumstances and according to the locality. Close upon this came the news that Bī-daulat, with the wretch K̲h̲ān-k̲h̲ānān, had turned his reins from the right road and gone towards the pargana Kotila, 20 koss towards the left, along with the brahman Sundar, who was his guide to the desert of error, with Dārāb, s. K̲h̲ān-k̲h̲ānān, and many of the Amirs who had accompanied him on the road of rebellion and rascality, such as Himmat K., Sar-buland K., S̲h̲arza K. ʿĀbid K., Jādo Rāy, Ūday Rām, Ātas̲h̲ K., Manṣūr K., and other mansabdars, who were attached to the Deccan, Gujarat, and Malwa, the recital of whom would take too long, and all his own servants, such as Rāja Bhīm, s. Rānā, Rustam K., Bairam Beg, the Afghan Daryā, Taqī, and others whom he had left to confront the royal army. There were five2 armies (corps?). Although nominally the command was in the hands of the wretch (*bar-gas̲h̲ta-i-rūzgār*) Dārāb, yet in reality the leader and centre of the whole affair was Sundar, of evil deeds. These men of darkened fortune pitched in the neighbourhood of Balūchpūr to their ruin. On the 8th I pitched at Qabūlpūr. On this day the turn to take the rear fell upon Bāqir K. We had left him behind all the rest. A body of the rebels attacked him on the march, and stretched out the hand of plunder. Bāqir planted firmly the foot of courage, and succeeded in beating them back. K̲h̲wāja Abū-l-Ḥasan got news of this, and turned his reins to support him. Before the arrival of the K̲h̲wāja the rebels (*mardūdān*), not being able to stand, had taken to flight. On Wednesday, the 9th of the month, having separated 25,000 horse under the leadership of Āṣaf K., K̲h̲wāja Abū-l-Ḥasan, and ʿAbdu-llah K., I sent them to attack the rebels who did not look to the end of things. Qāsim K., Lashkar K., Irādat K., Fidā'ī K., and other servants, to the number of 8,000 horse, were appointed to Āṣaf K.'s force. Bāqir K., Nūru-d-dīn Qulī, Ibrāhīm Ḥusain Kāshgharī, and others, to the number of 8,000 horse, were appointed to support Abū-l-Ḥasan. Nawāzish K., 'Abdu-l-'Azīz K., 'Azīzu-llah, and many of the Bārha and Amroha Sayyids, were ordered to accompany 'Abdu-llah. In this army 10,000 horse were enrolled. Sundar had arranged the army of ruin and put forward the foot of shamelessness. At this time I sent my special quiver by Zabar-dast K., Master of Ceremonies, to 'Abdu-llah K., that it might be the means of animating his zeal. When the encounter of the two sides took place, that black-faced one to all eternity, in whom the tendency to rebellion and ingratitude was innate, taking to flight, joined the rebels. 'Abdu-l-'Azīz K., the son of the Khān Daurān, God knows whether knowingly or not, went off with him. Nawāzish K., Zabar-dast K., and Shīr-ḥamla, who were in the corps of that shameless one ('Abdu-llah K.), planted firmly the foot of courage, and were not disturbed at his going. As the aid of Almighty God is ever near this suppliant, at this crisis, when a leader of the army such as 'Abdu-llah K. threw 10,000 cavalry into confusion and joined the enemy, and there was nearly a great disaster, a shot from a mysterious hand reached Sundar. At his fall the pillars of the courage of the rebels shook. Khwāja Abū-l-Ḥasan also drove before him the army in front of him and defeated it. Āṣaf K., when Bāqir K. arrived, showing great activity, finished the affair, and a victory which might be the *ṭughrā* (sign manual) of the victories of the age showed its face of purpose from the hidden world. Zabar-dast K., Shīr-ḥamla, Shīr-bacha, his son, and the son of Asad K., the architect, and Muḥammad Ḥusain, brother of Khwāja Jahān, and a number of the Sayyids of Bārha who were in the corps of the black-faced 'Abdu-llah, having tasted the sweet-flavoured wine of martyrdom, obtained everlasting life. 'Azīzu-llah, grandson of Ḥusain K. (Tukrīya), being wounded by a gun-shot, got off safely. Although at this time the desertion of that rejected hypocrite was a secret help, yet it is probable that if he had not performed this detestable action in the crisis of the battle, many of the rebel leaders would have been killed or captured. It chanced that he was known to the common people by the title of La'natu-llah (God's curse), and as he had received this name from the hidden world I also called him by it. Hereafter, wherever the expression *La'natu-llah* is used it refers to him. Briefly, after the rebels, whose end was evil, took to flight from the field of battle, and turned their faces towards the valley of ruin and could not reassemble, La'natu-llah, with all the rebels, did not turn his rein till he reached Bī-daulat, who was at a distance of 20 koss.

When the news of the victory of the servants of the State reached this suppliant to God, he prostrated himself in thankfulness for this gift, which was from the renewed favour of Allah, and summoned the loyal ones into his presence. On the next day they brought before me the head of Sundar. It appeared that when the ball struck him he gave up his soul to the lords of hell, and they took his body to a neighbouring village to be burnt. When they were about to light the fire, an army appeared in the distance, and for fear lest they should be taken prisoners, everyone took to flight. The Muqaddam (head man) of the village cut off his head, and for his own acquittal took it to Kh̲ān Aʿẓam, as it occurred in his jagir. He was brought to me (with the head): the head was quite recognizable and had as yet undergone no change, but they had cut off the ears for the sake of the pearls in them. No one knew by whose hand he had been shot. In consequence of his destruction, Bī-daulat did not gird his loins again. One might say his good fortune and courage and understanding lay in that dog of a Hindu. When, with a father like me, who in truth am his ostensible creator, and in my own lifetime have raised him to the great dignity of Sultanship, and denied him nothing, he acts in this manner, I appeal to the justice of Allah that He may never again regard him with favour. Those servants who in this disturbance had done fitting service were honoured with more and more favours, each according to his degree. Kh̲wāja Abū-l-Ḥasan was raised to the mansab of 5,000, original and increased, Nawāzish̲ K. to that of 4,000 and 3,000 horse, Bāqir K. to that of 3,000 and 500 horse, with drums, Ibrāhīm Ḥusain Kāsh̲gh̲arī to that of 2,000 and 1,000 horse, ʿAzīzu-llah to that of 2,000 and 1,000 horse, Nūru-d-dīn Qulī to that of 2,000 and 700 horse, Rāja Rām Dās to that of 2,000 and 1,000 horse, Luṭfu-llah to that of 1,000 and 500 horse, Parwarish̲ K. to that of 1,000 and 500 horse. If all the servants were to be written in detail it would take too long. Briefly I remained at that place one day and marched on the next. Kh̲ān ʿĀlam, having marched from Allahabad, had the good fortune to kiss the threshold. On the 12th of the month I encamped at the village of Jhānsa (?).

On this day Sar-buland Rāy came from the Deccan and waited on me, and was honoured with a special jewelled dagger, with a *phūl katāra*. ʿAbdu-l-ʿAzīz K. and some of those who had gone with Laʿnatu-llah released themselves from the hand of Bī-daulat, and paid their respects, and represented that when Laʿnatu-llah charged, they thought it was for a cavalry encounter. When they found themselves in the midst of the rebels they saw nothing for it but to submit and pay their respects, but now they had found an opportunity and had obtained the good fortune of kissing the threshold. Though they had taken 2,000 muhrs from Bī-daulat for their expenses, as the times were critical I made no inquiry, but accepted3 their statement.

On the 19th the Feast of the culmination was held, and many of the servants of the State were raised in mansab, and had suitable favours conferred on them.

Mīr ʿAẓudu-d-daulah, having come from Agra, waited on me. He brought a vocabulary4 of words that he had prepared. In truth he had taken much pains, and collected together all the words from the writings of ancient poets. There is no book like this in the science.

Rāja Jay Singh was raised to the mansab of 3,000 with 1,400 horse, and a special elephant was presented to my son S̲h̲ahriyār. The post of ʿArẓ-mukarrir (examiner of petitions) was conferred on Mūsawī K. Amānu-llah, s. Mahābat K., was given the title of K̲h̲ān-zād K̲h̲ān, was favoured with a mansab of 4,000 personal and horse, and was honoured with a flag and drums.

On the 1st of the Divine month of Urdībihis̲h̲t I pitched on the bank of the lake at Fatḥpūr. Iʿtibār K. came from Agra and waited on me, and was graciously received. Muẓaffar K., Mukarram K., and his brother also came from Agra, and had the good fortune to wait on me. As Iʿtibār K. had done approved service in the charge of the Agra fort he was dignified with the title of Mumtāz K., and I gave him the mansab of 6,000 personal and 5,000 horse, and having bestowed on him a dress of honour, a jewelled sword, a horse, and a special elephant, I sent him back to his duty. Sayyid Bahwa was promoted to the mansab of 2,000 and 1,500 horse, Mukarram K. to that of 3,000 and 2,000 horse, and K̲h̲wāja Qāsim to that of 1,000 with 400 horse. On the 4th Manṣūr K. Farangī, whose circumstances have been recorded5 in the preceding pages (?), with his brother6 and Naubat7 K. Dakhanī, by the guidance of good fortune separated themselves from Bī-daulat, and came into my service. I sent K̲h̲awāṣṣ K. to my fortunate son S̲h̲āh Parwīz. Mīrzā ʿĪsā Tark̲h̲ān, having come from Multan, had the good fortune to kiss the threshold. A special sword was given to Mahābat K. On the 10th the camp was pitched in the pargana of Hindaun. Manṣūr K. (the Farangī) was raised to the mansab of 4,000 personal and 3,000 horse, and that of Naubat8 K. to that of 2,000 and 1,000 horse. On the 11th was a halt. As on this day a meeting with my fortunate son S̲h̲āh Parwīz had been arranged, I ordered that the powerful princes and the illustrious Amirs and all the devoted servants should go out to meet him, and bring him to wait on me in a fitting manner. After midday had passed, at an auspicious chosen hour he kissed the ground and illuminated the forehead of his sincerity. After the usual salutations had been performed and the customary ceremonies gone through I embraced my fortunate son with the greatest pleasure and affection, and loaded him with more and more favours. At this time news came that Bī-daulat, when he was passing through the township (ḥawālī) of the pargana of

Amber, which was the hereditary abode of Rāja Mān Singh, had sent a band of scoundrels and plundered that cultivated spot.

On the 12th I pitched outside the village of Sārwalī. I had previously sent Ḥabash K. (Abyssinian) to repair the buildings at Ajmir. I promoted my fortunate son Shāh Parwīz to the high mansab of 40,000 and 30,000 horse. As it was reported that Bī-daulat had sent off Jagat Singh, s. Rāja Bāso, to his own country to raise disturbances in the hills of the Panjab, I promoted Ṣādiq K., chief Bakhshi, to the governorship of that province, and ordered him to punish him, giving him a dress of honour, with a sword and an elephant, and making up his mansab, original and increased, to 4,000 personal and 3,000 horse. I also honoured him with a standard (*tūgh*) and drums.

At this time it was reported to me that the younger brothers of Mīrzā Badīʿu-z-zamān, s. Mīrzā Shāhrukh, who was known as Fatḥpūrī, had attacked him unawares and killed him. About this time his brothers came to Court and paid their respects. His own mother also waited on me, but did not make a claim, as was proper, for her son's blood, and (so) proceedings9 could not be taken according to law. Although his disposition was so bad that his murder was not to be regretted, but on the contrary was opportune and advantageous, yet, as these wretches had shown such audacity with regard to their elder brother, who was to them in the position of a father, I ordered them to be put in gaol, and afterwards what was deemed proper should be done to them. On the 21st Rāja Gaj Singh and Rāy Sūraj Singh arrived from their jagirs, and had the good fortune to kiss my stirrup. Muʿizzu-l-mulk, whom I had sent to Multan to summon my son Khān Jahān, came and waited on me, and presented me with a letter about his severe illness and weakness. He had sent his son Aṣālat K. with 1,000 horse to wait on me, and expressed great regret at being deprived of the honour of meeting me. As his apology was evidently sincere, I accepted it. On the 25th my fortunate son Prince Parwīz, with the victorious army, was sent in pursuit to overthrow Bī-daulat. The reins of authority over the powerful Prince, and the centre of the ordering of the victorious army, were given into the hand of Muʾtaminu-d-daula Mahābat K. Of the illustrious Amīrs and life-sacrificing brave men who were in attendance on the Prince of lofty fortune, this is the detail.

Khān ʿĀlam, Mahārāja10 Gaj Singh, Fāẓil K., Rashīd K., Rāja Girdhar, Rāja Rām Dās Kachhwāha, Khwāja Mīr ʿAbdu-l-ʿAzīz, ʿAzīzu-llah, Asad K., Parwarish K., Ikrām K., Sayyid Hizbar K., Luṭfu-llah, Rāy Narāyan Dās, and others to the number of 40,000 horse, with much artillery. Rs. 20,00,000 (twenty lakhs) of treasure were sent with them. At a propitious hour they were started with my son, and bridle to bridle with victory. Fāẓil K. was appointed Bakhshi and newswriter to the victorious army. A special dress of honour was bestowed on the Prince, with a *nādirī* of gold brocade, and pearls on the collar and skirt worth Rs. 41,000, prepared in the royal establishment, and a private elephant of the name Ratan Gaj, ten[11] female elephants, a private horse, and a jewelled sword, the value of the whole of which was Rs. 77,000. These were all given to the Prince. Nūr Jahān Begam also gave him a dress of honour, a horse, and an elephant, as is the custom. To Mahābat K. and the other Amirs, according to their standing, horses, elephants, and dresses of honour were presented. The immediate attendants of the prince were also honoured with favours. On this day Muẓaffar K. received a dress of honour on appointment to the post of chief Bakhshi. On the first of the Divine month of Khurdād Prince Dāwar-bakhsh, s. Khusrau, was appointed to Gujarat, and Khān Aʿẓam to the high dignity of tutor to him. I conferred on the prince a horse, an elephant, a dress of honour, a private jewelled dagger, a standard (*tūgh*), and drums. Khān Aʿẓam, Nawāzish K. and other servants were honoured with presents according to their standing. Irādat K. was appointed Bakhshi in place of Fāẓil K. Ruknu-s-salṭana Āṣaf K. exalted his head with the dignity of the Subadarship of Bengal and Orissa. A special dress of honour, with a jewelled sword, were conferred on him. Abū Ṭālib (*i.e.*, Shaista K.), his son, was appointed to accompany him, and promoted to the mansab of 2,000 with 1,000 horse. On Saturday, the 9th, corresponding with the 19th Rajab, A.H. 1032 (May 9, 1623), the camp was pitched at the Anā-Sāgar lake outside Ajmir. Prince Dāwar-bakhsh, being honoured with the mansab of 8,000, and 3,000 horse, was granted Rs. 2,00,000 of treasure for the expenses of the army which accompanied him. Rs. 1,00,000 I also gave as an advance to Khān Aʿẓam. Allah-yār, s. Iftikhār Beg, who was in the service of my fortunate son Shāh Parwīz, was at his request granted a standard. Tātār K. took leave on his appointment to the charge of Fort Gwalior. Rāja Gaj Singh was appointed to the mansab of 5,000, with 4,000 horse.

On this day news came from Agra that Her Highness (ḥaẓrat) Maryamu-z-zamānī,[12] by the decree of God, had died. I trust that Almighty God will envelop her in the ocean of His mercy. Jagat Singh, s. Rānā Karan, having come from his native place, had the good fortune to pay his respects. Ibrāhīm K. Fatḥ-jang, governor of Bengal, had sent thirty-four elephants by way of offering, and they were submitted to me. Bāqir K. was appointed faujdār of Oudh, and Sādāt K. to the Dū-āb. The Mīr Mushrif was made Dīwān-i-buyūtāt.

On the 12th of the Divine month of Tīr a report came from the officials of Gujarat with the good news of victory and conquest. The particulars of this summary are that I had granted the Subah of Gujarat, the abode of Sultans of high dignity, to Bī-daulat as a reward for his victory over the Rānā, as has been fully related in the preceding pages. Sundar, the brahman, administered and protected the country. When futile ideas entered his ungrateful mind, he sent for that dog of a Hindu, who was always shaking the chain of enmity and perversity, along with Himmat K., Sharza K., Sar-afrāz K., and many of the royal servants who were fiefholders in the province. Sundar's brother Kunhar was appointed in his room. When Sundar was killed, and Bī-daulat retreated after his defeat to Māndū, the province of Gujarat was put in the charge of La'natu-llah as his fief, and Kunhar was sent for along with Ṣafī K., the diwan. At the same time the treasure, the jewelled throne on which five lakhs had been expended, and the *pardala* (belt) on which two lakhs had been spent—and which things had been prepared as a present for myself—were also sent for. Ṣafī K. was the brother's son (text says "brother") of Ja'far Beg, who received in my father's service the title of Āṣaf K., and was married to a daughter of Nūr Jahān's brother, who by my favour had received the title of Āṣaf K. An elder daughter was the wife of Bī-daulat. Both daughters were by one mother, and Bī-daulat expected that on account of this connection Ṣafī K. would be on his side. But an eternal decree had gone forth for Ṣafī K.'s loyalty and prosperity, and that he should attain to high rank! Accordingly, Almighty God made him loyal and the performer of good deeds, as will now be described. In short, the faithless (*bī-wafā*) La'natu-llah sent his eunuch named Wafā-dār to be governor of that country, and he, with a few ragamuffins (*bī-sar-u-pā*) entered Ahmadabad, and took possession of the city. As Ṣafī K. had made up his mind to be loyal, he courageously looked after the servants, and collected a force, and won the hearts of the people. Some days before Kunhar came out of the city he (Ṣafī) encamped on the bank of the Kankariyā lake, and thence hastened to Maḥmūdābād, giving out openly that he was going to Bī-daulat. Secretly, he opened communication and made arrangements to be loyal with Nāhir K., Sayyid Dilīr K., Nānū13 K., Afghan, and other devoted servants of the State, who were waiting in their own jagirs. He awaited his opportunity. Ṣāliḥ, a servant of Bī-daulat, who was faujdār of the Sarkar of Pitlād, and had a good force with him, heard rumours that Ṣafī K. entertained other ideas. Kunhar14 had also discovered this, but as Ṣafī K. soothed them and was very cautious and careful in his conduct, they could not move hand or foot. Ṣāliḥ, for fear lest Ṣafī K., abandoning dissimulation, should stretch his hand towards the treasure, exercised foresight, and went farther on with the treasure, taking nearly Rs. 10,00,000 to Bī-daulat at Māndū. Kunhar (or the younger brother?) also, having seized the jewelled *pardala*, started after him, but could not take the throne on account of its weight. Ṣafī K., knowing this was his opportunity, changed his place from Maḥmūdābād to the pargana of Karang,15 which is to the left of the usual road, where Nānū K. was, and arranged by letter and verbal messages with Nāhir K. and other loyal servants that each of them should ride from his jagir with the force that he had, and at the hour of sunrise, which was the morning of prosperity for people of good fortune, and the evening of ruin to those who practised villainy, enter the city by the gate to which each was opposite. He (Ṣafī) left his women in the aforesaid pargana, and, in company with Nānū (Bābū?) K., came at dawn to the outskirts of the city. He halted for a short time in the S̲h̲aʿbān16 garden until it had become light and friend could be distinguished from enemy. After the world-illuminating sun of good fortune (had risen), when he found the gate of prosperity open, though he could see no trace of Nāhir K. and the other loyalists, yet lest possibly the enemy might obtain information and fasten the gates of the fort he placed his confidence in God who gives victory, and entered the city by the Sārangpūr gate. About this time Nāhir K. also arrived, and, entering by the gate, came into the city. The eunuch of Laʿnatu-llah, having ascertained the unfailing good fortune of (Jahāngīr), took refuge in the house of S̲h̲aik̲h̲ Ḥaidar, grandson of Niẓām Wajīhu-d-dīn. The royal servants of approved service, having proclaimed their victory with loud voices, set to work to strengthen the towers and gates. They sent men to the houses of Muḥammad Taqī, Bī-daulat's diwan, and of Ḥasan Beg, his Bakhshi, and seized them. S̲h̲aik̲h̲ Ḥaidar himself came and informed Ṣafī K. that the eunuch of Laʿnatu-llah was in his house, and they tied his hands to his neck, and brought him. Having imprisoned a number of Bī-daulat's servants and dependants, they engaged in keeping order in the city. The jewelled throne, the cash of Rs. 2,00,000, and the property and effects of Bī-daulat and his men in the city, came into their possession. When this news reached Bī-daulat, he sent off Laʿnatu-llah with Himmat K., S̲h̲arza K., Sar-afrāz K., Qābil Beg, Rustam Bahādur, Ṣāliḥ Badak̲h̲s̲h̲ī, and other criminals. What with royal servants and his own men, he had some 5,000 or 6,000 horse. Ṣafī K. and Nāhir K., becoming aware of this, planted firmly the foot of courage, and employed themselves in encouraging their men and collecting forces. Whatever cash and valuables they could obtain, even to the throne, which they broke up, they divided amongst both the old and new troopers as pay. Rāja Kalyān, Zamindar of Īdar (printed wrongly "Andūr"), and the son of Lāl Gopī (?)17, and all the Zamindars from every quarter, were summoned into the city. A good number was thus assembled. Laʿnatu-llah did not wait for auxiliaries, and in the space of eight days came from Māndū to Baroda. The loyal party, by the guidance of their courage, and in reliance on God, came out of the city and encamped on the bank of the Kānkariyā Lake. It occurred to Laʿnatu-llah that if he came on quickly, the rope of order of the loyal might be broken. When he obtained news of the coming out of the loyal servants, drawing in the reins of ruin, he delayed in Baroda till the arrival of help. After the evil-ending criminals collected together at that chief place of mischief, he put forward the foot of error and deviation from the right path, and the loyal party, marching from the Kānkariyā tank, encamped outside the village of Batoh, near the mausoleum of Quṯb ʿĀlam. Laʿnatu-llah traversed a road of three days in two,18 and arrived at Maḥmūdābād. As Sayyid Dilīr K. had seized the women of S̲h̲arza K. and brought them from Baroda to the city, and the women of Sar-afrāz K. were also in the city, Ṣafī K. sent a secret message to both of them that if by the guidance of good fortune they would rub off the stain of sin (rebellion) from the tablet of their foreheads, and would enrol themselves among the loyal servants, their position in the present and future worlds would approach salvation; otherwise he would subject their wives and children to all kinds of indignities. Hearing this, Laʿnatu-llah sent for Sar-afrāz K. on some excuse to his house, and imprisoned him. As S̲h̲arza K., Himmat K., and Ṣāliḥ Badak̲h̲s̲h̲ī were in league together, and had alighted at the same place, he could not get S̲h̲arza K. into his hands. Briefly, on the 21st of S̲h̲aʿbān, A.H. 1032, June 10, 1623, Laʿnatu-llah mounted and arrayed the forces tinged with calamity. Those who were loyal also arrayed their forces and prepared for the fight. It occurred to Laʿnatu-llah that if he were to go, their foot of courage would not stand firm, and, without a battle taking place, they would be dispersed in a miserable condition. When he saw the firm attitude of the loyal, he could not screw up his courage (*tāb nayāwarda*), but turned his rein towards the left, and gave out that they had hidden gunpowder under the ground of that plain, and that his men would be destroyed by it—that it would therefore be better to go into the plain of Sarkhej and deliver battle there. These futile ideas were due to the aid of good fortune, for on the turning back of his rein a rumour of his defeat was spread abroad, and the horsemen of the plain of victory attacked him in flank, and that ill-omened one was unable to reach Sarkhej, and halted in the village of Nāranja. The loyal party arranged their forces in the village of Bālūd, which is nearly three koss off. At dawn on the next day they went to battle after the approved manner, their forces being drawn up in this way. In the vanguard were Nāhir K., Rāja Kalyān, the Zamindar of Īdar, and other valiant men; on the left wing Sayyid Dilīr K., Sayyid Sīdū, and other loyal servants were stationed; and on the right wing Nānū K., Sayyid Yaʿqūb, Sayyid G̲h̲ulām Muḥammad, and the rest of the life-sacrificing devoted ones, whilst in the centre were Ṣafī K., Kifāyat K. Bak̲h̲s̲h̲ī, and some other servants of approved service. It so happened, fortunately, that in the place where Laʿnatu-llah had halted, the land was undulating, full of thorn brakes and narrow lanes. The forces, accordingly, were not in compact order. He had sent on most of the experienced men with Rustam Bahādur, and Himmat K., and Ṣāliḥ Beg were amongst the foremost in (the ranks of) error. The army doomed to calamity first of all came in contact with Nāhir K. and S̲h̲ams K., and a notable fight took place. By chance Himmat K. fell in the dust of destruction from a gun-shot wound, and a fight ensued between Ṣāliḥ Beg, and Nānū K., Sayyid Yaʿqūb, Sayyid G̲h̲ulām Muḥammad, and other servants. In the height of the battle the elephant of Sayyid G͟hulām Muḥammad came and threw him (Ṣāliḥ) from his horse; he fell severely wounded to the ground, and about a hundred of his men were slain. At this moment an elephant which was in the van of the rebel army turned round at the noise of the rockets and the lightning of the guns, and got into a narrow lane, on both sides of which were thorn brakes, and trod down many of the rebels. By the turning back of the elephant the ranks of the enemy were disordered. At this moment Sayyid Dilīr K. came fighting from the right wing. Laʿnatu-llah did not know of the killing of Himmat K. and Ṣāliḥ, and, with the idea of helping them, urged on the steed of ruin. As the brave ones in the van, having displayed activity, had been mostly wounded, they could not stand the onset of Laʿnatu-llah, and turned back their rein, and it nearly happened that there was a great disaster. At this time the assistance of God displayed itself, and Ṣafī K. hastened from the centre to the support of the van. Just then Laʿnatu-llah heard of the killing of Himmat K. and Ṣāliḥ Beg, and, on the appearance of the centre and the attack of Ṣafī K., his courage failed him, and he became a vagabond in the desert of defeat and disaster. Sayyid Dilīr K. pursued him for a koss, and made many of the defeated the harvest of the sword of vengeance. Qābil Beg, unfaithful to his salt, with a body of rebels, became captives in the claws of retribution. As Laʿnatu-llah was not sure about Sar-afrāz K., he on the day of battle placed him in chains on an elephant and put him in charge of one of his slaves, with orders that if a defeat occurred he should kill him. In like manner he placed in chains on one of the elephants Bahādur, s. Sulṭān Aḥmad, and gave permission to kill him. When the fight took place the man in charge of Sulṭān Aḥmad's son put him to death with a dagger, but Sar-afrāz K. threw himself down off the elephant. The man in charge of him in that confusion aimed a blow at him in his bewilderment, but it was not effectual. Ṣafī K., finding him in the fight, sent him into the city. Laʿnatu-llah did not turn back till he arrived at Baroda. As the women of S͟harza K. were captives of those who were loyal, he was helpless, and came and waited upon Ṣafī K. Briefly, Laʿnatu-llah hastened from Baroda to Broach. The sons of Himmat K. were in the fort there. Although they did not admit him, yet they sent him 5,000 *maḥmūdīs* by way of maintenance. For three days he remained outside the fort of Broach in a wretched state, and on the fourth went to Surat by sea. For nearly two months he remained there assembling his scattered men. As Surat was in Bī-daulat's jagir, he took nearly 4 lakhs of *maḥmūdīs* from his officials there, and took possession of whatever he could by oppression and injustice. He again collected together those whose fortune was reversed and whose stars had been burnt, and betook himself to Bī-daulat at Burhanpur.

In fine, when this approved service performed by Ṣafī K. and other loyal servants in Gujarat became known, each one was exalted with favours and kindnesses. Ṣafī K. held the mansab of 700 personal and 300 horse: having given him that of 3,000 personal and 2,000 horse, I honoured him with the title of Saif K. Jahāngīr-s͟hāhī, and conferred on him a standard and drums. Nāhir K. had 1,000 with 200 horse; having given him the mansab of 3,000 with 2,000 horse, I bestowed on him the title of S͟hīr K., and raised his head of honour with a horse, an elephant, and a jewelled sword. He is the (descendant?) grandson of (?)19, the brother of Pūran Mal Lūlū (?), who was governor of Rāysīn and Chanderī. When S͟hīr K., the Afghan (*i.e.*, S͟hīr S͟hāh), besieged the fort of Rāysīn, it is well known that he killed him (Pūran Mal) after promising him quarter, and that his women burnt themselves, committing "*Johar*," according to the Hindu custom, in the fire of fame and modesty, so that the hand of no unlawful person should touch the skirt of their chastity. His sons and caste fellows went off to various20 places. The father of Nāhir K., whose title was K͟hān Jahān, having gone to Muḥammad K., governor of Āsīr and Burhanpur, became a Musalman, and when Muḥammad K. died, Ḥasan, his son, when in tender years, succeeded him. Rāja ʿAlī K., brother of Muḥammad K., put the child in confinement, and took possession of the government. After some time news reached Rāja ʿAlī K. that K͟hān Jahān and a body of the servants of Muḥammad K. had leagued together to attack him, and had determined to take Ḥasan K. out of the fort and raise him to power. He was beforehand with them, and sent Ḥayāt K͟hān Ḥabas͟hī, with many brave men, to the house of K͟hān Jahān, either to take him alive or to kill him. He, planting his foot firmly on his good fame, took to fighting, and when things went badly with him committed *Johar*, and passed from this borrowed life. At that time Nāhir K. was very young. Ḥayāt K͟hān Abyssinian, having asked ʿAlī K.'s permission, adopted him as his son, and made him a Musalman. After his death Rāja ʿAlī K. brought up Nāhir K., and took good care of him. When my revered father conquered Āsīr, Nāhir K. joined his service. He (Akbar) discerned the signs of bravery on his forehead, and raised him to a suitable mansab, and gave him in jagir the pargana of Muḥammadpūr in Malwa. In my service he advanced more and more. Now that the grace of gratitude has been bestowed upon him, he has found the advantage of doing what was right.

Sayyid Dilīr K. is of the Sayyids of Bārha; formerly his name was Sayyid ʿAbdu-l-Wahhāb. I raised him from the mansab of 1,000 and 800 horse to 2,000 and 1,200 horse, and presented him with a standard. They call twelve *bāra* in Hindi. As in the Dū-āb there are twelve villages near each other which are the native country of these Sayyids, they have become known as the Sayyids of Bārha. Some people make remarks about their lineage, but their bravery is a convincing proof of their being Sayyids, for there has never been a battle in this reign in which they have not been conspicuous, and in which some have not been killed. Mīrzā ʿAzīz Koka always said the Sayyids of Bārha were the averters of calamity from this dominion, and such is in reality the case.

Nānū K. Afghan held the mansab of 800 personal and horse: it was ordered to be one of 1,500 personal and 1,200 horse. In the same manner the other loyal servants, according to their services and sacrifices, were promoted to high mansabs, and obtained the desire of their hearts in lofty employments. At this time Aṣālat K., s. Khān Jahān, was deputed to the assistance of my son (grandson) Dāwar-bakhsh in Gujarat, and I sent Nūru-d-dīn Qulī into the Subah to bring Sharza K., Sar-afrāz K., and the other leaders of the rebel army who had been made captive in the land of retribution, chained, to the Court.

On this day it was reported to me that Minū-chihr, s. Shāh-nawāz K., had separated himself from Bī-daulat under the guidance of good fortune, and had joined the service of my fortunate son Shāh Parwīz. Iʿtiqād K., governor of Kashmir, was promoted to the mansab of 4,000 personal and 3,000 horse.

As the huntsmen brought news that in this neighbourhood a tiger had made its appearance, I felt disposed to hunt it. After entering the forest three other tigers became visible. Having killed all four, I returned to the palace. I have such a liking for tiger shooting that whilst I can get it I do not go after other sport. Sulṭān Masʿūd, s. Sulṭān Maḥmūd (of Ghaznin) (may the lights of Allah be his testimony!), was also much inclined to tiger shooting. With regard to his killing of tigers strange tales have been recorded, especially in the history of Baihaqī,21 who has kept a diary of what he saw with his own eyes. Among these things he writes that one day he (Masʿūd) went to hunt tigers in the borders of Hindustan, and was riding an elephant. A very large tiger came out from the wood, and made for the elephant. He threw a javelin (*khisht*) and struck the tiger's chest. The tiger, enraged at the pain, came up on the elephant's back, and the Amir knelt down and struck him such a blow with his sword that he cut off both the tiger's fore-feet, and the tiger fell backwards and died. It happened to me once when I was prince that I had gone out in the Punjab to hunt tigers. A powerful tiger appeared out of the wood. I fired at him from the elephant and the tiger in great fury rose and came on the elephant's back, and I had not time to put down my gun and seize my sword. Inverting the gun, I knelt, and with both hands struck him with the stock over the head and face so that he fell on to the ground and died.

One of the strange things that happened was that one day I was on an elephant, and was hunting wolves in Aligarh22 in the Nūh forest. A wolf appeared, and I struck it with a bullet on its face (*mana*) near the lobe of the ear. The bullet penetrated for about a span. From that bullet it fell and gave up its life. It has often happened in my presence that powerful (*jawānān*) men, good shots with the bow, have shot twenty or thirty arrows at them, and not killed. As it is not right to write about oneself, I must restrain the tongue of my pen from saying more.

On the 29th of the month I presented a string of pearls to Jagat Singh, s. Rānā Karan. At this time it was reported to me that Sulṭān Ḥusain, Zamindar of Paklī, had died. I gave his mansab and jagir to S͟hādmān, his eldest son.

On the 7th of the month of Amurdād Ibrāhīm Ḥusain, a servant of my fortunate son S͟hāh Parwīz, came from the victorious army, and brought news of the victory of the chiefs of the everlasting State. The report of my son laid before me the particulars of the fight, and the exertions of the brave and distinguished men in it. I performed the dues of thanksgiving for this favour, which was of God's grace alone. The details of this are as follows: When the royal troops in the army of the prince of high degree crossed the pass of Chānḍā,23 and entered the province of Malwa, Bī-daulat, with 20,000 horse, 300 fighting elephants, and a large force of artillery, left Māndū in order to fight. He dispatched a body of the Bargīs (Mahrattas) of the Deccan with Jādū Rāy and Ūday Rām, Ālas͟h K., and other rebels to make a raid (*qazzāqī*) on the royal camp. Mahābat K. made proper arrangements. He placed the illustrious prince in the *g͟haul* (centre), and he himself proceeded with the whole army, and in marching and in halting observed the conditions of caution. The Bargīs kept at a great distance, and did not put forward the foot of bravery. One day it was Manṣūr K. Farangī's turn to be with the rear-guard. At the time of pitching the camp Mahābat K., by way of caution, was standing with his army drawn up outside the camp, in order that the men might fence it in at their ease. As Manṣūr K. had been drinking on the road, he was coming to the stage drunk with the wine of pride. It happened an army was seen in the distance, and the wine put the idea into his head that he must charge. Without telling his brothers or his men, he mounted and charged, and drove off two or three Bargīs, and came to where Jādū Rāy and Ūday Rām were standing with two or three thousand cavalry drawn up. As was their custom, they attacked him from all sides and surrounded him. He fought as long as there was breath in his body, and gave up his life on the path of loyalty.

During these days Mahābat K. was continually capturing, by messages and letters, the afflicted hearts of a number of men who out of timidity and confusion had accompanied Bī-daulat. When men read the lines of despair on the page of his (S͟hāh Jahān's) condition, letters also came from that side, asking for agreements (*qaul*). After Bī-daulat came out of the fort of Māndū, he in the first instance sent forward a body of Bargīs, and after them he sent

Rustam K., Taqī, and Barq-andāz K. with a body of musketeers. Then he sent Dārāb K., Bhīm, Bairam Beg, and his other active men. As he could not resolve to give battle in person, he was continually looking backwards. He crossed the war-elephants over the Narbadda with the artillery waggons, and went himself unattended behind Dārāb and Bhīm, turning his face of ruin towards the battle. On the day when the royal camp was pitched at Kāliyādaha, Bī-daulat sent his army against the victorious forces, and stationed himself with K͟hān-k͟hānān and a few men at the distance of a koss in the rear. Barq-andāz K., who had made an agreement with Mahābat K., was lying in wait. When the armies were ranged opposite to each other, he got his opportunity, and attacked with a body of musketeers, and joined the royal army, crying out, "Success to King Jahāngīr!" When he reached Mahābat K., the latter took him to wait on my fortunate son Parwīz, who bestowed royal favours upon him. Previously he bore the name of Bahā'u-d-dīn, and was a servant of Zain K. After the latter's death he enlisted among the Turkish gunners. As he was active in the performance of his duty, and had a band of men with him, considering him worthy of patronage, I gave him the title of Barq-andāz K. When I sent Bī-daulat to the Deccan, I put him at the head of the artillery, and sent him with him. Although in the beginning he placed the scar of curse on the forehead of his obedience, yet in the end he turned out well and came at a good time. On the same day Rustam, who was one of his (S͟hāh Jahān's) chief servants and on whom he had perfect reliance, when he found that Fortune had turned away from him, made a compact with Mahābat K. By the guidance of good fortune and reliance on God, he, with Muḥammad Murād Badak͟hs͟hī and other mansabdars, left the ill-fated army, and joined that of the illustrious prince. Bī-daulat's hand and heart were paralyzed on hearing this news, and he suspected all his own servants, and still more the royal servants he had with him, of faithlessness and unreliability. During the night he sent for the men who were in front, and decided on flight, and in bewilderment crossed the Narbadda. At this time, again, some of his servants took the opportunity of separating themselves from him, and joined the service of my fortunate son. Each of them received favours according to his condition. On the day that he crossed the river Narbadda, a letter fell into the hand of one of his men, that Mahābat K. had written in answer to Zāhid's K. letter, making him hopeful of the royal favour, and urging him to come in. This they sent direct to Bī-daulat, and he, becoming suspicious of Zāhid K., imprisoned him with his three sons. Zāhid K. is s. S͟hajā'at K., who was one of the Amirs and trusted servants of my revered father. I had patronized this wretch in consideration of his claims of service and of his position as a house-born one (*khāna-zād*), and given him the title of K͟hān and the rank of 1,500, and had sent him with Bī-daulat for the conquest of the Deccan. When I summoned the Amirs of that quarter on account of the business of Qandahar, although a special farman of urgency was sent to him, the wretch did not come to Court, and gave himself out as an adherent and devoted servant of Bī-daulat. After the defeat near Delhi, he turned back. Though24 he had not a family, he had not the good fortune to pay his respects, or to cleanse the dust of shame and the stain of sin from the tablet of his forehead. At last the True Recompenser caught him on this day, and his property, to the extent of one lac and Rs. 30,000, was confiscated by Bī-daulat.

When25 thou hast done evil, think not thyself free of calamities

For retribution is according to natural law.

Briefly, Bī-daulat having quickly crossed the Narbadda, drew all the boats over to that side, and having secured the fords with men that he trusted, he left Bairam Beg, his Bakhshi, with a force of trustworthy men and a body of the Bargīs from the Deccan on the bank of the river. Taking the artillery-waggons, he himself went towards the fort of Āsīr and to Burhanpur. Meanwhile Taqī, his servant, caught the runner whom Kh̲ān-kh̲ānān had sent to Mahābat K., and took him to Bī-daulat. This couplet was written on the margin of the letter:

Hundreds are watching me

Otherwise I'd fly away from trouble.

Bī-daulat sent for him with his sons from his quarters, and showed him the writing. Although he made excuses, he could give no answer that could be listened to. In short, he kept him with Dārāb and his other sons in surveillance near his own station, and the lot he had himself drawn—viz., that hundreds were watching him—happened to him. At this time I gave Ibrāhīm Ḥusain, the servant of my prosperous son who had brought the report of the victory, the title of Kh̲ūsh̲-kh̲abar K., with a dress of honour, and an elephant, and sent a gracious farman to the Prince and Mahābat K. by Kh̲awāṣṣ K. I also sent with him a *pahūnchī*26 (bracelet) of great value to my son (Parwīz) and a jewelled sword to Mahābat K. As Mahābat K. had done approved service, I gave him the mansab of 7,000 personal and horse.

Sayyid Ṣalābat K., having come from the Deccan, had the good fortune to pay his respects, and received special favours. He was one of those employed in the Deccan. When Bī-daulat, having been defeated near Delhi, went to the fort of Māndū, he placed his children in independent territory under the protection of God, and went off by secret routes to pay his respects (to me). Mīrzā Ḥasan, s. Mīrzā Rustam Ṣafawī, having obtained leave to proceed to his appointment as faujdār of Bahraich, was given the mansab of 1,500 personal and 500 horse, original and increased. Having sent La'l Beg,

Superintendent of the Record Department, to my fortunate son S͟hāh Parwīz, I sent with him a special dress of honour and a *nādirī* for him, and a turban for Mahābat K. K͟hawāṣṣ K., who had previously been sent to him and had returned, waited upon me with good news (of him). K͟hāna-zād K., s. Mahābat K., was given the mansab of 5,000 personal and horse.

At this time I enjoyed myself for a day with hunting nīlgāw. Whilst I was hunting I saw a snake the length of which was 2½ yards, and its girth equal to three cubits (*dast*). He had swallowed half a hare, and was in the act of swallowing the other half. When the huntsmen picked him up and brought him to me, the hare fell out of his mouth. I ordered them to put it into its mouth again, but they could not do it, however much they exerted themselves; but by using great violence the corner of his mouth was torn to pieces. After this I ordered them to open its belly. Thereupon another entire hare came out. They call this kind of snake *chītal*27 in Hindustan, and it grows so large that it swallows a hog-deer (*kotāh-pācha*) entire; but it is not poisonous, and does not bite. One day during the same hunt I shot a female nīlgāw, and two fully formed young ones were found inside. As I heard that the flesh of nīlgāw fawns was delicate and delicious, I ordered the royal cooks to prepare a *dū-piyāza*28 (a kind of rich fricassee). Certainly it was not without flavour.

On the 15th of the Divine month of S͟hahrīwar Rustam K., Muḥammad Murād, and several other servants of Bī-daulat, who under the guidance of good luck had separated themselves from him and entered the service of my fortunate son S͟hāh Parwīz, according to orders came to Court, and had the good fortune to kiss the threshold. Having promoted Rustam K. to the mansab of 5,000 personal and 4,000 horse, and Muḥammad Murād to that of 1,000 personal and 500 horse, I made them hopeful of daily increasing favours. Rustam K. by extraction is a Badak͟hs͟hī. His name was Yūsuf Beg. He is connected with Muḥammad-qulī of Isfahan, who was agent for and prime minister of Mīrzā Sulaimān (of Badakhshan). He was first of all in the service of the Court, and passed his days mostly in the Subahs. He was included among the smaller mansabdars. Having been deprived of his jagir for some reason, he came to Bī-daulat, and entered his service. He had a perfect knowledge of tiger-hunting. He also did good service with him, especially in the affair of the Rānā. Bī-daulat selected him out of all his servants, and made him an Amir. As I bestowed much favour on him (S͟hāh Jahān), at his request I gave him the title of K͟hān, with a standard and drums. For some time he conducted as his agent the government of Gujarat, and did not manage badly. Muḥammad Murād is the son of Maqṣūd Mīr-āb (butler), who was one of the old servants of Mīrzā Sulaimān and Mīrzā S͟hāh-ruk͟h.

On this day Sayyid Bahwa came from Gujarat, and waited on me. Nūru-d-dīn Qulī brought in chains to the Court forty-one of the rebels, who had been taken prisoners at Ahmadabad. S̲h̲arza K. and Qābil Beg, who were ring-leaders of the seditious, I executed by throwing them under the feet of warlike (*mast*) elephants. On the 20th of the same month, corresponding with the 18th of the month of Z̤ī-qaʿda, a daughter was given by the grace of God to my son S̲h̲ahriyār by the granddaughter[29] of Iʿtimādu-d-daula. I hope that her advent[30] will be propitious and blessed to this State. On the 22nd of the month the feast of my solar weighment took place, and the 55th year of the age of this suppliant began auspiciously and happily. According to annual custom, I had myself weighed against gold and other valuables, and gave them to deserving people. Among these I gave Rs. 2,000 to S̲h̲aik̲h̲ Aḥmad[31] of Sihrind. On the 1st of the Divine month of Mihr Mīr Jumla was promoted to the mansab of 3,000 personal and 300 horse. Muqīm, the Bakhshi of Gujarat, was given the title of Kifāyat K. As the innocence of Sar-farāz K.[32] was established to my satisfaction, I took him out of prison, and allowed him to pay his respects. At the request of my son S̲h̲ahriyār, I went to his house. He had prepared a grand entertainment, and presented suitable offerings, and gave dresses of honour to most of the servants.

At this time a report came from my fortunate son S̲h̲āh Parwīz that Bī-daulat had crossed the river of Burhanpur (the Taptī), and was wandering in the desert of error. The particulars are that when he crossed the Narbadda and drew all the boats to that side, and fortified the banks of the river and the ferries with cannon and muskets, he left Bairam Beg on the bank with a large number of the rebels, and withdrew towards Āsīr and Burhanpur. The K̲h̲ān-k̲h̲ānān and Dārāb he took with him under surveillance.

And now, for the sake of enlivening my narrative, a few words must be said about Āsīr. The said fort, in its great height and strength, is not in want of my praise. Before Bī-daulat went to the Deccan it was in the charge of K̲h̲wāja Naṣru-llah, s. K̲h̲wāja Fatḥu-llah, who was one of the household slaves and ancient servants. Afterwards, at the request of Bī-daulat, it was handed over to Mīr Ḥusāmu-d-dīn, s. Mīr Jamālu-d-dīn Ḥusain.[33] As the daughter of Nūr Jahān Begam's maternal uncle (*taghāʾī*) was married[34] to him, when Bī-daulat, having been defeated in the neighbourhood of Delhi, turned his rein towards Malwa and Māndū, Nūr Jahān Begam wrote to him and strictly urged him, saying: "Beware, a thousand times beware, not to allow Bī-daulat and his men to come near the fort, but strengthen the towers and gates, and do your duty, and do not act in such a manner that the stain of a curse and ingratitude for favours should fall on the honour or the forehead of a Sayyid." In truth, he strengthened it well, and the arrangements of the fort were not of such a sort that Bī-daulat's bird of thought could fly up to its border, or the conquest of it be quickly accomplished. In brief, when Bī-daulat sent one of his attendants, of the name of S̲h̲arīfā, to the above-mentioned, he (S̲h̲arīfā) seduced him by means of promises and threats, and it was settled (between S̲h̲āh Jahān and S̲h̲arīfā) that when Ḥusāmu-d-dīn should come down to take the letter and dress of honour which had been sent, he should not be allowed to go up again. That wretch, immediately S̲h̲arīfā arrived, put away on the shelf of forgetfulness what he owed on account of his bringing up and the favours conferred on him, and without opposition or effort handed over the fort to S̲h̲arīfā, and with his wife[35] and child went to Bī-daulat, who made him accursed of the Faith and in the world by bestowing on him the mansab of 4,000 personal, and a standard and drums, and the title of Murtaẓā K.—a disgraceful name to all eternity.

In short, when that one of reversed fortune reached the foot of the fort of Āsīr, he took with him K̲h̲ān-k̲h̲ānān, Dārāb, and all his evil-minded offspring up to the fort, and remaining there for three or four days, and having set his mind at ease about provisions, etc., handed it over to one Gopāl Dās, a Rajput, who had formerly been an attendant of Sar-buland Rāy, and entered his service when he went to the Deccan. He left the women and his superfluous baggage, and took with him his three wives with their children and some maid-servants. At first he proposed to imprison K̲h̲ān-k̲h̲ānān and Dārāb in the fort, but at last changed his mind, and bringing them down with him, hastened to Burhanpur. At this time Laʿnatu-llah, after suffering disgrace and contempt, came from Surat and joined him. In great perplexity, Bī-daulat employed Sar-buland Rāy, the son of Rāy Bhoj Hārā, who is one of the brave Rajput servants, and who is fed from the royal table (?), as his mediator, and by letters and messages made proposals of peace. Mahābat K. said that until K̲h̲ān-k̲h̲ānān came, peace was impossible. His (Mahābat's) sole purpose was by these means to separate from him that head of deceivers who was the ring-leader of trouble and sedition. Being helpless, Bī-daulat brought him (K̲h̲ān-k̲h̲ānān) out of prison, and satisfied himself by taking an oath from him on the Qoran. In order to please him and strengthen his promises and oath, he took him inside the female apartment and made a confidant[36] of him, and brought his own wife and son to him, and made use of all kinds of entreaty and lamentation. The gist of his (S̲h̲āh Jahān's) remarks was: "My times are hard, and my position difficult; I make myself over to you, and make you the guardian of my honour. You must act so that I no longer undergo contempt and confusion." The K̲h̲ān-k̲h̲ānān, with a view to bring about peace, parted from Bī-daulat and proceeded to the royal army. It was settled that he should remain on the other side of the river, and arrange matters relating to peace in writing. According to fate, before K̲h̲ān-k̲h̲ānān arrived on the bank of the river, some of the brave warriors and victorious youths one night found an opportunity and crossed over at a place where the rebels were careless. On hearing this news the pillars of their courage trembled, and Bairam Beg could not keep firm the foot of error and ignorance, or engage in driving them back. Whilst he was in this agitation37 many crossed the river, and on the same night the rebels of evil fortune were separated from each other like the *Banātu-n-na'āsh*,38 and took to flight. By the unfailing good fortune (of Jahāngīr) the Khān-khānān fell into perplexity (lit. fell into the *shash-dar*39 position), and could neither go nor stay where he was. At this time again letters arrived from my prosperous son mingling threats with promises. The Khān-khānān, finding only despair and ruin in the page of Bī-daulat's affairs, hastened, through the mediation of Mahābat K., to wait upon my fortunate son. Bī-daulat, on hearing of the departure of Khān-khānān and the crossing of the Narbadda by the victorious army and the flight of Bairam Beg, lost courage, and, notwithstanding a flood in the river and the violence of the rain, crossed the Taptī in a state of wretchedness, and went off towards the Deccan. In this confusion many of the royal servants and his own attendants willingly or unwillingly separated, and did not accompany him. As the native country of Jādo Rāy and Ūday Rām and Ātash K. was on the route, they thought it better for themselves to keep with him for some stages, but Jādo Rāy did not come into his camp, and followed him at the distance of one stage. He took possession of such property as the men in this confusion and fear for their lives abandoned. On the day he (Shāh Jahān) started from the other side of the river (the Taptī) he sent a message by one of his immediate attendants of the name of Ẕū-l-faqār K. Turkmān, summoning Sar-buland K. Afghan, with the message that it seemed to him contrary to courage and the due performance of his engagements that he had as yet not crossed the river. "Fidelity was the glory of men; the faithlessness of no one has touched me (Shāh Jahān) so much as yours." He (Sar-buland) was standing on horseback on the river-bank when Ẕū-l-faqār40 K. came and delivered the message. Sar-buland did not give a precise answer, and was undecided as to whether to stay or go. In his perplexity and by way of objection he told Ẕū-l-faqār to let go his bridle. Ẕū-l-faqār drew his sword, and struck at his waist. At this crisis an Afghan interposed a short spear which the people of India call a *barchhā*, and the blow of the sword caught the shaft, and the point of the sword did not reach Sar-buland's waist. After swords were drawn, the Afghans attacked Ẕū-l-faqār and cut him in pieces. The son of Sulṭān Muḥammad, the treasurer, who was Bī-daulat's page, for friendship's sake had come (with Ẕū-l-faqār) without Bī-daulat's permission, and was also killed.

Briefly, when the news of his leaving Burhanpur and of the victorious army's approaching that city reached me, I sent Khawāṣṣ K. on the wings of haste to my loyal son, and strongly impressed upon him that he must not relax his efforts, but must determine either to take him alive or to drive him out of the imperial territory. It was said that if things went badly with him on this side, it was probable that he would throw himself by the road of Quṭḇu-l-mulk's country into the provinces of Orissa and Bengal. This, too, was in accordance with military plans. So out of caution, which is becoming to a ruler, I appointed Mīrzā Rustam to be governor of Allahabad and dismissed him with orders that if such circumstances should so occur (as S̲h̲āh Jahān's going to Bengal), he should rectify matters.

At this time my son *(farzand)* K̲h̲ān Jahān came from Multan, and had the good fortune to pay his respects. By way of nazar he presented 1,000 muhrs and a ruby of the value of Rs. 100,000, a pearl, and other jewels. I gave an elephant to Rustam K. On the 9th of the Divine month of Ābān K̲h̲awāṣṣ K. brought a report from the prince and Mahābat K. to the effect that when my son (Parwīz) reached Burhanpur, though many of his men had remained behind in consequence of the heavy rains, he, according to orders, without delay had crossed the river (Taptī), and gone in pursuit of Bī-daulat. Bī-daulat, on hearing this terrible news, was marching on. On account of the heaviness of the rain and the excessive quantity of mud and constant marching his beasts of burden had become exhausted. If any baggage was left behind no inquiries were made, and he (S̲h̲āh Jahān) and his children and dependents thought themselves lucky to save their lives and did not trouble about their goods. The army of good fortune having come down the pass of Bhangar, hastened after him as far as the pargana of Ankot,41 about forty koss from Burhanpur. Bī-daulat in this state reached the fort of Māhūr, and when he knew that Jādo Rāy and Ūday Rām and the other Dakhanis would not go with him any farther, he did not disgrace them, but let them go. Leaving the heavy elephants with the goods and chattels with Ūday Rām in the fort, he himself started for Quṭḇu-l-mulk's territory. When his departure from the royal territory was ascertained, my fortunate son, with the approval of Mahābat K. and other loyalists, turned rein from that pargana. On the first of the Divine month of Ābān he entered Burhanpur. Rāja Sārang Deo was sent to my son with a gracious farman.

Qāsim K. was raised to the mansab of 4,000 personal and 2,000 horse. Mīrak Muʿīn, Bakhshi of Kabul, at the request of Mahābat K., was honoured with the title of K̲h̲ān. Alf K. Qiyām-k̲h̲ānī, having come from the Subah of Patna, paid his respects, and was appointed to the charge of the fort of Kāngṛa. I presented him with a standard. On the 1st of the Divine month of Āẕar Bāqī K. came from Jūnāgaṛh and waited on me.

As I was at ease with regard to the affair of Bī-daulat, and the heat of Hindustan did not agree with my constitution, on the 2nd of the month, corresponding with the 1st of Ṣafar42 my camp started from Ajmir for a tour and to hunt in the pleasant regions of Kashmir. Before this I had appointed the chief of the state Āṣaf K. Subahdar of Bengal, and gave him leave. As I had taken a great liking to his society, and he was distinguished above all the other servants for ability and good disposition and tact, and is moreover unequalled in all kinds of propriety, and I regretted separation from him, I had broken through that purpose, and had sent for him to wait upon me. He came on this day, and had the good fortune to kiss the threshold. Jagat Singh, s. Rānā Karan, took leave on his return to his native country, and was given a dress of honour and a jewelled dagger. Rāja Sārang Deo brought a report from my fortunate son S̲h̲āh Parwīz and Mahābat K. Madāru-s-salṭ̤ana, and kissed the threshold. It was written that their minds were at ease with regard to the affair of Bī-daulat, and that the rulers of the Deccan, willingly or unwillingly, were performing the dues of obedience and submission. His Majesty (Jahāngīr) might make his mind at ease about that quarter and enjoy himself in hunting and travelling in whatever place in the royal dominions he might approve of and which was good for his health. On the 20th of the month Mīrzā Wālī, having come from Sironj, waited on me. Ḥakīm Mūminā was raised to the mansab of 1,000. Aṣālat K., s. K̲h̲ān Jahān, according to order, came from Gujarat, and had the good fortune to pay his respects.

At this time a report came from ʿAqīdat K., Bakhshi of the Deccan, containing the news of Rāja Girdhar's having been killed. The particulars of this event are that one of the brothers of Sayyid Kabīr Bārha, who was an attendant of my fortunate son S̲h̲āh Parwīz, gave his sword to brighten and put on the wheel (to sharpen) to a cutler who had a shop close to the house of Rāja Girdhar. The next day, when he came to fetch his sword, a conversation took place as to the charge for the work, and the people of the Sayyid struck the cutler some blows with a stick. The Raja's people in supporting him used their whips on them. By chance two or three young Sayyids of Bārha had lodgings in that neighbourhood, and hearing of this disturbance, went to the assistance of the aforesaid Sayyid. The fire of strife was lighted, and a fight took place between the Sayyids and Rajputs, ending in an encounter with arrows and swords. Sayyid Kabīr, becoming aware of this, came to assist with thirty or forty horsemen, and at this time Rāja Girdhar, with a body of Rajputs and his caste people, according to the custom of the Hindus, were sitting barebodied and eating their food. Becoming aware of the coming of Sayyid Kabīr and the violence of the Sayyids, he brought his men inside the house and firmly closed the door. The Sayyids, setting fire to the door, forced their way inside and the fight went to such a length that Rāja Girdhar and twenty-six of his servants were killed and forty others wounded. Four of the Sayyids were also killed. After Rāja Girdhar was killed, Sayyid Kabīr took the horses out of his stable to his own house and returned. The Rajput officers, when informed of the slaying of Rāja Girdhar, came on horseback in great numbers from their houses, and all the Bārha Sayyids came to the aid of Sayyid Kabīr. They assembled in the plain outside the citadel, and the fire of trouble and calamity increased, and it nearly came to a great disturbance. Mahābat K., being informed of it, immediately mounted and went there, and bringing the Sayyids into the citadel, and soothing the Rajputs in a manner suitable to the occasion, took some of their chief men with him and went to the house of Khān ʿĀlam, which was near there. He soothed them down in a proper way, and promised and became security for an inquiry into the matter. When this news reached the prince he also went to the quarters of the Khān ʿĀlam, and soothed them with words appropriate to the state of affairs, and sent the Rajputs to their own houses. Next day Mahābat K. went to the house of Rāja Girdhar, condoled and sympathized with his sons, and having contrived to get hold of Sayyid Kabīr put him into confinement. As the Rajputs would not be consoled without his being put to death, after a few days he executed him.

On the 23rd I appointed Muḥammad Murād faujdār of Ajmir, and sent him off. On this road I continually enjoyed myself in sporting. One day, while hunting, a *tūyghūn* (albino) partridge, which till now I had never seen, came to my sight, and I caught it with a hawk. By chance the hawk that caught it was also a *tūyghūn*. I ascertained by trial that the flesh of the black partridge was better than that of the white, and that the flesh of the large quail (*būdana*), which the people of India call *ghāghar*,43 is better than that of the quail, which is a fighter. I compared the flesh of a fat kid with that of a lamb; the flesh of the fat kid is more delicious. By way of test I ordered them both to be cooked in the same way, so that I might discern the matter accurately. On this account I have recorded it.

On the 10th of the month of Dai, in the neighbourhood of the pargana of Raḥīmābād,44 the huntsmen brought in news of a tiger. I ordered Irādat K. and Fidāʾī K. to take with them some of the guards (*ahl-i-yātish*) and surround the wood, and mounting (an elephant) I followed them and went towards the hunt. From the number of trees and thickness of the jungle it could not be well seen. Driving the elephant forward, the tiger's flank came into view, and with one wound from my gun he fell and gave up his life. Of all the tigers I have shot from the time when I was a prince until now I never saw a tiger like this for size and majesty and the symmetry of its limbs. I ordered the artists to take its portrait according to its real form and body. He weighed 8½ Jahāngīrī maunds; his length, from the top of his head to the end of his tail, was 3½ cubits45 and 2 *ṭassū* (1/24 of a yard).

On the 16th it was reported that Mumtāz46 K., the governor of Agra, had died. At first he was in the service of Bahādur K., the brother of Khān Zamān. After they were killed he entered the service of my revered father. When I placed my foot in the world of existence that revered person favoured me with making him the Nāẕir (Superintendent) of my establishment. For a period of fifty-six years he served me sincerely and zealously and in a manner to please me, and at no time did a speck of dust from him settle on the fringe of my heart. What is due to him for the excellence of his service is more than a clerk could write. May God Almighty overwhelm him in the ocean of His forgiveness!

Having conferred on Muqarrab K., who is one of the old officials,47 the government and administration of Agra, I gave him his leave. In the neighbourhood of Fatḥpūr, Mukarram K. and his brother ʿAbdu-s-Salām had the good fortune to pay their respects. On the 22nd the entertainment for my lunar weighment took place in the town of Mathura, and the fifty-seventh year of my age began auspiciously and happily. At Mathura I went on by boat seeing what was to be seen, and hunting. On the way the huntsmen reported that a tigress with three cubs had appeared. Disembarking from the boat I engaged in the pleasure of sport. As the cubs were small I ordered them to be taken by hand, and killed the mother with my gun. At this time it was reported to me that the villagers48 and cultivators on the other side of the river Jumna had not given up stealing and highway robbery, and, passing their time in the shelter of thick jungles and difficult strong places in stubbornness and fearlessness, would not pay their rents to the jagirdars. I gave an order to K͟hān Jahān to take a force of mansabdars with him and give them exemplary punishment, and having slaughtered, imprisoned, and plundered them, raze to the ground their strongholds and forts, and tear up from the root their thorn-brakes of mischief and disturbance. The next day the force crossed the river and made a hot attack on them. As they had no time for escape by flight they planted firmly the foot of folly, and showed fight. Many of them were slaughtered: their women and children were taken prisoners, and much booty fell into the hands of the victorious army.

On 1st Bahman, having promoted Rustam K. to the faujdārship of the Sarkar of Qanauj, I sent him there.

On the 2nd ʿAbdu-llah, s. Ḥakīm Nūru-d-dīn, of Teheran, was ordered to be capitally punished in my presence. The explanation of this brief announcement is as follows: When the ruler of Persia, on suspicion of his having money and other property, tortured his father, the aforesaid fled from Persia, and with a hundred miseries and adversities threw himself into Hindustan, and by the patronage of Iʿtimādu-d-daula was enrolled among the servants of the Court. By the aid of good fortune, having in a short time become well known, he was included among those who were in immediate attendance, and obtained a mansab of 500 and a fertile jagir, but as his capacity was small (lit., his digestion was narrow) he could not stand such great good fortune, and assumed ingratitude and unthankfulness and constantly defiled his tongue with abuse49 of his lord and master. At this time it was continually reported to me that as my kindness to him and observance of what was due to him increased, that ungrateful one blamed and abused me the more. When I considered the favours I had bestowed upon him, I could not believe these stories about him, but at last I heard from impartial and disinterested persons the disrespectful language which he had used with respect to me in assemblies and companies. The charge was thus confirmed, and accordingly I summoned him to my presence and had him executed.50

"A red51 tongue gives the green head to the winds." As the huntsmen reported that there was a tigress in this neighbourhood, by the mischief caused by which the inhabitants were oppressed, I ordered Fidā'ī K. to take elephants with him and surround it. Mounting myself, I followed him into the forest. It soon came to view, and with one shot from my gun its affairs were finished. One day I was enjoying myself with sport, and caught a black partridge with a hawk. I ordered them to open its crop in my presence. A mouse it had swallowed whole came out of its crop, and which was not yet digested. I was greatly astonished that the pipe of its gullet, small as it was, should swallow a whole mouse and how it had done so. Without exaggeration, if anyone had told me the tale I should not have believed it. As I saw this myself I have recorded it on account of its strangeness. On the 6th of the month Delhi became the abode of good fortune.

As Jagat Singh, s. Rāja Bāso, at the instigation of Bī-daulat, had gone out into the hills in the north of the Panjab, which is his hereditary abode, and raised a disturbance there, I appointed Ṣādiq K. to punish him, as has been related in the preceding pages. At this time Mādho Singh, his younger brother, was promoted to the title of Raja, and given a horse and robe of honour. An order was given for him to go to Ṣādiq K. and attack the rebels with him.

Next day I marched from the outskirts of the city, and alighted at Salīmgaṛh. As the house of Rāja Kis̲han Dās was on the road, and he had made great efforts and entreated me to do so, I at his request threw the shadow of prosperity on his dwelling, and gratified the desire of that old servant. A few of his offerings were accepted in order to dignify him. Marching on the 20th from Salīmgaṛh, I appointed Sayyid Bahwa Buk̲hārī to the governorship of Delhi, which is his ordinary residence. In fact, he had already done this service well, and I had given him high rank.

At this time ʿAlī Muḥammad, s. ʿAlī Rāy,52 ruler of Tibet, by his father's order came to Court, and had the good fortune to pay his respects. It was clear that ʿAlī Rāy had a great affection for and attachment to this son, and held him dearer than his other children. He wished to make him his successor, and he was consequently envied by his brothers, and disputes arose between them. Abdāl, s. ʿAlī Rāy, who was the eldest of his children, through this jealousy sought the patronage of the K͟hān of Kashghar and made him his protector, so that when ʿAlī Rāy, who was very old and decrepit, should die, he might, under the protection of the Wālī of Kashghar, become ruler of Tibet. ʿAlī Rāy, suspecting that the brothers might attack ʿAlī Muḥammad, and a disturbance might arise in his country, sent him to Court, his desire being that he might be attached to this Court, and his affairs might prosper by service to and kindness shown by the Court.

On the 1st of the Ilāhī month of Isfandārmuẕ I pitched in the pargana of Umbala. Las͟hkarī, s. Imām-wirdī, who had run away from Bī-daulat, and joined the service of my auspicious son S͟hāh Parwīz, having come on this date to Court, kissed the threshold. A report came from my son and Mahābat K. It contained the recommendation and the offer of service of ʿĀdil K., with a letter which he had sent to Mahābat, in which were set forth his submissiveness and loyalty. Las͟hkarī was sent back to Parwīz with a dress of honour, a *nādirī* with pearl buttons for the prince, and a dress of honour for K͟hān ʿĀlam and Mahābat K. At the request of my son I wrote a gracious farman to ʿĀdil K. showing great favour to him, and sent him a robe of honour with a special *nādirī*. I gave an order that if they thought fit they should send the above-mentioned53 to ʿĀdil K.

On the 5th I alighted at the garden of Sihrind. On the bank of the Beas Ṣādiq K., Mukh͟tār K., Isfandiyār, Rāja Rūp Chand of Gwalior, and other Amirs who had been appointed to support him, having succeeded in restoring order in the northern hill-country, had the good fortune to kiss the threshold. The facts, briefly, are that Jagat Singh, at the instigation of Bī-daulat, had taken to the hills above-mentioned, and engaged in stirring up sedition and strife. As the field was clear (*i.e.*, there was no one to oppose him) he passed over difficult mountains and defiles, and by attacking and plundering peasantry and the weak, heaped misfortune on them until Ṣādiq K. arrived. He brought the Zamindars under control by means of fears and hopes, and made the overthrow of that wretched creature the object of his exertions. Jagat Singh strengthened the fort of Mau, and was protected by it. Whenever he found an opportunity he left that fortress and fought with the royal servants. At last his provisions were exhausted, and he came to despair of assistance from the other Zamindars. The elevation of his younger brother became a source of disturbance and anxiety to him. Helplessly he then sought for patronage, and begged the protection of Nūr Jahān Begam, expressing shame and contrition, and sought a refuge in her mediation. In order to please and satisfy her, the pen of pardon was drawn through the record of his faults.

On this day reports came in from the officials in the Deccan that Bī-daulat, with La'natu-llah, Dārāb, and other wretched (with broken wing and feathers) creatures in miserable condition, with blackened faces, had gone from the borders of Quṭbu-l-mulk's territory towards Orissa and Bengal. In this journey great loss fell on him and his companions, many of whom, when a chance offered, with bare heads and feet, and having washed their hands of life (desperate), took to flight. Out of these one day Mīrzā Muḥammad, s. Afẓal K., his Diwan, with his mother and his family, ran away during the march, and when the news reached Bī-daulat, he sent Ja'far and K͟hān-qulī Uzbeg and some others of his confidential men in pursuit of him, that, if they could take him alive, well and good, or otherwise they should cut off his head and bring it into his presence. They with all speed proceeded and caught him up on the road. Becoming aware of this, he sent his mother and family into the jungles and hid them there, and himself with a body of young men whom he relied on as companions, planted manfully the foot of courage and stood with their bows. In front of them there was a canal and a swamp (*chihlā*). Sayyid Ja'far K. wished to approach near him and take him with him by deceiving him, but however much he tried to persuade him by threatening and holding out hopes, it had no effect, and he answered him with life-taking arrows. He made a good fight of it, and sent K͟hān-qulī and some others of Bī-daulat's men to hell. Sayyid Ja'far also was wounded. Finally Mīrzā Muḥammad received severe wounds and gambled away the cash of his life. But as long as he had breath he deprived many thereof. After he was killed, they cut off his head and took it to Bī-daulat.

When Bī-daulat was defeated near Delhi and went to Māndū, he sent Afẓal K. to get assistance and support from 'Ādil K. and others, forwarding with him an armlet (*bāzū-band*) for 'Ādil K., and a horse, an elephant, and a jewelled sword for 'Ambar. He first went to 'Ambar. After delivering his message he produced what Bī-daulat had sent for him, but 'Ambar would not accept them, saying he was the servant of 'Ādil K., who was at present the head of those in power in the Deccan: he should go first to him and explain what he desired. If he agreed, his slave would ally himself to and obey him, and in that case he would take whatever was sent, otherwise not. Afẓal K. went to 'Ādil K., who received him very badly, and for a long time kept him outside the city and did not look into his affair, but put all kinds of slights upon him, but secretly asked for what Bī-daulat had sent for him and 'Ambar, and took possession of it. The aforesaid (Afẓal K.) was there when he heard the news of the killing of his son and the ruin of his family, and so fell upon evil days. In short, Bī-daulat, in spite of all his (original) good fortune and happy auspices, undertook a long and distant journey, and came to the port of Machhlī Paṭan (Masulipaṭam), which belongs to Quṭbu-l-mulk. Before reaching this place, he sent some of his men to Quṭbu-l-mulk, and besought him for all sorts of assistance and companionship. Quṭbu-l-mulk sent him a small amount of cash and goods for his support, and wrote to the warden of his frontier to conduct him in safety out of his territory, and encourage the grain-sellers and Zamindars to send grain and all other necessaries to his camp.

On the 27th of the month a strange event took place. Returning from the hunting-place, I had come back to the camp at night. By chance I crossed a stream of water, the bed of which was very rocky and the water running violently. One of the servants of the *sharbat-khāna* (wine-cellar) was conveying a huntsman's relish. He had a gold tray, which contained a salver and five cups. There were covers to the cups, and the whole was in a cotton bag. When he was crossing, his foot slipped and the tray fell out of his hand. As the water was deep and running rapidly, however much they searched and beat their hands and feet (exerted themselves), no trace of it could be found. Next day the state of the case was reported to me, and I ordered a number of boatmen and huntsmen to go to the place and make a careful search, and it perhaps might appear. By chance, in the place where it had fallen it was found, and more strange still, it had not been turned upside down, and not a drop of water had got into the cups. This affair is similar to what happened when Hādī was seated on the throne of the Khalifate. A ruby ring had been inherited by Hārūn from his father. Hādī sent a slave to Hārūn and asked for it. It happened that at that time Hārūn was seated on the bank of the Tigris. The slave gave the message, and Hārūn, enraged, said: "I have allowed thee54 to have the Khalifate, and thou dost not allow me one ring." In his rage he threw the ring into the Tigris. After some months by the decree of fate Hādī died, and the turn of the Khalifate came to Hārūn. He ordered divers to look for the ring in the place where he had thrown it. By the chances of destiny, and the aid of good fortune, at the first dive the ring was found, and brought and given into Hārūn's hand!

At this time one day on the hunting ground the chief huntsman Imām-wirdī brought before me a partridge that had a spur on one leg and not on the other. As the way to distinguish the female lies in the spur, by way of testing me he asked whether this was a male or a female. I said at once "A female." When they opened it an egg appeared inside (*pīshīna*) its belly. The people who were in attendance asked with surprise by what sign I had discovered this: I said that the head and beak of the female are shorter than the male's. By investigation and often seeing (the birds) I had acquired this dexterity.55 It is a strange thing that the windpipe in all animals (*ḥaiwānāt*), which the Turks call *ḥalq*,56 is single from the top of the throat to the crop (*chīna-dān*), while in the case of the bustard (*jarz*) it is different. In the bustard it is for four finger-breadths from the top of the throat single and then it divides into two branches and in this form reaches the crop. Also at the place where it divides into two branches there is a stoppage (*sar-band*) and a knot (*girih*) is felt by the hand. In the *kulang* (crane) it is still stranger. In it the windpipe passes in a serpentine manner between the bones of the breast to the rump and then turns back from there and joins the throat. The *jarz* or *charz* (bustard) is of two kinds: one is a mottled black and the other *būr* (a kind of dun colour). I now57 discovered that there are not two kinds, but that which is a mottled black is the male, and that which is dun-coloured is the female. The proof of it is this, that in the piebald there are testicles and in the dun one there are eggs; this has been repeatedly found on examination.

I have a great liking for fish, and all kinds of good fish are brought for me; the best fish in Hindustan is the *rohū*, and after that the *barīn*.58 Both have scales, and in appearance and shape are like each other. Everyone cannot at once distinguish between them. The difference in their flesh also is very small, but the connoisseur discovers that the flesh of the *rohū* is rather more agreeable of the two.

---

1 He was the great-grandson, being the son of Mahā Singh s. Jagat Singh s. Mān Singh. ↑

2 *Panj fauj*. But perhaps the word is *binj*, or *bīkh*, "root." Or it may be *pīchhā fauj*, "the hinder army." Apparently the reference is to the arrangement of the royal army into five divisions. ↑

3 "Bought it as if it were genuine." ↑

4 The Farhang-i-Jahāngīrī, Rieu Cat., p. 496 b. ↑

5 Where is this account? He is mentioned later, p. 359 of text. Perhaps he is the Armenian mentioned in the 15th year as Zū-l-Qarnain. But an Armenian would hardly be called a Farangī. ↑

6 The MSS. have "his brother Maghrūr." ↑

7 The MSS. have a name that is not Naubat, and perhaps is Yūnas or Yūnash Khān. ↑

8 Yūnas or Yūnash in MSS. ↑

9 Perhaps it means that *qiṣāṣ* or retaliation could not be inflicted. See Ma'āṣiru-l-umarā, III. 335, and Iqbāl-nāma, 204. Evidently the mother did not want to prosecute. It is probable that his murderers were only his half-brothers. ↑

10 The MSS. have Mahārāja Gaj Singh, and they also have the names Manṣūr Khān, Sar-buland Rāy and Lashkar K. ↑

11 "Two" in MSS. ↑

12 Jahāngīr's mother. ↑

13 MS. 181 has Bābā Khān. ↑

14 MS. 181 has Kuhnar or Kunhar, and it seems that it is a name, and not merely "younger brother." The Iqbāl-nāma, 205, has Kunhar Dās. ↑

15 Karīj in text. See Jarrett, II. 253. But perhaps it should be Kaira. ↑

16 It is Shaʿbān in Nos. 181 and 305. The famous garden of Ahmadabad is the Shāhī, for which see the Bombay Gazetteer, vol. for Ahmadabad, p. 283. But besides being Shaʿbān in the MSS. it is also Shaʿbān in the Iqbāl-nāma, 207. The Shāhī garden lies to the north of Ahmadabad, and Ṣafī was at the south or south-east of the city. Perhaps the Shaʿbān garden was near the Malik Shaʿbān lake, which was east of the city, and is referred to in Bombay Gazetteer, p. 18. The Bāgh Shaʿbān is also referred to in Bayley's Gujarat, 236. ↑

17 Name very doubtful. MSS. seem to have Pīr Lāl Kolī, or it may be Bīr Lāl. ↑

18 The MSS. have "in ten." ↑

19 Text, Nar Singh Deo. But the MSS. seem to have another name, Silhadi Deo (?). The name Lūlū is also doubtful. The MSS. seem to have Bulur. In Elliot, IV. 402, Pūran Mal is called Bhaia. ↑

20 *Har kudām ba-ṭarafī aftādand.* ↑

21 Rieu, Cat., I. 158 b. ↑

22 Text has Kūh-i-Kūl. But the I.O. MSS. show that the true reading is Kūl Nūh ban, and it appears from the Āyīn, Jarrett, II. 186, that Nūh is a district in Kūl—*i.e.*, Aligarh. *Gurg* is a wolf, and *Kurag* a rhinoceros, but probably a wolf is here meant. It is not likely that there were rhinoceros in Aligarh, though Abū-l-Faẓl says there were rhinoceros in Sambhal (Jarrett, II. 281). Tīr means an arrow as well as a bullet. The word *mana*, "face," is not in text, but occurs in both the I.O. MSS. ↑

23 Chāṇḍā Ghāt between Ajmere and Malwa. ↑

24 Apparently the meaning is that he had no family with Shāh Jahān's army, and so could not be deterred from leaving Shāh Jahān through fear of their fate. See below, the reference to S. Ṣalābat's arrangements about his family. ↑

25 This couplet comes from Niẕāmī's K͟husrau u S͟hīrīn, and is quoted by Bābur. ↑

26 See Jaʿfar S͟harīf's Qānūn-i-Islām. App., p. xxiv. ↑

27 Dhāmin, python (?). ↑

28 See Blochmann, 60. ↑

29 Daughter of Nūr Jahān. ↑

30 Blochmann, p. 311, calls her Arzānī Begam. The Iqbāl-nāma (306) calls her Lāṛdilī Begam. A MS. of the Iqbāl-nāma in my possession calls her Walī Begam. She was born on September 4, 1623. ↑

31 The holy man formerly mentioned. ↑

32 He had been captured in Gujarat when Ṣafī K. defeated ʿAbdu-llah. ↑

33 The author of the dictionary. ↑

34 See Maʾāṩiru-l-Umarā, III. 382. His wife was the sister of Aḥmad Beg, the brother's son of Ibrāhīm K. Fatḥ-jang. But if so would she not be the daughter of S͟harīf and niece of Nūr Jahān? See Blochmann, 512. ↑

35 I.O. MS., 381, and the Iqbāl-nāma mention the wife. ↑

36 *Maḥram sāk͟ht*, "made him one who could enter the Harem." ↑

37 The text wrongly has *ba-chand* instead of *ba-jambīd.* ↑

38 Daughters of the Bier—*i.e.*, the constellation of the Plough. ↑

39 *S͟has͟h-dar* is the name of an impasse in the game of *nard.* ↑

40 The Muḥammad Beg of Roe? ↑

41 Jarrett, II. 239. ↑

42 1 Ṣafar, 1033 = November 14, 1623. ↑

43 Jerdon states that the black partridge is called *ghāghar* about Benares. ↑

44 Probably Raḥīmābād in the Bārī Dū-āb. Jarrett, II. 332. ↑

45 *Daraʿ* or *ẕaraʿ*, yards? The text gives his weight as 20½, but *bīst* must be a mistake for *has͟ht.* ↑

46 He was a eunuch, and originally had the name of Iʿtibār K. He received the title of Mumtāz K. in this year. Tūzuk, 359. See Blochmann, 433. ↑

47 *Aẕ qadīmān u bābariyān* (properly *bairiyān*). ↑

48 *Ganwārān u muẕāriʿān.* ↑

49 Text *ba shukr u shukūh*, but the Iqbāl-nāma, 213, has *ba-shakwa*, "with complaints," and this must be correct. ʿAbdu-llah indulged in abuse of his lord and master, *khudā u khudāwand-i-khwīsh—i.e.*, Jahāngīr. ↑

50 *Cf.* Iqbāl-nāma, 213–214. ↑

51 A proverbial expression. It is quoted by Niẓāmu-d-dīn in the Ṭabaqāt. ↑

52 ʿAlī Rāy was ruler of Little Tibet (Baltistan). Jahāngīr had married his daughter. Blochmann, 310, and Akbar-nāma, III. 603. The marriage took place in A.H. 1000 (1592). ↑

53 That is, Lashkarī. ↑

54 Hādī was Hārūnu-r-Rashīd's elder brother. ↑

55 Text *mulka*. Perhaps the word may be *malka-i-ān*, "possession of it"—*i.e.*, possession of such knowledge. The MSS. have *ān* after *malka*. ↑

56 Text *hanaq*. But the MSS. have merely *ḥaqq*, and it is said in the dictionaries that there is a bird called the *ḥaqq*. ↑

57 This corrects a previous statement to the effect that the black and red bustards were two species. ↑

58 The MSS. have either barīn or parīn. I cannot find the name in the dictionaries, but my friend Sir K. C. Gupta suggests that the word may be *bāns* (*Labeo calbasa*). This fish is also a carp, and resembles the *rohū* (*L. rohita*), but is smaller. It may also be the catla. ↑

# The Nineteenth New Year's Feast after the Auspicious Accession

On Wednesday, the 29th Jumādā-l-awwal, A.H. 1033, March 10, 1624, after one watch and two gharis of day had passed, the sun, that bestows bounty on the world, passed into its house of honour in Aries. The royal servants obtained promotions and increase of mansab. Aḥsanu-llah, s. Kh̲wāja Abū-l-Ḥasan, received as original and increase that of 1,000 and 300 horse. Muḥammad Sa'īd, s. Aḥmad Beg K. Kābulī, the same, Mīr Sh̲araf Dīwān-i-buyūtāt, and Kh̲awāṣṣ K., each of them that of 1,000. Sardār K., having come from Kāngṛa, had the good fortune to pay his respects. At this time I gave orders to the *yasāwuls* and men of the *yasāq* (guards) that hereafter at the time when I came out of the palace they should keep away defective people, such as the blind, and those whose noses and ears had been cut off, the leprous and the maimed, and all kinds of sick people, and not permit them to be seen. On the 19th the feast of the culmination was held. Ilāh-wirdī, the brother of Imām-wirdī, had run away from Bī-daulat and came to Court, and was honoured with great favours.

As the news of Bī-daulat's coming to the border of Orissa was constantly repeated, a farman was issued to the prince and Mahābat K. and the Amirs who had been sent to the support of my son, that they should set their minds at ease about the administering the provinces (of the Deccan), and go quickly to Allahabad and Behar, and if the Subahdar of Bengal could not forestall him, and he should put forward the foot of audacity, he must be made a wanderer in the desert of disappointment by the blows of the victorious army which is in the shadow of the flag of my son. By way of precaution on the 2nd Urdībihish̲t I gave my son Kh̲ān Jahān leave to proceed to Agra to remain in that neighbourhood and wait for a sign. If there should happen to be any necessity for a particular service and an order should be given him, he must act as occasion might require. I sent him a special dress of honour, with a *nādirī* with pearl buttons, a special jewelled sword, and to Aṣālat K., his son, a horse, and a dress of honour.

On this day a report came from 'Aqīdat K., Bakhshi of the Deccan. He wrote that, according to order, my prosperous son Sh̲āh Parwīz had married the sister of Rāja Gaj Singh. I hope that her coming will be auspicious to the State. He also wrote that, having sent for Turkumān K. from Pattan he had appointed 'Azīzu-llah in his place. Jān-sipār K., also by order, came and waited on me. When Bī-daulat crossed the Burhanpur river and took the road of ruin, Mīr Ḥusāmu-d-dīn, considering his own evil deeds, could not remain at Burhanpur. Taking his children with him, he conveyed the goods of ruin to the Deccan, in order that he might pass his days under the protection of

ʿĀdil K. By chance, as he passed by Bīr, Jān-sipār K. obtained information, and sent a body of men to head him off. He seized him and his dependants, and brought them before Mahābat. Mahābat placed him in confinement, and took from him Rs. 1,00,000 in cash and goods. (Also) Jādo Rāy and Ūday Rām had taken the elephants which Bī-daulat had left in Burhanpur and brought them to the prince (Parwīz).

Qāẓī ʿAbdu-l-ʿAzīz, who had come to Delhi from Bī-daulat in order to state his objects, had not been allowed by me an opportunity to speak and I had handed him over to Mahābat K. After his (Bī-daulat's) defeat and ruin Mahābat K. had made him his own servant. As he was an old friend of ʿĀdil K., and was for some years at Bījāpūr as Vakil of Kh̲ān Jahān. Mahābat K. now sent him again as his representative[1] to ʿĀdil Kh̲ān, and the leading men of the Deccan, *nolentes volentes*, looking to the necessities of the time and the upshot of affairs, were contented and professed loyalty and desire for service. The rebel ʿAmbar sent one of his confidential men of the name of ʿAlī Sh̲īr, and displayed great humility. He (ʿAmbar) wrote in the capacity of a servant to Mahābat K., and engaged that he (ʿAmbar) should come to Dewalgāon[2] and wait upon Mahābat. He would make his eldest son a servant of the State, and keep him in the service of my auspicious son. About this time there arrived a letter from Qāẓī ʿAbdu-l-ʿAzīz that ʿĀdil K. from the bottom of his heart had elected for service and loyalty, and agreed that he would send Mullā Muḥammad Lārī, who was his principal agent and minister, and whom both in spoken and written messages he called Mullā Bābā, with 5,000 horse, that he might remain continually on duty, and they might know that other[3] troops would follow (?). Urgent farmans had been sent that my son should proceed to Allahabad and Behar in order to overthrow Bī-daulat. At this time news arrived that notwithstanding the rainy season and the violence of the rain, that son, on the 6th Farwardīn had marched out of Burhanpur with the army of fortune, and had taken up his quarters in Lāl Bāgh̲,[4] and that Mahābat K. was awaiting at Burhanpur the arrival of Mullā Muḥammad Lārī, so that when he arrived he would relieve himself of the care of the maintenance of order in that neighbourhood, and come with him (Muḥammad Lārī) to wait on my son. Lash̲kar K., Jādo Rāy, Ūday Rām, and other servants of the State had been ordered to go to the Bālāgh̲āt (the country above the Ghats), and remain at Ẓafarnagar. Having given Jān-sipār K. leave as before, he (Parwīz) kept Asad K. Maʿmūrī at Elichpur. Minūchihr, s. Sh̲āh-nawāz K., was appointed to Jālnāpūr. He sent Riẓawī K. to Thālner, to guard the province of Khandesh.

On this day news came that Lash̲karī had taken the farman to ʿĀdil K., and he, having decorated the city, had gone out four koss to meet him, and had performed salutations and prostrations for the farman and the dress of honour. On the 21st I sent dresses of honour for my son Dāwar-bakhsh and Khān A'ẓam and Ṣafī K. Having appointed Ṣādiq K. to the government of Lahore, and given him a dress of honour and an elephant, I gave him leave. An order was given that he should have the mansab of 400 personal and 400 horse. Multafat K., s. Mīrzā Rustam, raised the head of distinction with the mansab of 1,500 personal and 300 horse.

One day while hunting it was reported to me that a snake with a black hood (*kafcha*) had swallowed another hooded (*kafcha?*) snake and gone into a hole. I ordered them to dig up the place and bring out the snake. Without exaggeration I had never seen a snake of this size. When, they opened its belly, the hood of the snake that it had swallowed came out whole. Although this snake was of another kind, in length and girth little difference was visible.

At this time it was represented to me in a report5 by the news writer of the Deccan that Mahābat K. had ordered 'Ārif s. Zāhid to be executed, and had put him (*i.e.*, Zāhid), with two other sons, in prison. It appeared that that wretched man had written with his own hand a petition to Bī-daulat representing on the part of his father and himself his loyalty, sincerity, repentance, and shame. By fate that letter fell into the hands of Mahābat K. Having sent for 'Ārif into his presence he showed him the letter. As he had written a decree for his own blood, he could not make any acceptable excuse, and of necessity he was executed, and his father and brothers imprisoned.

On the 1st Khurdād it was reported that Shajā'at K. 'Arab, had died a natural death in the Deccan.

At this time a report came from Ibrāhīm K. Fatḥ-jang that Bī-daulat had entered Orissa. The particulars of this are that between the boundary6 of Orissa and the Deccan there is a barrier. On one side there are lofty mountains, and on the other swamps and a river. The ruler of Golconda had also erected a wall (*dar-band*) and a fort, and armed it with muskets and cannon. The passage of men by that closed route was impracticable without the leave of Quṭbu-l-mulk. Bī-daulat, with the guidance of Quṭbu-l-mulk, having passed by that route, entered the country of Orissa. It happened that at this time Aḥmad Beg K., nephew of Ibrāhīm K., had attacked the Zamindars of Khurda. At this strange occurrence, which happened without precedent or news or information, he became confused and bewildered and without seeing a remedy gave up his campaign, and came to the village of Bulbulī7 (Pīplī), the seat of the governor of that Subah (Orissa). He then took his women with him and hastened to Cuttack, which is 12 koss from Pīplī towards Bengal. As the time was short, he had not leisure to collect troops and arrange his affairs. He did not feel himself equal to a war with Bī-daulat, and he had not with him associates such as were necessary, so he went on from Cuttack to Bardwan, of which Ṣāliḥ, nephew of Āṣaf K. deceased, was the Jagirdar. At first Ṣāliḥ was astonished8, and did not believe that Bī-daulat was coming, until a letter came from Laʿnatu-llah to conciliate him. Ṣāliḥ fortified Bardwan and remained in it. Ibrāhīm K. was surprised on hearing the terrible news. Though most of his auxiliaries and soldiers were scattered in the villages round about and unprocurable, he yet planted the foot of courage firmly in Akbarnagar (Rajmahal), and set himself to strengthen the fort and collect troops, and encourage the heads of tribes and retainers. He prepared the things necessary for his guns and other weapons and for battle. In the meanwhile a notice came to him from Bī-daulat that by the decree of God and the ordinances of heaven what was not suitable to him had appeared from the womb of non-existence. By the revolving of crooked-moving time and the changes of night and day his passage towards these regions had come to pass. Although to the view of manly courage the extent and breadth of that country were not more than an exercising-ground, or rather than a rubbish-heap (*pur-kāhī*, "full of straw"), and his aims were higher, yet as he had to pass by this way, he could not pass for nothing. If it were Ibrāhīm's determination to go to the royal Court, he (S͟hāh Jahān) would hold back the hand of injury from him and his family, and he might go to Court with an easy mind. If he considered it advisable to stay, he would bestow upon him any corner of the country he might ask for.

Addendum by Mīrzā Muḥammad Hādī, the Writer of the Preface

The MS. states: "Up to this place is the writing (*taʾlīf*) of the deceased king Jahāngīr. The rest, up to the end of the book, is written by Muḥammad Hādī from some trustworthy MS. collected together to complete the book.

---

1 *Ba-rism-i-ḥajābat.* ↑

2 Dewalgāon is about 60 miles S. of Burhanpur, Elliot, VII. 11. ↑

3 Or, perhaps, they might be sure he was coming shortly. ↑

4 Lāl Bāg͟h was on the outskirts of Burhanpur. Though the rainy season is spoken of, the date Farwardīn is in March. ↑

5 Perhaps the meaning is that Mahābat had imprisoned ʿĀrif, the son of the Zāhid whom Jahāngīr had condemned to death, for in the 18th year Jahāngīr speaks of Zāhid as a rebel. But the sentence is not clear. ↑

6 Elliot, VI. 390. It seems probable that this is the place mentioned in the Maʾāṣiru-l-umarā, I. 410, in the biography of Bāqir K. Najm Ṣānī, and also in the Pādis͟hāh-nāma, I. 333. It is called there "the Pass of Chhatar Diwār," and

is described as the boundary between Orissa and Telingana, and is two koss from Khairapāra. One Manṣūr, a servant of Quṭḅu-l-mulk, had built a fort there, and called it Manṣūr-garh. ↑

7 *Bulbulī.* I had supposed this to be Pīplī, but the latter place is in the Balasore district, and nearer Bengal than Cuttack. Curiously enough Pipli or Pippli is not given in the I.G. new ed., though it is given as Pippli in the old. There is also a Pipli in the Puri district (I.G., new ed., XX. 404). In the Ma'āṣịru-l-umarā, I. 137 and 194, in the biographies of Ibrāhīm Fatḥ K. and Aḥmad Beg, the place is taken to be Pipli. It is also Pipli in the Iqbāl-nāma, 217, where also Cuttack is described as being 12 koss off, towards Bengal. The maps show a Pipalgaon between Puri and Cuttack, and about 30 m. from the latter place. A Pipli in the Puri district is mentioned in the I.G., new ed. ↑

8 Text *isti'dād*, but the true reading is *istib'ād. Istib'ād namūda*, "regarded the thing as at a distance," or "was surprised." The I.O. MSS. end here, their last words being "Till at length there came a conciliatory letter from La'natu-llah ('Abdu-llah)." The R.A.S. MS. continues with Muḥammad Hādī's supplement. ↑

---

Milton Keynes UK
Ingram Content Group UK Ltd.
UKHW032232011124
450424UK00008B/915

9 789362 517692